PERFORMANCE ANALYSIS FOR JAVA™ WEB SITES

PERFORMANCE ANALYSIS
FOR JAVA™ WEB SITES

Stacy Joines, Ruth Willenborg, and Ken Hygh

◆◆Addison-Wesley

Boston • San Francisco • New York • Toronto • Montreal
London • Munich • Paris • Madrid
Capetown • Sydney • Tokyo • Singapore • Mexico City

The publisher offers discounts on this book when ordered in quantity for bulk purchases and special sales. For more information, please contact:

U.S. Corporate and Government Sales
(800) 382-3419
corpsales@pearsontechgroup.com

For sales outside of the U.S., please contact:

International Sales
(317) 581-3793
international@pearsontechgroup.com

Visit A-W on the Web: www.awprofessional.com

Library of Congress Cataloging-in-Publication Data

Joines, Stacy.
   Performance analysis for Java Web sites / Stacy Joines, Ruth Willenborg, Ken Hygh.
     p. cm.
   Includes bibliographical references and index.
   ISBN 0-201-84454-0 (alk. paper)
   1. Web sites. 2. Java (Computer program language) I. Willenborg, Ruth. II. Hygh,
Ken. III. Title.

TK5105.888.J648 2003
005.2'762—dc21

2002071655

ISBN 0-201-84454-0
Text printed on recycled paper
1 2 3 4 5 6 7 8 9 10—CRS—0605040302
First printing, September 2002

CONTENTS

FIGURES AND LISTINGS

Note: Code listings are numbered in a separate series in each chapter and gathered in their own subsection, following the figures.

Listings

FOREWORD

About a year ago I was sent out to a large Fortune 500 WebSphere customer to solve a critical "WebSphere performance" problem. The customer was close to putting a WebSphere application into production, and believed they had discovered—with less than a week to go before the application was to go into production—that WebSphere "did not perform well."

No one seemed to have many details about the problem, but we were assured by the highest levels of management at both the customer's company and IBM that this was indeed a critical situation. So I dropped everything and headed out the next morning on a 6:30AM flight. At the company I met with the customer representative, who showed me an impressive graph (the output of a popular load-testing tool) that demonstrated that their application reached a performance plateau at five simultaneous users, and that response times increased dramatically as more load was placed on the system.

I asked if they could run the test while I watched so that I could see the numbers myself. I was told no—the hardware they were using for performance testing was also being used for user-acceptance testing. It would not be available until after 4PM that day. So I asked if I could see the test scripts themselves. to see how they were testing the application. Again the answer was no. The fellow who wrote the scripts wouldn't return until 5PM, and no one else knew where he kept them.

Not wanting to seem like I was wasting time, I next asked for the source code for the application. They were able to provide it, and I spent the next eight hours reading through it and making notes about possible bottlenecks. When the script author returned at 5PM, we reconfigured the test machine and ran the script. Sure enough, the performance curve looked like what the test had caught the previous night. I asked him to walk me through the code of the test script. He showed me what each test did, and how the results were captured. I then asked him about one particular line of code in the middle of the script: "So, here you seem to be hard-coding a particular user ID and password into the test. You never vary it, regardless of the number of simultaneous users the load testing tool simulates?"

He said that this was true and asked if that could be a problem. I explained to him that their test setup used a third-party security library, and that one of the "features" of this library was that it restricted users with the same user ID and password from logging in twice. In fact, it "held" requests for the second login until the first user using that login has logged out. I had picked up on this fact by reading the code that morning. I then asked if he could rewrite the script to use more than one login ID. In fact, if they wanted to test up to a hundred simultaneous logins, could he rewrite the script so that it used a hundred different login IDs? He ended up doing just that, and the next night, after a few more such adventures, we reran the modified test.

This time WebSphere performed like a champ. There was no performance bottle-neck, and the performance curve that we now saw looked more like what I had expected in the first place. There were still some minor delays, but the response times were much more in line with other, untuned customer applications I had seen.

So what was wrong here? Why did this company have to spend an enormous amount of money on an expensive IBM consultant just to point out that their tests weren't measuring what they thought they measured? And why were we working under such stressful, difficult circumstances, at the last possible moment, with a vendor relation-ship on the line?

What it came down to was a matter of process. Our customer did not have a proper process in place for performance testing. They did not know how to go about discov-ering performance problems so that they could be eliminated. The value that this company placed on performance testing was demonstrated by the fact that the per-formance tests were scheduled for after hours, and were done on borrowed hardware. Also, the fact that this problem was not discovered until less than a week before the planned deployment date of the application showed the priority that performance testing had among other development activities; it was an "afterthought," not a criti-cal, ongoing part of development.

I have repeatedly seen large, expensive systems fail—and thousands or millions of dollars lost—because of this attitude. As a wise man once said "failing to plan is plan-ning to fail." The book you hold in your hand can help you to avoid such failures. It offers concise, easy to follow explanations of the different kinds of performance problems that large-scale web applications face. More important, it provides you with a process and methodology for testing your systems in order to detect and fix such problems before they become project-killers.

The authors of this book are all respected IBM consultants and developers, with years of collective experience in helping solve customer problems. They've dealt with the foibles of application servers, customer application code, network configuration issues, and a myriad of other performance-stealing problems. They convey their experiences and recommendations in a laid-back, easy to understand way that doesn't require that you to have a Ph.D. in stochastic modeling to understand. I believe their greatest contribution to the world is a process for injecting performance testing into all stages of the development process—making it, appropriately, a key part of web site development.

If you are building a large web site using J2EE technologies—or even just a small, departmental application—buy this book. Performance problems can creep in to all sizes of applications, and the time that you will save by following the advice given here will easily repay the purchase price of this book many times over. I've come to rely on the authors for advice in this area, and I'm sure you will too.

—Kyle Brown
Senior Technical Staff Member
IBM Software Services for WebSphere

INTRODUCTION

How well does your Java web site perform? Does it have enough capacity to handle today's user demands on its busiest days? Can it support additional users in the future? Will you lose potential customers because your web application is too slow? Regrettably, many companies release web sites to their users without knowing the answer to these questions. Performance is a serious issue. If your web site becomes unresponsive, you may lose potential sales or customer loyalty. In fact, government regulations sometimes require some financial web sites to remain responsive regardless of the level of customer demand.

Obviously, the customer's experience with a web site affects the company the web site represents. We work with many people every year trying to make their web sites perform better. Often, these folks come from a background of building PC-based applications, and they struggle with the unfamiliar issues of concurrency and high user volumes. Likewise, we frequently engage with performance and quality assurance (QA) teams who have lots of skill in tuning high-volume web sites and back-end systems. Yet they lack experience with the Java environment and Java web applications and need help to tune them properly. Many sites use Java application servers to power their web applications, and we discuss the special considerations (garbage collecting, threading, heap management, to name a few) that are unique to the J2EE environment. Also, the book covers the special performance requirements of sites supporting handheld devices, as well as sites using Enterprise JavaBeans (EJBs).

We wrote this book to help you better understand how your Java web site performs. First, we don't assume you have a Ph.D. in performance tuning. We don't spend any time on the mathematical theories behind performance testing. (Remember Little's theorem?) Of course, it wouldn't hurt if you wanted to learn more about these theories, but that is not the point of this book. We want to give you a practical guide for managing the performance of your web site. Our combined experience with hundreds of public and private web sites worldwide can help you conduct an effective performance analysis of your web site. Learn how to design performance tests tailored to your web site's content and customer usage patterns.

This book treats your Java web site as a system. Your web site consists of server machines, network hardware, vendor software, and custom applications, just to name a few components. A performance problem might arise in any of these subsystems inside your web site. Instead of focusing narrowly on any one element, we discuss the potential performance impact of everything from your network to your Java web application software. We even discuss some tuning ideas for remote systems residing on other servers or even at your mainframe. We also offer some ideas for preparing each part of your web site system to handle your traffic.

Designed to benefit those with a little or a lot of performance testing background, this book helps you get the most from your performance analysis investment. We organized the book to give the novice the basics before plunging into more advanced topics. If you're new to performance work, start with a thorough reading of the first chapter to nail down the basic terminology and concepts you'll need to understand the more advanced material. (More advanced readers might want to skim this section for any new information before moving on to the advanced material.)

If you're new to Java web applications or to web sites in general, Chapters 2–5 cover most of the major components of your web site and explain the best practices for their tuning and deployment. Here you'll find some solid recommendations on how to assemble a Java web application, as well as the entire web site, with performance in mind. We also discuss some of the fundamental operational and performance differences between the major web site types you might encounter.

The subsequent chapters cover how to design, execute, and analyze the results of a performance test. We firmly believe an accurate performance test is the best possible way to find out how your web site will perform (or does perform) in production. However, a poorly designed or executed test provides misleading information. We discuss how to build a test appropriate to your web site. Through several chapters, we discuss how to plan for a performance test, including selecting performance test tools and building test scripts. A case study at the end of these chapters pulls the information together into a larger example.

Finally, we describe what to do during the test and how to use the data the test produces. These chapters include a discussion of the performance testing and tuning process we recommend, as well as a rough guide to some common bottleneck symptoms and their possible resolutions. Are you adding load but not seeing increased throughput? Do some machines in your environment work much harder than others? Use the common symptom reference to isolate bottlenecks and improve performance. The appendixes provide helpful checklists for planning and worksheets for capturing the data produced during a performance test, so you can more easily diagnose problems and estimate capacity needs.

In addition to designing better tests, the book provides helpful advice for monitoring tests and analyzing the data collected. We also explore how to use the data from the test to develop a capacity plan for your production web site, as well as a plan for future growth. The ongoing case study provides solid examples of how to use these concepts. Our aim is to show you how to determine the best your site will do under the worst of conditions. Moreover, the book is useful as a performance reference guide. The appendixes include a series of worksheets to help you through capacity planning formulas and summarize key performance testing concepts into a series of checklists. We also include a list of some tool vendors who provide performance testing, analysis, and monitoring tools.

We want to make performance testing accessible to anyone charged with the task. Performance concepts readily map to everyday experiences, and we believe a successful performance evaluation is within the grasp of anyone willing to learn some basics. Don't let your e-business become the next cautionary tale highlighted on the evening news because your site can't handle traffic on its busiest days. Learn how to make use of performance testing and capacity planning to prepare your site for success.

ACKNOWLEDGMENTS

This book would not have been possible without the generous help of many people. We cannot begin to name everyone who has provided us with assistance, but the following people especially merit our thanks. (Of course, any mistakes in the book are solely the authors' responsibility.) We are grateful to

Susan Hanis, who at one time or another mentored each author in performance tuning and analysis. We appreciate all that she has taught us about performance over the years, and we particularly recognize her contributions of networking and web site expertise to this project.

Harvey Gunther, for his continuing quest to identify the best practices for developing Java 2 Platform, Enterprise Edition (J2EE) applications and his willingness to educate and share his knowledge.

Carolyn Norton, for her expertise, attention to detail, and encouragement throughout this process. We thank her especially for helping us out with some of the trickier network calculations we attempted.

Kyle Brown, for his expertise, advice, encouragement, and assistance throughout this process.

Geoff Hambrick, for his expert advice in the area of best practices.

Ken McCauley and Tom Kristek, for their encouragement and understanding throughout the writing of this book.

Gennaro Cuomo, for his support and expertise, and also for providing some performance data for our examples.

Leo Cai, for his assistance in creating the LoadRunner scripts and reviewing Chapters 7 and 8.

Stephan Asboeck, for his assistance in creating the SilkPerformer script and reviewing Chapters 7 and 8.

Dave Peterson for helping us through the publication process.

The five technical reviewers, Thomas Alcott, Kyle Brown, Susan Hanis, Scott Rich, and Paul Tyma, for valuable suggestions that dramatically improved the quality and accuracy of the book.

Also, we would like to thank Mary O'Brien, Amy Fleischer, Mary Cotillo, Alicia Carey, as well as the rest of the publication team at Addison-Wesley for their efforts in making this book possible. We would especially like to thank Nick Murray, our copy editor, and Robin Kibby, our illustrator, for their terrific work.

We recognize all our colleagues in the IBM WebSphere development and enablement teams for making high-performance J2EE applications a reality. Finally, we thank our families for their support and sacrifices during this endeavor.

Chapter 1
BASIC PERFORMANCE LINGO

L et's begin our discussion of performance with a quick review of key performance terminology. We say "key" because we use this terminology throughout the book. If you're new to performance, you should read this chapter thoroughly. If you're an experienced performance analyst, you should at least glance through it for new terms or to be sure you understand our use of the more ambiguous performance terms. This chapter acquaints you with the concepts and the specific performance "lingo" used to define the concepts. We begin by defining the most basic measurement terminology including *load*, *throughput*, and *response time*. Next, we explore the terminology for performance optimization, including *path length*, *bottlenecks*, and *scalability*.

The terminology used in performance analysis may be new to you, but you already know the underlying concepts from everyday life. In this chapter, we apply performance terminology to familiar experiences. We use analogies based on "brick and mortar" stores in our neighborhoods to describe performance concepts found in the virtual world of web site software. These analogies also demonstrate how performance terminology really describes everyday reality.

Measurement Terminology

Load: Customers Using Your Web Site

Traditional Store

Let's consider a traditional brick and mortar bookstore. A traditional bookstore serves customers and contains a certain number of customers at any point in time. If we use the store's security camera to take a snapshot of the sales floor at some point during the day, we get a picture similar to Figure 1.1.

In this picture, we see some of the customers browsing the shelves, while others interact with the store clerks. The customers ready to make purchases go to the clerks operating the cash registers. Other customers needing assistance with a book selection go to the clerk at the information desk.

The bookstore frequently contains more customers than clerks. Specifically, the bookstore contains more customers than cash registers. Intuitively, we know it usually takes some browsing time on the customer's part to pick out a selection for purchase, so we don't need a clerk for every customer.

On-Line Store

An on-line store also serves customers, though these customers are represented by requests to the web site instead of a physical presence in a store. The on-line store uses computing resources to handle customer requests (the electronic equivalent of our bookstore clerks).

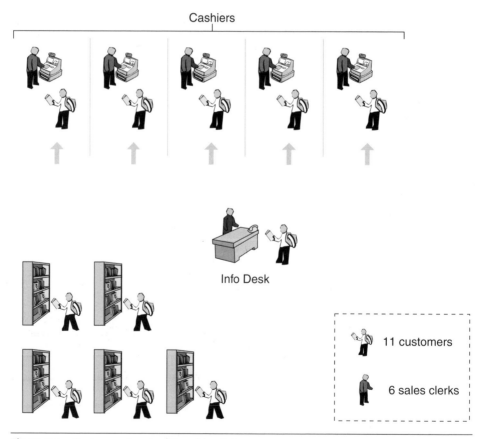

Figure 1.1 Customers in a traditional bookstore

Surprisingly, the customers using our on-line bookstore behave much like the customers visiting a brick and mortar bookstore. The on-line customers request pages from our web site (like asking the clerk at the info desk for help), and then spend some amount of time looking at a given page in their web browsers before making their next request. As they do in our brick and mortar store, the on-line customers may browse for a while before they make a purchase and often they make no purchase at all.

Figure 1.2 shows an on-line bookstore with a total of 11 customers: 2 with requests being handled by computing resources and 9 browsing recently created web pages. As this figure shows, at any point in time, an on-line store typically has more customers than the number of requests being handled. In fact, for some web sites, the customers reading pages far exceed those actively making requests to the web site.

So how does this all relate to load? *Load* is all of the customers using your web site at a point in time. Load includes customers making requests to your web site as well as those reading pages from previous requests. For example, the customer load in our bookstore snapshot in Figure 1.1 was 11 customers. (A performance expert might tell you the store is under an "11-customer load" at this point). In performance testing, we often "put the system under load." This means we plan to generate customer traffic against the system, often by using special test software to generate customers.

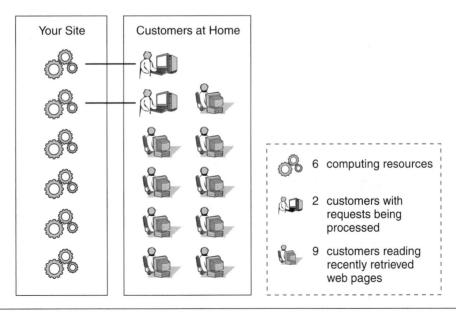

Figure 1.2   Customers using an on-line bookstore

Obviously, a term such as a *lightly loaded* system means the web site has few customers. Likewise, a *heavily loaded* system means the web site has many customers. Also, we often drop the term *customer* in the web space, preferring the terms *user, client,* or *visitor* instead. (Not all web sites actually sell things, so "customer" is not always appropriate.) However, we do need some way of differentiating between all clients and those clients actually making requests to our web site. We use the terms *concurrent load* and *active load* to make this distinction. Let's discuss these terms in more detail.[1]

Concurrent Load: Users Currently Using the Web Site

Traditional Store

As we noticed earlier, inside our traditional bookstore some customers look for books, while others interact with the clerks. For example, look at a security camera snapshot in Figure 1.3. At this point in time, the store contains 11 customers: 5 customers browsing, 1 requesting help from the info desk clerk, and 5 interacting with clerks at the cash registers to make purchases. *Concurrent load* refers to all of the customers in the store at a point in time, regardless of their activity.

On-Line Store

Web site visitors reading a previously requested web page resemble customers browsing in our traditional bookstore—they're using the web site, but not actively engaging it to satisfy a request. The concurrent load for your web site includes the customers browsing previously requested pages in addition to the active clients. Figure 1.4 shows an on-line bookstore with 6 active client requests, and 5 users browsing previously created pages for a total of 11 concurrent clients.

You may wonder why we care about the total users rather than just those making requests. Look at the traditional store example. All of the customers in the store use resources, even if they're not interacting with a clerk. For instance, the store owner provides floor space where browsing customers can stand as well as parking places out front for their cars. Likewise, web site visitors often require web site resources even when they're just reading a web page on their browsers. The web site often uses memory and other resources to keep information about users during their visit. (We expand this topic in Chapter 2's discussion of HTTP sessions.) Since any user potentially consumes resources, regardless of her current activity, we sometimes need to consider all of the users visiting our web site. This is concurrent load.

---

1. We know of no authoritative standard for defining concurrent vs. active clients. We prefer these terms. However, don't be surprised if you encounter others in your organization either using these terms differently, or using different terms altogether. In any case, make sure you *all* agree on definitions when planning your tests and your production web site.

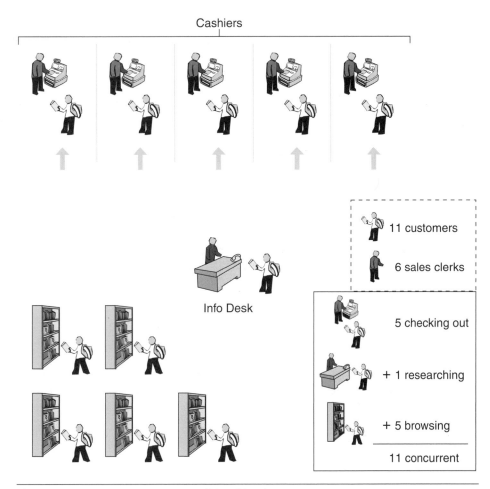

Figure 1.3 Concurrent users in a traditional bookstore

Active Load: Customers Making Requests of the Web Site

Traditional Store

Active load refers to customers currently making requests. In a brick and mortar store, the active customers are interacting with the sales staff. The bookstore may contain many customers, but only a subset of these actually is at the cash registers or at the information desk interacting with the sales clerks. We call these customers "active" because they actively want some service from the store to buy or find a book. Figure 1.5 shows a traditional bookstore with six active customers.

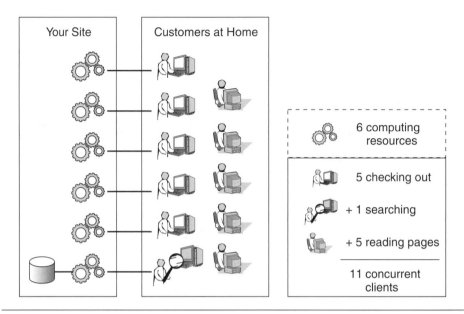

Figure 1.4   Concurrent web site load

On-Line Store

Much as they do in the traditional bookstore, on-line customers also make requests of the web site. These requests require web resources, particularly processing resources, to complete. For example, the on-line customer might request a search for books by a particular author, or request to purchase the items in an on-line shopping cart. See Figure 1.6 for an example. By definition, the term *active* applies to the user from the moment the request arrives at our web site until the requested information returns to the user.

Peak Load: Maximum Concurrent Web Site Customers

Traditional Store

After the bookstore opens, customer traffic rarely remains constant throughout the day. The store usually receives more customers during lunchtime or after school than in the morning or late at night. Over the course of a week, the store probably receives most of its traffic on Saturday. Over the course of a year, the Christmas holiday represents the store's overall busiest period, with the day after Thanksgiving being the busiest day of the year.

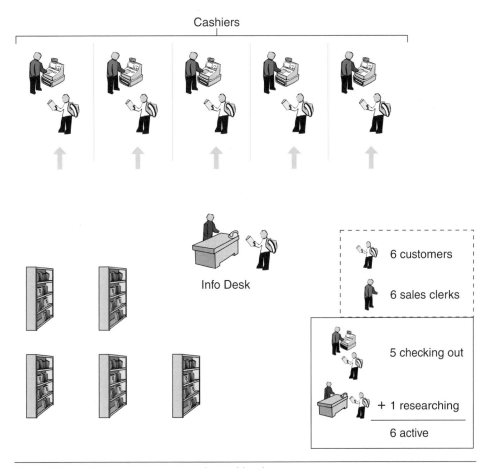

Figure 1.5   Active customers in a traditional bookstore

Peak load refers to the maximum concurrent customers in the store within some time period. For example, Figure 1.7 shows a graph of hourly customer visits during the course of a day. Notice that the store experiences two activity "spikes" during lunchtime and between 4 PM and 5 PM each day. The peak period, however, is the hour between 4 PM and 5 PM each day. The store receives its peak load (50 customers) during this period.

Peak load is not the average load. The store shown in Figure 1.7 averages 25 customers an hour during the day. If we only consider averages, the store might not schedule enough sales clerks to handle the 50 customers arriving between 4 PM and 5 PM. Note

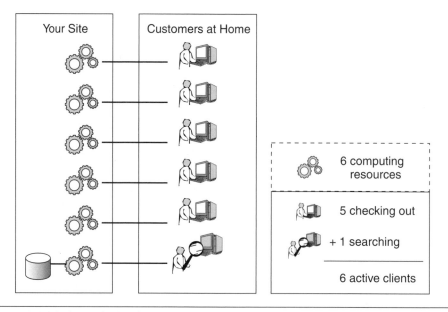

Figure 1.6   Active web site clients

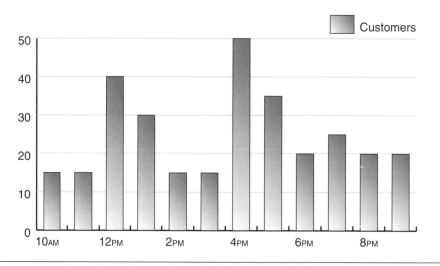

Figure 1.7   Traditional store customers per hour

that our concerns about averaging apply to the time scale as well. Perhaps Figure 1.7 represents an average day at the bookstore. While this information proves useful for scheduling most of the year, it doesn't tell us how many people arrive on our peak day (the day after Thanksgiving) or their arrival distribution during that day.

On-Line Store

Like a traditional bookstore, web sites experience an uneven distribution of users throughout the day. The peak user arrival times vary from web site to web site. For example, brokerage web sites receive intense load every day at market opening, while an on-line bookstore receives most of its traffic at lunchtime or after the workday ends. Also, web sites, like their brick and mortar counterparts, experience unusually high traffic during peak times such as the Christmas holidays or a stock market rush. However, web site traffic patterns differ significantly from those of traditional stores. An on-line bookstore's lunchtime spike often lasts three hours as lunchtime rolls across time zones from the East Coast to the West Coast.

Again, the peak load is our planning focus. A web site unable to support its peak traffic is an unsuccessful web site. When planning your performance test, find the peak loading goals for your web site, and build the test to exercise this load. (See Chapter 6 for details on developing an accurate performance test.)

Throughput: Customers Served over Time

Traditional Store

A clerk sells a customer a book at the cash register. This transaction requires one minute. Let's assume it *always* takes one minute to complete a customer sale, regardless of how many books the customer buys. In this case, if the store contains five cashiers, the store serves five customers per minute. (Figure 1.8 illustrates this scenario.) In performance terms, five customers per minute is the store's *throughput*. Throughput measures the customers served relative to some unit of time. It is a unique metric because it has an upper bound. No matter how many customers come to the store, the maximum number handled during a specific time interval remains unchanged. (We know from experience the clerk cannot check out two customers simultaneously.)

So with five clerks operating five cash registers, our store serves a maximum of five customers a minute. This represents our maximum throughput, regardless of how

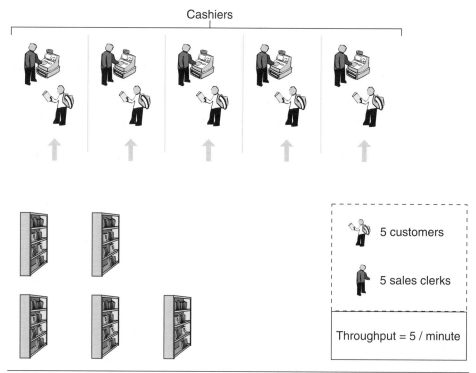

Figure 1.8   Throughput dynamics without waiting

many customers actually want to checkout during this time. For example, Figure 1.9 shows the same store, only now with ten customers; however, the clerks still sell at a rate of one customer per minute. So, with five clerks, we still only serve five custom-ers per minute (our store's maximum throughput remains unchanged). Thus five of the customers must wait or queue. After reaching the throughput upper bound, add-ing more users to the store does not increase throughput. This is, as you might guess, an important concept to grasp.

On-Line Store

An on-line site exhibits the same throughput dynamics as the traditional store. An on-line store handles requests, typically initiated by a customer using a web browser. For example, a customer may search for particular books or purchase the contents of a shopping cart. A web site handles a specific number of requests in parallel; for example, a web site may handle 20 customer requests simultaneously. If each request takes one second to process, the on-line store throughput is 20 requests per second.

Just as in our traditional store, adding more requests does not increase throughput after we reach our throughput upper bound. If the web site receives 30 requests per

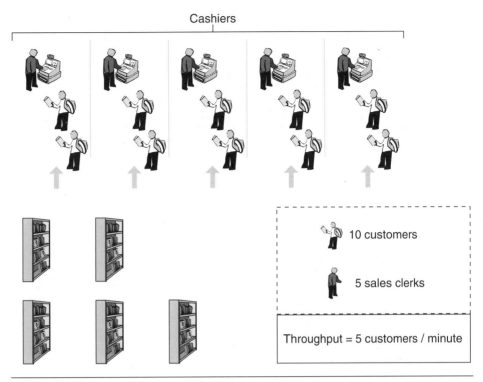

Figure 1.9   Throughput dynamics with waiting

second, but the maximum throughput is 20 requests per second, some of the requests must wait or queue.

Throughput Curve: Finding the Throughput Upper Bound

A performance test uses a series of test runs to understand the relationship between load and throughput. A graph of the data from these runs establishes the *throughput curve* for your system. As the load on your system increases, the throughput usually increases as well until it reaches the throughput upper bound (maximum throughput). On the graphs shown in this section, we plot the load on the *x*-axis and the throughput (requests per second or customers per second) on the *y*-axis.

Traditional Store

Figure 1.10 shows the throughput curve for the bookstore. With one customer, the throughput is one customer per minute; at two customers, it is two customers per minute. This pattern continues through five customers, with a throughput of five customers per minute. The graph shows that as the load increases between one and five customers, the throughput increases to a maximum of five customers per minute. Once the load reaches five customers, all five clerks are busy at the cash registers. Throughput then remains a constant five customers per minute, even as the number of customers increases. After we reach maximum throughput, we have reached the throughput plateau. Beyond maximum throughput, adding load, or users, results in a consistent, flat throughput curve (a plateau). For the bookstore, the throughput plateau is five customers per minute.

On-Line Store

Web sites produce a similar throughput curve with a throughput plateau. Figure 1.11 shows a typical throughput curve for a web site. (Obviously, this graph contains more data points than the bookstore throughput graph.) The "Light load zone" in the figure shows that, as the number of user requests increases, the throughput increases almost linearly. At light loads, requests face very little congestion for resources. After some point, congestion starts to build up, and throughput increases at a much lower rate until it reaches a saturation point. This is the throughput upper-bound value.

The throughput maximum typically represents some bottleneck in the web site, usually a saturated resource (the on-line equivalent of all sales clerks being busy). The CPU often becomes the constraining resource on your web site. After your CPU(s) reach 100% utilization, the web site lacks processing capacity to handle additional requests.

As client load increases in the "Heavy load zone" in Figure 1.11, throughput remains relatively constant; however, the response time increases proportionally to the user

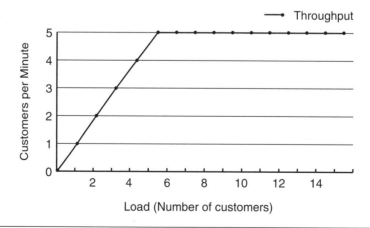

Figure 1.10   Throughput curve: brick and mortar store

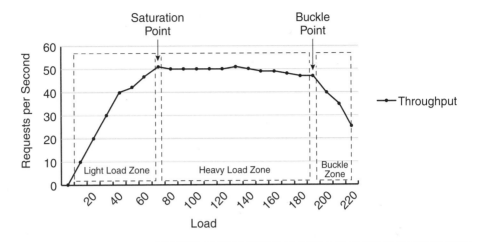

Figure 1.11 Typical web site throughput curve. From Gennaro Cuomo, "A Methodology for Production Performance Tuning," an IBM WebSphere Standard/Advanced White Paper. Copyright 2000 by IBM Corp. Reprinted by permission of IBM Corp.

load (see the next section on response time for more details). At some point, represented by the "buckle zone," one of the system components becomes exhausted, and throughput starts to degrade. For example, the system might enter the buckle zone if the network connections at your web server exhaust the limits of the network adapter, or if you exceed the operating system limits for file handles.

So far, we've discussed throughput generically as "requests per second." We often hear throughput discussed in terms of hits, transactions, pages, or users in some unit of time (usually a second, but sometimes in terms of a day or week). Not surprisingly, how you measure your throughput makes a big difference in how you set up your tests, and also affects your hardware plan. We briefly discuss the differences between hits, transactions, pages, and users in the next sections. A more thorough discussion, with an example, appears in Chapter 6.

Hit

A *hit* may mean one of several different things. For an HTTP server specialist, a hit means a request to the HTTP server. Because HTML (Hyper Text Markup Language) pages usually contain embedded elements, such as gifs or jpegs, one HTML page might require multiple HTTP "hits" as the browser retrieves all of the elements from the server to build a page.

Regrettably, the rest of the world uses the term *hit* in very ambiguous ways. Sometimes *hit* refers to an entire page, including embedded elements. Also, many companies routinely use *hit* to mean an entire site visit by a given user. (A site visit usually encompasses many pages, not to mention the embedded elements and frames included in those pages.) Therefore, you must first make sure everyone discussing a "hit" is discussing the same thing. Any misunderstanding on this point drastically impacts the success of the performance test and the production web site.

Transaction Rate

Transaction rate is the most common measurement of throughput. (Web sites often measure their throughput in transactions per second.) Usually, web sites define a *transaction* as a single HTTP request and response pair. However, the definition for *transaction*, like that for *hit*, often means different things to different people. Sometimes transactions involve more complex behavior than dealing with a simple request/response pair. Within your team, establish your definition of a transaction, and use it consistently.

Page Rate

Page rate measures the pages returned by a web site during a specified period of time. For a web site, a web page is the fully formatted content of one page as displayed in a browser. As noted above, web pages almost always contain embedded elements such as gifs, jpegs, JavaScript, and, in the case of frames, other pages.

In order to complete a web page, the browser makes multiple HTTP requests to retrieve imbedded elements. For example, the first request returns the basic page content, and the browser issues additional requests for each embedded gif file or JavaScript element. Again, almost all web pages contain embedded elements. (See Chapter 5 for an expanded discussion of web page construction based on web site function.)

Since it is important to look at your web site as a whole, understanding throughput in terms of pages per second makes sense. Your web site may handle a high request volume in terms of HTTP requests during the day. However, if each of your web pages contains many embedded elements, this request volume may not translate into a high page volume. (It takes many requests, in this case, to build a single page.) From a user's perspective, the throughput of your web site could be much lower than your transaction volume.

User Rate

The *user rate* measures the users visiting the web site during a period of time. The web site receives many visitors over the course of the day. They interact with the web site to perform one or more tasks, which may involve navigating through several pages.

The most common definition of *user* refers to one of potentially many visits a user might make to the web site over the course of day. The user visit includes the set of web pages navigated while using the web site. Because a user visit encompasses multiple pages, the user rate is usually lower than the page rate or transaction rate for a web site.

In practice, the definition of *user* varies from team to team. For example, web masters frequently interchange *user* with *hit* (a single request/response pair, not a multipage web site visit). See Chapter 6 for an expanded discussion. Again, you and your team need to pick a consistent definition and stick with it.

Response Time: Time to Serve the Customer

Traditional Store

In the traditional store, each customer sale takes a certain amount of time. For example, it may take a sales clerk one minute to check out a customer and complete a sale. Prior to actually purchasing a book, you may wait in line for an available clerk. This wait time adds to the length of time required to complete a purchase. Figure 1.12 shows the last customer in line waiting four minutes to reach the sales clerk. After the customer reaches the clerk, the sale requires the standard one minute of processing time to complete. Therefore, this customer's total checkout time includes the four minutes of waiting, plus the one minute of actually checking out, resulting in a total checkout time of five minutes.

On-Line Store

A customer who initiates a request from a browser waits a certain amount of time before the web page resulting from the request appears in the browser. For example, if the on-line customer issues a request to purchase a book, the browser submits the request to the web site, and the customer waits until the web site returns an order confirmation page to the browser. Note that this works much like our traditional bookstore: Our purchase takes some quantity of time, regardless of whether we wait in line or not prior to making the purchase.

Web site *response time* refers to the time from when the customer initiates a request from his browser until the resulting HTML page returns to the browser. (Technically, response time refers to the time between the request and the display of all the page's content. However, the user's perceived response time spans the request to the first appearance of returning page data in the browser.)[2]

Remember that the customer's request shares the web site with potentially many other simultaneous requests. If the request finds the processing capacity of your web

---

2. See Patrick Killelea, *Web Performance Tuning.*

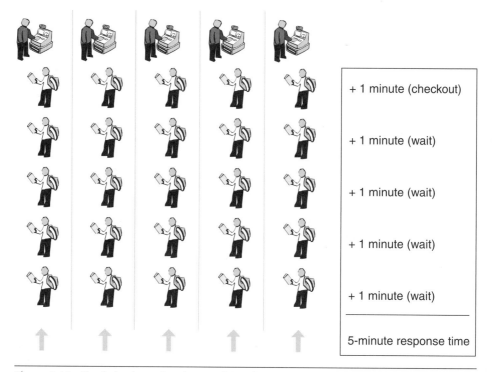

Figure 1.12   Total checkout time in a traditional store

site fully engaged, the request "waits." (Actually, the web site usually queues the request until processing capacity becomes available to satisfy it.) Just as in our traditional bookstore, the time spent waiting adds to the actual service time of the request. The total response time in this case is the wait time plus the actual service time.

Again, response time is the time it takes to serve the customer. In both the brick and mortar example and the on-line store, the response time consists of the total time it takes to purchase the book. For example, if a customer submits a request to purchase a book, we measure the response time from when the user submits the request via a browser until the browser displays the confirmation page. This time includes any "wait time" for busy resources. Figure 1.13 shows the response time for a typical web request.

Also, in either a traditional or on-line environment, customers come with limited patience. If response time grows too long, the customer stops waiting and leaves, maybe never to return to your store or web site. Therefore, response time is the critical measurement for most web sites. Performance testing strives to minimize response time and ensure it does not exceed your web site objectives, even during peak loading.

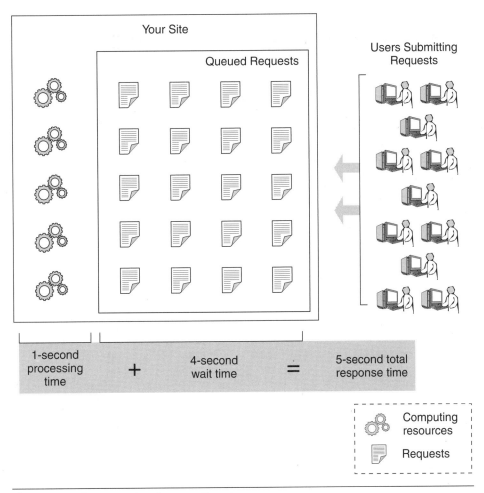

Figure 1.13   Response time in an on-line store

Think Time

Think time is the time a user takes between submitting requests. Think time and response time represent two different concepts. Response time measures the time the user waits for a response to return from the web site (including any wait time for server resources). Think time, however, measures the interval between a user's requests. During the think time, the server performs no work for the user because the user has not made a request.

For example, the user's first request to search for a book may require five seconds to process. After the server returns a list of books matching the search criteria, the user reads through the list and decides what action to take next. Maybe the user chooses to submit another search, or maybe he requests more details about a particular book on the list.

During this think time, the user may read material previously obtained from the server, choose further server activity, or even go for a snack. Regardless, from your web site's perspective, the user is not active during this time. For example, Figure 1.14 shows a user making two separate requests, one minute apart. The response time for each request is only five seconds, but the total time the user spends shopping is one minute and ten seconds. Chapter 7 contains a more detailed discussion of think time and the important role it plays in performance testing and capacity planning.

While think time is beyond the scope of our control, we can (and must) carefully control and monitor our web site's response time. Make no mistake: Response time is the critical performance measurement for any web site because it represents how long users wait for a given request. Like their traditional store counterparts, on-line customers often refuse to wait patiently for an overworked server. If your site cannot deliver pages quickly, even under heavy load, you lose customers. Discouraged customers often never return to an underperforming web site. The primary objective of

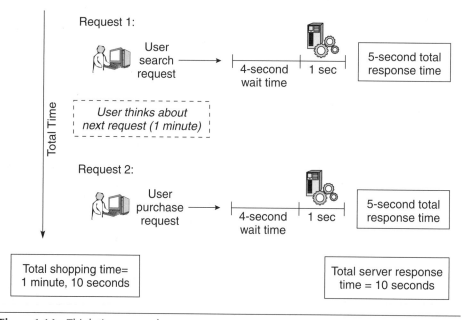

Figure 1.14   Think time example

your performance test should be to minimize and measure your web site's response time. Even at peak load, keep your web site's response time under its responsiveness objectives.

Response Time Graph

Understanding your web site's response time requires an understanding of the relationship between load, throughput, and response time. As discussed earlier, your web site does not possess infinite throughput potential, but achieves its maximum throughput at a certain user load. Beyond this point (known as the throughput saturation point), throughput remains constant. However, the response time begins to increase. Response time increases after throughput saturation because of resource constraints. Additional load waits for these limited resources before actually doing useful work.

Traditional Store

Let's look at the load, throughput, and response time dynamics in a brick and mortar store. If only one customer wants to check out, she receives immediate service from the cashier. If we require one minute to complete her sale, the store's throughput becomes one customer per minute. Let's extend our example by assuming that the store contains five cashiers. If five customers arrive at the same time for checkout, they all receive simultaneous service from the individual cashiers (see Figure 1.15). Since these five customers did not wait, they experienced one-minute response time (the time required to check out). Likewise, since our store served multiple customers in parallel, our throughput increased to five customers per minute.

This throughput (five customers per minute) represents our store's throughput upper bound. A cashier cannot check out multiple customers at once, so our store experiences a resource constraint (cashiers) that prevents it from exceeding this boundary. If a sixth person arrives while all five cashiers are busy with other customers, the sixth person waits, or queues, until a resource (in this case, a cashier) becomes available. Time spent in the queue waiting for a resource is called *wait time*. In our store, the maximum wait time for the sixth person in line is one minute (the time required to check out the person currently being served by the cashier). Figure 1.15 shows an example of customers experiencing wait time.

Wait time also influences the response time for the sixth customer. We must add the wait time to his overall service time. In the case of our sixth person, the response time increases to two minutes: one minute waiting for a cash register to clear plus one minute actually spent checking out (yes, 1 + 1 = 2). However, because of limited resources (again, the cashiers), the store's throughput does not increase as more customers arrive. This demonstrates our previous claim about throughput: Once you hit the throughput upper bound, response time begins to increase as additional load enters the system. As Figure 1.15 shows, the response time doubles as the number of customers doubles past the throughput saturation point.

On-Line Store

The on-line store exhibits the same dynamics in the relationship between throughput, response time, and load. If our on-line store handles a maximum of 5 requests per second with a one-second response time, the next 10 simultaneous requests experience a maximum response time of two seconds, while 20 simultaneous requests experience a maximum response time of four seconds, and so forth. Figure 1.16 shows the linear relationship between response time and load after reaching the

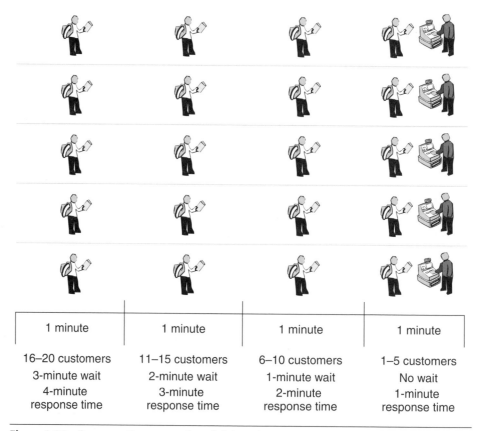

1 minute	1 minute	1 minute	1 minute
16–20 customers	11–15 customers	6–10 customers	1–5 customers
3-minute wait	2-minute wait	1-minute wait	No wait
4-minute response time	3-minute response time	2-minute response time	1-minute response time

Figure 1.15 Response time queue for a brick and mortar store

throughput upper bound. (This graph does not show the throughput buckle zone, as displayed in Figure 1.11, but it still exists. Once the load goes beyond a certain point, average response time growth is more than linear.)

Understanding how many customers your web site may handle simultaneously and how long your waiting lines and response times become at your busiest times is the primary motivation behind performance load testing. This understanding, in our opinion, forms the basis of "due diligence" for any commercial web site. Clearly, we need more than a throughput curve like the one shown in Figure 1.11. We also need a response time graph to show the relationship between load, response times, and the throughput upper bound, like that shown in Figure 1.16.

This graph resembles the throughput graph in Figure 1.11 in several ways. The left *y*-axis plots our throughput, while the *x*-axis plots our load. However, we add another *y*-axis on the far right to plot our response times. As you see, with one to five customers, the response time averages one second. However, the web site reaches throughput saturation at this point. Beyond this point, the graph shows unchanging throughput despite increased load (a sure sign of throughput saturation). The response times for the increased load, however, grow linearly beyond the response time at the throughput saturation point. (Again, watch out for the buckle zone, where response times often grow exponentially.)

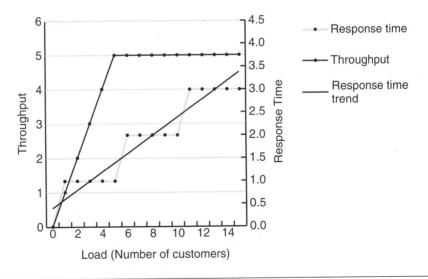

Figure 1.16   Throughput curve and response time graph

Throughout the rest of the book, we discuss what to do if your throughput and response time numbers do not meet your expectations. In fact, few web sites start with ideal throughput and response times. Usually, the first performance tests show throughput much lower and response times much higher than you actually require. The process of performance tuning focuses on improving these numbers and giving your web site the performance your customers demand. Even if your results fall well below expectations by a factor of 10, or even 100, don't despair. Keep reading. Sometimes very small performance adjustments make a tremendous difference in overall performance.

Steady State

Traditional Bookstore

Most bookstores open for limited periods during each day, for example, 10 AM to 9 PM. Although the store opens at 10 AM, the manager might panic if a large number of people arrived at 10:01 AM to buy books. Why? Because the store needs time to fully prepare. Before the bookstore works at optimum efficiency, the staff must complete some opening activities. The bookshelves need dusting and straightening. Returned books need reshelving. The cash tills in the registers might be low on change, so the manager makes a quick trip to the bank for coins. Maybe a few employees get stuck in traffic and arrive a few minutes late. In any case, the store works most efficiently after the store staff arrives, and finishes these start-up activities. Also, the traffic levels at off-peak times tend to be low. The store rarely experiences peak traffic at 10 AM or 9 PM simply because customers do not come in large numbers during those hours.

When we measure the response time for our store, we want to measure at a time when the store operates efficiently and when it experiences significant (even peak) loading. Otherwise, our data may not be valid. For example, if we measure response time at 10:01 AM, just after opening, we may get mixed results. A customer might experience terrific response time because she's the only customer in the store. However, on some days, a customer might wait an unusually long time if the store is out of change and the manager must go to the bank for coins. If we take measurements at 10:01 AM, our measurements are outside the store's *steady state*. The store needs more load, or more preparation, to demonstrate its typical behavior.

On-Line Store

Surprisingly, our performance tests must also consider steady-state issues to obtain valid data. The web site under test also experiences "opening the store" activities, albeit quite different than dusting shelves. "Opening activities" for web sites include loading servlets into memory, compiling JavaServer Pages (JSPs), priming caches, and other activities with a one-time cost. Since the vast majority of your web site users never experience the cost associated with these activities, try factoring them out of your tests by selecting your measurements carefully.

Just as the web site requires preparation time, your test usually requires time to reach full loading. Most tests start with a few virtual users and increase the load over time until achieving the maximum load for the test. We call this the ramp-up period; the load ramps up to maximum users. Likewise, all virtual users in your load may not stop at the same time, but finish the test scenario over some time period. We call this the ramp-down period as you wait for the test to complete.

We want to capture data only after all of the users start. We also want to delay the measurement slightly after starting all of the users to give the system time to adjust to the load. Figure 1.17 demonstrates this concept. The ramp-up occurs as the user load increases up to 100 users. During this time, our web site goes through its "opening activities," such as bringing servlets into memory and priming caches. Again, we do not include this time in our measurements because the data tends to be ambiguous. Likewise, we do not want to take measurements while the tests finish during the ramp-down period. Instead, note the time period during full loading when we actually take measurements. This gives us an accurate picture of how the web site operates under this load. In this case, we take measurements from our full load period, giving ourselves two time periods of buffer after ramp-up and before ramp-down.

Remember, you want measurements best representing your site under load. Failing to account for the ramp-up and ramp-down periods of your performance test may invalidate the entire test.

Optimization Terminology

Now that we've covered some of the basic performance measurement terms, let's discuss some of the terminology associated with optimizing your web site. After all, we want not only to know about our web site's performance, but also to improve it. So how do you improve your web site's performance? For example, recall our earlier discussion of performance issues such as the throughput upper bound. What do you do after you find the upper bound, and it is lower than you hoped? At this point, you need to optimize your web site or apply scaling techniques to push the site beyond its current performance.

Optimization usually focuses on the web application. You may reduce the number of steps the application performs (known as "shortening the application's path length") to save time. You also may eliminate key resource bottlenecks by pooling resources, or making other adjustments to improve resource availability. Optimizing a web site requires a knowledge of how it behaves for any given user, as well as how it behaves

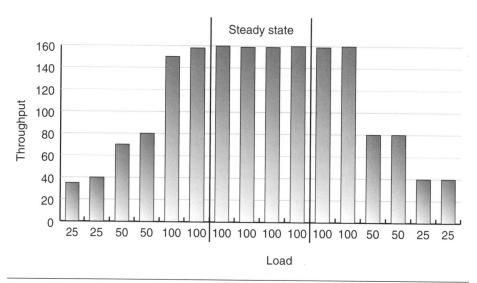

Figure 1.17   Steady-state measurement interval

under load from many users. For example, we might discover our web site's "check-out" function requires 20 seconds to complete for a single user. We must optimize this function to improve the response time. Likewise, under a light load of ten users, we find our search function response time increases from 3 seconds to 50 seconds. In this case, we need to remove a resource contention only present under load.

Scaling techniques, on the other hand, focus on adding resources to increase the web site's capacity. For example, we might double our throughput capacity by doubling the number of available servers. However, not all web sites scale well, so we must test the web site before assuming additional hardware provides any capacity benefit. This section covers the basic terminology of optimization. Later chapters give more detail on how to apply one or all of these techniques to your web site.

Path Length: The Steps to Service a Request

Traditional Store

In the previous section, we measured key activities in our brick and mortar store. In this section, we discuss some optimizations we might make now that we better understand the operation of the store. Let's look first at the checkout process, which takes one minute per customer to complete. So what happens during the checkout process? During this one minute, the clerk performs multiple actions, such as greeting the customer, entering her name and address, entering the price of the book into the cash register, taking money from the customer, providing change, and putting the book into a bag. Figure 1.18 outlines this list of activities, or *path*. Keep in mind that if we reduce checkout time from 1 minute to 30 seconds, we not only reduce the store's response time but also increase its overall throughput. For example, assuming five cashiers, throughput increases from five to ten customers per minute. (One customer every 30 seconds results in two customers per minute. Multiply by five cashiers, and you get an overall throughput of ten customers per minute.)

We decide to reduce the checkout time by reducing the path length of the checkout activity. The *path length* is the number of steps required to complete an activity, as well as the time each step takes. We reduce the path length either by (1) speeding up a step or (2) removing a step entirely. For example, as shown in Figure 1.18, the clerk types in the customer's name and address as part of the checkout process. The store never uses this information, so we remove this step, which reduces the number of steps required and removes ten seconds from every checkout. While entering the customer's name proved optional, entering the price of the customer's purchases remains mandatory. Entering the price takes 30 seconds, a significant part of our processing time, because each clerk manually enters the price from a tag on the item. Purchasing a bar-code scanner and automating this step speeds up the checkout process by 20 seconds. These adjustments cut the checkout time in half and doubled throughput. However, these long-term performance gains required an investment in a detailed understanding of the checkout process.

On-Line Store

Much like the cashier, your web application code executes "steps" to complete each request. These steps form the path through your code for each request. Likewise, making the path through your code shorter or more efficient improves both response time and throughput. Of course, before improving web application code, you must first understand it. Code analysis requires both programming skill and time, particularly if you did not originally develop the software under analysis. While it does require an investment, *code path optimization* is usually the most effective technique for improving web site performance. Just as with the brick and mortar store, reducing a web application's code path involves two tactics: (1) Removing unnecessary code and (2) improving the performance of the remaining code. Again, the *path* is the execution path your code takes. A code path might include the following steps: initialization, reading data, comparing values, and writing updates.

In order to optimize the code, we want to remove any unnecessary code from the path a given request takes. For example, the code path for our checkout function may contain a loop. At each pass through the loop, several statements execute. (If we loop ten times, we execute the statements ten times each.) Sometimes we find a statement, such as a constant declaration or the like, that does not need to be repeated inside the

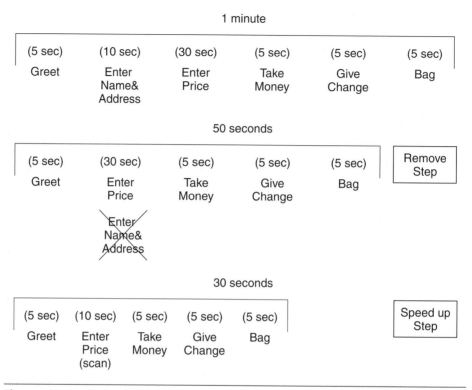

Figure 1.18   Reducing the checkout process path length

loop. Moving this statement outside the loop reduces the steps we execute on our code path (in ten iterations, we reduce the path length by nine statements.)

However, just as with our brick and mortar store, we cannot always change the number of steps we execute. In these cases, we consider making the steps themselves faster. For example, we might pool database connections to make obtaining a connection in our code faster. If we frequently manipulate String objects, we might build our own lightweight parser rather than using StringTokenizer throughout our code. (See Chapter 4 for specific Java tuning advice.)

Bottleneck: Resource Contention under Load

Bottleneck refers to a resource contention inside your web site. As the name implies, a bottleneck chokes the flow of traffic through your site as requests contend for one or more limited resources.

Traditional Store

In order to uncover bottlenecks, we need to look at our store as a whole rather than focusing on individual areas. Our store's response time and throughput rely on more than just the number of customers going through the checkout line.

For example, during Christmas, the manager receives many complaints from customers about long lines. However, the cashiers say they often wait for customers and never see more than one or two people waiting to check out, even during the busy part of the day. The manager decides to explore other areas of the store, such as the information desk, for long lines. As Figure 1.19 shows, he finds the line in the gift-wrap department. While customers make it through checkout quickly, they experience long delays if they want their purchases wrapped. The gift-wrap desk acts as a bottleneck on the throughput and response time of the entire store. Sufficient resources in one part of your store do not guarantee acceptable overall throughput and response time. The store operates as a system: A bottleneck in one resource often impacts the throughput and response time of the whole.

Removing bottlenecks is both an iterative and ongoing process. It is iterative because we may find that removing one bottleneck introduces a new one. For example, if the information desk became a bottleneck, improving that situation may put more pressure on the cashiers (people move more quickly to the cash registers rather than stalling at the information desk). After removing a bottleneck, be sure to reevaluate the system for new sources of contention. The process is ongoing because usage patterns change. Our gift-wrap department probably doesn't get a lot of traffic in August, but at Christmas it becomes a bottleneck because our customers' use of the store changes. Instead of purchasing books for themselves, they buy gifts for others. Constant monitoring allows you to identify usage shifts, and reallocate (or add) resources as needed to meet the new traffic patterns.

On-Line Store

On-line stores frequently experience bottlenecks. We discussed earlier tuning the code paths throughout your web application. However, code path tuning focuses on single-user performance; bottlenecks emerge only when we put the system under load. While code path tuning gives us more efficient code, we also must study the system under load to look for these resource sharing issues.

Technically, we find a bottleneck wherever the code processing a request must wait for a resource. For example, when your web site receives a request to purchase a book, the code path to handle this request probably includes a database update. If the database update locks rows needed by a request from a second user who wants to purchase a different book, the processing of the second user's request waits until the

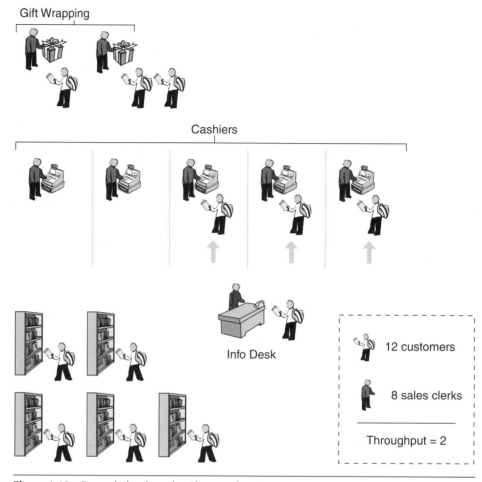

Figure 1.19   Example bottleneck: gift-wrap department

desired rows become available. This locking design works great in a single-user test, giving us problems only when we add load (additional users). This example again underscores the importance of concurrency and load testing prior to releasing your web site.

While poor database sharing strategies often develop into serious bottlenecks, you may also uncover bottlenecks associated with sharing hardware resources. Each request requires CPU and memory resources from your web site. If you handle many simultaneous requests, these hardware resources may quickly deplete, forcing request processing to wait. CPU and memory often become bottlenecks under load. For more information on identifying and resolving bottlenecks, see Chapter 13. Bottle-necks often produce unusual symptoms, so check this chapter for more details on how to spot resource sharing problems.

Scaling: Adding Resources to Improve Performance

Scaling a web site simply means adding hardware to improve its performance. Of course, this only works if your hardware resources, such as CPU and memory, present the largest bottleneck in the web site's system. If your code spends most of its time waiting for CPU resource or memory, adding more hardware improves performance. Regrettably, web site teams often upgrade or add hardware only to find little or no performance benefits after they finish the upgrade. We recommend tuning the web site and performing at least fundamental bottleneck analysis before adding hardware. Dedicate some time to making your web applications more efficient. Most important, find and eliminate any major bottlenecks, such as database locking issues. If you perform these optimization steps well, your hardware resources eventually become your only remaining bottlenecks. At this point, scaling provides real performance benefits.

In a perfect world, scaling does not affect your application. You simply add new machines, or increase memory, or upgrade your CPUs. However, adding resources often changes the dynamics of your application. For example, if your application used to run on a single server, adding a new server may introduce remote communications between the application and a naming service or a database. Because of these unknowns, we recommend performing a scalability test prior to scaling your web site. This test tells you how well the web site performs after you add new hardware and whether the new configuration meets your performance expectations. Also, before purchasing new equipment, decide which form of scaling works best for your web application. Most scaling focuses on two basic approaches: vertical scaling and horizontal scaling.

Vertical Scaling

Traditional Store

In scaling, we increase throughput by handling more customers in parallel. Inside a bookstore, this means additional cash registers and cashiers. Figure 1.20 shows five additional cash registers, giving the store a total of ten registers. This raises the throughput of the store to a maximum of 20 customers per minute (two customers per minute per cashier multiplied by ten cashiers, assuming—here and in the rest of this chapter's examples—our improved response time of 30 seconds per customer). We call adding resources to our existing store *vertical scaling*. We relieve resource contention within our physical store by increasing the constrained resource (in this case, cashiers and cash registers).

On-Line Store

On-line stores also use vertical scaling to process more requests in parallel. Vertical scaling at a web site helps us get the most out of each available server machine; it occurs at both the hardware and software levels. From a hardware perspective, we might increase the processors (CPUs) for each server. For example, we might upgrade a two CPU machine (also known as a *two-way*) to a four CPU machine (a *four-way*). In theory, this gives the machine twice the processing capabilities. In reality, we rarely

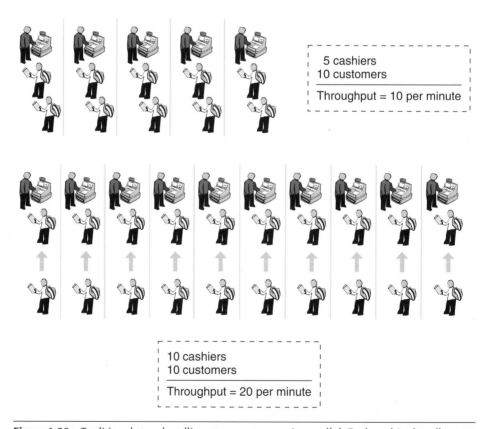

Figure 1.20   Traditional store handling more customers in parallel. Each cashier handles two customers per minute.

obtain a true performance doubling with this technique. Our ability to use extra CPUs inside an existing server depends on several factors:

- The existing servers must be upgradeable (they permit us to add more CPUs).
- The operating system and the Java Virtual Machine (JVM) support symmetric multiprocessing (SMP). Unless your OS and JVM support SMP, they cannot distribute work to multiple processors, thus making it difficult to take advantage of additional CPUs. (Happily, most newer operating systems and JVMs support SMP to a point.)

SMP is an important factor in vertical scaling. (In fact, you may hear the term *SMP scaling* as another name for vertical scaling.) As we mentioned, most modern operating systems and JVMs support SMP scaling, but only to a point. On extremely large servers (12 processors or more), a single JVM may not fully exercise all of the processors available. With such servers, we turn to *vertical software scaling*. Rather than one JVM, we execute two or more until all CPUs on the machine become fully engaged. Running multiple JVM processes allows us to better utilize all the resources of these large servers. (Chapters 2 and 11 discuss vertical scaling in more detail.)

Horizontal Scaling

Traditional Store

At some point, the bookstore may physically exhaust the available floor space and be unable to add more cashiers. When this happens, we cannot continue to increase the capacity of the store, even though the store does not meet the demands of our peak customer loads.

In the brick and mortar world, one of the following three alternatives typically transpires in this situation:

1. The store relocates to a larger facility.
2. A competitor opens a store nearby and takes customers from your store.
3. Your company opens a second store some distance away and customers shop at the most convenient location.

In any case, we expand our physical resources to meet customer demand. Either we provide more facilities, or our competition does. By opening the second store, we anticipate increasing our throughput, or at least reducing our response time, by distributing the customers between multiple stores.

For example, Figure 1.21 shows our throughput if a second store opens with ten checkout lines and a throughput of 20 customers per minute. If the first store continues to handle ten customers per minute, the overall throughput increases to 30 customers per minute. We call this *horizontal scaling*. We cannot continue to grow inside a single store (vertical scaling), so we add more stores.

On-Line Store

When it comes to horizontal scaling, on-line stores beat traditional stores hands down. Web sites grow by adding servers, not by building new bookstores. It's much easier and cheaper for a web site to grow to meet explosive customer demand (and fend off the competition) than for a traditional store.

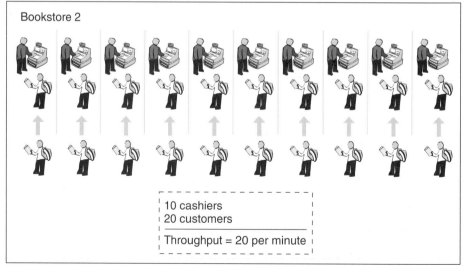

Throughput Bookstore 1 (10) + Throughput Bookstore 2 (20) = 30

Figure 1.21 Scaling with multiple bookstores. Each cashier handles two customers per minute.

Horizontal scaling in the web world means adding duplicate resources (servers, networks, and the like) to handle increasing load. If you employ the clever technique of load balancing, your users never know how many servers make up your web site. Your URL points to the load balancer, which picks a server from your web site's server pool to respond to the user's request. Load balancing algorithms vary from the simplistic (round-robin) to the highly sophisticated (monitoring server activity, and picking the least busy server to handle the next request). Because the load balancer interacts with a pool of servers, known as a *cluster*, we sometimes call horizontal scaling *cluster scaling*. Figure 1.22 show a small cluster of two servers. The load balancer sends incoming requests to Server A or Server B for resolution. This cluster also allows the web site to support double the throughput of either server acting alone. (See Chapter 3 for more details on horizontal scaling.)

Linear Scaling

In an ideal world, we experience *linear scaling* when we increase our web site's capacity. Linear scaling means that as our resources double, so does our throughput. In the real world, perfect linear scaling seldom occurs. However, horizontal scaling techniques come closest to ideal linear scaling. Vertical scaling, while often improving overall throughput, rarely achieves true linear scaling.

Traditional Store

In Figure 1.20, doubling the number of cash registers and cashiers doubled the throughput in our store. This is an example of linear scaling. In reality, linear scaling often depends on complex interactions among various resources. For example, in order to increase our throughput, we need more customers in the store. This

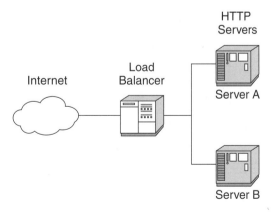

Figure 1.22   Horizontal scaling example

requires also increasing a range of other resources from the information desk personnel to parking spaces. If we fail to grow any of these resources, we probably won't experience true linear throughput growth.

On-Line Store

Scaling a web site also requires taking into consideration all required resources. You may want to double your throughput by upgrading your two-processor server to a four-processor machine. However, as you double your processors, you must also appropriately scale other resources such as memory and disk space.

Frequently, adding capacity also creates more complex concurrency issues within the server. More load often exposes new resource bottlenecks within your application. Again, consider testing your web site with its new capacity to determine the actual benefit of hardware upgrades.

Considerations for scaling your web site and setting appropriate expectations with respect to linear scaling are discussed in more detail in Chapter 11.

Summary

The same performance issues you encounter every day at brick and mortar stores also prevent your web site from achieving its full performance potential. In this chapter, we defined some basic performance terminology by showing how e-Commerce concepts also apply to the familiar world of traditional retail stores. By now you should understand the fundamental measurement concepts (load, throughput, and response time) of performance. You should also understand the relationships between these measurements, and how they impact each other. Also by now, you should be familiar with some basic optimization terminology (path length, bottlenecks, and scaling). The upcoming chapters expand and build on these basic performance concepts, so it is important to be comfortable with them before moving ahead.

While a traditional store and an on-line store share similar performance issues, resolving these issues on your web site requires a great deal more planning, testing, and analysis. The upcoming chapters cover in detail the knowledge and skills you need for measuring and tuning Java web sites.

Chapter 2
JAVA APPLICATION
SERVER PERFORMANCE

In Chapter 1, we discussed how code optimization requires an investment in understanding the code itself. If you're wondering if this investment is worth the potential dividends, keep this in mind: *The Java web application, more than any other single factor, determines web site performance.* (Tuning the site hardware or the application server rarely compensates for an underperforming application.) Frequently we find web site teams trying to tune their way around a poorly written or poorly designed web application. If these flaws prove severe, the web site cannot perform or scale until the underlying software receives the attention it needs from the development team.

The next three chapters cover the basics of Java web applications and the Java web site environment. We begin with a brief discussion of Java web application design and an overview of how Java web applications interact with Java web application servers. If you come from a quality assurance (QA) or performance background, this early material gives you an idea of how a Java web application functions based on accepted principles of good design. (Experienced developers might want to just skim for new information.) This overview material does not contain the level of detail you need to design and develop a new Java web application. If you plan to write a Java web application, the bibliography includes some excellent books that provide the detail you need regarding good design and development practices.

Next, we discuss some performance tips that cover many common problem areas in Java web applications, such as logging and poor HTTP session management. Most of these tips apply to any Java web application server implementing the J2EE (Java 2 Platform, Enterprise Edition) standard. (Any tips specific to a given Java web application server implementation receive special note.) If you need more specifics on a particular area of the J2EE standard, we suggest you start by reviewing the materials available on the Sun Java web site: <java.sun.com>.

Remember: The web site is a system. The Java web application plays a critical role in the performance of your web site, but it also interacts with the Java Virtual Machine and other hardware and software components. We suggest that you read this chapter and the next two as a unit to give you a good sense of how the web site components function together to deliver content. Also, let's settle on some terminology at this point. Rather than repeating the phrase "Java web application server" throughout the rest of the book, we're just going to call it an *application server*. Likewise with "Java web application": from now on we'll refer to it as a *web application*.

Web Content Types

Java web sites serve two types of content: *static* and *dynamic*. Before we get into the specifics of the application server, let's discuss the differences between these two types of content, and what they mean to the performance of your site. Static content refers to elements of your web content that rarely change. Familiar static elements include things like graphic elements (gifs, jpegs, and the like), stable HTML elements like banners and pages, and client-side elements like JavaScript, style sheets, and so on. Usually static content lives in files at your web site. Depending on the type of web site you operate, static content might make up the largest proportion of information your site serves.

Dynamic content refers to web pages or portions of web pages created by a web application. A program actually generates the content returned. For example, if the user requested a search based on a keyword, the web site uses a web application to perform the search and build the list of results to return to the user. Dynamic content requires computing cycles on the application server, and may need to call other programs on other machines in your network, like a database server, search engine, existing program, or something else. As we will see, the mix of static versus dynamic content drives design decisions not only for your applications, but also for the network you set up to support them.

Web Application Basics

The Model-View-Controller Design Pattern

Before we plunge into the various elements of a web application, let's first discuss a key concept in application design: the *Model-View-Controller*, or *MVC*, design pattern. (The J2EE world refers to this pattern as *Model 2*.) Regardless of what you call it, many web applications use MVC as a basis for their architecture and operation. Therefore, we want to describe briefly how this design pattern works. We'll be using MVC terminology throughout this chapter to describe the roles of various web application components, so you need to be familiar with this subject before we move ahead.

Architects and developers like MVC because it allows them to divide the application into pieces that can be assigned to different developers with different skill sets. These pieces map cleanly to easily understood subcomponents of the application. Traditionally, the design pattern breaks down as follows:

- *Model*: The model encapsulates business logic and database schemas. Naturally, developers skilled in database technology and business logic develop the model portion of the application. In J2EE applications, model code is often implemented using JavaBeans or *Enterprise Java Beans (EJBs)*. The model remains independent of the application using it; therefore, multiple applications sometimes share the same underlying model.
- *View*: The view focuses on the look and feel of the application. Your developers with skills in human interface design and implementation usually work on the view. These components focus on presenting dynamic information to the user, but they do *not* gather this dynamic information themselves. In the J2EE model, *JavaServer Pages*, or *JSPs*, handle the responsibilities of the view.
- *Controller*: The controller handles the flow of the application. Application developers usually handle the components comprising the controller functions of your application. These components guide the flow of the view and instantiate model objects in order to fulfill the application's requirements. In J2EE, the *servlet* and its associated classes play the role of the controller in the web application.

Because of the multi-tiered nature of web sites, MVC is an excellent choice for web application design. Using MVC yields applications that are flexible, easily maintainable, and extendable. MVC also makes it easy to divide the application among developers with different skill sets. In fact, web sites thrive under the MVC model. Many web sites change their look and feel constantly. By splitting out their presentation (view) components from their application (controller) code, they isolate the presentation of the web site from the logic flow. This allows the design team to make cosmetic changes to the web site without calling the programmers (who aren't generally known for their artistic abilities anyway). Changing a page's look not only doesn't require a programmer if you use MVC, but the update cannot impact the program's code. Likewise, if another application needs a column added to a database table, the resulting updates to the model do not impact either the controller or the view of other applications that use the same table.

Figure 2.1 shows how MVC works within a Java application server. (If some of the components are unfamiliar to you, we explain them later in this chapter and in the next.) The client, using a browser, makes a request for a URL that invokes a servlet. The network sends the request to the correct machine, and the HTTP server on that machine receives the request. The HTTP server passes it on to the plug-in, which determines that it is a request for the application server to handle. The application server takes the request and maps it to a servlet. The application server's web container instantiates the servlet, if required, and begins executing it to satisfy the request. During execution, the servlet calls model objects as needed to read or update data and forwards the resulting data to a JSP. The JSP formats the data into a web page and returns the generated page back to the client.

Many leaders in the field of Java web application design recommend the MVC approach for web site architecture.[1] While the J2EE model does not enforce this design pattern, we expect (and hope) that your web developers used this approach to assemble your web application. Keep in mind that MVC is a design strategy. By itself, it does not guarantee terrific performance for your web application. However, knowing your web application's overall design structure (even if you're not a developer) often proves helpful for several reasons:

- Understanding the design of the application allows you to follow its flow more easily. This is frequently useful in tracking down bottlenecks.
- Knowing the breakdown of responsibilities for the various components of the application allows your team to involve the right skills for problem solving.
- Proper application structure often proves an effective indicator of overall application quality.

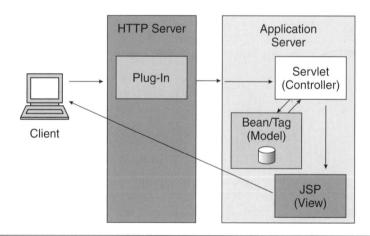

Figure 2.1   Model-View-Controller within a Java web application. From "WebSphere Programming Model: Best Practices for Http Servlets and Java Server Pages," paper presented by Ken Hygh at Solutions 2001, San Francisco, CA. © IBM Corp. 2001. Reprinted by permission of IBM Corp.

---

1. MVC is a cornerstone of both the J2EE Design Patterns, <http://java.sun.com/blueprints/patterns/ j2ee_patterns/model_view_controller/>, and the Apache Struts Project, <http://jakarta.apache.org/ struts/>. Also, check the bibliography.

Servlets

A *servlet* is a small Java program.[2] These little programs provide the intelligence behind Java web site applications. Each incoming HTTP request for a dynamic page goes to a servlet. The servlet decides how to satisfy the dynamic request by marshalling data from any number of sources and passing it to the presentation logic to generate the dynamic page. For any given request, the servlet might choose between multiple presentations to return to the user. For example, if the site supports both French and English pages, the servlet looks at the parameters on the incoming HTTP request and picks the correct format for the output. Or a servlet might choose an error page rather than the normally displayed page if the servlet couldn't communicate with the database or a validation error occurred.

Servlet Scope

Large web sites contain lots of functions for their users. Each function provided maps to a different request sent to the web application providing the intelligence behind the web site. How the web site maps these requests to functionality varies. Some web sites use a new URL for each request, while others generate one or more URLs with a series of parameters attached to differentiate between functions. Regardless of the form your requests take, your web site needs a strategy for dealing with a variety of requests. Specifically, you need a strategy for controlling how you map an incoming request to the function you must provide and to the JSP you eventually use to return the dynamic page to the requestor.

One popular strategy maps the incoming requests into a small set of servlets. Each servlet handles a small set of requests and uses one or two specific JSP pages to return dynamic pages to the requestor. The servlet contains only the logic required to satisfy the small set of requests it handles. This approach also allows you to update and add new function to the web site easily, as the logic for the function resides in discrete servlets and JSPs. Updating or adding functions does not impact other servlets. Another strategy uses a "front controller" to manage incoming requests.[3] The controller potentially handles all the requests for a functional area of your web site (say, the banking or brokerage areas of a finance web site). The controller uses "helper" objects, such as JavaBeans, to pull together data for the JSPs. (See Figure 2.2 for an example of the two common request management strategies.)

---

2. From Javadoc of the `javax.servlet.Servlet` class. Retrieved February 22, 2002 from the World Wide Web: <http://java.sun.com/j2ee/j2sdkee/techdocs/api/javax/servlet/Servlet.html>.
3. See Deepak Alur, John Crupi, Dan Malks, *Core J2EE Patterns.*

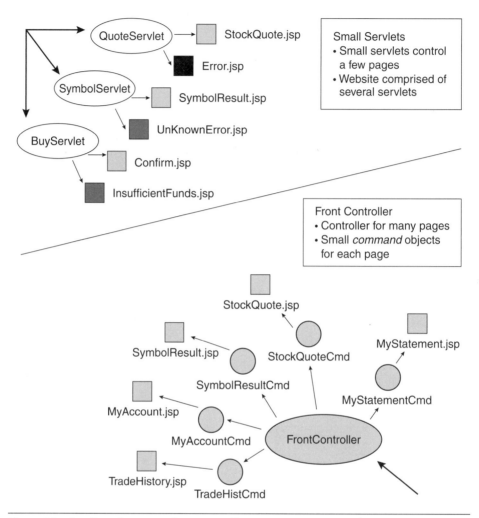

Figure 2.2   Small servlets versus front controller strategy. From IBM Software Group Services Performance Workshop presented by Stacy Joines, 2001, Hursley, U.K. © IBM Corp. 2001. Reprinted by permission of IBM Corp.

Regardless of the request management strategy you use, keep the following performance considerations in mind.

- *Keep code paths short:* Design your control logic to quickly recognize each request and begin meaningful processing to build a response. Some web applications traverse enormous "decision trees" (usually an enormous "if" construct) to determine how to answer the user's request. The decision trees often prove inefficient, especially if the site handles a lot of different URL/parameter combinations.

■ *Maintain the right granularity as your site grows:* As your web site grows, you add web application logic to support new features. For example, if you operate a web banking site, you might grow your web site to include brokerage functions. To support the brokerage functions, you need new web application logic.

How you grow your site really depends on the request management strategy you use (front controllers with helper objects versus a larger group of self-contained servlets). In any case, we recommend building new helper objects or self-contained servlets as you add new function. (Also consider adding a new controller for major new functional areas of your web site.)

Again, the idea is to keep the code paths in your web site short. Often, when developers shove significant new function into existing servlets or helper objects, the code paths within these objects become unnecessarily long. This results in not only suboptimal performance but also in maintenance difficulties for the development team. For example, in our banking web site, we might add new servlets to support our new brokerage functions. (For web sites using the front controller strategy, we might add another front controller and set of helper objects specifically for the brokerage functions.) Likewise you potentially need new JSPs, JavaBeans, and other objects to support this new feature.

As with any design practice, you want to avoid extremes of object creation as well. We sometimes encounter developers who create a servlet for every possible request permutation the web site might receive. Obviously, thousands of little servlets prove just as difficult to maintain and extend as one gigantic servlet. When your site grows, consider refactoring the web application classes if you're generating lots of classes containing similar logic. (Refactoring simply means reorganizing your application. It often involves centralizing common logic currently distributed throughout your objects.)[4]

Servlet Operation

Now that we better understand *what* servlets do, exactly *how* do they work? The application server loads the servlet either as the web container starts or when the servlet receives its first request, depending on administrative settings. (Note: JSPs and servlets share many runtime characteristics, although their roles at the web site differ. We discuss the specifics of loading and running JSPs in more detail later in this chapter.) When the servlet loads into memory, the application server calls the servlet's `init()` method. This gives the servlet an opportunity to obtain static resources and perform initialization steps. (As we'll discuss later in this chapter, good management of static resources often dramatically improves servlet performance.)

---

4. See Martin Fowler, *Refactoring: Improving the Design of Existing Code.*

The init() method only runs once, at servlet load time. The servlets we most commonly see inherit from javax.servlet.http.HttpServlet. They return HTML or other appropriate formats in response to an HTTP request. As the HTTP requests arrive for the servlet, they trigger execution of the servlet's doGet() or doPost() methods, depending on the request. The servlet programmer provides the logic inside these methods.

Servlets typically run as multi-threaded entities. That is, the application server creates only *one* instance of the servlet, and multiple threads may execute code in this instance simultaneously. For example, if your web site receives four simultaneous requests for the same servlet, those requests execute inside the doGet() or doPost() method on separate threads simultaneously. Because of this multi-threading, you *cannot* use instance variables inside your servlet to maintain state information.

The servlet specification does provide a single-threaded alternative. By implementing the javax.servlet.http.SingleThreadModel interface, your servlet becomes single-threaded. This means the application server creates an instance of your servlet for each simultaneous request. If you've never written a multi-threaded application before, you might feel tempted to use the single-threaded model. *Don't do it!* The single-threaded model does not perform well, particularly in high-volume web sites nor does it scale well. In this model, each request operates within its own fully instantiated servlets. This requires more memory and related overhead than the multi-threaded model. While the single-threaded model might seem like a shortcut, it is actually a performance dead end. Take the time and learn how to write good multi-threaded servlets instead.

Obviously, threading is an important issue for servlet developers. We discuss threading in more detail in Chapter 4. Other excellent books provide detailed tutorials on managing threading issues inside your servlets.[5] Take the time to learn and master these issues before writing your web application. You will reap returns in improved application performance, fewer application errors, and less rewriting.

Servlets, Threads, and Queuing

If the request specifies a page generated by a servlet or JSP, the HTTP server *plug-in* (see Chapter 3 for a more detailed discussion of HTTP servers) passes the request into the web container. The web container runs inside a J2EE application server running in a Java Virtual Machine (JVM) and has a limited number of threads available to handle servlet requests. Typically, the number of HTTP "listeners" (see Chapter 3) greatly exceeds the number of available servlet threads in the application

---

5. See Hunter and Crawford, *Java Servlet Programming*.

server's web container. (For example, a typical installation may have 150 HTTP server listeners, but only 20–50 servlet threads.) Figure 2.3 shows the different numbers of listeners and threads, including servlet threads, that make a call to a database through a *connection pool* (we'll discuss connection pools later in this chapter). The application server assigns the incoming request to a thread, and the requested servlet runs on this thread. After the servlet satisfies the request and returns the data to the user, the thread returns to the available servlet thread pool inside the application server's web container. If all of the threads in the web container are busy when a request arrives, the servlet request queues. Both queued requests and requests executing inside the servlet engine tie up the HTTP server listener thread originally assigned to them.

At runtime, you want a threading "funnel effect," as demonstrated in Figure 2.3.[6] You do not want equal numbers of worker threads at every layer in a multi-tiered application. At first, this seems counterintuitive, but keep in mind that the work occurring at one layer does not always involve the next layer. For example, if your HTTP server handles requests for both static and dynamic data, some of the HTTP listeners handle the static requests without involving the application server. Therefore, not all of your HTTP listeners engage the application server simultaneously. Likewise, not all the servlet threads make database calls simultaneously, so you need fewer database connections in the connection pool than configured servlet threads.

Application servers allow you to set the maximum threads allocated for executing servlets and JSPs. You may think the default setting for your application server thread pool is quite low (some vendors set the default as low as 15–20 threads), especially if you plan to handle a lot of user requests per second. Actually, the default settings, despite the small number of threads, probably represent the optimum number of threads for the average web application. This seems counterintuitive: If you want to handle more simultaneous requests through your web site, you should allocate more threads, right? Wrong. Actually, more threads often prove detrimental to web performance. As you allocate more threads, you create more work for the JVM, which manages the threads. Adding more threads generates more overhead as the JVM tries to give each thread its fair share of CPU and other resources. This is known as *context switching overhead*, and it increases as the number of threads increases, reducing the amount of useful work that the greater number of threads in the JVM can actually accomplish. So, start your performance testing by leaving the servlet/JSP thread pool sizes at their defaults. You might try adjusting these thread pool sizes up (and down) using *small* increments. If you see improvement, consider moving up a little bit more. However, keep in mind the key to servlet/JSP thread pools: *Less is often more.*

---

6. See Gennaro Cuomo, "A Methodology for Production Performance Tuning," an IBM WebSphere Standard/Advanced White Paper (March 2000): <www.ibm.com/support/manager.wss?rs=180&rt =0&org=SW&doc=7000616>.

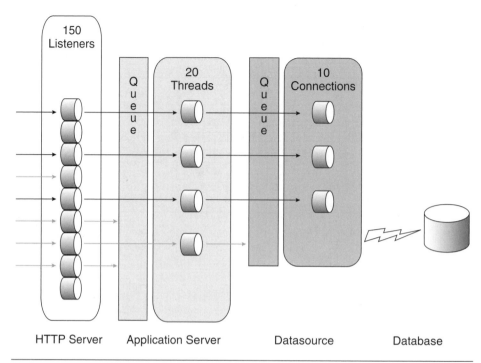

Figure 2.3   Threading/queuing "funnel." From IBM Software Group Services Performance Workshop presented by Stacy Joines, 2001, Hursley, U.K. © IBM Corp. 2001. Reprinted by permission of IBM Corp.

The Frozen Web Site Danger

Before we talk about specific servlet performance issues, let's talk about how poor programming practices sometimes literally stall web sites. We call this phenomenon the "frozen web site." The web site becomes nonresponsive to requests, even requests for static elements like gifs, jpegs, and static HTML pages.

How can failures in servlet programming impact the HTTP server? The answer lies in the queuing between the HTTP server plug-in and the application server engine. We discussed in the previous section how the HTTP server plug-in queues requests for the web application server until a servlet thread becomes available, as shown in Figure 2.3. However, poorly written servlets sometimes stall as a servlet waits indefinitely for a nonresponsive resource—perhaps a remote database or a remote system overloaded with traffic. In any case, the servlet programmer didn't provide an exit strategy for the servlet in this circumstance.

If the servlet stalls, the thread running the servlet never returns to the application server's thread pool. This reduces the resources available to perform useful work. The nonresponsive remote system may stall every servlet thread in the web site. The stall happens quickly if the servlets call the remote system on almost every servlet request. If the web site uses the remote system infrequently, it may lose threads over the course of hours or days before the stall finally occurs. As new requests arrive they queue to wait for an available servlet thread, occupying the HTTP server threads as they wait. Eventually, the HTTP server runs out of threads to respond to simple static requests. At this point, the web site is "frozen," as shown in Figure 2.4.

Frozen web sites exhibit some variety in symptoms. As we mentioned above, all of the available servlet/JSP threads might stall immediately if almost every request accesses the nonresponsive back-end system. In these cases, the web site appears to "hang" fairly quickly. That is, the site at first stops responding to dynamic requests, and shortly thereafter stops responding to static requests as well. However, other functions, which monitor the application server without using the HTTP interface, continue to function normally. (For example, depending on the application server vendor, the administrative interface may continue to work, although the application server no longer can serve pages.) If your web site only accesses the nonresponsive system infrequently, it may take hours or days to become nonresponsive. In these cases, the web site often experiences increasingly poor throughput and response time before it completely stops responding to requests.

The "acid test" for a frozen web site is a *thread trace*. A thread trace gives you details on the activity of the threads in a JVM. In the case of frozen web site, the thread traces shows the statement on which each thread is waiting. (See Chapter 12 for more details on thread traces.)

Avoid the frozen web site by planning for the eventuality of a back-end outage. Set time limits on any requests to a remote resource, and exit if the remote resource fails to respond during the time limit. If the remote resource doesn't respond, cut your losses and return an error page if you cannot obtain the data you need in a reasonable time. Do not stall your site waiting for resources. Some web containers automatically grow their thread pools in these situations. However, the thread pool cannot grow infinitely. Either performance becomes unacceptable, or the JVM collapses because of the number of running threads. Even with self-adjusting thread pools, then, the web application must prepare for and handle nonresponsive remote systems.

Web sites need short timeout periods. Unlike thick clients, which serve one user, web sites may have dozens or even hundreds of users making requests every second. The servlet often cannot afford to wait 30 seconds for a database or other back-end resource to respond. Keep the timeout values short (a few seconds at most). Place them in

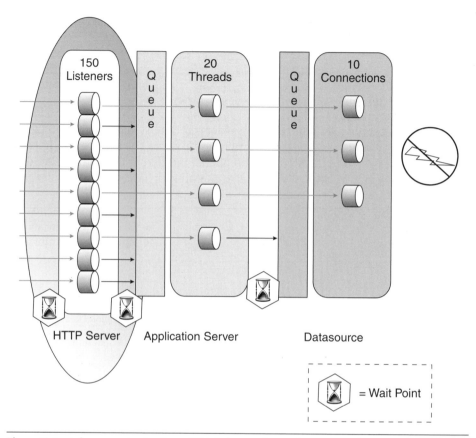

Figure 2.4 A frozen web site. From IBM Software Group Services Performance Workshop presented by Stacy Joines, 2001, Hursley, U.K. © IBM Corp. 2001. Reprinted by permission of IBM Corp.

external resource files, such as a resource bundle, and load them at servlet initialization (when the servlet's init () method executes). This allows the administrator to tune the timeout values later, if required, without modifying the code. A good web site keeps moving no matter what happens to remote resources. Plan for outages, and build an error path that allows your servlets to handle outages consistently. (Usually, the web site team sets up an error JSP to return to the user in these cases.) Again, it is far better to return an error page to a single user than to stall the web site and affect every user.

Servlet Performance Tips

As with most specifications, the servlet specification gives the programmer little guidance on the best way to write a servlet. We encounter many teams with strong backgrounds in thick client development struggling over the transition to server-based applications. Some "best practices" from the thick client world make for disaster when applied to a servlet application. A naive code port from a client-server application to a web application typically performs poorly.

Web sites amplify small programming errors and inefficiencies. For example, in the previous section we discussed thread management and thread stalls. In a thick client environment, an overly generous timeout for a back-end resource might annoy the end user but wouldn't create problems for the system as a whole. On a web site, an overly generous timeout might bring the entire site to its knees. In the client-server paradigm, one client's operation doesn't interfere with another's, but the same is definitely not true in server-side programming for Java web sites.

In this section we discuss some common application performance problems. Some of these issues might not make a tremendous difference in a thick client application. However, because of the volume of requests a large web site executes each day, these minor points become critical to the performance of a web application. Let's look at some of these best performance practices for your servlets.[7]

Use Servlets to Control Application Flow

Servlets control the flow of your application. Do not use the servlet to generate HTML or other output formats; use JSPs instead. This works even if you're not returning HTML, as JSPs can build XML or other output datastreams. This also keeps your view logic separate from the control logic of the web site, which makes it easier to change the look and feel of your web site over time.

From a performance perspective, using the servlet strictly as the controller often helps the web application avoid garbage collection issues. The outbound presentation layer usually consists of lots of strings. The JSPs generated by your application server build these strings efficiently, and efficient string handling generally reduces your garbage collection cycles. (See Chapter 4 for more details on string management and garbage collection.)

Acquire Static Resources at Initialization

Earlier we discussed the multi-threaded nature of servlets and noted that you cannot store state information in instance variables shared by multiple threads. However, some information fits very well into instance variables. For example, programmers often repeat the Java Name and Directory Interface (JNDI) lookup for a common resource such as a data source unnecessarily. The JNDI context is threadsafe, so if

---

7. See Harvey W. Gunther, "Application Server Development Best Practices for Performance and Scalability, Version 1.1.0," for many detailed servlet, JSP, and EJB best practices. Retrieved from the World Wide Web: <http://www-3.ibm.com/software/Webservers/appserv/ws_bestpractices.pdf> on March 23, 2002.

the programmer places it in a class variable, all the servlet threads may share it safely. We recommend performing any common lookups inside the servlet's init() method, and then storing the results in class variables. With this technique, the servlet only looks up the context for a given resource at initialization time. Given the performance overhead associated with JNDI lookups, this technique also significantly speeds up servlet processing.

In Listing 2.1, we use JNDI caching in a servlet example using the IBM WebSphere Application Server. This code gets the data source information once in the init() method and stores it in a class variable called myDataSource. Subsequently, every request that calls the doGet() method obtains a database connection from the data source defined in myDataSource. This spares each request from doing its own JNDI lookup of the data source. The IBM WebSphere Application Server (Version 3.5.2 and above) provides a JNDI lookup cache to speed up applications. However, doing the caching inside the servlet is even faster. (Check with your application server provider for more details about any similar JNDI caching strategies.)

Listing 2.1   Example of caching JNDI lookups inside a servlet

```
public class MyServlet extends HttpServlet {
  private static final String dsName = "myDataSource";
  private static Context context = null;
  private static DataSource myDataSource = null;

  public void init(ServletConfig config) {
    Hashtable parms = new Hashtable(2);
    parms.put(Context.INITIAL_CONTEXT_FACTORY,
              "com.ibm.websphere.naming.WsnInitialContextFactory");
    parms.put(Context.PROVIDER_URL, "iiop:///"); // local machine
      context = new InitialContext(parms);

      myDataSource = (DataSource)context.lookup("jdbc/" + dsName);

  }

  public void doGet(HttpServletRequest request,
                    HttpServletResponse response) {
    acctNumber = request.getParameter("account");
    if (acctNumber == null || "".equals(acctNumber)){
      // do error page
      }
    AccountInfo bean = new AccountInfo(acctNumber,myDataSource);
    // the AccountInfo bean will use the DataSource in order to get
    // its data from the database, by getting a connection, etc.
    .
    .

    .
    request.setAttribute("acctInfo",bean);
    getServletContext().getRequestDispatcher("foo.jsp").forward(
```

```
        request,response);
    } // doGet
} // class MyServlet
```

Manage Servlet Logging

The servlet standard lacks a detailed *logging strategy* at this point (see the discussion below on using the `servlet.log()` method). Until a standard exists, you might consider several of the free logging frameworks currently available, or you might implement your own custom framework. Regardless of your approach, your application needs a logging strategy. From a performance perspective, logs usually end up at the hard disk at some point. Of course, anything interacting frequently with the hard disk presents a potentially performance expensive operation. Before you choose a logging framework, or write one yourself, consider the following suggestions regarding logging.

- **Support Logging Levels and Use Them**   Sometimes you require more information than at others. Allow the application programmers to give a log message a weighted "importance" value. For example, severe application errors always rate a "Level 1" importance, while trace information always rates a "Level 4." Use code reviews to keep the team in synch as to the importance assigned to various classes of messages.
- **Reduce Production Logging**   When the application runs in production, keep logging to a minimum. At this stage, you only want to capture application errors, not trace information (unless you're trying to find a problem in production, which should be rare!). This greatly reduces the time the system spends interacting with the hard disk. (Remember, hard disk interaction is generally very performance expensive.) It also reduces the size of log files on the system, and avoids potential disk space issues.
- **Make Logging Levels Runtime Configurable**   If your system encounters an error, you probably want to record more detailed log information for awhile to capture the trace information around the error. However, turning the logging on for the course of the day might be too expensive in terms of performance. Instead, consider building a special "administration page" as part of your web application to toggle logging levels on the fly. (Actually, custom administration pages often prove useful for other things, such as setting various application parameters. Web site administrators use them to set everything from timeouts to the location of custom log files.)
- **Consider Buffered Writing**   Some logging mechanisms prevent disk overflows by setting an absolute maximum file size for the log file. After reaching this size, the log begins writing again at the top of the file. The danger, of course, lies in losing information in the history you might need. However, it does defeat any danger of stalling the system by running out of logging disk space.

- **Take Care with Memory Buffers**   Some logging systems write the log to a memory location, and dump to hard disk only on request, or only after the memory buffer fills up. While this is certainly faster than a pure disk I/O system, avoid overcoming your JVM heap with log data. Set a hard maximum for the buffer in memory, and make sure your applications still have enough room to run.
- **Avoid `servlet.log()`**   The standard provides a logging interface via the `servlet.log()` method. However, the implementation of this method varies greatly among application servers. Some servers just write the information to `stdout` while others write the information to their administrative database logs. The latter makes for a very, very expensive logging technique, and greatly impacts performance. We recommend avoiding the `servlet.log()` method, particularly if you plan to port your application to multiple application server vendors' platforms.
- **Avoid `system.out.println()`**   Many programmers place these statements in their application code for debugging or logging, and leave them when the code goes into production. This is a serialized resource, and requires file I/O on every call, which impacts performance. If you can't easily get these out of the code, consider setting your application server's standard out to `/dev/null` (depending on operating system) so these statements do not trigger file I/O.
- **Use an Available Logging Framework Rather Than Writing Your Own**   Rather than reinventing a logging framework, consider using one of the many available (for example, Apache's Log4j or JTrack's jLog). We do not recommend writing your own logger, as this tends to introduce errors and performance problems into many projects. Rely on existing technology if at all possible.

File-Serving Servlets

Many application servers include a servlet that acts as a miniature HTTP server. This servlet is a convenience feature, allowing the application server to serve static content. This permits the web site programmer to test web applications without defining the static content of the application to an external HTTP server. However, the file-serving servlet lacks performance efficiency. Normally, a request for static content stops at the HTTP server, which handles the request. However, if the file-serving servlet handles your static content, the request must travel through the HTTP server, the application server plug-in, and the application server itself before reaching the file-serving servlet. The increase in path length increases the overhead required to return the servlet.

Whenever possible, we strongly recommend using an HTTP server or similar server (such as a caching proxy server) to deliver static content to your users. However, if you plan on using your application server to provide security for static as well as dynamic content, you may require the application server's web container and the file-serving servlet to properly secure your static content. Of course, the J2EE 1.2 standard complicates this advice through the use of Enterprise Archive (EAR) and Web Archive (WAR) files to consolidate *all* the components of the application (including static elements). With this approach, the administrator deploys the web application into the application server, which serves both the static and dynamic content. While this approach might work for small web sites, or sites wanting to secure their static content, we still recommend using an HTTP server to serve your static content. Making this work with your application and packaging tools may require some effort, but is well worth the resulting performance gains.

JavaServer Pages (JSPs)

The previous sections discussed *JavaServer Pages (JSPs)* a great deal without really defining them or what they do. Let's briefly discuss the operation of a JSP, and its role in a Java web application. Early in the development of the servlet standard, the need for a mechanism to separate the logic layers of the web site from the presentation layers became apparent. The JSP developed out of this, and provides the presentation layer with sufficient abstraction to handle dynamic data output while keeping the feel of an HTML page. (Using MVC terminology, JSPs function as the *view*.)

A JSP exists to return dynamic data in a predefined format (often HTML). The JSP receives the data to display from a servlet and places the data into the format using special JSP tags defined by the specification. You may extend the function of the JSP by writing your own tags and creating your own "tag library," which is strongly recommended. This allows you to isolate Java code out from the body of your JSPs.

The JSP standard tries to keep the JSP page familiar to a less technical audience: the graphic designers and layout specialists for your site. These folks come with tremendous artistic talent but not a lot of Java programming skills. Good JSPs isolate the design folks from the programming team working on the servlets. As we mentioned earlier in our discussion of servlets, avoid putting presentation logic inside servlet code. Your layout team, the folks high in artistic talent but low in programming skill, cannot modify presentation logic managed inside a servlet. They do not know how to write or modify the servlet's Java code. Don't put the look and feel of your web site in the not-so-artistic hands of your servlet developers; use JSPs to build your presentation layer.

Basic JSP Runtime Operation

So how does the JSP work? Operationally, a JSP is just a special form of a servlet. The first time a request requires a JSP, the web application server runs the JSP page through a parser to turn it into a servlet. The web application server then compiles this intermediate "servlet state" of the JSP and launches it on a thread just like any other servlet. At this point, the web application server makes no differentiation between the JSP and any other runnable servlet. (Figure 2.5 illustrates the differences between servlet loading versus JSP loading.)

Usually the application server checks the file system periodically for a more recent copy of the JSP. If it finds one, it parses, compiles, and starts the newer version. The interval at which the application server checks for new JSPs is usually configurable via an administration setting.

JSP Performance Tips

Web applications servers execute JSPs much as they do regular servlets; thus, our previous discussions on good servlet programming techniques also apply to JSPs. Again we want to emphasize that you should not place Java code inside your JSPs. If you need to embed Java logic to control the layout of the page, use a tag library or JavaBean (see below) to hide the code from your presentation team. While JSPs

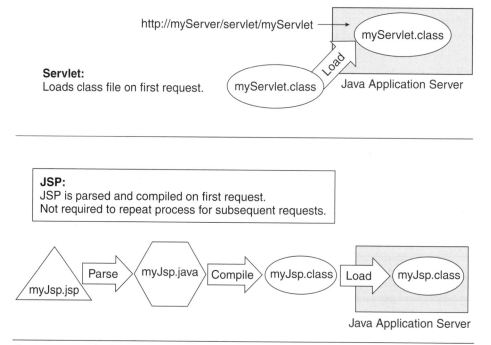

Figure 2.5   Servlet loading versus JSP loading

behave at runtime like any other servlet, they do involve a few unique performance considerations. Let's review the most important performance tips for your JSPs.

Reload Intervals

Application servers check for updates to the JSP and reparse and recompile the JSP if a more recent version exists. Of course, these checks require file I/O to look at time-stamps on the JSP files. Again, anything interacting frequently with the hard disk is performance expensive. If your application server permits, avoid auto-reloading JSPs in production (this is also a good practice for site security as well). If you cannot turn the auto-reload function off completely, set the reload interval as high as possible.

HTTP Session Created by Default

The J2EE specification supports creating "implicit" objects inside JSPs without requiring a formal declaration by the programmer. To support this feature, some application servers automatically create an HTTP session object for each JSP page if it does not already exist. As you will see, a session object remains in memory until it times out and is removed by the container. The default timeout is often as high as 30 minutes. Obviously, these session objects might take up a lot of heap space in the JVM without the web team even being aware of their existence!

Find out how your web application server manages this portion of the J2EE specification. If you do not use implicit objects and do not want an HTTP session object created in your JSP page, use a tag to prevent the web container from creating one automatically. The tag for turning off the HTTP session default creation is

```
<%@ page session="false"%>
```

Precompile or Preclick

The first time the web site receives a request for a JSP, the web application server parses, compiles, and starts the JSP as a running servlet. The parsing and compiling steps often require several seconds to perform and use significant amounts of CPU. If at all possible, get these parsing and compiling steps out of the way before the web site comes under load.

Some application servers provide JSP precompilers to eliminate the compile overhead at runtime. Make use of this feature if your web application server supports it. (The IBM WebSphere Application Server provides a batch compiler for JSP files.)

If your application server doesn't provide a JSP precompiler, consider developing a process to request as many JSPs as possible when your web application comes up. You might use an inexpensive load test tool for this, or it might just be a manual process performed quickly by the administrator after restarting the machine. Obviously, for large web sites, touching every JSP on restart isn't always feasible. However, the sooner the most frequently used JSPs become compiled, the sooner your web site gets back to normal response time and CPU utilization. (Also, precompiling your new or updated JSPs alerts you to any parsing or compilation errors *before* your user community encounters them.)

Using JavaBeans and Custom Tags

"Regular" JavaBeans make a nice complement to servlet/JSP programming by implementing the Model portion of MVC. Beans frequently play the role of a "contract" between a servlet and a JSP. The Bean defines the data the JSP might expect from the servlet, as well as methods available to access this data. Regular Beans also act as high-level wrappers for Enterprise JavaBeans (EJBs) by defining the data interface without revealing the EJB interactions underneath used to access the data or function.

JSPs use custom tags to camouflage their interactions with JavaBeans. The custom tag looks like just another HTML tag, only with special attributes defined by your development team. Behind the tag, your developers provide logic to interact with a JavaBean to retrieve dynamic data to populate the tag. Custom tags hide the Java implementation details from your design team and eliminate visible Java code in your JSPs.

Servlets pass JavaBeans to JSPs via the HTTP session or the `HTTPServletRequest` object. Again, the Bean contains the dynamic data the JSP will turn into an output page for the requesting user. Your design and programming teams may coordinate JavaBeans and custom tags manually, or they may use some of the tools available to perform "drag-and-drop" creation of JSPs with custom tags and JavaBeans.

JavaBean and Custom-Tag Performance Tips

Just as with any other feature, misusing JavaBeans and custom tags negatively impacts your web application's performance. Keep the following best practices in mind when using JavaBeans throughout your application and custom tags in your JSPs:

Avoid `bean.instantiate()` JavaBeans come with their own simplified "persistence" mechanism. Beans may place their contents in a file for "reconstitution" at a later time. For this reason, if your code creates a new JavaBean using the `bean.instantiate()` method, the servlet or JSP code checks the hard disk for any persistent Bean contents to load. Checking the hard disk takes a relatively long time, and greatly impacts the performance of your web application, so avoid using this method when creating Beans. Instead, use the `MyBean aBean = new MyBean()` technique to create a new JavaBean instance in your web application code.

Use a Database If You Need to Persist Bean Data   If you must persist the contents of your JavaBean, use a database, *not* the file system. Databases do a much better job of handling simultaneous updates than does a native file system. Again, think of the impact if thousands of servlets every hour tried to dump Bean contents directly to the hard drive. The native file system does not perform well enough to support this kind of burden, and web site performance would tumble. Instead, use a database or EJB (which interacts with the database) to store Bean contents persistently.

Use Custom Tags in Your JSPs   We discussed this earlier in the section, but it bears another brief mention here. Early JSPs depended heavily on embedded Java code to retrieve dynamic data from JavaBeans and to place the dynamic data into the page returned to the user. This usually involved liberal use of the `scriptlet` tag inside the JSP. It also required involvement by your development team to build this embedded Java and to maintain it as the look and feel of the web site changed over time.

The custom tag feature of the J2EE standard allows your developers to build a library of custom HTML tags to hide the Java required to retrieve dynamic data. These tags allow your designers to work with a familiar interface to place dynamic data in the JSPs' layout.

While custom tags provide no direct benefit to performance (we can't say a custom tag runs faster than a lump of code in a scriptlet tag), they do simplify the web application and make it more maintainable by the folks with the correct skill sets. Simplification and organization often go a long way in making your code run faster. Likewise, using custom tags might prevent your designers from making ad hoc updates to the Java code used to retrieve dynamic elements. `Scriptlet` tags make it much easier for folks outside the development team to add underperforming code to your web site.

JSPs and XML/XSL

Previous sections discussed JSPs returning HTML pages. Recently, however, many web sites are using XML (Extensible Markup Language) and XSL (Extensible Style Language) to generate dynamic pages for the user requests. For example, the JSPs might generate XML instead of full HTML pages. The XML contains only the dynamic data, while the XSL stylesheet defines how to translate this data into a format usable by the requesting client.

The XML/XSL concepts often proves beneficial for web sites supporting several user devices. With XSL, your web site might use one stylesheet to generate WML (Wireless Markup Language) for wireless devices such as mobile phones or personal digital assistants (PDAs), while another stylesheet provides the format for traditional

HTML pages. While XML/XSL allows you to readily support multiple device types, this flexibility comes at a cost. The XML/XSL approach requires repeated parsing of the XML to pull together the final output. Repeated string parsing in almost any language quickly becomes a performance drain. Java often incurs an even higher overhead because of the extra garbage collections sometimes required to clean up after string processing. (See Chapter 4 for more details on string management in Java.)

Some client devices and browsers support XSLT (XSL transformation). If *all* your clients support XSLT, consider offloading the page assembly to the client's machine. This pushes the parsing of the XML to the client machine, distributes the parsing penalty, and reduces the processing burden at your web site. However, many devices and browsers do not support XSLT. In these cases, you must parse the XML and build the output at the server.

Assorted Application Server Tuning Tips

Before we move ahead with our performance discussions, let's cover a few remaining performance topics. These tips mostly concern some performance settings available to your web application objects. Consult your documentation on how to manipulate these parameters for your application server.

Load at Startup

You choose when a servlet starts. If you so specify, the web container starts the servlet when the web container itself starts. Otherwise, the web container only starts the servlet if it receives a request for the servlet. Starting the servlet at web container startup often proves beneficial if the servlet's init() method performs significant initialization. This also proves beneficial if the servlet's init() method performs initialization that affects other areas of the web application. However, it comes at the expense of slowing the overall application server start-up time. Check your application server documentation on how to set the "load at startup" parameter for your servlets.

Web Container Thread Pool Size

The number of threads available in the web container to execute servlets, as we have noted, affects the throughput and performance of your web site. As we discussed earlier, less is often more when allocating threads because of the context switching overhead. Adjust the thread pool size for your web container in small increments to find the optimum size for your particular application and operating environment. Finding the optimal setting is an iterative process best addressed during your performance testing.

Servlet Reload

The J2EE specification requires the web container to detect updated servlets, and to start executing the new version automatically. Often, development teams use this feature during the development phase to quickly produce and test servlet updates. However, the automatic reload function is rarely desirable in production. Some points to consider include the following:

- *Performance:* Enabling this function causes the web container to check the timestamp on the Java .class file that contains the servlet, and compare it against the last known timestamp. This check either happens at regular intervals (see below), or every time the servlet receives a request. Either way, a file check takes processing time away from your application.
- *Seamless Operation:* Most application servers implement servlet reloading through the use of Java's custom class loaders. Some application servers will destroy all HTTP session objects when reloading any servlet to prevent mismatches in class definitions. Obviously, dropping all of the HTTP session objects on a production web site leads to high customer dissatisfaction.
- *Security:* Automatic reload allows the replacement of running code without stopping the application server. Whether innocently or maliciously, this gives people in your organization the opportunity to easily move unauthorized code into the production web environment.

   Turn off the automatic reload in production, if at all possible. However, if you choose to use automatic reload, consider increasing the reload interval. Some application servers set the interval quite low (as low as a few seconds in some cases). Increase the reload interval to several minutes, if possible, to minimize the application server's interaction with the file system, and improve performance.

   Note: Your application server may differentiate between servlet and JSP reload intervals and provide individual settings for servlet and JSP reload settings.

Beyond the Basics

In addition to the basic features we've discussed already, the J2EE standard provides additional features for the web application. In this section, we cover the best practices for using these features.

HTTP Sessions

We discussed earlier the multi-threaded servlet model, and some of the implications this model has for your servlets. To recap, the connectionless nature of HTTP and servlet multi-threading means the servlet cannot maintain state information for the user through normal programming techniques. For example, the servlet cannot store the user's name or account ID in an instance variable because each user does not obtain a unique instance of the servlet. Rather, multiple threads engage the same instance simultaneously.

Because the usual technique for keeping state information (instance variables) doesn't work with servlets, the servlet specification provides a different mechanism for maintaining this information. This mechanism is the `javax.servlet.http.HttpSession` class. A user's web site visit usually spans multiple, discrete requests, and sometimes lasts for an extended period of time (up to a day, in some cases). The `HttpSession` class allows the web application to keep a user's state information for the duration of the user's visit. The web application, through a servlet or JSP, requests the creation of an HTTP session for a visiting user. While the servlets and JSPs treat the HTTP session as a hash table, the application server manages the session and associates its contents repeatedly with the same user.

Application servers employ several techniques to maintain the association between users and their HTTP session data. In one commonly used approach, the application server gives the visiting user a "session ID", and returns it in a cookie to the user's browser. On subsequent visits, the browser passes the cookie back to the web site, and the application server pulls the session ID from the cookie to find the user's HTTP session data. (Also, using this technique, the cookie and HTTP session management remains invisible to the programmer. The servlet programmer merely requests the current HTTP session object without directly manipulating the cookie.) See Figure 2.6 for an example of HTTP session management using cookies. Some specialized web sites also support users who cannot or will not accept cookies. In these situations, the web sites use URL-rewriting or embed state information as hidden form fields within the returned HTML. Unlike cookie-based HTTP session support, these two methods are *not* transparent to the developer. Developers must add code to their servlets/JSPs in order to support URL-encoding or embed hidden state information in outbound data

While HTTP sessions solve a significant problem for your web application (how to keep state information about a user over the course of her visit), they introduce new considerations for your web site. HTTP session misuse often leads to web site performance and scalability issues.

HTTP Session Memory Usage

Most web application servers keep the HTTP sessions in memory. This allows the web application fast access to the user's state information. However, this also means

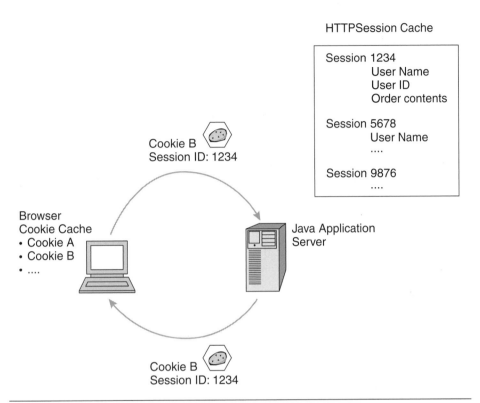

HTTPSession Cache

Session 1234
        User Name
        User ID
        Order contents

Session 5678
        User Name
        ....

Session 9876
        ....

Cookie B
Session ID: 1234

Browser
Cookie Cache
• Cookie A
• Cookie B
• ....

Java Application
Server

Cookie B
Session ID: 1234

Figure 2.6   Cookies and HTTP sessions. From "Changing Your Application Tactics: Successful Web Application Strategies for Production Websites," paper presented by Stacy Joines at Solutions 2001, San Francisco, CA. ©IBM Corp. 2001. Reprinted by permission of IBM Corp.

that the HTTP sessions share memory with the running web site applications inside the JVM heap. The J2EE specification provides no mechanism for controlling the size of an individual HTTP session. Some application servers, such as the IBM WebSphere Application Server, allow the administrator to limit the number of HTTP sessions held in memory, but they do not limit the memory allocated for each of these HTTP sessions.

We discussed previously how small indiscretions that might go unnoticed in a thick client application amplify to become serious issues on a high-volume web site. The HTTP session size often falls into this category. For example, thick client programmers routinely trade memory for performance. The developer might cache significant chunks of data in the client's memory to avoid repeated trips to a remote data source for retrieval. Because thick clients generally contain lots of dedicated memory (125MB or more, routinely), this approach makes sense.

However, this same paradigm does not work in server-side programming. We routinely encounter web applications attempting to store 10MB of data or more into each HTTP session object. 10MB of application data on a thick client presents no real problem, but 10MB spells disaster on a high-volume web site. Let's look at the math. If the HTTP session contains 10MB of data, and we have 10,000 users arriving on the site during the HTTP session timeout period, these users would require the following memory to hold their HTTP session data:

```
10,000 users * 10MB/user = 100GB
```

Since our optimum JVM heapsize often lies between 256MB and 512MB, one JVM cannot support this web site alone. In fact, if we assume a 512MB maximum heap size for each JVM, we need almost 200 JVMs to support this application!

Also, keep in mind that the objects you store in your HTTP session often contain other objects. Your actual HTTP session size depends on every object you store, including deeply nested objects. Make sure you understand the *full* extent of everything you place in the HTTP session. HTTP session bloat clearly demonstrates why you need a web site performance test before you enter production. This problem frequently goes undetected in both the programming phase as well as the functional test phase of your application's development. HTTP session bloat impacts your web site *only under load*, because it deprives the web site of memory resource as the user burden increases. Therefore, you need to introduce load from many unique users to your web site before you enter production to flush out problems of this nature.

HTTP Session Memory-Management Tips

So how do you defeat the engorged HTTP session problem? A few techniques are explained below.

Preserve Data That Must Persist   If you are using the class `HttpSession` to store things that will later go into a database, consider putting them into a database in the first place. For example, some programmers put all of a user's shopping cart data into HTTP session and then store this information into a database as well, "just in case." For these situations, consider just keeping keys in HTTP session and looking up the rest of the state information in the database if and when needed. (This technique is especially handy if the state information is referenced infrequently.)

Perform Code Reviews   Review the web application code for excessive HTTP session storage. Also, go over this problem with your web site team, especially programmers new to the web application space. Ideally, use the HTTP session to hold a few thousand bytes of data (under 2KB is ideal for most applications). If data is rarely used, and inexpensive to look up, then just leave it in the database and load it as needed.

Use Code-Profiling Tools   Many tools are available for profiling Java applications. Consider using these tools to get a handle on how much data the HTTP session uses. (See Appendix C for a list of popular code-profiling tools available for Java.)

Serialize the HTTP Session to a Stream   Many web sites use a specialized servlet to write a user's HTTP session data to a stream and then measure the size of the stream to determine the size of the HTTP session. This allows you to check the HTTP session size easily in a production environment without introducing specialized tools into the environment. It also allows you to check the contents of the HTTP session to be sure everything it holds implements the serializable interface. (If an HTTP session contains non-serializable elements, this restricts your ability to share it in a clustered environment.)

In addition to reducing the data kept in the average HTTP session, we also need to monitor *how many* HTTP sessions your web application keeps in memory at any given time. Optimizing this HTTP session cache reduces the total memory required by your HTTP sessions. Let's discuss a few techniques for managing the HTTP session cache.

Reduce HTTP Session Timeout   Most application servers allow the administrator to reduce the HTTP session timeout interval, which specifies how long the HTTP session exists after the user's last interaction with the web site. This interval gives the user an opportunity to read pages returned from the web site without losing their state information.

The interval also allows the web application server to recognize stale HTTP sessions. If the user does not return to the web site before the interval expires, the web application considers the user inactive and purges his corresponding HTTP session. Of course, the longer the timeout interval, the more unused HTTP sessions your site contains at any given point.

Usually the application server sets the timeout interval to a reasonably generous period of time. (The IBM WebSphere Application Server sets HTTP session timeout to 30 minutes by default.) Reducing the timeout might help the HTTP session pressure in your JVM, but avoid setting the timeout too low. You'll anger users if you drop their HTTP sessions while they're still using your web site. Also, setting the timeout *very* low sometimes negatively impacts performance. An extremely low timeout period may cause the application server's HTTP session management routines to run frequently. Often these routines incur a significant overhead, thus diminishing any benefit of frequently cleaning the HTTP session cache.

Before you change the timeout interval, however, check with the web application's development team. The J2EE specification also provides a method on the `HttpSession` class for modifying its timeout interval. The timeout set via this method overrides any value set administratively, so be aware of any timeout intervals set by the programming staff, and, of course, encourage them to externalize these interval values for tuning purposes.

Support a Logout Function   Consider supporting a logout function for your web site as either a button or menu item on your web pages. This lets users indicate when they've completed their visit, and allows your web application to immediately invalidate the user's corresponding HTTP session. (The web application invalidates the HTTP session via a method. Invalidation destroys the HTTP session right away rather than waiting for the timeout interval to elapse.) One caution regarding HTTP session invalidation: Earlier versions of the servlet standard allow web applications to share HTTP sessions. Don't remove HTTP session objects potentially in use by other web applications, if your application server supports the earlier spec level and your application uses this capability.

While we recommend a logout feature, we don't really expect it to solve HTTP session management for your web site. Sadly, most users never touch the logout buttons on web sites they visit. Most users just move to the next web site without formally logging out of yours. So, while it provides some benefits, the logout function is only a part of an overall HTTP session management strategy.

If your web application handles sensitive data (such as financial information) and may be accessed from a shared workstation or kiosk, consider a logout function to be a requirement. Logging out prevents subsequent users from obtaining a previous visitor's information via an existing HTTP session. Naturally, these applications generally support a very short HTTP session timeout interval and may force a logout after completing certain tasks.

Keep the HTTP Session Working Set in Memory   The working set of HTTP sessions belongs to the users *currently* engaged in using our web site. We want to keep these HTTP sessions available for fast access as the active users make requests. These HTTP sessions, therefore, need to remain in memory.

In the next section, we discuss in detail some techniques for sharing HTTP sessions and keeping them in persistent storage. At this point, however, let's discuss the most common *improper* use of a persistent HTTP session store. Sometimes web sites desperate for memory reduce their HTTP session cache size and off-load most of their HTTP session data to persistent storage. This works like an operating system paging scheme: As the web application needs an HTTP session, the application server retrieves it from the persistent store. After use, the application server stores the updates to the HTTP session back to the database.

While this sounds like a good idea at first, in practice it does not perform well. Accessing remote HTTP sessions takes time and increases network traffic. Particularly for web sites serving high request volumes or supporting large HTTP sessions, the remote HTTP session "retrieve on demand" approach quickly degenerates into abysmal performance. (Of course, these web sites are usually the most eager to try this technique.)

Always keep your working set of HTTP sessions in the memory cache. Use any persistence or sharing mechanism only to store/share HTTP sessions as an outage precaution. Do not try to use these mechanisms as an extension of the in-memory HTTP session cache. You may need to configure multiple application server instances (see Multiple Instances: Clones later in this chapter) to get enough total heap size to hold all the HTTP session data.

Sharing HTTP Sessions

Many application servers support sharing HTTP session data among many instances of the application server functioning in a cluster (see Clones below in this chapter, and Web Site Topologies in Chapter 3). Strategies for sharing session data vary. Sharing HTTP session data allows the cluster to *failover* a visiting user. If the web application server handling the user's requests fails, the web site may route the user's request to another application server in the cluster. If the user's HTTP session data resides in a common store, this application server pulls in the user's state data and continues the user's visit to the site without interruption. Figure 2.7 demonstrates HTTP session failover using database persistence.

Some vendors share the sessions through a shared network update, either to all other servers in the cluster or from a "primary" server to a "secondary" server. In this strategy, the session data resides in the memory of one or more application servers in the cluster. Another technique places all the HTTP sessions in the cluster in a shared, persistent datastore (usually a relational database). Yet another sharing method involves using flat files on a shared file system to store the session data.

Each strategy generates its own performance issues. Clustered network updates potentially generate lots of network traffic and spread the memory burden of the HTTP sessions throughout the cluster. Likewise, persistent session storage requires transfer of data between the application server instances and the datastore. Serializing HTTP session data and writing it to disk is also slow.

HTTP Session Sharing Tips

If you share HTTP session data within your application server cluster, keep the following performance pointers in mind.

Keep HTTP Sessions Small Moving HTTP session data across the network increases the need for small HTTP sessions. Small HTTP sessions reduce the database burden for persistent session storage and keep the clusterwide memory

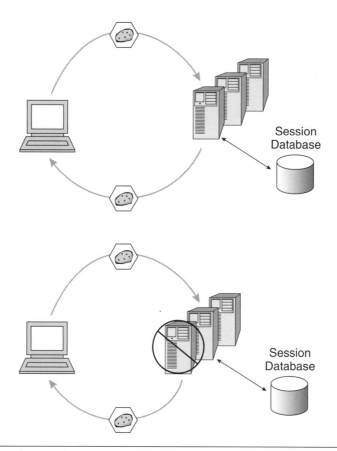

Figure 2.7   Failover with a persistent HTTP session database. From "Changing Your Application Tactics: Successful Web Application Strategies for Production Websites," paper presented by Stacy Joines at Solutions 2001, San Francisco, CA. © IBM Corp. 2001. Reprinted by permission of IBM Corp.

requirements manageable for a networked HTTP session sharing system. Small HTTP sessions also use less network bandwidth during their transfers.

Keep HTTP Session Data Serializable   Objects placed in the HTTP session should implement the `java.io.Serializable` interface. (This includes the objects themselves, as well as anything they include or from which they inherit.) The application server serializes the HTTP session data onto the network when transferring the data. If the data does not implement the `Serializable` interface, the web application server throws an exception when it tries to transfer it to a shared database or other store.

These serialization exceptions often take the web site team by surprise. HTTP session sharing, in theory, requires no programming changes to implement. (The application server administrator determines whether to enable this feature.) However, if the application developers did not prepare their code for HTTP session sharing, the first attempt by the administrator to use this feature often fails.

While enabling HTTP session sharing may seem as easy as "flipping a switch" in load testing or production, objects placed in the HTTP session actually determine whether HTTP session sharing works. Check the content of your HTTP sessions during code reviews to avoid encountering this problem in testing or production.

Avoid Nontransferable Data Sometimes HTTP session data does not transfer in a meaningful way to another web application server instance. For example, if your application programmers stuff the HTTP session with things like thread handles, this data provides no value to another web application server instance on failover. (Remember, each server instance lives in its own Java Virtual Machine.)

Mark nontransferable variables in your HTTP session objects with the `transient` keyword, so they won't be serialized. Of course, you must write your code to handle failover by recreating the transient data within the context of the new web application server instance, as needed.

This leads to a programming issue for your web application. Avoid using information specific to a machine or web application server instance whenever possible. In addition to thread handles and the like, avoid depending on a machine's IP address and similar data that make it difficult for your application to failover. Again, rigorous code reviews and programmer education provide your best protection for these scenarios.

Enterprise JavaBeans (EJBs)

Enterprise JavaBeans (EJBs) allow your web site applications and other traditional applications to gain access to centralized business logic contained in distributed components. They provide a layer of abstraction between your applications and your database. In fact, your EJBs may consist of data assembled from various datastores. This section covers the EJB basics so that we can discuss some of their performance characteristics. If you need more information about EJBs, we list several excellent books in the Bibliography.

EJBs exist inside an *EJB container*, which controls the life cycle of the Beans under its care. This management includes instantiating and destroying EJBs, managing EJB pools, and even interacting directly with databases on behalf of certain types of EJBs.

EJBs come in two basic flavors: *Session Beans* and *Entity Beans*. Session Beans live a transient existence inside the container. They contain business logic and may contain state for a specific client. Session Beans are either *Stateful* or *Stateless*.

- *Stateless Session Beans:* As their name indicates, Stateless Session Beans do not maintain state from one method call to the next. After executing a method, they return to their pool to await the next request, which might originate from any client.
- *Stateful Session Beans:* Again, as their name implies, Stateful Session Beans maintain state information. A client application or web application may reference the same instance of a Stateful Session Bean for multiple calls. Stateful Session Beans, while not as transient as the Stateless Session Beans, do not persist. If the Bean times out, or if the container experiences a failure, the Bean and its state go away. (Note: Some application servers actually support failover for Stateful Session Beans, so check your vendor's documentation.)

Entity Beans represent a persistent entity. The data contained by an Entity Bean generally originates from a single database row, although it could consist of an assemblage of data. Likewise, EJBs most commonly store persistent data in a database, although other persistence mechanisms also exist. The J2EE specification defines two types of Entity Beans: *Container-managed Persistence* (CMP), or *Bean-managed Persistence* (BMP).

- *Container-managed Entity Beans:* These Entity Beans require little or no coding to control their data retrieval and persistence. For example, when using a relational database as the persistent store, the CMP Bean requires little or no custom SQL to retrieve or store its contents from/to the database. The container manages the interaction with the persistent storage mechanism, and updates the contents of the EJB from the persistent store as required.
- *Bean-managed Entity Beans*, on the other hand, require custom-coded persistence interaction logic. These Beans contain their own logic for retrieval and storage with regard to their persistent storage mechanism. In the case of relational database interaction, these Beans require custom SQL provided by application developers to interact with the relational database.

EJB Performance Tips

EJBs give you excellent support for sharing your business logic between your web applications and thick client applications. EJBs also perform and scale very well in web applications if you plan ahead for performance and scalability. Let's discuss some of the best practices to ensure good EJB performance.

Use Stateless Session Beans as Façades Servlet or JavaBean programmers often interact directly with Entity Beans. On a typical user request, the servlet makes several calls to Entity Beans to gather the data required to satisfy the request. This, however, is not the best strategy for high performance. Direct interaction with Entity Beans from a servlet usually results in several remote method calls. These calls tend to be performance expensive, so reducing the number of remote calls in your code path makes sense.

Direct interaction also stresses the transactional boundary between the servlet and the EJB. Entity Beans synchronize their state after each transaction, often needing two database calls for each method called. When a servlet accesses the Bean directly, each "getter" method becomes a transaction. This usually means a database call to get the current data from the database and then another to update the database at the end of the method, as shown in Figure 2.8.

To circumvent these problems, use a Session Bean as a façade to Entity Beans. The Session Bean contains the logic to gather data from one or more Entity Beans and return this information to the calling application, which yields several advantages. The programming interface becomes much simpler: The client calls only one method on a single EJB to perform complex interactions. This reduces the remote method calls for these complex interactions (the Session Bean doesn't require a

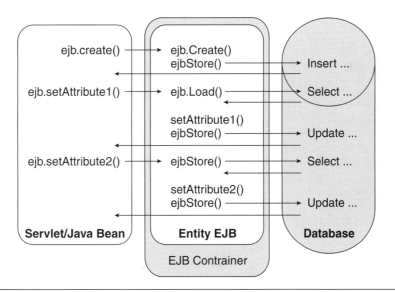

Figure 2.8 Enterprise JavaBean transactions without a façade Bean

remote call to Entity Beans in the same EJB container as itself). Likewise, if the Session Bean shares an EJB container with the Entity Beans, it also controls the transactional boundary for the entire interaction. The Session Bean controls the transaction for all other EJBs involved in implementing the function. The Entity Bean only synchronizes its state when the Session Bean reaches a transactional boundary (such as the completion of the Stateless Session Bean's method). Figure 2.9 shows an example of transactional boundaries using façade Beans.

Also, façade Beans prove useful when coordinating transactions across multiple Entity Beans, as well as other Session Beans performing direct JDBC calls. This requires the Entity Beans involved to implement the correct transaction setting, usually TX_SUPPORTS or TX_REQUIRED.

Use Direct JDBC Calls   If you manipulate multiple rows of your database when retrieving an Entity Bean, consider using direct JDBC calls from within a Stateless Session Bean to perform a "read" of the Bean's data. Later, if you need to update or delete the data (or create new data), use an Entity Bean to control these tasks. This approach sometimes saves time by reducing expensive "finder" overhead. It also provides performance benefits to applications that perform lots of read activity, but few updates, on a complex database table structure.

Avoid Fine-Grained EJB Data Models   Don't overdo it with the Entity Beans. In some cases, we've seen a simple application request use literally hundreds of different

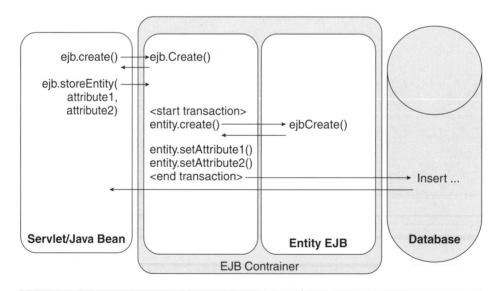

Figure 2.9   Enterprise JavaBean transactions using a façade Bean

Entity Beans. Obviously, your web site cannot handle high volumes if you load hundreds of EJBs on each call. Simplify the model and consolidate your data into larger Beans. Also, reduce the Beans involved by letting your SQL and the database do more work for you. Use database joins to consolidate your data at the database.

Mark Methods as Read-Only   This setting reduces the database interactions required to execute your EJB methods and provides performance benefits to your application. Check with your application server vendor for the implementation of this J2EE feature.

Consider Scalability Issues of Stateful Session and Entity Beans   Since these Beans have identity and state, each instance only exists in one EJB container in your web site. Stateless Beans, on the other hand, exist in any convenient container (often, the EJB container running in the same JVM as the web container), or in the container with the most processing power available. This flexibility often makes Stateless Session Beans more scalable than other EJB choices.

Cache Bean Contents in Custom Finders   Custom finders returning an Entity Bean collection make *n* + 1 database calls: one to perform the "find" and one call *per Entity Bean instance* to instantiate the Entity Bean's contents. Depending on the number of Entity Beans returned, their size, and the frequency with which you access them, you may decide to cache the results of a custom finder.

Before you implement a custom-finder cache, consider how much memory the cache requires. Again, caching at your server only works to your advantage if it does not consume excessive amounts of memory. Likewise, caching only works if the data retrieved does not change while cached.

Avoid EJB Passivation   We discussed earlier the inefficiencies of the file system in high-volume web sites. EJB containers passivate inactive Stateful Session Beans if the container begins to run out of room when creating new Beans. Passivation dumps the state of the Bean to a file. If a subsequent request needs the passivated Bean, the container must interact with the file system to reload it.

To avoid passivation, remove unneeded Stateful Session Beans as soon as possible. Of course, eventually the container times out and removes old Stateful Session Beans, but if your web site moves high volumes, the container may be forced to passivate the Bean before the time-out. Use the EJB `remove()` method to remove unneeded Stateful Session Beans from the container. Also, consider shortening the timeout period for the Stateless Session Beans.

Cache Homes for EJBs   As stated earlier in the discussion on servlets, avoid expensive JNDI lookups whenever possible. As we discussed in the servlet section, you should use caching techniques to reduce or eliminate repeated JNDI lookups. Consider `Broker` objects or other design patterns to manage JNDI lookups, as well as any other cacheable operations. (Caching EJB homes is always a good idea.)

Tuning EJB Containers

EJB containers from different vendors often include some unique settings that affect their performance, but some settings span all vendor implementations. Let's take a quick look at some of the more important EJB container settings. Of course, you should check your application server vendor's documentation for other tuning settings.

Pool Size

Containers maintain pools of EJB instances. You may configure the maximum size for these pools, which determines how many instances your EJB container controls at any point in time. (Some containers support a "per pool" setting, while others use a grosser measurement for the *total* EJB instances managed by the container.) Configure your pool size to contain the working set of EJBs your web application requires. Your pool should *at least* accommodate the EJB instances required to satisfy your maximum simultaneous requests. (Keep in mind that these requests may originate from multiple web containers in a large, distributed web site.) At the same time, you must prevent the EJB container from exhausting its JVM heap with excessive EJB instances.

Thus, the size of the EJB pool really depends on two factors: demand and data size. Use your performance test to help define an optimal setting for your EJB pool. Understanding how many EJB instances you need at peak loading, as well as the size of these instances, also gives you significant insight in setting an optimal EJB pool size. (Also, as with web containers, some EJB containers permit unbounded pool growth, which you should avoid because it eventually leads to memory exhaustion. Instead, enforce a hard maximum on the EJB pool size based on your testing. Different vendors support setting this hard maximum in different ways, so check the vendor's documentation for details.)

Cleanup Interval

Some containers allow you to specify how frequently the container sweeps its pool for old objects. Reducing the interval between sweeps reduces the number of old objects left in your pool and gives you more room to create new objects as needed. However, running the sweeping routine *too* frequently may degrade performance, depending on the "weight" of the sweeping routine. Consider adjusting this interval during your performance testing to find an adequate setting for your application.

Transaction Isolation Level

The *transaction isolation level* controls the visibility of uncommitted changes within the underlying database. You may specify the application level at the EJB or EJB method level. (Additional rules apply if your application calls multiple methods with differing transaction isolation levels.)

For best performance, use as liberal an isolation level as possible. However, this really depends on the application as well as the other objects and applications sharing the underlying database. Too low a setting may result in unexpected side-effects such as multiple, simultaneous updates to the same data row. (Obviously, performance considerations take a back seat to data correctness issues.) Likewise, too high a setting results in application deadlocks.

Local versus Remote Interfaces

As more vendors implement the EJB 2.0 specification, the features of this specification level become more important. For example, you may decide to call your EJBs via *local interfaces*, rather than *remote interfaces*. Local interfaces work when the calling client (such as a servlet or JavaBean) shares the same JVM as the called EJB. By avoiding a remote method call, this protocol provides significant performance benefits.

However, you cannot use local interfaces with widely distributed web sites. If your EJBs reside in a remote JVM, you must use remote interfaces to access them. (See the discussion on clones later in this chapter.) Relying on local interfaces for performance limits your web site scalability. If you anticipate scaling your web site in the future, develop a performance strategy that assumes the possibility of remote interfaces.

Message-Oriented Middleware (MOMs)

The EJB 2.0 specification also introduces *message-driven Beans*. This feature enables Message-Oriented Middleware (MOMs) like IBM's MQ-Series, to call functions implemented within EJBs. Because this technology is so new, very few performance guidelines exist regarding it.

However, the reverse practice, where EJBs access a MOM for data, is quite common. The best practice for accessing MOMs via an EJB, or from any other object in web application (servlet, JavaBean, etc.), for that matter, is the following. First, be aware that MOMs operate *asynchronously*, while web applications operate *synchronously*. Many web sites try to mask the asynchronous nature of a MOM within the synchronous operation of their web application by placing the web application in a wait state until the MOM completes the requested task. However, MOMs do not guarantee delivery within a particular time frame; they only guarantee eventual delivery. Therefore, you cannot count on the responsiveness of a MOM. Be *very* careful accessing an asynchronous MOM inside your synchronous web application. As noted earlier, indefinite wait within a web application often leads to disaster. Plan ahead for long response times and outages within the MOM system. Just because your MOM normally responds quickly, don't assume that it always will.

Database Connection Pool Management

Database connection management in the servlet world proves difficult for former thick client developers. Thick client best practices encourage the programmer to obtain a database connection once and cache it inside the client for all future requests. This works well inside a thick client because it costs a lot of time to obtain a new connection; however, it is not practical on a web site. Your web site may support thousands of logged-in users at any given time and may run dozens of different servlets over the course of a minute. Obviously, assigning a database connection to a given user, or even to a given servlet, isn't practical.

Instead, most web applications use pooled database connections. The most common pooling mechanisms are the `javax.sql.ConnectionPoolDataSource` or the `javax.sql.XADataSource`. The JDBC specification defines the `DataSource` class, which is in turn implemented by the vendors. Many early application servers also supported their own implementations of data sources, or similar pooling constructs, prior to the JDBC standard. The data source allows the administrator to define the number of database connections available to the running web applications. An example flow using a data source goes as follows:

1. A servlet obtains a database connection when required for database interaction.
2. The servlet uses the database connection to interact with the database and processes any returned data.
3. *Immediately* after completing the database interaction, the servlet returns the connection to the data source connection pool by issuing a `connection.close()` method.

By "immediately," we mean within the method that gets the connection. Don't pass a result set around to various layers (JSPs, other servlets, and so on) in order to manipulate the data from the database. Loop through the result set, pulling the data out into your own collection, and then close the result set, statement, and connection. (Failing to close the statement object before returning the connection to the pool sometimes results in an error for the next application reusing the connection.)

Database Connection Management Tips

The data source and its database connection pool make managing database connections trivial. However, many programmers fail to use the database connection pool properly, if at all. Let's discuss some of the best practices for database connection management.

Return the Database Connection to Its Pool Quickly   Many servlet writers return the database connection to the connection pool as an afterthought when all the processing inside the servlet completes. This makes the connection unavailable to other servlets for significant periods of time (a half second or more, in some cases). Return the connection as soon as possible to the connection pool. Also, consider optimizing your code to use database connections more efficiently.

Return Connections No Matter What Happens   Make sure you close everything within `finally` clauses in your code. Otherwise, if an exception occurs, you may "leak" a database connection or leave a statement open. While the connection pool may eventually "reap" the lost connection (discard it and create a new one), this process only starts after a generous timeout interval. Too many lost connections may consume all of the connections in your database connection pool, and this may result in a frozen web site. Try to return connections to their pools even in the event of an exception. Also, try to close statements to avoid returning a connection to the pool in an unusable state.

Use the Connection Pooling Feature   A few servlet writers refuse to use the data source at all. They continually obtain and release database connections inside their servlets. The performance overhead of this approach is breathtaking. Use a connection pool, even if you need to make some changes in your existing code. The extra effort almost always pays for itself in enormous performance benefits.

"Custom" Connection Pool Managers versus Data Sources   Sometimes we may encounter shops using custom connection pools. Often, these shops wrote their own pooling logic prior to the adoption of the `DataSource` object in the JDBC standard. Connection pools contain surprisingly complex logic for things such as recognizing and reaping dead connections, growing and shrinking the pool in accordance with demand, and refreshing connections after a database outage. Often home-grown data sources require considerable tuning, and they may not scale as the site continues to grow. Take advantage of the tuning and expertise built into your vendor's implementation and convert to the JDBC standard data source.

Web Services

Another relative newcomer to the web application space is the concept of *web services.* Regrettably, the web services technology lacks a body of performance expertise at this point. (Performance guidelines usually follow some number of practical experiences with a new technology.) Nonetheless, based on what we *do* know about web services in general, we tentatively offer some rough advice. Again, these touch web services performance at a high level. Use solid performance testing of your implementation to better understand your specific performance profile.

Use UDDI (Universal Description, Discovery and Integration) with Care

Repeatedly locating a web service, parsing the interface description, and mapping parameters to the interface seriously degrades the performance of your web application. For better performance, consider selecting the services you plan to use during the development of your web application. Directly code interactions with these services rather than repeatedly using UDDI at runtime. Of course, hard-coding services may result in some flexibility restrictions on your applications, but it may make sense as performance trade-off for heavily used web application functions.

Minimize SOAP Data Transfers   SOAP (Simple Object Access Protocol) is relatively slow. Web services applications often spend most of their time parsing and generating the XML used by SOAP rather than executing logic.[8] Reduce the parsing overhead by keeping the data transferred via SOAP to a minimum.

Monitor Changing Web Site Usage Patterns   Providing web services functions often changes the usage patterns of your web site. Most web site designs focus on direct interactions with a web user. However, web sites providing web services functions often find themselves playing the role of "middleware" for other web applications using their functions. For example, a search engine or sports site often handles more requests for information actually displayed by other web sites than direct requests from web users.

This new role as middleware often shifts the priorities of the web site providing the web services function. For example, key features such as the web site's home page become less important. However, other features, such as returning the high school basketball scores for all teams in a particular zip code become heavily used through the web services function.

---

8. From Harvey W. Gunther, "Web Services Best Practices for Performance and Scalability, Version 1.0.0," an IBM internal report (September 24, 2001).

If your web site provides web services functions, monitor the usage patterns of your web site. You may discover a need for additional resources, such as database connections, to support increased demand for certain web application functions. Also, this increased demand may require performance improvements in previously underperforming (but seldom-accessed) functions now receiving considerably more traffic.

Other Features

Your web application server might use other features not defined in the J2EE specification. We've included below some performance pointers for a few of the more common of these features.

Built-in HTTP Servers

Many web application servers include their own, built-in HTTP servers. By using the built-in HTTP server, the web site avoids the performance overhead of the plug-in processing normally associated with a stand-alone HTTP server. These built-in HTTP servers often run "out of the box" with little setup, which makes them particularly appealing to web site teams hard-pressed for time.

While the built-in HTTP servers have a lot going for them, we do not recommend them for high-volume, production web sites. Many high-volume web sites place the HTTP server inside a DMZ, and run the web application server behind the DMZ. Built-in HTTP servers cannot support this configuration. Also, stand-alone, commercial HTTP servers provide more features and support high volumes and static content requests more efficiently. (See the next chapter for more on HTTP servers and their performance.)

General Object Pool Management

The JDBC data source standard we discussed earlier applies only to database connections. Sometimes you need a custom pool manager in your web application to control sharing of other objects, such as connections to a non-JDBC-compliant data repository or other sharable objects. For example, if your web application launches threads, you need a thread pool. The thread pool reduces overhead from repeatedly creating and destroying threads, and prevents some runaway conditions.

General Object Pool Management Tips

If you find yourself writing a custom pool manager, consider the following best practices.

Use Configurable Limits   Load the parameters for your thread pool from an external source, such as an XML file or resource bundle, during initialization. This allows the administrator to fine-tune the pools in your application during performance testing or deployment without making a code change. Key parameters include the minimum and maximum pool size, timeout values, growth values, and so on. (Some web applications build their own custom administration function to update these values on the fly.)

Never Wait Indefinitely Inside the Pool   The servlet requests a thread from the pool, but none are available. The pool manager decides to grow the pool by another five threads (the pool has not reached its maximum size yet). What happens to the servlet request while the pool grows? Do not allow it to wait indefinitely. Time out the request and/or throw a "soft" exception if the pool cannot obtain new resources in a very short period of time (milliseconds, not seconds). *It is better to return empty-handed than not return at all from a resource request.* Avoid stalling the web site by leaving servlet threads in an indefinite wait state. (See the discussion on "frozen web sites" earlier in this chapter.)

Set Pool Maximums   To avoid runaway thread creation, set hard maximums for your thread pool. If your threads interact with a back-end system, they might stall if that system becomes nonresponsive. In this case, your thread pool might fill up with stalled threads waiting for a dead remote system. Creating more threads only makes the situation worse, and may lead to a system crash if you allow thread pool to create hundreds of threads. Instead, return an exception to the servlets requesting threads. Program the servlets to catch this exception and return the appropriate error page, if necessary. This is another example of making outages a normal part of your site's operation.

Set a Maximum Wait for Thread Execution   After retrieving the thread, take care when launching it. Again, you cannot wait indefinitely for a thread to return. Always manage the amount of time your servlet waits for a thread before continuing, particularly if your thread tries to access remote resources. Use a timeout on your threads. Instead of

```
myThread.join();
```

use the join with a timeout parameter:

```
myThread.join(500);
```

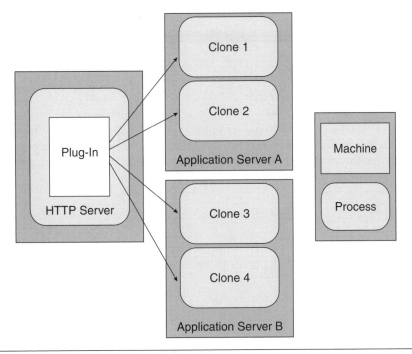

Figure 2.10   Clones in both vertical and horizontal scaling

(Note: This is just an example of a potential timeout value. Base your timeouts on your actual application needs.)

Again, whenever possible, make the timeout value externally configurable. Also, if you set a timeout, you may abandon threads over time. This is another reason to set an absolute maximum for your thread pool to avoid runaway thread acquisition.

Multiple Instances: Clones

Many larger Java web application server vendors provide an easy way to create and manage multiple application server instances (each running in a separate JVM) on your web site. These multiple JVMs may execute servlet applications, or EJB containers, or both. The IBM WebSphere Application Server, for example, calls these multiple JVMs *clones*; other products call them *instances*. Clones may share the same machine, or install across multiple machines, or both. Figure 2.10 shows multiple clones within a server cluster.

Clones play a useful role in the performance of your Java web site. For very large multiprocessor servers, clones allow you to take better advantage of the CPU and memory available on the server. Clones assist with large-server *vertical scaling*. As discussed in Chapter 1, a single JVM cannot take full advantage of the resources available on an extremely large server. For example, if you use a 24-way, 64GB RAM server machine, you cannot expect to get full utilization of this box with a single JVM. If the single JVM uses 50% of the CPU available, adding another cloned JVM might raise that to 80% or 90%.

Cloning also allows the administrator to manage application server instances spread across multiple machines. This gives the administrator flexibility to better allocate resources, as well as centralized control over the web applications executing on the server machines.

Cloning Performance Tips

As with any other feature, cloning requires careful use to avoid performance pitfalls. Let's discuss some cloning performance best practices. (See Web Site Topologies in Chapter 3 for more on clones and the best practices for their deployment.)

Too Many Clones, Too Little Resource   Cloning does not solve problems for overloaded servers. If your server machine uses 100% of the CPU capacity (or even close to 100%), *do not add clones to your server*. The CPU is saturated. Instead, add CPU capacity to your system, or tune your application. Do not increase the CPU burden by adding clones to the server.

Scale Your Resources as You Add Clones   If you add clones to your servers or web site, don't forget to add resources to support them. Each clone requires database connections, heap space, and network capacity. If you add clones, add the resources the clone needs to operate.

Summary

This chapter covered many aspects of Java application servers, including settings on the various containers, coding practices, and performance issues with various J2EE features. However, your web site is more than your Java web application. The next chapter discusses some of the other key "players" such as the HTTP server and the firewall. Again, your web site is a system. Tuning your web application while ignoring other web site components usually leads to an underperforming production system.

Chapter 3

THE PERFORMANCE ROLES OF KEY WEB SITE COMPONENTS

Your web site is a system of many interconnected components. So far, we've discussed only the performance issues surrounding the web application and the Java runtime environment while mostly ignoring the rest of the web site. This chapter begins looking outward from the web application to the many other components of your web site. Remember that a web site is only as fast as its slowest component. If you tune your web application but fail to tune an underperforming network, your customer still experiences poor performance. To make the web site fast, we must evaluate its performance as a whole and tune any element not meeting performance requirements.

In this chapter, we review the essential hardware and software components of a typical web site. We cover the basics of your network as well as discussing key web site elements like load balancers and HTTP servers. We also review some common web site topologies, along with the essentials of scaling and clustering.

Network Components

Let's start our review of the web site with the most underappreciated component: the network. The network acts as the arteries and veins of your web site. Every request entering your site moves across the network, as does every outbound response. In between, the HTTP servers, application servers, databases, content servers, and the like all depend on the network when sharing essential data required to handle the incoming requests. If something in the network hampers this flow of information, the web site does not work at peak efficiency.

Despite its essential function, the network plays an invisible role at the web site. Unlike noting problems with the servers, detecting an overworked network is not as easy as glancing at a CPU monitor. Many web site teams lack the skills for monitoring network performance or even for determining the network capacity their web site requires. For these reasons, network problems often go undetected until they become critical. This section covers some of the basic components of your network and their function. We suggest you also consult Chapter 9 for more details on network capacity planning and troubleshooting.

Routers

Routers connect your enterprise to the Internet, so they usually mark the start of your web site's network, as shown in Figure 3.1. When you select a router for your network, make sure it's rated to handle the full bandwidth of your upstream link to the Internet. Also, check the router's settings to ensure it's properly configured for your anticipated network traffic. Routers impact performance when they limit the network's potential bandwidth. Typical symptoms of a router problem include low network utilization and low machine utilization. If the router becomes a bottleneck, traffic simply does not reach the network and the servers attached to the network.

If you observe these symptoms in your environment, monitor your router. High CPU utilization at the router usually means you need a larger unit. Also, improper configuration may prevent the router from performing at capacity. Sometimes it's not

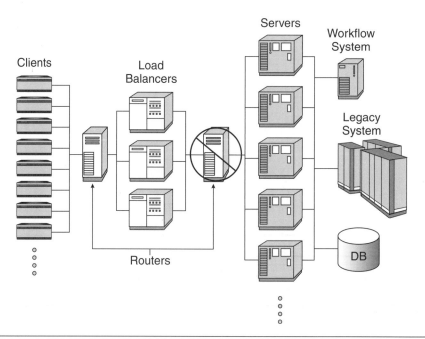

Figure 3.1   Router placement in a large web site

possible to monitor the router. In these situations, try moving your test clients so the router no longer lies between them and the servers under test. This technique eliminates the router from the test, and tells you if the router contributes to performance problems.

Firewalls

Usually, a firewall follows immediately behind the router in your web site's network. Firewalls prevent unauthorized network traffic from flowing between the external world and the enterprise. A typical installation adds a second firewall or set of firewalls between the servers and the enterprise's intranet. This configuration supplies an extra level of security in case of a hacker attack from the Internet against one of the server machines.

Figure 3.2 illustrates a typical network topology. The network segment between the two firewalls is known as the DMZ. (See the discussion on firewall usage later in this chapter in the section entitled Web Site Topologies for more details on firewall configuration.)

Much like routers, undersized or poorly configured firewalls act as bottlenecks in the network. The symptoms of a firewall problem resemble those of a router problem: poor network and server machine utilization. Sometimes firewall problems also result in refused connections at the browser/test driver, or dropped connections between the application server and the database. We recommend initially testing *without* firewalls in your environment. After obtaining a baseline of performance, add the firewalls to your configuration to gauge their impact on overall web site performance.

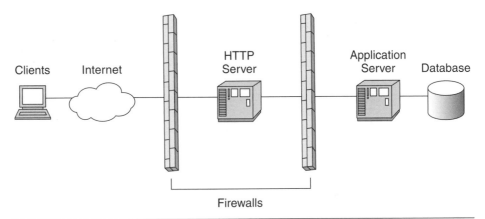

Figure 3.2 A typical web site firewall configuration

Proxy Servers

Proxy servers and reverse proxy servers commonly reside in the DMZ. Proxy servers hide the network addresses of machines configured to route traffic through them. Enterprises use regular proxy servers for outbound traffic, and these machines seldom impact web site performance. Reverse proxy servers, however, often act as security devices for funneling inbound traffic through the second firewall in a DMZ. (Figure 3.3 shows such a configuration.) Since the reverse proxy funnels all the traffic in this web site, it easily becomes a bottleneck if improperly configured.

Another common reverse proxy server configuration places it at the front of the network to cache content closer to the user. Figure 3.4 shows such a typical reverse proxy setup. In this configuration, the reverse proxy server caches the web site's static content (static HTML pages, jpegs, gifs, JavaScript, and so on). This produces several advantages for the web site.

- The reverse proxy server quickly responds to browser requests for static elements without passing the requests further into the web site for handling. This reduces the path length of the static requests and results in faster performance for the user. (Most web sites receive far more requests for static content than for dynamic.)
- This reduces the burden on the other portions of the web site. The HTTP servers and web application servers no longer handle the bulk of static requests (the reverse proxy server handles them instead). This gives the web site more bandwidth to handle requests for dynamic pages and decreases overall network and server load further into the web site.

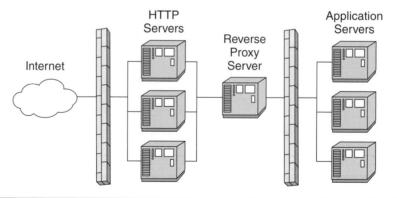

Figure 3.3   Reverse proxy server used for security

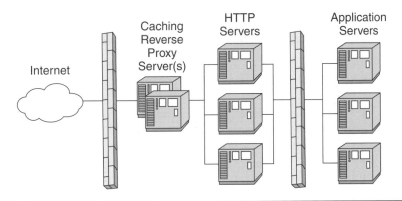

Figure 3.4 Caching reverse proxy servers

Some application servers also support pushing some dynamic content into the reverse proxy server. For example, a news web site might cache the site's "front page," since every visitor accesses this page. Whenever the page changes, the updated page replaces the original in the cache. This technique works well for dynamic pages that are accessed frequently but updated relatively infrequently. High-volume web sites serving lots of static content find reverse proxy servers particularly useful. In particular, e-Commerce web sites frequently use this configuration to support the gifs and jpegs embedded in their catalog pages.

Under the covers, a proxy server is just a highly specialized HTTP server. Many of the performance tips in the HTTP server section of this chapter also apply to the proxy server. In general, make sure your reverse proxy server supports the incoming traffic loads you anticipate. (Consider adding reverse proxy servers to support very large web sites.) Also, make sure you configure the reverse proxy with enough *listeners* to support the incoming traffic. Finally, the reverse proxy server needs enough capacity for its cache of static elements. As you add applications (or modify existing ones), check the impact of the new or updated pages and their static content on the proxy server. Note that the proxy server may require more network bandwidth than the portions of the web site returning dynamic content. (Graphic elements require more network bandwidth than HTML text because they're simply larger.)

As with the router, we suggest beginning initial performance testing without the reverse proxy server. Add it to the configuration after obtaining some baseline performance measurements. This gives you a reference point to determine the impact (if any) of the reverse proxy on overall performance.

Network Interface Cards (NICs)

Web site servers often use multiple network interface cards (NICs) to increase network throughput and decrease congestion. Keep in mind that web traffic is not balanced: The size of a request is usually many times smaller than the response. For this reason, web sites sometimes route incoming requests over a normal network while sending the outbound responses over a high-speed network. (Figure 3.5 shows such a topology.) Machines bridging the inbound and outbound traffic require two NIC cards, one for each network, in these topologies. Beyond the inbound and outbound request traffic, the web site sometimes uses multiple networks to support the site's DMZ or to separate web application traffic from database traffic. In all these cases, any machine bridging the networks requires multiple NICs.

NICs sometimes impact performance, especially that of systems using multiple NIC configurations. In many operating systems, the system administrator binds processes to particular NICs. Misconfigured bindings sometimes cause overloaded NICs, resulting in performance problems or application failures. To make matters worse, the NICs themselves vary in complexity and operation. For example, we once encountered a particularly difficult error involving improperly configured programmable NICs. (In this case, two machines contained cards with duplicate MAC addresses, and one NIC failed whenever the other started.) Likewise, we've encountered NIC cards with buffering or pacing algorithms, which interfere with the machine's network throughput.

Even simple NIC configurations sometime impact performance. An overburdened NIC card acts as a bottleneck. If the overburden card resides in a firewall server or HTTP server, it prevents traffic from reaching many other web site components. Test client machines frequently experience NIC overloads. The test client tries to

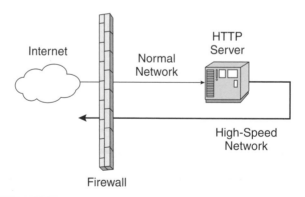

Figure 3.5   Different speeds for networks handling different loads

simulate the activity of many users all on a single machine. If the web site returns large pages, or if the test client tries to simulate a large number of concurrent users, the resulting traffic volume frequently swamps the NIC.

Network card problems prove incredibly difficult to diagnose and resolve. Many operating systems fail to provide any useful monitors for attached NICs, and CPU activity does not always act as an effective gauge of network activity. Hands down, a network protocol analyzer is the best tool for finding NIC problems. If you don't have a network protocol analyzer, or you can't use one on the network in question, try isolating or removing web site components until you find the machine causing the problem. Finally, avoid simple NIC errors. If you upgrade the network from 10Mbps Ethernet to 100Mbps, make sure the attaching NIC cards support 100Mbps.

Load Balancers

All but the most trivial web sites use load balancers. Also known as "IP sprayers," load balancers take incoming requests and distribute them across multiple servers. The distribution of requests hides the servers actually responding to the request, and allows the web site to add or reconfigure hardware behind the load balancer without affecting the inbound traffic. Figure 3.6 shows a typical load balancer configuration.

Your load balancer's implementation depends on the brand you choose. Some companies implement the load balancer in hardware, while others provide load balancing software. (If you use load balancing software, we recommend dedicating a machine to

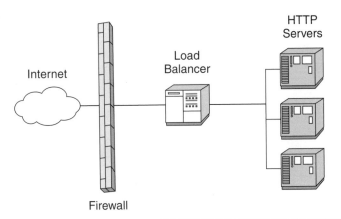

Figure 3.6 A load balancer distributing HTTP traffic

support this function.) Regardless of the implementation, the basic principle behind these products is the same. The load balancer operates at the IP level of your network, analyzing incoming request packets and passing them to the IP addresses of your web site servers. At this level, the load balancer really doesn't analyze the request itself; it only looks at the IP header information. This is a very fast operation, requiring little processing time. Load balancers handling simple IP spraying usually support high traffic volumes because they operate so efficiently. A properly configured load balancer rarely presents performance issues.

However, load balancers increasingly add more complexity to their functionality to support sophisticated distribution algorithms. Many support several configurable routing algorithms, as well as allowing customers to program their own routing algorithms. Among routing algorithms, the simplest—round-robin—is usually also the fastest for the load balancer to execute. In round-robin, each incoming request routes to the next server in turn. Most load balancers use this algorithm by default if no other is specified. Round-robin works reasonably well, but doesn't adapt well to runtime load problems or different machine capacities. If one server gets a disproportionate number of long-running or computationally intensive requests, this algorithm continues sending more requests to the overused server. Round-robin also proves ineffective when the web site uses a mixture of server machines with different load capacities.

To avoid this problem, some web sites use a weighted load distribution algorithm. This algorithm proves useful when balancing traffic among servers with different load capacities. Weighted distribution assigns a percentage of the overall load to particular downstream servers. This allows the load balancer to send the smaller servers fewer requests, while sending more work to larger or newer machines. Sophisticated load balancers support dynamic weighting of their distribution algorithms. These balancers actively monitor the downstream servers and determine their capacity for more traffic. The balancer makes adjustments to the load distribution so that busy servers receive less traffic, while idle servers receive more. Of course, as the complexity of the distribution algorithm increases, the throughput of the load balancer tends to decrease. Remote server monitoring and weighting computations make the load balancer less efficient. Before configuring sophisticated distribution algorithms, determine their impact on the load balancer's performance.

Not surprisingly then, the most flexible distribution scheme, content-based routing, is also the slowest. *Content-based routing* routes requests to servers depending on the data within the request. Typically, routing occurs based on the request's URL or parameters. Obviously, this requires more than an examination of the IP headers: The load balancer must actually examine the request content before making a routing decision. To examine the content, the load balancer must first collect all the request packets (in simple IP routing, the balancer usually sends the packets individually to the destination server) and retrieve the request content. After parsing the content for routing information, the load balancer forwards the request to the correct server. Because of the parsing activity, some load balancers pair with an HTTP server to support this algorithm. (Note: This routing technique does not work with SSL (Secure Socket Layer) because of the complexities of managing encryption keys between the web site and the browser.)

In addition to request distribution, load balancers also handle server failures inside the web site. If a downstream server stops responding to forwarded requests, most load balancers remove it from their distribution list and stop sending it requests. As you might guess, depending on the load balancer, the algorithms for detecting and managing a server outage vary in complexity and performance overhead. Likewise, your load balancer may support a hot-failover function. In this configuration, the web site configures two load balancers. One balancer monitors the other and takes over load distribution if the primary load balancer fails. This prevents the load balancer from becoming a single point of failure for your web site.

Affinity Routing

Sophisticated web sites frequently need more than a request distribution algorithm. These sites often require users to return to the same server machine in the web site cluster throughout their visit to the web site. In these cases, the load balancer keeps track of the server handling a particular user's requests and continually routes the user to the same server. We call this feature *affinity routing* (also called "sticky routing"). Affinity routing reduces SSL overhead by returning an incoming visitor to the same HTTP server repeatedly. This allows the browser to complete an SSL transaction with the same HTTP server, requiring only one SSL handshake sequence. As we'll discuss later, affinity routing also assists with returning a user to her session information throughout a web site visit.

Every incoming TCP/IP packet contains the IP address of the requesting machine. (Usually, this is the address of the browser machine, though there are times when the address is actually a proxy machine, not the browser.) When the load balancer gets the initial request from a browser, it uses one of the algorithms discussed above to decide which server receives the request. The load balancer then adds the browser's IP address to a table, along with the IP address of the server it chose to handle the request. When another request comes from the same IP address, the balancer looks up the server's IP address in the table, based on the browser's address, and routes all subsequent requests from the browser to the same server. (See Figure 3.7 for a diagram of a load balancer using an affinity algorithm.)

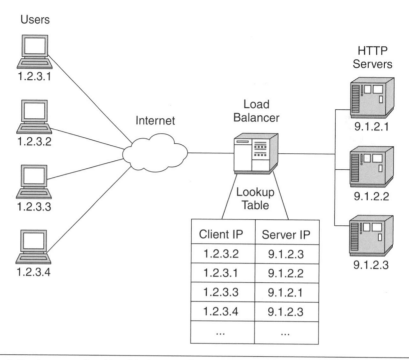

Figure 3.7   An example of load balancer affinity routing

Despite its simplicity, load balancer affinity routing sometimes encounters problems in production web sites. The most familiar problem arises when a disproportionate number of clients access the web site from behind a proxy server (for example, traffic originating from a large ISP or a large enterprise network). The ISP's proxy server hides the real IP addresses of all the browser machines accessing the network through it. Therefore *all* incoming requests from users of that ISP contain *the same IP address*. So instead of an IP address representing one user, the ISP's proxy address might represent hundreds or thousands of users.

This problem (sometimes called a "net quasar") results in wildly uneven loading of the web site's servers. The load balancer routes *all* of the users from the ISP or enterprise proxy to the same server machine because of the structure of the affinity routing table (one IP address maps to only one server). Figure 3.8 provides a small example of this problem. However, as more ISPs enter the market, overall traffic load becomes more evenly distributed, reducing the severity of this problem. Nonetheless, if you anticipate large volumes of traffic originating behind a proxy server, consider the impact of these users on any IP affinity routing at your web site.

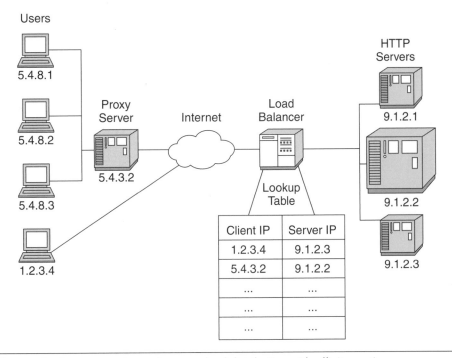

Figure 3.8 Proxy server impacting even load distribution with affinity routing

The second major affinity routing problem also involves proxy servers. Again, the client uses the ISP's proxy server to access the Internet. In this case, the ISP uses multiple proxy servers to support the client load. Figure 3.9 shows such a setup. In this example, a user's first request routes through a particular proxy server, but the second request routes through a different proxy server. This time, the load balancer sees a different incoming IP address and routes the request to a different HTTP server. This breaks affinity: The user request receives service from a different machine in the cluster. Some possible solutions to this problem include using more intelligent routing (based on cookies or content parameters) to uniquely identify the user or to share the user's critical information so it's available to any machine in the cluster. Application servers also provide software load balancing that alleviates this problem, as discussed below.

Recent improvements in vertical and horizontal scaling have changed the landscape of load distribution. In the early days of Java application servers, web sites used affinity routing to repeatedly send users to the server holding their HTTP session data. To accomplish this, the site paired each application server instance with its own HTTP server. This worked well because at that time each server machine typically

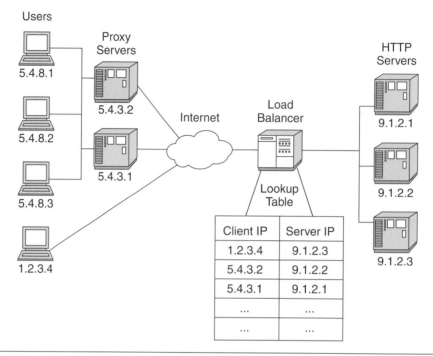

Figure 3.9   Users accessing a web site through a proxy server farm

ran only one application server instance (JVM). Thus the load balancer mapped the incoming user's IP address to the HTTP server machine's IP address, which corresponded to the single application server instance associated with the HTTP server.

Cloning changed the usefulness of load balancers in resolving HTTP session issues. Because multiple application server instances (JVMs) sometimes run on the same machine, mapping a user to a server's IP address does not suffice any more. Cloned application servers need more affinity support than the IP affinity provided by a load balancer. Usually, the application server vendor provides load distribution software to distribute load among the clones and to provide affinity routing if required.

HTTP Servers

Your HTTP servers play a critical role in the performance of the web site, as they handle large volumes of requests. HTTP serving is one of the older web technologies, and the popular HTTP servers enjoy the benefits of software maturity (stability, better performance, and improved usability). Web sites often improve performance by using the HTTP server directly to return static content, such as html, gif, and jpeg files. This allows these generally large pieces of content to be served earlier in the web site instead of forwarding requests on to the application servers. Knowing the relative number of requests for static content and dynamic content becomes important for sizing and configuring the HTTP servers. (Web sites often move static content to a caching proxy server, as discussed earlier, for even faster response to these requests.)

HTTP servers vary widely, from the extremely popular and open-source Apache web server to servers installed as standard components of software packages to commercial servers available for purchase. Refer to your documentation for parameters specific to your particular server. However, some basic performance settings remain fairly common across most implementations.

Threads or Processes (Listeners)

Different HTTP servers (sometimes even the same HTTP server brand running on different operating systems) use different models for handling large numbers of simultaneous requests. Some HTTP servers run as a single process and launch threads within the process to handle simultaneous requests. Others run as multiple, lightweight processes on the server, with each process handling a single user request. The HTTP server usually starts several threads or processes initially and opens more as needed to respond to incoming requests. We call these threads or processes *listeners*. An incoming request attaches to an available listener, which returns the information requested. After completing the request, the listener "listens," or waits, for the next request to arrive. HTTP servers typically respond very quickly to static content requests. Depending on the request and the data returned, an HTTP server on the right equipment may respond to hundreds or thousands of hits per second.

Your web site's configuration and workload determine the optimum settings for your HTTP server. If it receives only dynamic requests for the application server, you should define only slightly more HTTP listeners than the threads (processes) defined for your application server. If the HTTP server receives both static and dynamic requests, configure considerably more listeners. In general, for every dynamic page request, the web page receives several requests for static elements. Set the listener pool size for your HTTP server to support this ratio. As with every performance setting, just defining a lot of listeners is not always useful and often causes your server's throughput to decrease. Each thread or process competes with the others for machine resources, such as CPU or memory. Most HTTP servers use a default setting of 150–200 listeners. The default makes a good starting point for performance testing. Try adjusting this number during your testing to find the optimal listener settings for your application.

Much as the JVM does with heapsize parameters, many HTTP servers also allow you to define minimum and maximum listener pool values. Other HTTP servers add a profusion of settings to vary the number of listeners between the minimum and maximum values. For example, on some HTTP servers, the listener pool shrinks to a predefined value during times of low usage. Be sure you understand the listener controls for your HTTP server.

Timeouts

Most HTTP servers enforce a timeout setting for requests. If the requested function does not return before the timeout period finishes, the HTTP server assumes the process is stalled and terminates the request. Occasionally, long-running server-side processes require you to raise this timeout value. Note, however, that browsers also time out long-running processes, so raising the HTTP server timeout value only helps if it remains lower than the browser timeout. Bear in mind, however, that extremely long-running processes usually spell disaster for high-volume web sites. If you find yourself increasing the timeout value, consider tuning the offending process instead.

If you're forced to support an unstable web application, consider shortening the default timeout value. This reduces the wait in the likely event that a request fails, and it prevents your web site from "freezing" due to thread unavailability. (See Chapter 2 for details on "frozen" web sites.)

Logging

The HTTP server's logging settings impact performance, particularly on high-volume web sites. Verbose logging requires more disk I/O to write the logs, and disk serialization negatively impacts performance. Some other logging functions, such as converting date strings from their default format, become very expensive if done frequently. Keep your logging format simple, and limit it to reporting severe errors. If you want to convert the date strings, consider using an external conversion process after generating the log.

The logs generated by HTTP servers typically contain the TCP/IP address of the requesting client. Some servers perform a reverse lookup to get a full name instead of just the numeric address. Performing this lookup on every request, again, takes precious processing time from your web site in order to create nicer logs. If you really want this information, post-process your logs to do the lookups at a later time.

Keep-Alive

As mentioned previously, HTTP is a connectionless protocol. Each request opens a TCP/IP socket from the browser to the server, completes a request, and then closes the socket. Since every page typically requires multiple HTTP requests for embedded elements, the protocol supports an extension for longer-lived connections. The HTTP server supports this extension through the *keep-alive* configuration settings. These settings tell the HTTP server whether or not to allow long connections, the maximum requests any browser may make on one long connection, and even the maximum time the connection may stay active. Consider adjusting these settings if your web pages require a much higher or lower number of HTTP requests per page to complete. Sometimes browsers do not close these connections cleanly, leaving the listener unavailable for other work until the timeout completes. Lowering the timeout makes the listener available more quickly.

Operating System Settings

Operating system settings also impact HTTP server performance. We'll mention just a couple of them here, but, as always, you need to consult your HTTP server's documentation for more details.

TCP/IP Timeouts

As mentioned above, browsers and HTTP servers communicate through TCP/IP sockets. Some operating systems provide settings to control the duration of the connection between machines. This optimization allows two machines in constant communication to avoid the overhead of continually setting up and breaking down a socket connection by extending the time the connection remains viable. If you set the timeout too high, the server might run out of connections if many different browsers try to send it requests.

File Descriptors

HTTP servers open many files during normal operation. Operating systems, however, typically limit the number of files open at any given time. Depending on your web site, consider increasing the available file descriptors.

SSL/HTTPS

Secure transmissions between the HTTP server and the browser use the HTTPS protocol instead of HTTP. The HTTPS protocol flows HTTP over the TCP/IP Secure Sockets Layer (SSL), which encrypts all the traffic between the client and the server. Adding more bits to the encryption key makes breaking the encryption key more difficult but increases the processing overhead when computing the keys. Beyond key computation, SSL adds overhead in key negotiation between the server and the client. As Figure 3.10 shows, key negotiation requires multiple network round trips to accomplish. The handshake requires multiple processing steps as well at each machine. Let's briefly review the basics of SSL setup.

First, the server gives its public key to the browser in a server *certificate*. This public key is part of an asymmetric public/private key pair delivered from the *certifying authority (CA)*. However, runtime usage of this key for every request requires too much overhead. Symmetric keys provide more security and speed, but these keys need secure exchange. In the SSL handshake, the public key is first sent to the server, which uses it to encrypt the rest of the handshake. The server then computes the symmetric key, and transmits this key back to the client encrypted using the public/private key pair. After this exchange of the keys, the conversation flows relatively quickly between the browser and the server. The initial exchange of keys is slow, so you want to keep the number of times this happens to a minimum. Configuring your load balancer for affinity routing reduces the SSL handshake overhead. Returning requests to a server with an existing SSL session for your browser saves time over moving between servers on each request to the web site.

As you might expect, SSL processing adds significant overhead to your HTTP server's processing. The HTTP server needs more CPU to manage the encryption and decryption algorithm, and each request takes longer to process. All these factors potentially impact the number of HTTP listeners supported by the server machine, as well as the overall number of listeners required by the web site. HTTP servers handling large SSL traffic volumes run best on a dedicated server machine. Otherwise, the CPU overhead tends to rob other applications (particularly application servers) of valuable processing cycles.

In general, use SSL discriminately. Certainly, we recommend encrypting sensitive information such as passwords, financial data, or other private information. However,

Figure 3.10   A simplified version of the SSL handshake

a normal web site really only requires encryption for a small percentage of the site's content. For example, a shopping web site requires SSL encryption when taking the customer's credit card number, but not when showing them a selection of toasters. SSL encryption of large graphic elements is particularly expensive.

Plug-Ins

The application server receives web requests via an HTTP server. Most application servers provide a *plug-in* to connect with an existing HTTP server product. Using the HTTP server's own APIs, the plug-in allows dynamic requests to pass to the application server from the HTTP server. Figure 3.11 shows a typical plug-in at work.

The plug-in runs in the HTTP server's process, and its configuration potentially impacts the overall operation of the HTTP server, regardless of whether a given request passes to the application server. For example, some application servers' plug-ins perform security checks on every request. Likewise, plug-ins commonly grab incoming requests first before allowing the HTTP server to process them. The plug-in determines if the request goes to the application server and allows the HTTP server to process only those requests it cannot resolve (typically, the static requests). Of course, the plug-in processing increases the response time for static pages.

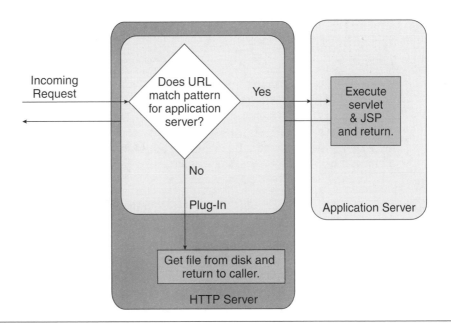

Figure 3.11 Plug-in operation

Sophisticated application servers often provide sophisticated plug-ins. As noted ear-lier, an application server supporting cloned instances may provide a smart plug-in to handle affinity routing and load distribution across these clones. These smart plug-ins often handle other tasks associated with the load balancer, such as failover. They may detect newly started application server instances and begin sending traffic to them. Regarding load distribution, sophisticated plug-ins frequently use distribution algorithms similar to those discussed earlier for load balancers. Plug-ins usually sup-port round-robin distribution, and many support dynamic distribution based on feedback from the application server instances. Some include optimizations to prefer local clones (application server instances sharing the same box as the plug-in) to avoid expensive remote calls across the network.

As we mentioned, plug-ins sometimes support affinity routing to specific application server instances. Unlike HTTP servers, this affinity does not benefit SSL handshak-ing, but exists to provide faster access to HTTP session data. Overall performance generally benefits (sometimes significantly) if the user returns repeatedly to a cached copy of their HTTP session data. Particularly if the cluster uses a centralized HTTP session sharing scheme (such as a persistent HTTP session database), returning to the cached copy avoids a relatively expensive database retrieval of the user's state information. For example, plug-ins sometimes add a cookie to facilitate affinity rout-ing. This allows the plug-in to track where it first routed this user at the start of his visit, and to return him to the same clone repeatedly until the visit is over.

Application Servers

Java application servers form the core of any J2EE-based web site. Application serv-ers extend the ability of an HTTP server from simply returning static content to implementing complex tasks requiring the coordination of diverse applications run-ning on geographically dispersed machines. Most, if not all, of the programming logic associated with a web application executes within an application server. Ensur-ing that the application server has undergone proper performance tuning is crucial for good web site performance.

Chapters 2 and 4 cover the specifics of web application and application server perfor-mance. Again, application server performance frequently plays the largest role in web site performance, so tuning your applications, the application server, and the JVM often proves very beneficial to your overall performance and throughput. Chapter 2 covers most of the common J2EE tuning parameters. Your application server proba-bly comes with a tuning guide to cover any vendor-specific features or tuning adjust-ments. We refer you to these resources rather than repeating this information. However, one feature not discussed in Chapter 2 merits some coverage here. The

J2EE specification provides a security infrastructure for application server components. Let's briefly discuss the basics of this security architecture.

Security

The J2EE security infrastructure specification covers all application server container types. Web containers must implement security for callable servlets and JSPs down to the HTTP request type. EJB containers implement security on each callable method. Client containers may require authentication on invocation. Security of this granularity (for example, enforcing access at the method level) usually implies a significant performance overhead.

Additionally, security within an application server cluster encrypts all traffic between servers within the cluster, as well as traffic between the HTTP server's plug-in and web containers within application servers. As discussed in the preceding section, SSL requires encryption and decryption, so these algorithms incur a heavy performance penalty. Therefore, enabling SSL for all transmissions within your web site incurs a significant performance cost.

The application server uses security for both authentication and authorization. Authentication verifies that the users (both humans and computer processes) are who they say they are. HTTP servers and web containers sometimes require users to authenticate themselves. (We're all familiar with the pop-up from a browser asking us for a user ID and a password). Using a password known only to a single user is a common method for authentication, but is not the only solution. Client-side certificates provide even more security, but they require additional administration effort to obtain and distribute.

Authorization occurs when a process decides whether to permit a specific user access to a resource. As you can imagine, checking for authorization on every access by a client proves quite time-consuming. Specialized security servers often manage authorization data. Mainframes often use IBM's *Resource Access Control Facility (RACF)* or other specialized databases to manage their authorization data; other types of systems commonly use a server running an implementation of the *Lightweight Directory Access Protocol (LDAP)*. Regardless of which product you use, the performance characteristics of your authorization server become important to the overall throughput of your web site. During your performance testing, include a similar server in your test environment for more accurate test results. We see many web sites using various LDAP servers to support security. These servers frequently become a bottleneck, so some web sites try to improve performance by writing their own LDAP connection pools. If you choose to write such a pool, make sure you follow the guidance in Chapters 2 and 4, as well as other works, for proper pool implementation and use.[1]

Databases and Other Back-End Resources

Java application servers rarely exist in a vacuum. In fact, the value of an application server lies in its ability to connect with other subsystems, such as databases, MOMs, and other existing processes. The application server usually interacts with these resources through a remote connection. The web application often creates this connection implicitly by using client interface code, such as a JDBC (Java DataBase Connectivity) connection, provided by the remote resource vendor. (As discussed in Chapter 2, connection creation incurs lots of process overhead. Most application servers use pooling to reduce this burden.) These remote systems often limit the number of concurrent connections they'll accept, while some remote systems do not support concurrent access at all. In any case, take care with the number of connections allocated against a remote system to avoid exceeding these limits, especially as your web site grows. As you increase web site capacity, coordinate your growth with the teams supporting remote resources to avoid overwhelming these systems.

Most likely your back-end systems existed originally to support thick client applications for a limited number of users. For example, financial institutions used to provide account information via thick client applications or dumb terminal connections for their brokers and customer-support agents. With the boom of self-service financial web sites, this same mainframe application may find itself supporting a large, multi-threaded web site. Not surprisingly, these applications sometimes need tuning or upgraded hardware to support Internet traffic volumes.

Some remote systems require an intermediate gateway for connection (often the gateway provides some service, such as protocol conversion, to support communications between the server and the remote system). We recommend dedicating a machine to the gateway whenever possible to avoid resource contention (mainly CPU and NIC access) with other applications. Of course, an improperly configured gateway easily becomes a bottleneck in your web site. Monitor this component as you would any other during your performance testing. (Some web sites provide a failover mechanism for the gateway software to eliminate it as a single point of failure during operation. We recommend planning enough capacity on failover to handle the peak site traffic volumes.)

Caching

Production web sites often improve their perceived response times by the extensive use of caching. Many processes throughout a web site's network establish caches, and

---

1. See M. Daconta, *et al., Java Pitfalls: Time-Saving Solutions and Workarounds to Improve Programs.*

understanding their roles becomes important when predicting performance. Caches clearly have the most impact when they are close to the user. Browsers use caching extensively by putting images and other content into both memory caches as well as caches on the local disk. This dramatically shortens the interval between a user's click on a link or button and the complete display of the resulting page. (This helpful function can cause headaches when testing dynamic content, as the browser may display a cached copy instead of getting new content from the server.) The browser periodically makes a special request to the server to see if the content has changed since the copy was put in the cache, and only if that is true does the browser request a new copy.).

As discussed above, caching proxy servers, located close to the edge of your network, not only speed up response times to your users, but also decrease the load on your servers and network. If static content makes up a large fraction of your web site's total content, setting up caching reverse proxy servers greatly increases your web site's total throughput and decreases response time. (Some HTTP servers also cache static content.) Some very popular sites contract with other enterprises to cache their content. The data is pushed to caches located within a large ISP's own network, and the requests then go to these caching machines. This technique proves especially useful for graphics-heavy web sites.

Web Site Topologies

Now that we've discussed all the parts, let's put them together to build a web site. High-volume, high-availability web sites deploy across multiple machines and processes for both reliability and workload management purposes. As the request volume increases over time, the web site grows (scales) by adding more resources to meet the demand. Successful scaling requires planning and forethought. A good web site configuration maximizes flexibility while avoiding single points of failure. (A component is a single point of failure if its outage results in most or all of the web site becoming unavailable.)

Most large web sites plan for scalability and redundancy by isolating key software components to dedicated machines. While you might find it useful to run an HTTP server, an application server, and a database on one machine for development purposes, most web sites give each of these components a dedicated machine in production. Splitting these functions across their own servers delivers several benefits:

- The applications do not contend with each other for system resources.
- Each application runs on a machine tuned to its particular performance needs. For example, a database server may require faster DASD than an application server.

▪ The web site gains configuration flexibility. You may place the HTTP server inside the DMZ, while moving the application server and database behind the DMZ for additional security. Many companies also place business databases within their own firewalled networks to protect them from unauthorized internal access.

Of course, exceptions to this rule exist. Some companies prefer to run a few, large server machines with multiple web site components sharing each machine. This approach requires a good understanding of the performance characteristics of each application sharing the box, or an unusually big box. In fact, running web sites with mainframe equipment is becoming increasingly popular for many reasons. However, that's a topic for another book.

Most web sites set up a basic topology similar to the one shown in Figure 3.2. A firewall restricts access to the DMZ containing the HTTP server, and another firewall restricts intranet access to only those machines with network addresses within the DMZ. Sometimes, as noted above, another firewall exists between the application server and the database server for additional security. The HTTP server delivers static content from within the DMZ and passes dynamic requests to the application server behind the second firewall. This very flexible configuration allows specific server tuning for maximum throughput based on the type of content each machine handles. Likewise, none of the web site components contends with another application for CPU, memory, or other machine resources. Assuming sufficient network capacity and proper component tuning, nothing hinders this configuration from achieving top performance. Despite these positives, this setup is not without problems. If any of the servers involved fail, the web site cannot deliver dynamic content. Likewise, if we want to upgrade some software or add memory to a server, the web site becomes unavailable until we finish the upgrade.

Perhaps we need more capacity to handle increasing request volumes; how do we increase the web site's capacity? Duplicating web site resources eliminates potential failure points and allows us to add capacity as required to meet growing demand. Let's cover two of the most common ways to duplicate resources and grow a web site: vertical and horizontal scaling.

Vertical Scaling

As we discussed in Chapter 1, one type of vertical scaling increases processes to better utilize the web site's hardware. To scale vertically, we create more application server instances on a single machine. (These instances may contain web containers, EJB containers, or both, as required.) Figure 3.12 shows a web site using two application server instances on one server machine. The plug-in provided by the application server manages the flow of requests to the two instances (sometimes called *clones*), including any affinity routing required by the traffic. In this case, the plug-in acts as a load balancer for the two application server instances. Vertical scaling also provides limited failure protection for the web site. If a software bug causes a failure in one of the instances, the other instance remains available to serve requests. Obviously, if the server machine experiences a failure, both instances also fail.

This type of vertical scaling provides performance benefits only if the server machine has enough capacity for both instances. If a single application server instance drives your CPU to 90% utilization, you gain nothing by burdening the machine with another instance. In this case, the instances contend for the CPU, which usually results in worse performance. For very large machines (12 processors or more), vertical scaling allows the web site to better utilize the box's processing power. Again, a single JVM cannot fully utilize the processing power of a very large server machine. However, with vertical cloning, multiple JVMs (in the form of application server instances) obtain higher CPU utilization. As long as other resources, such as memory and NIC capacity, remain unconstrained, vertical scaling on large machines improves performance.

As we mentioned earlier, vertical scaling rarely provides perfect scaling. Adding two application server instances seldom produces a perfect doubling of throughput. Vertical scaling allows you to get more out of your large server boxes, but it may not allow you to exercise their full potential, because of machine resource limitations and hardware architecture issues. In many cases, we need more hardware to grow our web site.

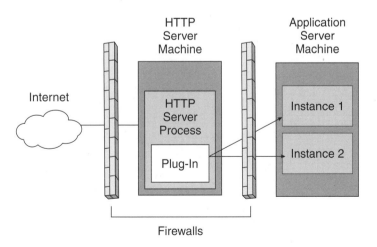

Figure 3.12 Vertical scaling of the application server

Horizontal Scaling

Horizontal scaling increases web site hardware and the processes executing on the hardware. Scaling usually adds similar servers with similar configurations (operating systems, installed applications, and so on) to the web site. Most large web sites try to keep their servers and server configuration homogenous throughout. This reduces maintenance overhead and simplifies capacity planning.

Figure 3.13 gives an example of a web site implementing horizontal scaling. The site uses multiple HTTP server machines and application server machines to support the traffic volume. The load balancer provides an entry point to the web site, and distributes the requests across the HTTP servers. The end user never knows that multiple machines or servers exist behind the web site's URL; the load balancer hides the complexity of the web site. Each application server in this diagram runs one or more application server instances. Some web sites combine vertical and horizontal scaling by using multiple server machines and multiple application server instances on each machine. If this web site requires affinity routing, a combination of load balancer affinity and plug-in affinity makes it work. The load balancer routes consistently to the same HTTP server, and the plug-in routes consistently to the same application server instance. Some plug-ins, however, automatically route to the right application server instance and thus do not require load balancer affinity.

We refer to a group of server machines as a *cluster*. The machines in a cluster, as well as the software running on them, work together to support a seamless web site visit for the end user. The small cluster pictured in Figure 3.13 includes duplicate load balancers and databases to provide for *failover*. If one machine or service in this cluster fails, another takes its place to avoid interrupting service to the end user. Ideally,

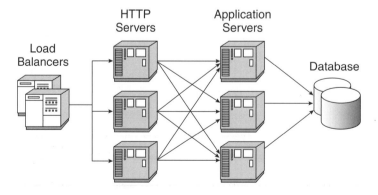

Figure 3.13   A small web site using horizontal scaling

failover happens instantaneously, although some lost requests are not uncommon except in the most sophisticated systems.

Note, however, that failover only works if the remaining machines and software contain enough capacity to cover the work of the failed component. If all your application servers routinely run at 100% CPU utilization, a failure of one application server machine leaves insufficient capacity to support your total traffic volume at the same level of performance. Failover preparedness requires extra capacity: You need at least one additional machine beyond your capacity projections for each web site component. Keep your network infrastructure in mind as you grow your web site, and add the necessary capacity to support your expansion. Also, don't forget the impact of the expansion on back-end servers, such as your database. More web site capacity means more database activity, so give the database the capacity it needs to handle web application requests.

Horizontal scaling typically produces near linear scaling. That is, doubling the web site's hardware usually yields close to double the throughput. Of course, we base this statement on some very important assumptions:

- Other web site systems (network, database, and so on) have enough capacity to support the expanded web site. Otherwise, increase the capacity of these systems to prevent bottlenecks.
- Your web applications scale. Some web application designs prohibit growing the application across multiple application server instances. Test your application in a clustered environment prior to growing the production web site.

We've kept our web site purposefully simple for this discussion. Very large sites often develop very complex topologies. Within large corporations, the corporate web site often consists of many smaller web sites tied together through a series of load balancers and routers. Growing these web sites, or even adding new features, sometimes proves very difficult.

Choosing between a Few Big Machines or Many Smaller Machines

Web site teams frequently struggle with hardware selection. A common debate centers on the merits of operating the web site on a few very large servers versus using many small servers. Let's consider a few guidelines to help you with this decision.

Get More of What You Already Have If your production environment already uses large machines, and your staff knows how to install, configure, and maintain these boxes, then add additional machines of this caliber. Staffing and training costs usually outweigh any other considerations.

More Machines Means More Labor   Smaller machines cost less, but dozens of small servers require more administration than a single large machine. This cost difference often dwarfs the equipment savings for large installations. Consider additional staffing as part of your analysis.

Machine Selection Impacts Licensing Fees   Software pricing sometimes drives equipment purchase decisions. Some software packages charge per CPU, while others charge per installation. Depending on the licensing fees involved, picking a machine to minimize licensing fees sometimes generates significant savings.

Don't Forget Failover Costs   A web site usually needs at least three application server machines. Having only two machines leaves a thin margin for failover, particularly if you take one server down for maintenance or upgrades. Two large machines often handle normal loads just fine but create tricky maintenance problems, especially for round-the-clock web sites.

Best Practices

So, what do we recommend? A configuration similar to that shown in Figure 3.13 is a good start. Each web site component receives a dedicated machine, giving us more flexibility. As we stated earlier, most web sites configure a minimum of two machines for each major component (HTTP server and application server). Three machines per component give you some buffer to perform maintenance and upgrades while still providing failover capacity. Of course, you need to weigh availability requirements against the additional costs. Many web sites need far more than two or three machines to support their traffic volumes. Regardless of your capacity sizing, consider additional capacity for failover and maintenance concerns.

Earlier we discussed proxy servers. If your web site serves predominantly static content, adding a proxy server to your site may give you tremendous performance and capacity benefits. Place the proxy server as close to the users as possible, preferably just inside the first (outer) firewall. Proxy servers reduce the traffic within the interior of your web site and reduce the burden on your HTTP servers.

Avoid using your application server as a static content server. We realize this advice is a bit controversial, given the new J2EE packaging schemes (`.ear` and `.war` files); however, the HTTP server remains the best component for serving static content. Serving static content from the HTTP server places the content closer to the requester and reduces the burden on the application server. Also, modern HTTP servers deliver static content much faster than an application server. Most web pages contain many static elements; optimizing their service improves overall web site performance.

Some sites direct static content requests to HTTP servers dedicated to serving static content. For instance, requests to the main web site have the form

```
<http://www.enterprise.com/myservlet>,
```

while requests for graphics have the form

```
<http://graphics.enterprise.com/mystuff.gif>.
```

This allows a completely different set of HTTP servers to satisfy these requests and reduces the contention for listeners on the HTTP servers supporting requests for dynamic pages. Also, because the HTTP servers that handle only static content don't require an application server plug-in, they respond even faster.

Finally, we want to show you a configuration using EJBs in addition to servlets and JSPs. Some enterprises implement their business logic solely in EJBs, with the view and a thin controller layer in the presentation tier, deployed in the DMZ. This works especially well when both internal and Internet applications share some business logic. Figure 3.14 shows such a configuration, where the Internet applications reside in the DMZ and connect to EJB containers behind the DMZ. Of course, for security purposes, both the application servers and the EJB components often lie behind the DMZ, leaving only the HTTP server between the firewalls.

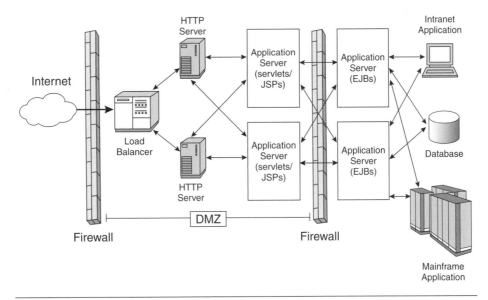

Figure 3.14   A DMZ configuration with servlets, JSPs, and EJBs

Summary

This chapter covered some common hardware and software elements found in many production web sites. We discussed various low-level components, such as NICs, routers, and firewalls, which frequently go unnoticed in performance discussions, but nevertheless must be configured properly for your site to operate at peak efficiency. We also discussed more familiar components, such as proxy servers, HTTP servers, application servers, and database servers. The chapter covered their performance issues as well as special considerations such as caching and security.

Finally, we looked not only at your site as it is today but also at how it might grow to support its future traffic burden. The chapter included the trade-offs between vertical and horizontal scaling, as well as some guidelines for selecting servers for your web site.

Having read Chapters 2 and 3, you should now have a basic understanding of how the web application server and the web site function. You should also have a feel for some key tuning points within each of them. In the next chapter, we focus on the key performance issues of the Java virtual machine. Because the application server uses the JVM as its execution platform, JVM performance plays a critical role in your web application's success.

Chapter 4

JAVA SPECIFICS

In Chapter 2 we discussed the performance issues surrounding Java web applications, including key features of the J2EE specification. However, Java, unlike many other languages, also comes with its own runtime environment. Properly tuning the Java runtime environment often impacts the overall performance of your web site. This chapter presents some of the most common Java runtime performance issues that affect Java application servers. In particular, we discuss Java memory management, garbage collection, and memory leaks. We also cover key programming techniques, such as string management, multi-threading, and synchronization. These programming techniques often make the difference between a slow web site and a successful one.

In addition, we focus on Java runtime issues and parameters common across mid-tier platforms (NT, Windows 2000, AIX, Solaris, and HP/UX). However, your Java runtime provider may include other tuning parameters not mentioned in this chapter. (This is especially true for HP/UX.) Check with your JVM provider for additional tuning settings.

The Java Virtual Machine

Java web applications differ from programs encoded in most other languages. In other languages, an executable compiles to native machine code, which runs directly on the operating system. Java executables compile to binaries, which run inside a virtual machine. A *virtual machine* is really just another program providing a layer of abstraction between the code you write and the operating system. This powerful mechanism gives Java its "write once, run anywhere" capability at the expense of some additional runtime overhead. Because the Java virtual machine (the JVM) insulates Java applications from operating system specifics, your Java code moves easily between many different hardware platforms and operating systems.

Heap Management

Since the JVM runs as a process on the operating system, the JVM allocates memory at runtime from the operating system just as any other process does. However, this memory is used not only to run the JVM itself, but also to execute Java applications *inside* the JVM process. Therefore much of the memory allocated usually goes to build the JVM's internal *heap*. The JVM manages this heap and allocates memory from it to new objects as they are created by Java applications running inside the JVM. Unlike other languages, Java does not allow the programmer to explicitly release memory back to the heap when an object is no longer needed. Instead, the JVM periodically cleans up unused objects automatically. This process is called *garbage collection*.

The JVM provides controls for the heapsize via tuning parameters given to the JVM at startup. These parameters allow us to specify both the minimum heapsize the JVM obtains, as well as the maximum heapsize. Optimal JVM heapsize settings often prove counterintuitive. The next sections cover the basics of these settings, as well as a simple process for finding the best values for your specific web application.

Minimum and Maximum Heap Settings

As mentioned previously, the JVM accepts both maximum and minimum heapsize settings. The maximum setting prevents the heap from growing too large (we'll discuss later why too much memory can impact performance). The minimum setting tells the JVM how much memory to obtain as it starts up. However, to begin our discussion of JVM tuning, let's first focus on the maximum heapsize. The maximum heapsize setting comes from the –Xmx parameter. For example,

```
-Xmx512m
```

sets the maximum heapsize to 512MB on some systems (again, check with your JVM provider for the proper syntax). The JVM reads this parameter at initialization, so there's no changing the maximum heap after the JVM starts. Keep in mind that this parameter sets a maximum. The JVM using this setting never obtains more than 512MB of heap memory during its operation, so even if your application requires more memory, the JVM cannot obtain it.

Too much memory often causes as many performance problems as too little. Large heaps require longer garbage collection cycles, which impact the performance of the applications running in the JVM. Also, keep in mind the memory available on your machine. If the JVM grows larger than the available memory, the operating system begins paging the JVM process out of memory. A paging JVM delivers abysmal performance.

The minimum heapsize, set with the –Xms parameter, is less problematic. For performance testing, we typically recommend that it be set equal to the maximum heap setting. This forces the JVM to acquire all the memory for the maximum heapsize at startup. Acquiring more memory to increase the heap later takes time and may trigger more frequent garbage collections as the heap approaches the current memory allocated. In production, some experts recommend setting –Xms to between 25% and 30% of the maximum heapsize defined by –Xmx.[1] In theory, starting with a smaller heap allows the JVM to build a cleaner object table as the heap grows, which improves garbage collection times.

However, the actual minimum heap setting depends on several factors, including your application's memory footprint (which we discuss in the next section), and the traffic arrival patterns of your web site. For example, many brokerage web sites receive intense traffic loads early in the morning, so slowly growing the heap in these web sites proves difficult. Instead, preallocating a large heap often makes the web site faster during intensive loading periods. In these cases, we recommend setting the –Xms to at least 75% of the –Xmx value. (Figure 4.1 shows some different loading patterns.)

Tuning the Heap Settings

Now that we understand how to set the heap for the JVM, let's try to find the *optimal* setting for our web application. In order to optimally tune the JVM's heap settings, you first need to determine the *application footprint* of your web site application. The footprint defines how much memory the application requires to execute at peak load. Begin the optimization process by defining a generous maximum heapsize. Usually one-half the machine's physical memory, or 512MB, whichever is smaller, makes a good starting point for the maximum heapsize.

Run the application at peak load for a significant period of time (at least 20 minutes, but for an hour or more if possible). Assuming there are no memory leaks, after some time the application stabilizes in memory, allowing you to record the maximum memory used during the peak loading. Determine maximum memory used either by running profiling software to measure the heap used by the application or by turning on Java's verbose garbage collection. Use the verbose garbage collection output to calculate the value based on the maximum amount of memory used during the application's steady-state execution. This is the application's footprint. (See Figure 4.2 for an example, and see Chapter 12 for more information about obtaining verbosegc information.)

---

1. See Ken Ueno, *et al.*, WebSphere Version 3 Tuning Guide for AIX, an IBM Redbook, published by the IBM International Technical Support Organization (February 2000, SG24-5657-00) or *WebSphere Application Server 3.0 Standard/Advanced Tuning Guide*, 1999.

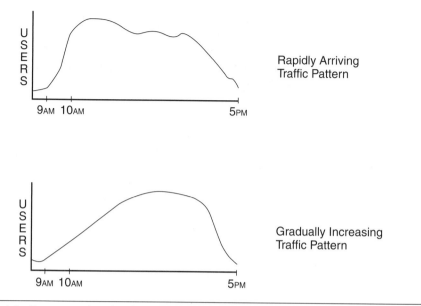

Figure 4.1   Two examples of web site traffic patterns

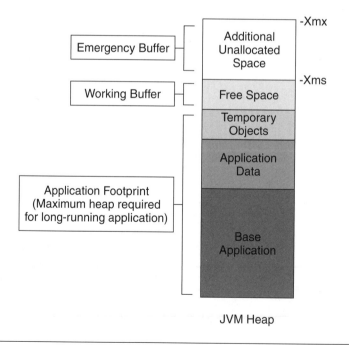

Figure 4.2   A conceptualized JVM heap and corresponding settings

After establishing a footprint, adjust the maximum heapsize to give the application some headroom in case of unexpected spikes, but not so much as to unduly increase the garbage collection time. For example, if the application requires 256MB at peak loading, you might specify 450MB as the maximum to give the application a bit more room for excess capacity in case an extreme spike occurs. (See Sun's Java site for more information about tuning the heap.)[2]

If the application never stabilizes during your testing, but continues to acquire memory throughout the run, your application has a memory leak. *Memory leaks* occur in Java when an application maintains references to objects it no longer needs, thus denying the garbage collector the opportunity to return them to memory. (We'll talk more about memory leaks later in this chapter.) Obviously, you cannot establish a memory footprint for your application until you resolve the memory leak.

Also, keep in mind any other applications sharing the same JVM, and establish a heapsize to accommodate all of your simultaneously executing applications. Remember that some functions require more memory than others. Make sure you establish your memory baselines using realistic scenarios.

In addition to other applications sharing a JVM, we must be aware of any vertical scaling issues on the server machine. If you plan to run multiple JVMs on the server, remember that the sum of all your JVM heaps must be smaller than the physical memory (usually no more than 50%–75% of available memory). So, based on the memory baselines you establish for one JVM, add more memory to your server machine as required if you plan to run multiple JVMs.

Also, remember that the JVM itself requires some memory for execution. Thus, when you view your JVM process using operating system monitoring tools, the process usually requires more memory than the amount specified by the –Xmx parameter (assuming, of course, the heap is fully allocated to the extent defined by –Xmx). Keep this overhead in mind when planning the memory required by your server machine.

Garbage Collection

Heap optimization, however, is about more than using a server's available memory effectively. An optimized heap also benefits from more efficient garbage collection cycles. As we mentioned earlier, garbage collection makes Java different from most languages. The inventors of Java took into account that human programmers often

---

2. See "Tuning Garbage Collection with the 1.3.1 Java™ Virtual Machine," retrieved January 14, 2002, from the World Wide Web: <http://java.sun.com/docs/hotspot/gc/>.

have difficulty with memory management inside their applications. Often, in traditional programming languages, poor memory management by the application developer leads to memory leaks or other very obscure memory-related problems.

To avoid these issues, Java omits programming statements for allocating or releasing memory. Instead, the JVM runtime itself manages memory reclamation. Developers find this feature particularly appealing, as they no longer have to programmatically return every byte of memory they allocate inside an application. (However, Java memory reclamation doesn't cover every class of memory problem. Thus, Java applications may experience memory leaks if they progressively acquire objects without also eventually releasing them for garbage collection.) The memory reclamation occurs when the garbage collection process executes. The garbage collector looks for any object not currently referenced by any other object and assumes it is no longer in use. The garbage collector destroys the unreferenced object and returns its memory to the heap. Garbage collection affects every application running inside a JVM. Although the newer JVMs work more efficiently than earlier models, garbage collection still stops all useful work inside the JVM until the memory reclamation process completes. (Future JVMs may allow processes to continue execution during the garbage collection cycle.)

Most JVMs collect garbage as needed. An application creates an object either explicitly with the new keyword, or implicitly to satisfy an instruction. If enough memory exists in the heap, the JVM allocates the object and returns it to the application. If not enough memory exists, the create request might trigger a garbage collection cycle to reclaim memory, or the JVM might immediately request more memory from the operating system (assuming the current heap is smaller than the allowable maximum heapsize). However, if the JVM doesn't have enough heap to satisfy the create request, and the heap is already at its maximum allowable size, the JVM must trigger a garbage collection to reclaim memory. After the garbage collection completes, the JVM satisfies the create request from the reclaimed memory.

Remember, all other activities inside the JVM stop while some or all of the garbage collection cycle (depending on the JVM version in use) completes. This becomes a problem if the collections take a long time or happen frequently. In either case, your web application users perceive large response time variances as they request pages from your web site. Figure 4.3 shows a normal garbage collection cycle that runs at infrequent, regular intervals and lasts for a relatively short period of time. This graph indicates a reasonable heap setting for this application.

As a general rule, the larger the heapsize, the longer the garbage collector runs. In the field, we've witnessed garbage collection cycles lasting over 20 seconds (yes, we're serious). Setting a large maximum heapsize is likely to cause infrequent, but long, garbage collection cycles. While the JVM collects garbage, your web application remains nonresponsive to pending and incoming requests. Your visitors perceive good response

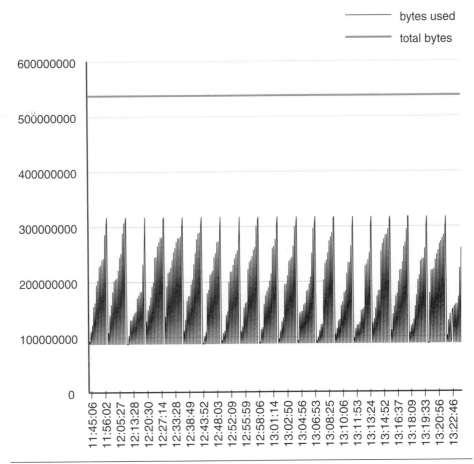

Figure 4.3   Typical garbage collection cycles

time for some pages, but occasionally requests take much longer. This sometimes generates complaints about the web site "freezing up" periodically. If your web site receives high traffic volumes, these long pauses in service may make the site unusable.

To avoid prolonged garbage collection cycles, keep your maximum heapsize within a reasonable limit. Heaps of 512MB or less usually exhibit good garbage collection cycle times for most classes of processors. Sometimes large servers with extremely fast processors support heaps in the range of 750MB to 1024MB. If your application requires more heap to support your user load, consider creating additional JVMs (and their corresponding memory heaps) to support the application.

While setting the heap too high promotes long garbage collections, setting the heap too *low* leads to *frequent* garbage collection. The chart in Figure 4.4 shows a system with an undersized memory heap experiencing frequent, short garbage collection cycles.

With an undersized JVM heap, the application frequently uses all of the memory available, which forces the JVM to run garbage collection to reclaim space for pending memory requests. This proves to be only a temporary solution, however, as the application quickly consumes the reclaimed space, forcing yet another garbage collection cycle. Although each garbage collection may complete quickly, their frequency means the JVM spends most of its time garbage collecting rather than doing useful work.

If you see this garbage collection pattern, consider extending the JVM's maximum heapsize. Of course, this assumes you have the machine memory to support such an extension. It also assumes your current heap is reasonably sized (in the 512MB range). This gives your application more room to execute without triggering frequent garbage collections. If the heap is already at its practical limit, consider reducing the load on the JVM by creating additional JVMs (scaling) to support your application. Also, if your application continues to consume heap space, regardless of how large the heap, check the application for memory leaks.

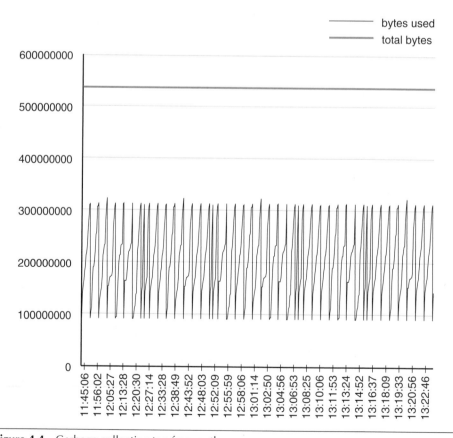

Figure 4.4   Garbage collecting too frequently

Minimizing Garbage

Beyond setting the heapsize, consider how much "garbage" your application generates. Wasteful applications use more heap and require larger memory footprints. This translates to more garbage collection, and less useful work from your application. Efficient applications require less memory and usually exhibit a better garbage collection profile. These applications minimize the number of objects they create and discard for each request. We discuss these memory-management techniques for your application in an upcoming section.

Memory Leaks

Java enthusiasts often point to automatic memory management using the garbage collector when discussing Java's advantages over other languages, such as C++. However, as we mentioned earlier, just because Java manages memory does *not* mean that memory leaks are impossible in Java applications. Remember, the garbage collector looks for abandoned objects. Specifically, it only "reaps" objects currently without references from any other objects. So, although programmers no longer *explicitly* release unneeded objects, they still must manage an application's objects to de-reference unneeded objects, which otherwise remain in memory indefinitely.

For example, consider one of the most frequent causes of Java memory leaks: caching. Applications often use hash tables or collections as quick data caches. However, programmers sometimes forget to clean up these cached objects periodically. As long as an object remains in a collection or hash table, it is ineligible for garbage collection (the collection or hash table references the object). Only by explicitly removing the object from the cache, or by de-referencing the collection or hash table as a whole, can a programmer make the object available for reclamation by the garbage collector.

Similarly, misuse of certain J2EE objects frequently leads to memory leaks. For example, HTTP session objects function as hash tables from a programming perspective. Programmers frequently cache data in the HTTP session but never subsequently release the cached data. Given the longevity of an HTTP session object (often 30 minutes or more), a web site visitor may hold onto part of a JVM's memory long after she has stopped interacting with the web site. Misusing HTTP session objects sometimes produces symptoms similar to memory leaks. We mentioned in Chapter 2 the dangers of creating large HTTP session objects. An application that builds such objects for every user may consume all of the heap available just to hold HTTP session objects.

Observing this externally, we may conclude the application has a memory leak. However, the real problem lies in sharing our heap resources among all the users of our application server. The "per user footprint," as defined by the size of the HTTP session kept for each user, is too large for our heap. The web site is simply trying to keep too much data for each visitor. In these cases, reduce the size of the HTTP session, or open more JVMs to accommodate the user volume. In the long term, however, a reduction in the HTTP session size provides more benefits and reduces the overall hardware cost for the web site. (See Chapter 2 for a more in-depth discussion of HTTP session management.)

Regardless of how your application leaks memory, the symptom is always the same. The application consumes increasingly more memory over time, and depletes the heap. Figure 4.5 shows a typical memory leak pattern. Notice that the garbage collector frees less and less memory after each collection cycle. Some memory leaks occur quickly, while others take days of continuous application execution to find. Code-profiling tools are usually essential in resolving memory leaks. Also, we recommend long-run testing of your web site under simulated load to flush out these problems.

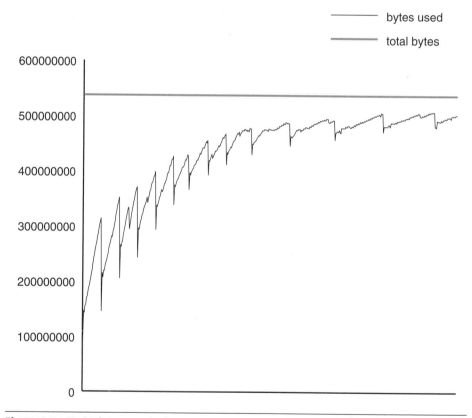

Figure 4.5   Typical memory leak pattern

Java Coding Techniques

Previously, we addressed how to avoid memory leaks by understanding how our application impacts Java's memory management strategy. Likewise, good Java programmers understand how their application interacts with the Java compiler and the Java runtime environment. Programming with the compiler and the runtime environment in mind often makes the application faster and more memory efficient without compromising the application's readability or portability. This section covers some programming techniques for improving application performance. We focus, of course, on those techniques most beneficial to the web application environment.

Minimizing Object Creation

One of the best mechanisms for minimizing time spent in garbage collection is, as mentioned previously, to minimize the amount of garbage created. Let's discuss some common techniques for reducing the objects an application creates, as well as covering some common object creation mistakes.

String Usage

If you want to build a string from several fragments, you might concatenate them together using code similar to this:

```
1 final static String a = "<p>";
2 final static String b = "</p>";
3 String c = a + "some text" + b;
4 c += a + " this is some more text." + b;
5 c += a + " and another paragraph" + b;
6 return c;
```

Taking the code at face value, we expect it to create object c just once. As subsequent statements append string fragments to c, we expect the code to add these fragments to our existing object c.

In Java, however, objects of class String are immutable. That is, once we create a String object, we cannot change it. So, in line 4, we cannot append more characters to the object c we created in line 3. Instead, Java creates a new object under the covers and places the contents of the existing object c plus the newly appended text into this object. This new object becomes c, and the old c object is discarded. The same process repeats for line 5: Java creates a new c object to hold the contents of the old c object plus the newly appended text. The old c object (created just previously in line 4) is discarded. Obviously, whether we know it or not, our code generates a lot of "garbage" objects. Extrapolate this example to a web application receiving 20 user requests per second. If each request generates 50 "garbage" objects, we generate 1,000 discarded objects per second. This directly impacts our garbage collection overhead.

A better solution uses the `StringBuffer` class. Unlike objects of the `String` class, these objects are mutable, so they change as their contents change. If we use `StringBuffer` objects, the previous example looks like this:

```
1 static final String a = "<p>";
2 static final String b = "</p>";
3 StringBuffer c = a + "some text" + b;
4 c.append(a + " this is some more text." + b);
5 c.append(a + " and another paragraph" + b);
6 return c.toString();
```

Note that we still use the string concatenation operator, +, *within* a line. This is safe because the Java compiler internally uses a `StringBuffer` object just to construct this part of the string.[3] If you wish, you can use `StringBuffer.append()` for all the fragments, but this technique makes the code more difficult to read without improving the performance.

Also, remember that string literals are `String` objects too. If you use string literals throughout your program, consider declaring them all as `static final String "…"` (as we did in the example above). This declaration assures only one instance of the literal string in your application, and this instance never becomes a candidate for garbage collection. Other techniques for managing string literals include placing them in singleton objects or storing them in resource bundles. (However, if you place them in resource bundles, consider caching them to avoid repeated reads from disk.)

Unused Local Variables

Over time, programs change. If you refactor your code, clean up unnecessary local variables. Otherwise, your methods allocate these "dead" variables for each method call. Some compilers recognize unused variables and avoid them automatically. Many compilers, however, do not, so check with your vendor for details. If your compiler does not provide this feature, consider using a profiling tool to identify unused variables. These tools often prove most useful for large or unfamiliar applications.

---

3. See the discussion on `String` and `StringBuffer` usage at `java.lang.StringBuffer`. Retrieved January 16, 2002, from the World Wide Web: <http://java.sun.com/products/jdk/1.1/docs/api-java.lang.StringBuffer.html>

Pooling

Chapter 2 discussed the specifics of thread pooling. However, you may benefit from pooling other objects as well. First, consider your application's objects, and determine if any fit the following pattern:

- Creating the object is expensive, either because of the object's size or initialization complexity.
- The application uses this object frequently, but only for brief, limited activities.
- After the application finishes with the object, it becomes a candidate for garbage collection.
- The object is stateless.
- If the object does change with use, the object reinitializes to its original state quickly and easily.
- The application never places the object inside an HTTP session or similar long-lived object.

Basically, if you create and destroy the same objects frequently, these objects make good candidates for a pooling strategy. However, pool management also incurs overhead. Before investing in a custom pool strategy, be sure the benefits outweigh the costs.

Of course, using custom pools works the same as using connection pools or a custom thread pool: The application requests an object from the pool, uses it briefly, and returns it to the pool. This pattern allows multiple web application threads to share expensive objects and to reduce the create/delete overhead associated with these objects. If you want a custom object pool, check out the information in Chapter 2 regarding thread pools. Many of the hints and cautions mentioned there apply to any type of pool. Again, let us caution you to first try a small sample application using the pool. Profile this sample to determine if pooling truly provides benefits for your application or if the pool management overhead negates any potential pooling benefits.

Multi-Threading Issues

Java designers built multi-threading into the base language. J2EE also embraces multi-threading: J2EE containers create new threads to handle the current request burden. (As noted in Chapter 2, we suggest setting a hard maximum on the number of threads a container may create to avoid resource congestion.) Multi-threading allows a web server to support multiple, simultaneous requests. However, programmers more familiar with the "one user, one application," single-threaded world of the thick client frequently experience difficulties in moving to a multi-threaded design.

Usually, these folks trip over issues such as how to maintain state information properly and how to use shared resources correctly.

To complicate matters, multi-threading issues usually come to light only under load testing. While the developers write their code and perform simple single-user tests against it, everything works beautifully. However, when we run 20 simultaneous users through the same application, things begin to break. (That is, hopefully things begin to break. Some race conditions may only appear after very long runs, and under extremely specific scenarios.)

This section covers the basics of multi-threaded programming for a web application, including good programming practices for servlets and the proper use of synchronization in your application. However, keep in mind that good programming does not always eliminate multi-threading problems. You must also check any third-party code your web application references for multi-threading support. Also, you must verify that your remote systems (content servers, databases, and so on) accept simultaneous traffic. Good multi-threading support in your web application does not guarantee excellent performance. However, improper multi-threading support (particularly the improper use of synchronization) frequently creates performance bottlenecks. Also, an awareness of multi-threading issues usually proves useful to the performance test team. Remember, threading problems only emerge under load, so the performance team may be the first to discover these problems in an application.

Multi-Threaded Servlets

As stated in Chapter 2, multi-threaded servlets give Java web sites the best performance. However, one of the drawbacks of multi-threaded servlets is their inability to maintain state information in instance or class variables. By way of review, recall that the container only creates a single instance of a multi-threaded servlet and allows multiple threads to execute against this instance. Therefore, we cannot keep state information in instance or class variables because all execution threads have access to these variables, and they may try to update them simultaneously. This potentially leads to terrible error states, such as one visitor receiving another visitor's financial or medical information in the returned HTML.

Here's a poorly coded servlet ready to create just such an error state.

```
public class MyServlet extends HttpServlet {
   private String acctNumber = null;
   public void doGet(HttpServletRequest request, HttpServletResponse
➡ response) {
     acctNumber = request.getParameter("account");
     if (acctNumber == null || "".equals(acctNumber)){
       // do error page
```

```
      }
    AccountInfo info = doDatabaseCall(acctNumber);
    request.setAttribute("acctInfo",info);
    getServletContext().getRequestDispatcher("foo.jsp").
    forward(request,response);
    } // doGet
} // class MyServlet
```

Let's walk through this servlet and observe the multi-threading problems it contains. First, a request comes in, and executes through the following statement:

```
acctNumber = request.getParameter("account");
```

(Let's say the new value of acctNumber is "1234" after the first request executes the statement.) Let's assume another request arrives *simultaneously* and executes through the same line just slightly after the first request, also updating the value in the variable acctNumber. Let's say the second request sets the value of acctNumber to "5678".

As the first thread continues, it executes the database call to get the account info:

```
AccountInfo info = doDatabaseCall(acctNumber);
```

However, because the first thread and the second thread *share* the same instance of the variable acctNumber, the database call retrieves the account information of *second requestor*! (The database retrieves account data for account number "5678", its current value, instead of "1234".) The servlet then sends the wrong person's account information to a JSP for display to the *first* requester!

To solve this problem, move the declaration of acctNumber inside the doGet() method. Method variables are unique to the method *and thread* on which they were invoked.

Synchronization

Because many programmers feel uncomfortable with multi-threaded programming, they overuse or misuse the synchronized statement in their servlet code. The synchronized statement allows only one thread to enter a code block at a time. Other threads trying to access the code block must wait until the thread inside the block exits. If you must use the synchronized statement, minimize the code inside the synchronized block. The longer the synchronized code requires to execute, the longer other threads wait to enter the block. Limit the code inside the block to the essential elements requiring synchronization. For example, synchronize moving objects in and out of a pool, but not the use of an object itself after it leaves the pool. (The pool is actually the shared resource, not the object obtained from the pool.)

For example, let's assume we create a sharing crisis in our code similar to the one in the previous example:

```
1  public class MyServlet extends HttpServlet {
2     private String someString;
3     public void service(HttpServletRequest req, HttpServletResponse res) {
4        someString = req.getParameter("myParameter");
5        ...
6     }
7  }
```

This code is not *threadsafe* (that is, it does not support multi-threading). Just as in our previous example, as multiple threads execute through the service() method, they overwrite each other's value of the variable someString. So, for multiple simultaneous requests, this code behaves in a nondeterminate manner. (Given a fixed set of inputs, we do not get predictable output.)

Sometimes, when the developers discover this problem, they look to synchronization to solve their threading problem. Surprisingly, as a result, we sometimes find this very example solved by marking the entire service() method as synchronized! (See the code sample below.) Of course, this strategy makes the method threadsafe, but it also forces requests through the servlet serially rather than in parallel. In short, this technique turns a multi-threaded servlet into a single-threaded servlet. The synchronized statement acts as a bottleneck, and for web sites of almost any size, this results in terrible performance.

```
1  public class MyServlet extends HttpServlet {
2     private String someString;
3     public synchronized void service(HttpServletRequest req,
➡        HttpServletResponse res) {
4        someString = req.getParameter("myParameter");
         ...
6     }
7  }
```

As we discussed in the previous section, the best solution removes the instance variables, and places them within the scope of the method, as shown in the code sample below. This eliminates the threading problems.

```
1  public class MyServlet extends HttpServlet {
2     public synchronized void service(HttpServletRequest req,
➡        HttpServletResponse res) {
3        String someString = req.getParameter("myParameter");
4        ...
5     }
6  }
```

This works nicely for simple problems, but what if you're calling code that isn't threadsafe, and you need to implement some thread safety yourself? You might use the following synchronization technique to protect a class (MyClass in the following example) that isn't threadsafe.

```
1  public class MyServlet extends HttpServlet {
2      public void service(HttpServletRequest req, HttpServletResponse
➡   res) {
3          String stuff;
4          synchronized(this) {
5              MyClass myObject = MyClass.getObject();
6              myObject.performTask();
7              stuff = myObject.getSomething();
8              }
9          ...
10          }
11      }
```

This protects the instance of the single-threaded class (myObject), and allows the service() method to use the contents of the variable stuff after line 8. However, by using synchronized(this), we prevent any other thread from executing a method of our class MyServlet while another thread is in the synchronized block. If many threads use this code block, we in effect make this servlet single-threaded.

The following solution provides a better alternative with minimal synchronization:

```
1  public class MyServlet extends HttpServlet {
2      Object lock = new Object();
3      public void service(HttpServletRequest req, HttpServletResponse res) {
4          String stuff;
5
6          synchronized(lock) {
7              MyClass myObject = MyClass.getObject();
8              myObject.performTask();
9              stuff = myObject.getSomething();
10              }
11          ...
12          }
13      }
```

Here we provide a shared object for synchronization rather than the servlet class itself. This allows other threads to continue executing other methods of the MyServlet servlet while another thread is inside the synchronized block.[4]

---

4. Double-checked locking inside a singleton requires more consideration. See http://www.cs.umd.edu/~pugh/java/memoryModel/DoubleCheckedLocking.html for more details.

Summary

Developing a high-performance Java application requires an understanding of how the Java runtime operates in order to avoid correct but underperforming code. In this chapter, we addressed the issues of implicit object creation, synchronization, and threading, and their potential impact on performance.

We also discussed how to determine the optimal heap settings for your application, as well as how to determine the frequency and duration of the garbage collection cycle. Of course, after you determine the memory footprint and garbage collection profile of your application, you may want to tune your application further to use memory resources more efficiently.

Again, our goal is not to teach Java or J2EE programming but to make you aware of the key performance issues of various programming techniques. For more information about the issues raised in this chapter, we encourage you to examine some of the books in our bibliography.

This chapter also closes our introductory material. Hopefully, you understand a bit more about performance terminology and Java web sites after completing these chapters. Next, we begin a more detailed examination of web site performance with a discussion of some basic types of sites and their key stress points.

Chapter 5

PERFORMANCE PROFILES OF COMMON WEB SITES

N ow that we understand how a Java web site works, let's move on to evaluating the web site's performance. Web applications and web sites differ, and their performance requirements vary widely. Therefore, the single most important question to ask before beginning a web site performance test is this: *What does the web site need to do well?* For example, some web sites exist to return graphics-laden catalog pages, while others exist to provide textual information about stocks and bonds. Obviously, the performance requirements of these web sites differ, and so should their performance tests. Often, test teams assume their job is to find the maximum throughput the site supports, and they build a test accordingly. However, the actual measure of the web site's success may be how quickly it returns pages or how well it supports a large number of logged-in users. In short, performance testing is not "one size fits all." Every web site requires a test designed to exercise its key performance criteria.

This chapter explores the performance characteristics of some popular types of web sites. Using these characteristics, we discuss how to design a relevant performance test for the web site. Even if your site doesn't quite match the ones covered here, these examples might help you think about your specific performance requirements.

Financial Sites

Most financial sites handle large request volumes. Often their customers log on when the market opens, and remain active all day. These users repeatedly check the value of their portfolios and obtain price updates on stocks they're following. They also review (with less frequency) news and research materials on companies, currencies, and other instruments of interest. All of this information is very time-sensitive, requiring real-time quotes, up-to-the-minute market news, and the latest analysts' reports. Much of the information displayed by the web site comes from remote databases and third-party systems.

While all of these functions provide value to the users, the financial web site's real purpose is trading. A large portion of the site's traffic volumes results from trade requests. On busy market days, these trading volumes grow dramatically, often to many times the average load. (See Figure 5.1 for an example.) Trading volumes translate to commissions revenue for the financial institution behind the web site. This gives the web site's owners incentive to focus on trading performance. Additional incentive often comes from the government. Failure to support timely trades, regardless of the circumstances, may attract the attention of regulatory agencies. Financial web sites also like to convey the same sense of reliability and responsiveness to their customers as their brick-and-mortar counterparts. Media scrutiny, the threat of poor publicity, and the resulting lack of customer confidence all play a role in pressuring financial web sites to be fast and reliable, despite frequent wide swings in traffic volumes.

Financial trading heavily engages the dynamic portions of the web site. The trading application uses a variety of external resources to prepare the trade, including the customer account database and quote servers to pull the trade information together. However, the actual trade usually occurs outside the web site in a trading engine. The engine usually resides on a mainframe, or it may belong to a third-party trade clearing house. The web site must maintain fast access to this central trading engine, and the engine must keep pace with the trading demands from the web site as well as other trading software inside the brokerage

Caching Potential

Financial web site pages usually contain few graphics. A typical page may display the institution's logo and some aesthetically pleasing navigational aides (tabs, buttons, shading graphics, and so on). The page frequently contains JavaScript and a few advertisements for related services. However, users sometimes request customized graphics, and generating these requires the involvement of the web application. (For example, a graph of portfolio gains and losses over the past 30 days requires dynamic generation.)

This leads to the next major characteristic of financial web sites: They cannot rely on long-lived data caches. The data returned by a financial web site actually falls under a "freshness" hierarchy. Real-time data such as stock quotes or market indices changes frequently and must be current. Any cache of such data must refresh constantly, and it only benefits the web site if it receives large, simultaneous request volumes requiring this information. Next in the hierarchy comes market news and bulletins. These bulletins arrive continuously, but their information remains relevant longer than an "old" stock quote. Caching these bulletins makes sense, but the cache requires frequent refreshing as well to load the latest bulletins. Finally, at the bottom of the information hierarchy lies longer-lived data such as analysts' reports or company quarterly statements. Given the size of these reports, as well as their low access rate, most web sites retrieve them only as needed from a database.

Special Considerations

Financial web sites deal with time-critical and confidential information. Therefore these web sites operate differently in some important areas, as we'll discuss in this section.

Security

Security is a very important consideration. Financial web sites contain, manipulate, and display sensitive information about their users. The data returned routinely contains account numbers, trading history, portfolio content and value, and other highly personal information. To defend this data, the web site uses SSL to encrypt sensitive communications. To protect the site from unauthorized internal or external access, the institution shields the site with other security measures such as multiple firewall layers and internal security features (authentication and/or authorization). Of course, all this security impacts performance. More than other web site types, financial sites use SSL on a higher percentage of page requests. This increases overall response time as well as the burden on the HTTP servers.

Traffic Patterns

The traffic pattern for a financial web site tracks to major market operating hours. Request volumes spike around the market opening, and again just before closing. Also, traffic tends to be high around lunchtime. Before and after the major U.S. East coast markets close, significantly smaller traffic volumes visit the web site to check portfolios and research investments. Market upheavals result in abnormally large, sustained traffic volumes during the market day. Figure 5.1 in the next section shows an example of financial web site traffic patterns.

Financial web sites plan for market upheavals rather than the normal days. For this reason, these sites invest significantly in reserve hardware capacity. The web applications occupying this hardware undergo stringent performance and scalability tests to gauge their performance under extreme loading.

Auditing

Financial sites track detailed information about every trade, both within the web site and within the trading system. Often such auditing results from government mandate, but it also proves useful when settling disputes with customers.

Customers occasionally try to renounce a trade if it results in losses. If the customer claims they never executed the trade, the web site needs detailed logging to track the trade from initiation through every step until completion. This includes following the trade across multiple, distributed systems.

Logging adds overhead to web site processing. However, nonrepudiation is so important that logging is a must for these transactions. Use performance testing to evaluate the impact of logging on trading performance.

Performance Testing Considerations

Financial web site performance testing stresses the limits of throughput and user logins for the web site. Generating the traffic necessary to stress the systems under test frequently requires a large client environment. See the suggestions in Chapter 6 on managing these types of performance tests.

Also, your test needs test data. Obviously, you don't want to make hundreds of stock trades from real accounts while testing performance. Many financial companies use specially designed test accounts for these situations. Make sure you have enough data in the test system to avoid artificially inflating your results through data caching.

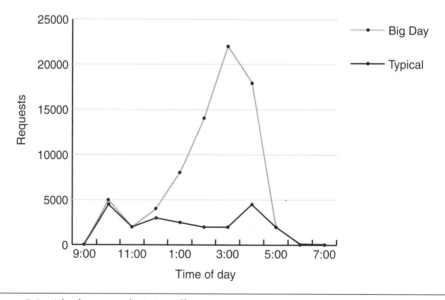

Figure 5.1   A brokerage web site's traffic patterns

(For example, using the same customer IDs repeatedly often leads to caching of these accounts at the customer database. This artificially improves their average retrieval time.)

Since financial web sites incorporate many distributed systems, consider the availability of these systems when planning your test. Overloading a quote server with your testing leads to unhappy customers on the existing web site. Schedule off-shift testing for these elements, or develop test simulators for these systems.

B2B (Business-to-Business) Sites

While financial sites and their requirements get plenty of publicity, other types of web sites exist, and they have different usage patterns. B2B sites, for example, exist to provide services from one company to other companies. The B2B site is not designed for retail but for wholesale operation. For example, purchasing agents for client companies might use a B2B site to obtain order quotes, check shipping status, and the like.

B2B web site users often log on and stay active throughout the day, much like the users of financial sites. However, the *level* of activity per user differs significantly from the brokerage scenario. A typical day for visitors on some B2B sites might include checking the inventory status of a purchase under consideration, placing an order, and checking the shipping status of an outstanding order. That's all the activity for the entire day. These low-utilization B2B sites do not experience huge swings in traffic and user volumes, as many financial or e-Commerce sites do. These sites generally have only hundreds or a few thousands of users known to the system. Depending on their markets, some B2B sites receive a worldwide set of users, which also flattens any daily traffic variation (and also implies round-the-clock web site availability).

B2B users generate fewer interactions with the web site, but each interaction usually requires "heavier" processing than a financial transaction. A B2B transaction might include processing a large order or receiving a large XML (extensible markup language) document for processing. Also, the web site interacts with a variety of back-end systems to handle each request. The B2B web application interacts with order processing, workflow management, inventory, and third-party systems (such as the shipping company's tracking database) to satisfy user requests.

Regardless of the weight of the transaction, the B2B user expects a responsive web site. While the user may be willing to wait longer than a day trader at a financial web site, the B2B user demands a site available when needed, and responsive to requests.

Caching Potential

Pages returned by B2B sites rarely contain heavy graphics content (unless, of course, the B2B site provides a "catalog feature"). The pages contain graphics merely as presentation aids rather than as content. Also, because the users interact with the web site infrequently throughout the day, maintaining large data caches for each user proves memory expensive. However, caching references to key data elements (such as the customer's account ID) speeds retrieval when the customer does make a request, and requires very little memory per user.

Special Considerations

B2B web sites focus on providing convenient access for their users. They also interact extensively with existing ordering systems. Let's discuss how these factors influence the performance tests.

User Pressure

B2B web sites support many concurrent users. Because their users want constant availability, many B2B web sites allow their users to log on to the web site just once in the morning and retain access to their accounts all day. Overall web site performance depends on the web application managing these users properly. If each user's HTTP session accumulates a large data cache over the course of a visit, the memory available to run applications quickly disappears.

Asynchronous Interactions

B2B systems often interact asynchronously with back-end resources such as the order processing system or the workflow system. Communication with these systems often involves a messaging service, such as IBM's WebSphere MQSeries product. These services support asynchronous communication to remote systems: The message gets delivered, but there's no guarantee of how long it takes to make the delivery. Web application developers frequently make the mistake of waiting indefinitely for asynchronous calls to return. This opens the door for "freezing" the web site (see Chapter 2) if the messaging service begins responding slowly.

Performance Testing a B2B Site

The performance tests for B2B sites differ from those for high-transaction web sites, as the number of logged-on users is much higher in proportion to the number of requests. The critical success factor becomes the number of logged-on users the site is able to support. Of course, the response time at this high-water mark of users must still fall into the acceptable range.

These tests typically involve lots of simulated users. Consider some of the suggestions in Chapter 6 for managing large user loads. Fully exercise each major user scenario during the test: ordering, checking order status, reviewing payment history, and the like. Also, provide sufficient capacity to simulate the logged-on user pressure, and use realistic think times during the scenario. Also, as with financial web sites, use test data during your performance tests. Coordinate your testing with any third-party resources (such as the shipping company), or simulate their resources in your environment.

e-Commerce Sites

e-Commerce web sites exist to sell products. Users visit these sites to view items, place orders, and use customer service features (for example, checking order shipping status, or requesting a return authorization). Most users browse the on-line "catalog" of items or perform searches to view item selections. Only a small percentage of visitors (typically less than 5%) actually make purchases.

Response time is the critical factor for e-Commerce sites. These web sites compete with other e-Commerce sites as well as brick-and-mortar stores for customers. Rapid page responses give users a better shopping experience and allow them see more pages in less time. Users frustrated by slow response times find another place to shop.

Large commercial e-Commerce sites often receive large traffic volumes. These sites require good throughput to handle this traffic while maintaining good response times.

Large traffic volumes also imply a large number of concurrent users. Web sites creating an HTTP session for each visiting user must manage these sessions carefully to avoid excessive memory consumption.

Caching Potential

By now you might think there's little difference between an e-Commerce web site and a financial site. However, unlike their financial counterparts, e-Commerce sites typically return large pages created by embedding many sizeable static elements. An e-Commerce site exists to sell things, and showing customers pictures of these things moves merchandise.

Happily, e-Commerce sites also differ from financial sites in content stability. The selection of toaster ovens at most retail sites doesn't change much from moment to moment. This allows the web site to cache much of its static content using one of the techniques we discussed in Chapter 3. (Some very large e-Commerce web sites actually cache content inside the networks of some very large ISPs. However, that's really beyond our discussion here.)

Special Considerations

e-Commerce web sites deal with confidential user information, as well as potentially large volumes of users. Both these factors influence performance test design.

Traffic Patterns

Much like the financial web sites, e-Commerce sites experience daily traffic cycles. Traffic for these sites tends to be the heaviest around lunch hours and in the early evenings. Of course, for web sites with national appeal, these peak hours may span several time zones. The largest traffic fluctuations for an e-Commerce web site actually occur over the course of a year, with many retail web sites experiencing huge spikes in daily traffic because of seasonal influences. Figure 5.2 shows a web site experiencing a prolonged traffic spike at the holiday season. Web sites may also receive more traffic during the "back-to-school" period in August, as well as at other times, depending on the type of merchandise they sell.

As they do on financial web sites, these peak events dramatically raise the traffic handled by e-Commerce sites. They may also represent a large part of a retailer's yearly revenue, so planning for these sustained peak loads is essential. Basing your performance test on data for March may mean the site fails when holiday shopping begins in November.

Security

As we discussed earlier, e-Commerce web sites must secure the financial transactions that customers make on the site. However, these transactions normally make up a small fraction of the overall traffic (typically, less than 5% of our daily visitors actually buy anything).

You should use security (particularly SSL) to protect any financial transactions, but try to avoid encrypting graphics-intensive pages, as this requires more overhead. Keep the checkout pages relatively simple for faster processing.

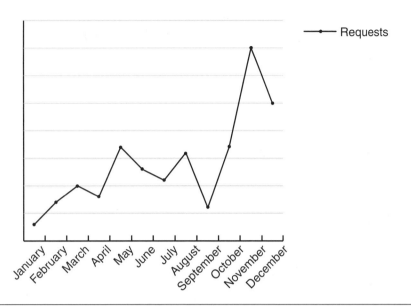

Figure 5.2 Yearly traffic patterns for an e-Commerce site

Performance Testing an e-Commerce Site

e-Commerce sites require thorough exploration of their transaction rates, response times, and user pressures. This requires an investment in user simulation licenses and test equipment. Usually, e-Commerce web sites interact with large catalog databases, and the site visitors look at a wide variety of items in the database throughout the day. Set up your performance tests to mimic this behavior. Use a large set of test data to fuel your simulated searches and purchases rather than repeatedly going after the same small set of items. This testing approach more accurately recreates the impact of database interaction on performance.

Repeatedly using as small set of test items often artificially improves your performance numbers. The catalog database quickly loads these items into its cache, reducing their retrieval time. This caching benefit does not generally apply under production conditions, so use enough test data to defeat any artificial caching benefit. Similarly, use a copy of the production database rather than a scaled-down version in your testing. By exercising the full database, you get a more realistic idea of its actual production responsiveness.

Also, be sure to correctly simulate the user pressure during your testing. These web sites receive many different users throughout the day, so your test must simulate this to uncover any user management problems.

Portal Sites

A portal behaves differently from other sites in that it offers a personalized "home page" to users. Much as they do on the B2B web site, users tend to log on at the beginning of their day and stay logged on all day long. They refresh their customized page from time to time during the day and drill down into items that catch their interest. These sites often display a customized view of news, entertainment features, a few selected stocks or other investment data, weather, and so on.

Such sites may forward requests for page segments to other systems and web sites. For example, a portal might have a page link that forwards requests to a news or stock price site. Public portal sites sometimes support millions of registered users, while enterprise portals frequently support tens of thousands of users.

Although portals support many users, these users make fewer requests against the portal than e-Commerce or financial users. In fact, the traffic patterns for a portal web site often resemble those for a B2B web site: many concurrent users making infrequent requests.

Caching Potential

Portals make extensive use of caching. They cache static content for faster display and refresh the cache periodically to reflect updates. The dynamic portions of the portal web site often cache small, dynamic components of the portal page for faster display, particularly if all the portal users see many of the same components.

Special Considerations: Traffic Patterns

The web sites accessed via a portal server impact the portal's behavior. However, the portal traffic pattern often differs from that of the other web sites we've discussed thus far. While the overall daily traffic patterns for a portal mimic the B2B traffic patterns we discussed earlier, portals also often experience peak traffic periods. Especially for enterprise portals, most users arrive at work within a one- or two-hour interval and log on to the portal web site for the first time. User log-on is the most expensive operation for many portals. During this process, the web site interacts with security servers (like LDAP) to retrieve information needed to confirm the log-on. The web site creates the user's session information during this time and also loads any personalization data for the user.

Beyond the morning log-on traffic, these web sites often receive event-based load spikes. For example, if the CEO makes an important speech, or the company releases a hot new product, an enterprise portal receives more traffic as employees clamor to see this information. In addition, portals sometimes generate their own load. Often portal pages include JavaScript to refresh key page components periodically. Also, some components include applets, which generate load against the web site. Understanding the typical configuration of a portal page helps in designing the performance test.

Performance Testing a Portal Site

Many of the principles behind testing a B2B web site also apply to testing portal web sites. The test requires many users to simulate the user pressure, and it usually benefits from scaled-down testing. However, portal web sites sometimes run two sets of performance tests. The first test resembles typical daily activity (the user logs in and makes infrequent requests). The second test just simulates log-on activity to accurately test the log-on peak in the morning.

Because these web sites rely on remote systems to supply content, security, and personalization data, coordinating your test with the support organizations for these systems is critical. As with the e-Commerce web sites, testing at off-shift hours often works best. Likewise, portal performance tests often simulate content from third-party providers.

Information Sites

Information web sites receive anonymous user traffic. Unlike financial, B2B, or portal web sites, these sites don't require users to have an account with the site to make full use of its features. (e-Commerce sites also allow anonymous browsing, but generally require the user to create an account for purchases.) Examples of information sites include news, weather, entertainment, and major sports event web sites. These web sites focus on excellent response times and high throughput. These sites compete for advertising revenue; the more traffic they handle every day, the happier the advertisers. Advertising content sometimes comes from third-party sources, complicating the site's performance characteristics.

Caching Potential

Information web site caching resembles a hybrid between e-Commerce and portal caching. The pages returned contain graphic elements such as aesthetic graphics (buttons, menu bars, and so on), advertisements, and often information graphics (charts, news photos, and so on.). These sites cache their static elements and also frequently cache prebuilt dynamic pages. For example, news sites often cache their front page until the content changes. The site then builds the new page, and "pushes" it out to the cache.

The high-end information sites use very elaborate hardware configurations to route users to their nearest regional cluster. Within the cluster, the web site uses multiple servers and caches to handle user requests. In these cases, simultaneously updating the distributed machine cluster to give all your users consistent content often proves to be a significant challenge. The cache refresh rates vary depending on the information site's function. Large sports event sites refresh their caches continuously to reflect the latest scores. An entertainment site, however, probably reports accurate TV programming listings using only hourly, or even daily, cache refreshes.

Special Considerations: Traffic Patterns

Information web sites provide information. The largest considerations with these sites revolve around the "when" and "how" of information retrieval. Traffic patterns on information web sites vary widely depending on the site. In general, these sites receive most of their traffic throughout the business day with spikes during the lunch hours. However, if the site's information suddenly becomes more interesting, traffic volumes grow dramatically. Entertainment sites experience traffic spikes if a major celebrity makes headlines. Sports event sites receive potentially crushing loads of traffic during the actual event.

Since no traffic pattern fits all information sites, we typically look to the traffic handled by similar web sites for guidance when planning a test. Also, discuss traffic patterns with your marketing department to get more ideas. Finally, consider the information on your web site: Can you foresee any circumstances that would create unusually high demand for this information? If so, plan for this demand.

As we mentioned previously, many information sites now act as providers to other sites or portals. For many information web sites, the traffic generated by these sites far exceeds their usual traffic rates. If your site acts as a provider to other sites, the traffic patterns of those sites become your traffic patterns as well. Make your capacity and test plans fit the projected peak loads of sites using your content.

Performance Testing an Information Site

Information web site performance testing focuses on throughput and response time. User visits tend to be very brief at such sites, unlike visits to other web sites, and require little or no HTTP session information. Web sites fitting this pattern make good candidates for think time reduction within the test client, which reduces the number of user licenses actually required to stress the system. (See Chapter 6 for more details.)

Pervasive Client Device Support

Users increasingly want to access Internet information from portable devices such as cell phones or PDAs (personal digital assistants). Known as *pervasive client devices*, they represent the latest major trend in Internet access. We mention them here because they present special performance issues for web sites supporting their access. Not surprisingly, cell phones and PDAs do not provide the same graphical and functional support as traditional web browsers. Pages viewed on pervasive devices often contain less content and few (if any graphics). Also, many of these devices simply do not support HTML or cookies.

Many web sites provide special areas in the site for pervasive users. The applications in these areas generate content for the devices, and they may use different page flows or logic to eliminate the need for cookies. Other web sites often use special pervasive gateways to provide cookie support, as well as other functions. These gateways manage the cookies for each user, and provide protocol conversion between the pervasive device and the web site. Also, the gateways manage any SSL traffic between the web site and the pervasive device. (Many pervasive devices do not support SSL encryption/decryption.)

Figure 5.3 shows such a gateway in action. In this case, the gateway provides HTTP/WAP protocol conversion. The pervasive requests enter the web site using the WAP protocol; the gateway converts them to HTTP. This allows the web site to process the request using its existing HTTP servers. Likewise, the gateway converts the outbound request from HTTP to WAP for display at the device.

Caching Potential

Because many pervasive devices support only text formats, caching graphics and other static content provides little benefit to the web site. However, caching frequently accessed pages (like a common homepage) may provide some benefits to very busy sites.

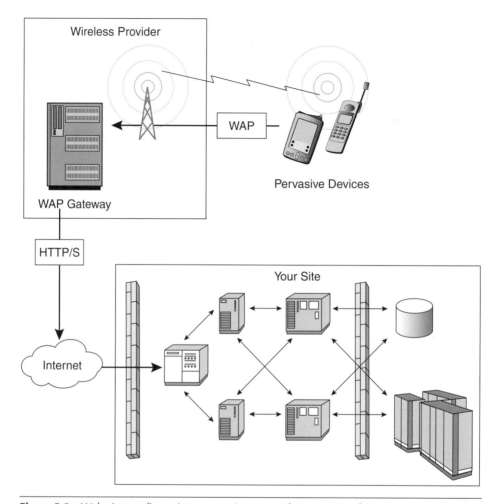

Figure 5.3 Web site configuration supporting access by pervasive devices

Special Considerations

Pervasive device support requires work at the web site to deliver palatable information to these special devices. Also, providing such support frequently changes web site traffic patterns.

Traffic Patterns

Adding pervasive support to your web site often dramatically increases your daily user visits. Most pervasive device visitors interact with the site very briefly (but perhaps frequently) throughout the day. If you use existing web applications to handle pervasive visitors, proper user management becomes a critical concern. Existing applications may create an HTTP session for each visitor. As the number of visitors surges, the application may run out of memory.

Also, pervasive devices tend to be slow. If your site currently receives most of its traffic from LAN-connected users, adding support for pervasive devices often changes your network landscape. Consider the potential impact of longer connection times in your network planning.

Conversion Overhead

Some web sites support pervasive devices through translation servers. Rather than change their web applications to support an ever-changing variety of pervasive devices, they simply convert the web application's output to fit the device. These servers automatically remove or convert graphics elements, trim the pages to the right size, and generally make the page ready for viewing at the device. Translation servers must process every page returned, adding significant overhead to the web site and impacting response times. Caching provides some relief for common pages, but custom pages still require the translation step.

Performance Testing Sites That Support Pervasive Devices

Pervasive performance testing begins by ignoring the pervasive devices themselves. The initial testing generates the HTTP normally sent from the pervasive gateway device, and drives the appropriate load against the web site.

Simulating lots of brief users visits is the goal of pervasive performance testing. Some of the think time strategies for reducing virtual user licenses discussed in Chapter 6 apply to these test situations.

Testing the full web site, including the gateway, from a device's perspective often proves difficult. The small test simulators provided by many pervasive vendors do not drive enough load to test a large system. However, some commercial test driver products have recently added support for scripting and testing with pervasive protocols.

Nonetheless, testing as a pervasive device drives load against the gateway and any auxiliary systems it uses. For example, some gateways use a database to assist with cookie tracking. Driving load through the gateway exercises the performance of both the gateway and its database. This testing gives us a complete end-to-end understanding of the web site's performance, including the components interacting directly with the pervasive devices.

Web Services

Web services, despite their name, do not comprise what is normally thought of as a web site. Rather than supplying content viewed by a person, they provide a way for programs to invoke one another. Though they often use HTTP, you may invoke web services over almost any protocol, including asynchronous messaging and e-mail. We mention web services here because they often use web sites to make their function available to the world. As mentioned before, they use the HTTP protocol to wrap some kind of functionality in a servlet that understands the SOAP (simple object access protocol) encoding used by web services. If your web site serves up both web pages and web services, you need to understand the performance impact that the web services have on the rest of your site.

There are several areas where web services potentially impact a web site. First, they expose more function, and as more clients invoke that function, your site obviously receives more load. In addition, the XML decoding and encoding to pass the SOAP messages around puts considerable CPU load on your application servers. In addition to the raw CPU load, these "heavy" requests tend to tie up servlet threads for longer times, so you may need to tweak the number of threads in your web container to compensate for the additional workload.

Summary

This chapter covered the differing performance concerns of a few major web site types, as summarized in Table 5.1. We consider pervasive device support a special case of these web sites, so it is not listed separately in Table 5.1. However, be sure to consider the impact of pervasive requests as required when designing or testing any web sites.

Of course, many other types of web sites exist, all with their own performance profiles. The larger lesson is that your performance test must fit your web site. In the next few chapters, we discuss how to plan and execute a relevant performance test for your site.

Table 5.1 Comparing Performance Characteristics of Several Web Site Types

Web Site Type	User Pressure	Throughput Dependent	Response Time Requirements	Caching Potential
Financial	High	High	High	Medium
B2B	High	Medium	Medium	Low
e-Commerce	High	High	High	High
Portals	High	Medium	Medium	High
Information	Low	High	High	High

Chapter 6

DEVELOPING A
PERFORMANCE TEST PLAN

Performance tests require a test plan. Before writing the first test script or starting the first test run, you need to develop test goals and a plan for obtaining the desired measurements. Well-designed tests tell you if the site achieves key goals, as well as how the site needs to grow in the future as traffic increases. A poorly designed test usually provides misleading information.

In Chapter 5, we discussed the different performance issues and priorities of various web sites. Keep these differences in mind as you begin your test planning. While understanding throughput and response time is important, some web sites require additional testing to determine the maximum logged-on users they support. Like-wise, each site needs realistic test scenarios in order to accurately stress key components such as caches, databases, and application servers. A good test plan manages all of these requirements.

Beyond the measures, we need goals before entering the performance test. Perfor-mance tests, as more thoroughly described in Chapter 11, cycle through an iterative process of testing, resolving bottlenecks, and retesting. Without goals, the cycle of testing and resolution often continues indefinitely. You must identify the point of diminishing returns for your testing before you start.

This chapter discusses how to interpret rough performance requirements to develop test goals. Also, we discuss the basics of response time measurements, as well as test-ing for maximum logged-on users. Beyond setting goals, the chapter covers strategies for test implementation. For very large sites, generating the full, peak user load proves impossible. We cover strategies for validating web site performance by testing small portions of the site. Finally, we discuss how to use the performance test for planning future site growth. Properly designed tests uncover the weakest points in the web site and teach us how to better manage these weaknesses as the site grows.

Test Goals

First, before starting performance testing, complete a rigorous function and integration test of your web applications. This ensures that the applications function properly (at least in the single-user case) before you begin load testing. Remember: You cannot performance test broken applications. They behave erratically and may exhibit much better or much worse performance than a correct version. After completing function and integration testing, it's time to make sure that your application and supporting infrastructure supports the expected traffic volumes.

Start your performance test planning by setting performance goals. Without clearly defined goals, performance tests tend to continue indefinitely. Any web site contains an infinite number of bottlenecks. Solving one bottleneck merely exposes the next one. Without clear targets, your test team never knows if and when the web site reaches a sufficient level of performance to support its expected traffic. Setting goals lets you know when the web site is ready for production.

In Chapter 1, we discussed some of the basic performance concepts, such as peak load, throughput, response time, and scalability. In this chapter, we discuss how to develop performance goals for each of these concepts.

Peak Load

The performance test must simulate the web site's peak load. As we discussed in Chapter 1, if the web site does not perform well at peak loading, it does not really perform at all. We use the performance test in conjunction with the anticipated peak load to accomplish the following:

- Determine if the web site currently supports this goal.
- Tune an underperforming web site so that it supports peak loading.
- Determine the hardware capacity required by the web site at peak.

Surprisingly, many performance tests overlook the importance of peak loading. These tests frequently use average load numbers as their performance test targets. However, as Figure 6.1 demonstrates, average load often differs dramatically from the peak. Merely testing for average load sometimes means your web site cannot support key periods over the course of a year or even a day.

Also, use the numbers from your web site's peak usage period. As we discussed in Chapter 5, many e-Commerce web sites experience their busiest days during the Christmas shopping season. Take your peak daily load from the busiest day of your busiest season.

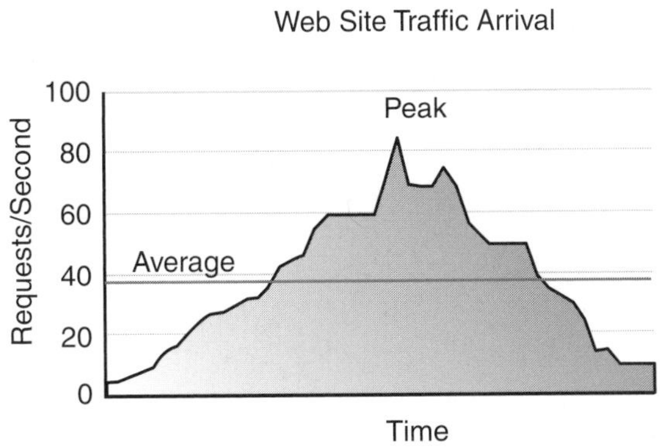

Web Site Traffic Arrival

Figure 6.1   Peak versus average web site load

While determining the peak load sounds simple enough, in practice it often proves challenging. If the site currently exists in a production environment, use data from the existing site to gauge traffic patterns and peak usage. Having said this, we should say as well that we encounter many web masters and web site teams who have no idea how many users access the site per hour, per day, or even per year! If the web site team lacks this data, many tools exist to pull site usage statistics from HTTP access logs.

An existing thick client application also presents another avenue for predicting peak load. For example, reviewing the host database transactions generated by the thick client often provides insight into peak loading. (To generalize a bit, DBAs tend to keep much better records than web site teams anyway.) Of course, this technique works best when the web site under test is the planned replacement for the thick client application.

Even data from similar web sites frequently proves useful. If these sites serve the same target audience as your web site, or provide a similar class of functionality, their traffic patterns might help you set expectations for your site. The key word here is *similar.* Arbitrarily selecting a web site as a pattern for a completely different site rarely works, as we discussed in Chapter 5. For example, assume your company supports both an e-Commerce site selling retail clothing and a site supporting financial interactions. These two web sites receive very different patterns and peak load volume; you cannot use the data from either site to predict the peak load of the other. However, the traffic patterns from the "shoe store" portion of the e-Commerce site probably apply quite well to a new "handbag store" function on this same site.

If you performance test a completely new web site or function (or target the web site to a new user market), estimating peak load becomes more difficult. In these cases you rely heavily on projections based on any available market research. This includes any public data available on similar web sites operated by other companies. However, in the end, you end up with a best guess in these situations. We suggest generously buffering any peak load estimate you develop for a completely new web site.

As you gather these numbers, don't forget about growth data as well as current usage data. Predicting future usage is also tricky, but important. By the time you finish a performance test, today's peak load no longer applies. Analyze past growth, and discuss your early estimates with marketing and development to generate your growth targets. In particular, check with marketing for any plans that might dramatically increase load. Promotional mailings, television advertising, or new products all stand to dramatically impact web site loads. Again, generously buffer any load-growth estimates you develop.

Even though the performance teams we advise often begin their test planning without good peak loading estimates, these same teams usually develop reasonable and relevant estimates after consulting the available data. Teams without loading estimates often release web sites without sufficient traffic capacity. At the other extreme, we sometimes find teams building enormous web site infrastructures to support tiny user loads. Good loading estimates lead to a properly sized web site.

Peak loading also provides the basis for throughput estimates. In the next section, we discuss how to use rough load data to develop some estimates for both peak loading and throughput.

Throughput Estimates

As you begin your search for load and throughput estimates, expect an influx of ill-defined goals. For example, we often hear requirements such as, "The site needs to support 10,000 hits a day," or "We expect 10 million users per year," or (the most ill-defined) "We anticipate 100,000 users a day." You must turn this data into reasonable estimates for building a performance test. In this section, we demonstrate some of the formulas we use for turning rough guesses into the estimates you need. Appendix A also presents these calculations in spreadsheet format to help you better organize your data.

Important! After developing rough loading and throughput estimates, *feed them back* to the other teams involved with the web site (such as marketing or management) for validation. These numbers only work if they reflect reality. All of those involved with the web site must agree with the targets you develop for the performance test and, ultimately, for the production web site itself.

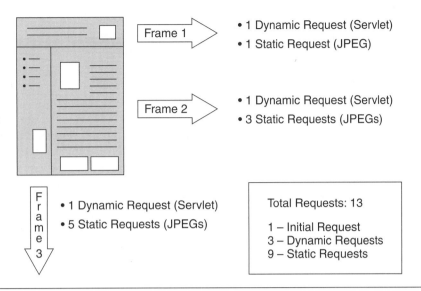

Figure 6.2 One HTML assembled from multiple HTTP requests

Hits per Day Estimates

So the marketing team tells you, "Expect 10,000 hits per day for the site." Before you take this estimate at face value, we suggest asking a few questions. As mentioned in Chapter 1, Internet terminology often varies between companies or even between departments in the same company. Let's use the marketing team's statement to explore how terminology usage impacts performance estimates.

What Is a Hit?

A "hit" potentially means a couple of different things. For an HTTP server specialist, a hit means any request sent to the HTTP server. Because HTML pages usually contain embedded elements such as *gifs* or *jpegs*, one HTML page might result in multiple HTTP "hits" as the browser retrieves all of the elements from the server to build a page. Figure 6.2 shows a web page constructed from multiple HTTP requests.

If your web master tracks site activity via the HTTP access logs, a hit might actually mean just an HTTP request rather than a full page. For example, if the average page on the site contains four embedded elements, our marketing team's "10,000 hits per day" number translates to become as few as 2,000 page requests per day:

```
Requests to display a full page = 1 page request + 4 embedded element requests

                                 = 5 requests

10,000 requests per day / 5 requests per page = 2,000 pages per day
```

This assumes every request for a page also requires the browser to retrieve all the embedded elements. This isn't always the case, as most browsers cache static page elements so they do not have to request them repeatedly. If a web site's pages contain many of the same embedded static elements on every page (for example, a banner common to all pages), the user's browser may not retrieve this element again after the first page of the user's visit.

These considerations become important as we try to find out how much dynamic content our web site serves. We need these estimates to develop some key capacity planning ratios for our web site. We want to know how many HTTP servers we require as compared to application servers. This also allows us to predict the value of specialized components, such as caching proxy servers, within our web site.

In the example above, let's assume our page request is a dynamic page request requiring service by the application server. Let's also assume the static elements do not require interaction with the application server (they're handled by the HTTP server, not the application server). In this case, our dynamic request to static request ratio is 1:4. Establishing this ratio helps us to better tune our web site (for example, configuring the ratio between HTTP server listeners and application server threads). It also helps us to plan capacity for the application servers if we understand how much traffic they receive.

Returning to our example of 10,000 hits per day, we know this number resolves to 2,000 page hits (representing dynamic content) *if* the browser requests all the embedded static elements for each page. If the browser caches static elements, the 10,000 hits per day measurement contains a higher percentage of dynamic page requests versus static elements. Consider the impact of caching on your request ratios.

Regrettably, the rest of the world uses the term *hit* in very ambiguous ways. We've seen *hit* used to refer to an entire page, including embedded elements or even entire framesets. Also, many companies routinely use *hit* to mean an entire site visit by a given user. A site visit usually encompasses many pages, not to mention the embedded elements and frames included in those pages.

This leads us to an important point: *Use performance terminology consistently.* However you define a hit, define it explicitly, and stick with the definition uniformly throughout your planning and testing. Terminology misunderstandings make for unsuccessful performance tests.

What Is a Day?

Beyond the concept of a hit, what does the marketing team mean by the term *day?* In the world of web sites, even the concept of a day lies open for interpretation. A day usually defines the primary period of activity for a web site. Many, many web site teams wrongly assume their site will be fully populated by happy users 24 hours a day. With few exceptions (such as worldwide sporting event sites), the average web site does not receive a great deal of traffic on a round-the-clock basis. Instead, most users arrive during the period of a business day. Defining the day becomes very important for determining the peak load on the web site. As shown in Figure 6.3, overestimating the length of the day conversely underestimates the peak pressure on the site. Determining the period of time when most users arrive on the system becomes critical for estimating peak load.

Determining Peak Throughput from Hits per Day

Given 10,000 hits per day, how can we turn this number into a peak throughput estimate? The ideal estimate comes from the traffic patterns of an existing web site or application, as mentioned above. For example, if the web master tells us to expect 30% of the traffic during the peak hour,[1] expect 3,000 hits per hour during the peak

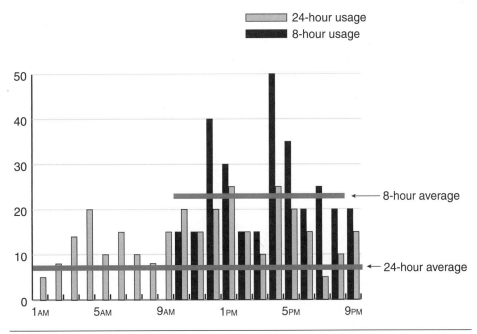

Figure 6.3 The same daily traffic volume spread over both 8- and 24-hour days

---

1. Your web site may track a smaller or larger peak time interval. Use the peak interval your team can describe with the most confidence.

period. This number gives us 0.8 hits/sec during the peak hour. Here's the math to get these numbers:

```
10,000 hits/day * 30% of traffic at peak hour
= 3,000 hits during peak hour

3,000 hits per hour / 60 minutes per hour / 60 seconds per minute
= 0.83 hits/second
```

Again, keep in mind, depending on the definition of *hit*, this may resolve to more traffic. For example, if a hit really represents a whole page containing 30 embedded elements, this number resolves to as many as 24 HTTP requests per second. Understanding the meaning behind the number makes the difference in these estimates.

Frequently, however, you receive a daily or yearly traffic rate but no guidance on how much of the traffic arrives during the peak period. In these cases, applying some calculations to the available information yields a rough peak estimate. This algorithm first spreads the traffic evenly over the web site's workday. For this example, let's assume the web site receives most of its traffic during an eight-hour period:

```
10,000 hits per day / 8 hours per day = 1,250 hits/hour
```

Notice that this gives us an even distribution with no consideration for peak loading. To estimate the peak, we normally assume three to five times the weight of the daily average. For safety, in this case, let's assume the peak is five times the average.

```
1,250 hits/hour * 5 = 6,250 hits/hour
```

This gives us the following value for the per second hit rate at peak:

```
6,250 hits per hour / 60 minutes per hour / 60 seconds per minute
= 1.7 hits/second
```

After arriving at this step, we proceed as follows.

- Convert the number to peak HTTP requests. For example, if our numbers represent page requests instead of HTTP requests, we do more work. If each page request translates to seven HTTP requests, the peak HTTP request rate becomes

  ```
  6,250 hits per hour * 7 HTTP requests per hit
  = 43,750 HTTP requests per hour

  43,750 HTTP requests per hour ➜ 12.15 HTTP requests per second
  ```

- After converting to HTTP requests, apply the dynamic to static ratio. From an earlier example, we know each dynamic page request generates four additional static requests. This means that, of our 12.15 requests/second:

```
12.15 hits per second * 1/5 = 2.43 dynamic hits per second
```

```
12.15 hits per second * 4/5 = 9.72 static hits per second
```

- Validate these calculations with others involved in the site, such as marketing or management. Always review the calculations in light of the real site.

Users per Day Estimates

Regrettably, the *hit* does not reign as the most ill-defined term in web site performance. The term *user* leads the pack as the most misunderstood performance metric. Often, the web site team receives guidelines for site performance such as "the site needs to support 100,000 users per day." Of course, this doesn't give us any information about what these 100,000 users will be doing on the web site.

So, once again, we must dig into the number to determine how the users interact with the site. Likewise, we need to develop some idea of how the site is constructed to understand the burden the typical user interaction places on the web site. Finally, we use all of this information to develop peak load estimates.

What Is a User?

User usually means one of three things in terms of web site usage:

1. One of potentially many "visits" the user will make to the web site over the course of a day
2. A complete set of activities accomplished by the user on the site for the whole day
3. A hit

Users as Hits

Let's start with the last definition: a hit. Many web masters and web site teams use *hit* and *user* interchangeably. So when they say "user," they really mean "user request." So, in this case, they expect 100,000 user requests per day. Usually, this translates best to pages, but, as with the discussion above, hit can mean a variety of things.

All Day Visitors

The second definition is often used in B2B, portal, and some other classes of web sites where the users log on to the site for the entire day. In these cases, a *user* represents a complete set of activities accomplished by the user for the whole day. These users may or may not be very active. If they infrequently make requests throughout the day, the primary web site burden may well be the "footprint" of the user on the system.

This user "footprint" includes any resources required to keep the user active on the system all day. For example, the system sometimes uses memory to keep HTTP session data about the user. Also, the web site may save the user's session to a persistent HTTP session database. The performance team must design a test for these systems simulating the burden of logged-on, but largely dormant, concurrent users.

User Visits

The term *visit* defines the most common usage of *user*. The web site receives many visitors over the course of the day. These visitors interact with the web site, performing one or more tasks that usually involve navigating through multiple pages. The user stays logged on to the site until shortly after his activity finishes (usually 15 or 30 minutes after the last request the user makes). After this timeout period, the web site removes the user's transient information (the HTTP session data) from the site. If the user wants to interact with the site later, he must log on to the site again.

User Scenarios

Regardless of the loading goal (users, hits, or transactions), eventually you must determine the load's distribution, or *how* the users interact with the web site. Usually, this requires developing several scenarios and determining the percentage of traffic executing each scenario at any given time.

For example, an e-Commerce site might receive users who want to browse, purchase, or check the status of an order. A financial site might receive visitors who want to check their portfolio value, trade stocks, or do research on a particular company. We then develop these usage scenarios as test scripts for each of these tasks, and estimate their relative execution frequency.

Scenarios come from several sources. Usability testing or analysis of site logs gives the most reliable data about usage patterns. For new web sites without the benefit of usability testing, we often look to use cases from the analysis/design phase of the web application to provide scenarios. However, the best scenarios involve real data on how the users interact with the web site. (See Chapter 7 for more details on developing test scripts.)

On the basis of these scenarios, we develop an idea of how many pages the users access for each scenario. However, we also need an estimate for the duration of the average visit. A good choice for this number is how long it takes us to run the scenario manually (see the caveats applying to this in Chapter 7). Even better, we might obtain some data from early usability testing. However, most sites do not perform rigorous usability testing, so a rough guess from walking through the scenarios is a good first start.

The frequency of each scenario is important as well. We must determine how many users execute each scenario over the course of the day. The scenario utilization becomes very important if some scenarios require "heavier" activities, such as database interactions, or a large number of page visits per scenario. Usually, we derive the scenario mix from the existing web site or receive this weighting from the marketing team. Scenarios tell what our traffic is doing. For "users per day" estimates, we also need the scenarios to tell us how much traffic our users generate during peak periods.

User Visit Projections

So what do user arrival numbers mean for web site load and throughput projections? Let's assume the following information from the marketing team:

- 100,000 user visits per day
- 30% of traffic arrives during peak hour

After some clever and dedicated investigation work, you uncover the following information about the web site:

- Average user visit: 10 minutes
- Session timeout: 15 minutes
- Average pages per visit: 5

During the peak hour, the web site has the following new user arrival rate:

```
100,000 users * 30% peak users = 30,000 peak users

30,000 peak users/hour  ➔  8.33 new users/second
```

Over a ten-minute visit, at a minimum, the web site contains the following concurrent users:

```
8.33 new users/second * 10 minutes * 60 seconds/minute
= 4,998 concurrent users (approx. 5,000)
```

These users typically stay active for ten minutes and visit five pages during that time. This gives us the following page rate:

```
5000 users * 5 pages per user / 10 minutes / 60 seconds per minute
= 41.667 pages/second

  (approx. 42 pages/sec)
```

If each page contains an average of five embedded static elements per page, the overall throughput (in requests per second) is as follows:

```
((1 initial request) + (5 static requests)) * 42 pages/second
= 252 requests/second
```

Obviously, browser caching might reduce this request burden, but it serves as an upper bound for testing purposes.

User arrival rates and active log-on rates also help determine the HTTP session pressure of these users. If the Java web site uses HTTP sessions, each user may use memory on one or more application servers. This memory only frees after the user's HTTP session times out (or, in some cases, when the user logs out of the web site).

Let's assume each concurrent user requires about 2KB of memory. Since the average user visit is 10 minutes and, in this case, the HTTP session timeout is 15 minutes, the average session stays in memory a total of 25 minutes. Therefore, the server requires the following memory to hold these sessions:

```
8.33 users/second * (25 minutes) * 60 seconds/minute
= 12,495 users (let's say 12,500)

12,500 users * 2KB/user = 25MB of memory
```

Of course, this equation does not take into account any users still logged on from previous arrivals outside the 15-minute window. (Remember, the 10-minute visit time is an average.)

Response Time Measurements

The web site requirements consist not only of load, but also responsiveness to the load. Response time requirements may be very general, such as "no more than five-second response time for any page at peak load." Some teams receive requirements broken out by pages. For example, a financial site might require two-second response time on stock quotes, but accept ten seconds for research pages.

Response time requirements change as the industry changes. The goal is to keep your response time consistent or better than the customer's experience at other web sites. Usually your QA or marketing teams provide response time targets based on current industry "standards."

Defining the Test Scope

After determining the peak loading and throughput, we start designing the performance test. A good performance test, as we mentioned earlier, tells us how to build the web site to support peak loading. It also tells us how to prepare the web site for future growth. To make these preparations, we need detailed information on how key components of the site, such as the servers, databases, and networks, perform under increasing load.

The test requires a starting point. Even for the most complex web sites, the best tests begin with a single server. Determining the capacity of just one machine tells us the following:

- The accuracy of capacity estimates on a per server basis
- The database and other back-end resources required by one server
- The network capacity consumed by this server
- Front-end resources such as HTTP server and router capacity consumed to support this server

For example, if we estimate we need ten servers to support the 100,000 user day from the previous section, let's validate this estimate early in the performance test. Begin the validation process by determining how much load each server can support. (If you want to learn how to actually estimate the equipment required by your web site, see Chapter 15.)

The estimates calculated previously from this loading estimate show a peak load of 5,000 users over a ten-minute period. These users request 42 pages/second at peak, which translates to 252 requests/second to the web site. The web site requires 50% *headroom* (double the capacity it needs for the projected peak). This gives the site a generous margin for error in case the initial capacity estimates are wrong, and it also gives the site capacity in case of a pathological surge in traffic caused by some unforeseen event.

Given this, we estimate each server handles 8.4 pages/second or 50.4 HTTP requests/second:

```
(42 pages/second * 2 headroom cushion) / 10 servers
= 8.4 pages/second

(252 requests/second * 2 headroom cushion) / 10 servers
= 50.4 requests/second
```

Likewise, this transaction rate represents the workload generated by a fraction of the peak users. Using a similar calculation, we get an estimate for the number of users supported by a single server. In this case, the test for a single machine simulates the workload generated by 1,000 users:

```
(5,000 peak users * 2 headroom cushion) / 10 servers
= 1,000 concurrent users/server
```

This number represents the maximum number of concurrent users expected per server during peak loading.

Building the Test

After some analysis to develop peak loading estimates, we build the actual test to simulate peak conditions. We want to begin the test with a single server and determine how many requests per second and users the server can support. Based on preliminary pen-and-paper estimates, we expect to get 1,000 users and 50.4 requests/second with this server. Testing is the only way to determine if these estimates are valid.

Setup

In order to simplify this example, let's map each concurrent user to one virtual user. This means we'll need 1,000 virtual users to perform our testing. (Later in the book, we'll discuss some techniques for reducing the number of virtual users required for a test.) Next, let's establish the scenarios these virtual user will execute, as well as the proportion of users assigned each scenario. For our example, let's assume we're testing a financial web site, and we want the following test scenarios and weighting:

- Check portfolio—50% of users
- Perform trade—30% of users
- Perform market research—10% of users
- Setup new account—10% of users

The next step, of course, is to turn these scenarios into test scripts. At this point, we also need to answer some key questions about the scripts, such as whether they should include think time, cookies, or browser caching. After completing scenario preparation and validating that the performance test scripts execute *correctly* and *without generating errors on the server*, the test actually begins against our single server.

Simple-to-Complex Strategy

If at all possible, start with a very simple test configuration, and work outward to more complex scenarios. Consider the test configuration shown in Figure 6.4.

Begin with a simple configuration of one application server, one HTTP server, and a database. If possible, start the tests without firewalls and SSL. After resolving bottlenecks in this environment and doing initial tuning on key components, begin increasing complexity by adding components to the test environment incrementally. After adding each new component, retest to determine its impact on performance, tuning as necessary, before adding another component.

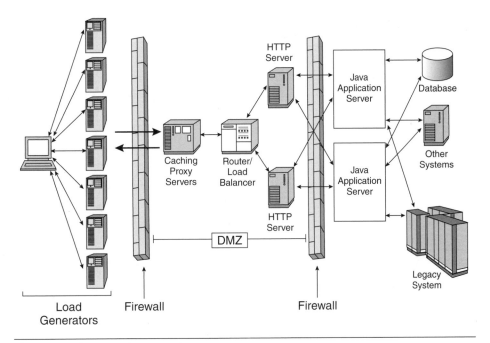

Figure 6.4   An example test environment

By working from the inside of the web site outward, and reducing the complexity of initial tests, we learn

- How the fundamental components of the system perform. If key components such as the web application suffer from severe performance problems or require substantial tuning, we need to find and address these problems as early as possible in the testing. Web applications tend to have the greatest impact on site performance, and they merit careful performance analysis.
- The impact of each component on performance. By knowing the capacity of the base systems, we can measure the impact of additional components, such as a firewall, on the test environment's performance. This also proves very useful in planning for site growth, and for determining problems in production.

The performance test provides validation for capacity planning estimates. It also helps us identify underperforming components in test environment.

Scalability Testing

So far, we've discussed testing with a subset of the production web site. We begin by testing and tuning this subset of equipment, and continue until we reach our performance goals for this portion of the web site. However, we cannot assume the performance we achieve for the subset applies to the web site as whole. To achieve this confidence, we need a *scalability test*. During this test, we add capacity to our test environment and determine whether the web application actually takes advantage of this capacity. That is, does the web application *scale* to use additional resources?

Scalability testing usually doubles capacity at each step of the test. We start with a subset of our web site that supports some amount of user load. If we double the subset's capacity, we also expect to double the traffic the subset supports while maintaining the same response time. We call this *linear scaling*: As you multiply capacity, the throughput and users handled by the web site multiply as well, while maintaining the same responsiveness.

Scalability determines the behavior of the web site as a system, including its growth characteristics and limiting factors. These tests tell us how adding capacity at one point in the web site impacts the capacity of other components. We need this knowledge as we build our web site, as well as when we grow it in the production environment.

Building the Performance Team

When we consider building a performance test, we often overlook the people who make the testing successful. Testing requires skills from every component used by your web site throughout all phases of the testing cycle (planning, execution, measuring, analysis, and tuning).

For new web applications with links to existing data or function, it's fairly common to focus exclusively on the newly created function and to ignore what's happening inside the existing components. This myopic approach to testing frequently proves disastrous. Web applications work differently than existing thick client applications: They exert more simultaneous requests, and often use the existing applications differently. In short, legacy applications often require tuning for the web environment.

For example, consider a legacy application used by in-house stock brokers. Customers call the brokers, who then use a thick client application to create orders, retrieve pricing, or check the customer's account. The company decides to build a web application giving customers direct access to these functions over the Internet. However, your new web application uses the same business logic at the mainframe as the old thick client application.

Not surprisingly, this web application generates many more transactions per day than the thick client application. Along with more transactions comes the need for more connections to your back-end database—which implies potential licensing and performance impacts not only on the new application, but also on those who continue to use the old system.

Obviously, you need to get the team supporting the mainframe business logic involved with your testing. Involving them early in the test planning phase gives them time to understand your performance goals and to do some tuning in preparation for your testing. As you continue the testing, they assist by capturing data at the mainframe and performing additional tuning.

Beyond this one example, consider the peripheral systems involved in your test, and pull together the right people to make the test successful. Below is a list of folks we often find useful as part of the larger test team. Review this list and consider the relationships you need for a thorough and accurate test.

Quality Assurance People

We consider quality assurance people first because they're often overlooked. Some enterprises relegate performance testing to something outside their standard QA processes and only assign the application programmers to the task. This is a mistake.

Performance testing really operates as an extension of QA, assuming that your QA team is in the business of assuring that applications behave satisfactorily when put into production. Many QA groups actually own the performance test. This includes creating the test scripts based on either the design or current customer usage patterns.

Even if QA does not own the test, they often make a good resource for test scenarios, as mentioned above. They also often provide many of the performance targets (such as maximum response time) used in the testing.

Web Application Programmers

Use the application programmers to troubleshoot the application during testing. Problem analysis usually becomes one of the biggest headaches in deploying a distributed application. The test team needs someone intimately familiar with the application's internals to fix problems as they arise.

Web Application Architect

You need the application architect's input to build a good test. For large applications, use the architect's guidance to identify the subset of function and infrastructure required to accurately model the entire application's behavior. The architect also understands how users *should* interact with the web site. Use this information when designing your test scripts. However, always try to back up this information with observation of actual users interacting with the system.

Finally, the architect knows all the systems, such as databases and content servers, that are interacting with the web application. Use this information both in designing your test system and in resolving any performance problems you encounter during the testing.

System Administrators

System administrators set up and configure the test machines. During the test, they monitor the resource consumption on all the machines in order to identify machines and processes that are acting as bottlenecks.

Network Administrators

Just as your system administrators install, configure, and monitor the servers and clients, the network administrators do the same for the network. They validate your capacity estimates, set up an isolated network (hopefully), and monitor the network during testing.

Systems Analysts

Systems analysts monitor the legacy systems used by your web site. As we discussed earlier, new web applications often drive legacy systems much harder than existing thick client applications. You need a systems analyst to monitor these legacy components during your performance testing. They also provide important information about planned outages and backups of the systems, which you need for scheduling performance tests. Also, they manage the legacy resources and help you schedule your testing so that you do not interfere with existing production applications.

Database Administrators

Almost all web applications connect to databases. Large web sites may connect to a variety of databases on multiple systems, including mid-tier and host systems. Each database used by your web site often has a different DBA or support team. Find these folks, and include them on your team before the testing begins.

Work with the DBAs to configure the database for the traffic you're planning to send its way. In particular, coordinate available database connections to match the size of your web site's database connection pools. During the testing, use the DBAs to monitor the databases for potential performance problems.

The DBAs are very important players on the web site performance team. These folks, along with the systems analyst, have skills you cannot reproduce on your team in the short term. Call on them early to help you understand the issues regarding their systems *before* a problem occurs.

Legacy Application Programmers

Often web applications use legacy applications in ways unforeseen in the legacy applications' original designs. Having a legacy application programmer assigned as a point of contact and assistance is important. It's important to build teamwork and a sense of ownership for the performance test within this broad group of support personnel. Obtain commitments from this varied group of folks and their management to make your testing successful.

Summary

Performance testing requires planning. Responsible performance targets, accurate test scenarios, and a reasonable testing strategy all lead to accurate test results. In this chapter, we covered some of the highlights of performance test planning. Everyone uses terms like *hit*, *user*, and *day*, but regrettably we often use them to describe a variety of different concepts. It's important to get agreement ahead of time on the definition of these terms as they are used in your planning.

We also provided some examples of developing performance estimates for your web site. Starting with interpreting data from your existing web site or working with estimates provided by your marketing team, we showed how to create rough estimates for your planning and testing. We also discussed the difference between peak and average load, and emphasized the importance of planning for peak load usage. Appendix A contains worksheets for most of these estimates to help you better organize your data and develop a test plan We suggest you use this plan to drive discussion with the various parties involved with the web site (marketing, management, development, etc) in order to achieve consensus on your performance goals before beginning the test.

Also, we discussed the basics of scenario development and scalability testing. Upcoming chapters explore these topics in greater detail, complete with a case study applying best practices. However, as you learn more in these chapters about executing a performance test, keep in mind the importance of a good test plan. If your fundamental goals and assumptions prove erroneous, your test results are worthless.

Chapter 7
TEST SCRIPTS

Test scripts drive the performance test. The scripts simulate the series of requests a user makes during a visit to the web site. In order to develop test scripts, you need to understand the expected behavior of your production users. Usually, the performance test requires a series of scripts to represent a range of production users. In this chapter, we'll walk through this process for a sample application that you may already be familiar with, the Pet Store demo from Sun Microsystems.[1] As we mentioned in the previous chapter, a poor understanding of your users leads to poor test scripts. During your test planning phase, find out how users interact with your web applications.

Getting Started

Pet Store Overview

Important! We do *not* recommend Pet Store as a performance benchmark application for running under load conditions. See Sun's Java web site for suitable performance benchmarks, such as ECperf.[2] However, Pet Store contains classic e-Commerce functions such as Browse, Search, Sign-in, Add-to-Cart, Checkout, and Update Account, and it provides a good example for discussing test script concepts. The home page for Pet Store, shown in Figure 7.1, contains the following choices:

1. Browse from one of five categories (Fish, Dogs, Reptiles, Cats, Birds)
2. Search
3. Sign-in
4. Shopping cart
5. ? (Help)

---

1. Pet Store is a sample J2EE application provided by Sun Microsystems, and is available from <http://developer.java.sun.com/developer/releases/petstore/>.
2. ECperf is a performance benchmark developed under the Java Community Process. See <http://java.sun.com/j2ee/ecperf/>.

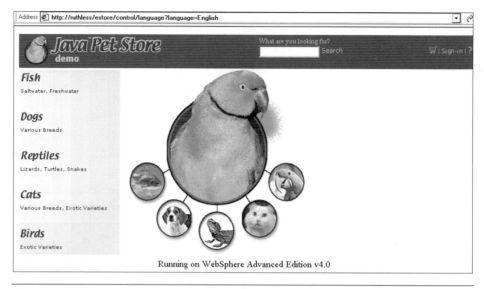

Figure 7.1   Java Pet Store demo home page. © Sun Microsystems 2002. Reprinted by permission from Sun Microsystems.

If the user wants to browse and chooses one of the categories, a list of pets in this category returns. Similarly, if the user selects Search, a list of pets containing the search attribute returns. Figure 7.2 shows the high-level browse and search hierarchy for Pet Store. As shown in this diagram, the browse for Fish displays four fish, Angelfish, Goldfish, Koi, and Tiger Shark, whereas the browse for Reptiles only returns two reptiles, Iguana and Rattlesnake. Search returns a variable number of pets, depending on the search criteria entered.

Pet Store functions resemble those of many e-Commerce applications. In addition to the Browse and Search capabilities, the application provides the capability to make purchases, which requires a log-on (called Sign-in by Pet Store). A purchase requires standard information such as address, credit card, and number of items. With this background on how Pet Store works, let's start developing test scripts for a web site.

Determining User Behavior

As mentioned previously, the best starting point in developing test scripts is analysis of an existing web site's traffic patterns. Your HTTP server typically generates logs of all requests made through it. For example, Listing 7.1 shows a subset of an access log from IBM HTTP Server taken from a run of the Pet Store web application. The HTTP server logs URL requests, including any parameters.[3]

---

3. Assuming your web site logs requests at this level. Not every web site does, making this level of log analysis impossible.

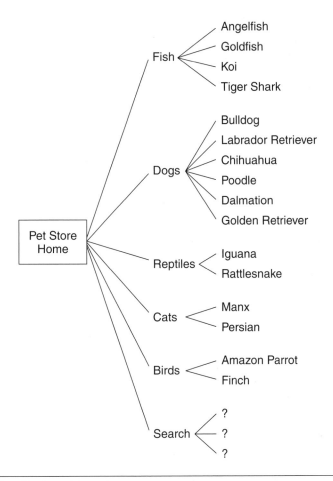

Figure 7.2   Java Pet Store hierarchy

The first log entry references a query on the Fish category. A bit further down, the log contains an entry for a purchase of an item labeled EST-3. By examining the logs, we begin to see the activities the users typically perform against the web site, as well as the ratio of one type of activity compared to another. Listing 7.1 also shows some of the difficulty in examining logs. This log represents a very small snippet of activity, yet it is hard to identify particular users or to correlate static requests with dynamic requests. Analysis tools exist to automatically scan logs and organize their information into usage patterns. These tools often prove useful when trying to extract this information for large web sites.

Listing 7.1   Sample HTTP server log

```
127.0.0.1 - - [28/Dec/2001:17:26:30 -0500] "GET /estore/control/cate-
               gory?category_id=FISH HTTP/1.0" 200 6467
127.0.0.1 - - [28/Dec/2001:17:26:34 -0500] "GET /estore/control/white
               HTTP/1.0" 200 0
127.0.0.1 - - [28/Dec/2001:17:26:34 -0500] "GET /estore/control/prod-
               uct?product_id=FI-SW-02 HTTP/1.0" 200 6388
127.0.0.1 - - [28/Dec/2001:17:26:34 -0500] "GET
               /estore/images/button_cart-add.gif HTTP/1.0" 200 481
127.0.0.1 - - [28/Dec/2001:17:26:38 -0500] "GET /estore/control/white
               HTTP/1.0" 200 0
127.0.0.1 - - [28/Dec/2001:17:27:00 -0500] "GET /estore/control/productde-
               tails?item_id=EST-3 HTTP/1.0" 200 6038
127.0.0.1 - - [28/Dec/2001:17:27:00 -0500] "GET /estore/images/fish4.gif
               HTTP/1.0" 200 7501
127.0.0.1 - - [28/Dec/2001:17:27:04 -0500] "GET /estore/control/white
               HTTP/1.0" 200 0
127.0.0.1 - - [28/Dec/2001:17:27:04 -0500] "GET /estore/control/cart?
               action=purchaseItem&itemId=EST-3 HTTP/1.0" 200 7760
127.0.0.1 - - [28/Dec/2001:17:27:04 -0500] "GET
               /estore/images/button_checkout.gif HTTP/1.0" 200 534
127.0.0.1 - - [28/Dec/2001:17:27:04 -0500] "GET
               /estore/images/button_remove.gif HTTP/1.0" 200 1189
127.0.0.1 - - [28/Dec/2001:17:27:04 -0500] "GET /estore/images/cart-
               update.gif HTTP/1.0" 200 489
127.0.0.1 - - [28/Dec/2001:17:27:16 -0500] "GET /estore/control/white
               HTTP/1.0" 200 0
127.0.0.1 - - [28/Dec/2001:17:27:16 -0500] "GET /estore/control/checkout
               HTTP/1.0" 200 6981
127.0.0.1 - - [28/Dec/2001:17:27:16 -0500] "GET
               /estore/images/button_cont.gif HTTP/1.0" 200 1275
127.0.0.1 - - [28/Dec/2001:17:27:18 -0500] "GET /estore/control/white
               HTTP/1.0" 200 0
127.0.0.1 - - [28/Dec/2001:17:27:18 -0500] "GET /estore/control/placeor-
               der HTTP/1.0" 200 6617
127.0.0.1 - - [28/Dec/2001:17:27:19 -0500] "GET
               /estore/images/button_submit.gif HTTP/1.0" 200 455
127.0.0.1 - - [28/Dec/2001:17:27:24 -0500] "GET /estore/control/white
               HTTP/1.0" 200 0
127.0.0.1 - - [28/Dec/2001:17:27:24 -0500] "POST /estore/control/verify-
               signin HTTP/1.0" 200 10038
127.0.0.1 - - [28/Dec/2001:17:27:29 -0500] "GET /estore/control/white
               HTTP/1.0" 200 0
```

The more realistic the scenario, the better the test scripts. Pulling data from logs generally gives you the best understanding of how users interact with an existing web site. (Of course, don't forget to account for new features or functions in your web site test scenarios.) Log analysis works well for existing web sites; it proves less useful for new or significantly modified web sites. In these cases, the results of usability testing often provide better scenario data.

Also keep in mind that the smallest details matter in building a scenario: Does the user enter the web site through the home page or bookmark another entry point? Does the user log out of the web site or just leave for another site? Accurately representing your users in your test scripts influences the throughput rate and user loading that your test achieves. This in turn corresponds to how accurately you portray your web site's production performance.

A Typical Test Script

Using the data on how you expect users to walk through your site, you create test scripts to simulate these paths. A test script represents an execution path through a set of web pages. During the test, this same script is executed over and over again, simulating multiple users. In order to simulate many users executing many different paths through a web site, a collection of scripts is typically used. In this chapter, we call this collection of scripts the *test scenario*. Using the data on how you expect users to walk through your site, you actually create test scripts to simulate these paths. Typically, we create test scripts by "recording" a user's activities while performing a series of tasks at the web site.

Many test tools provide script recording capability. In this chapter, we use two common products, LoadRunner, from Mercury Interactive Corporation, and SilkPerformer V, from Segue Software, Inc., to provide our examples. Chapter 8, Selecting the Right Test Tools, covers test tools and script generation capabilities in more detail, and Appendix C also contains a broader list of vendor tools.

A typical test script consists of a variety of things, including URLs, think times, and cookies.

- URLs—The test script contains the actual URL requests it issues against the web site. Some of the URLs represent the simulated user's explicit requests, and some represent embedded elements (such as *gifs* and JavaScript) in the HTML pages returned in response to the simulated user's requests.
- Think Times—A user on your web site typically reads a returned web page prior to issuing another request. During testing, a test tool makes page requests and does not require the same amount of time to analyze a page and make the next request. The test tool, in fact, doesn't require any time to send the next request; it can do so immediately.

  To accurately simulate the user environment, you want the test tool to wait just like a real user before sending the next request. Most tools allow you to specify a think time or range of think times between requests.

  Some tools actually capture the user's think time while recording the script. However, providing your own think time value usually yields better results. (Script recorders sometimes click through the script too quickly, or take coffee breaks between pages during the recording session.)

- Cookies—If your web site uses cookies, your scripts must also utilize and process cookies correctly. Some web applications or functions require the cookies they generate to function properly. Failure to return a required cookie usually results in testing errors.

    Typically, the test tool records any cookies the user receives from the server during the script recording session. During script execution, the test tool retrieves cookies for each virtual user and returns them to the server on each request, as required.

Let's look at an example of a recorded test script. Listing 7.2 shows a subset of a LoadRunner test script for Pet Store.[4] The test script specifies a sequence of two URL requests and also a think time of two seconds between submitting the URL requests. The first URL retrieves the Pet Store home page, and the second URL requests a selection of Fish.

Listing 7.2   Example script. © 2002 Mercury Interactive Corporation.

```
//subset of Pet Store browse script
//first URL request to Pet Store home page
   web_url("language",
           "URL=http://ruthless/estore/control/language?language=English",
           "TargetFrame=",
           "Resource=0",
           "RecContentType=text/html",
           "Referer=",
           "Snapshot=t1.inf",
           "Mode=URL",
           LAST);

//think time
   lr_think_time( 2 );

//browse for fish
   web_url("nav-fish.gif",
           "URL=http://ruthless/estore/control/category?category_id=FISH",
           "TargetFrame=",
           "Resource=0",
           "RecContentType=text/html",
           "Referer=http://ruthless:80/estore/control/language?language
➥=English",
           "Snapshot=t2.inf",
           "Mode=URL",
           LAST);
   return 0;
}
```

---

4. Thanks to Leo Cai for his assistance with all the LoadRunner example scripts.

Test Scripts Basics

Before going into the complexity of how to make individual test scripts represent multiple users, let's discuss the basic test script design best practices.

Model the Real Users

As we discussed early in this chapter, the closer your test scripts mimic actual user behavior, the more accurate your performance test. Again, use logs and usability data whenever possible to build accurate test scenarios. Failing the availability of this data, consult your marketing team or conduct your own research to understand how your user visits typically flow.

Develop Multiple, Short Scripts

Some script writers try to cover all possible user activities for a site visit with one script. Generally, the best scripts cover about three to five page requests. For example, for an e-Commerce site like Pet Store, your scripts might include a Search script that searches for an item and views it, a Browse script that browses for an item and views it, and a Purchase script that selects an item and adds it to a shopping cart.

Developing short scripts results in more flexibility later in the process when you actually define the test scenarios. Here are a few specific reasons for writing smaller scripts:

- Smaller scripts allow you to assign different weights to different activities on the web site. For example, maybe 70% of the customers use a Browse scenario, while only 30% use the Search scenario. Recording these activities in different scripts allows for greater flexibility in assigning user activity at test execution time.
- Smaller scripts allow you to build more elaborate scenarios for the virtual users. For example, if the marketing team discovers a large number of users use both Search and Browse prior to making a purchase, you easily build this new scenario by combining three smaller ones (Search, Browse, and Purchase).
- Maintenance for larger scripts often proves difficult. For example, if a portion of the web site changes, the entire script often requires regeneration. With smaller scripts, only the scripts using the new feature require regeneration.

Write Atomic Scripts

Along the same lines as developing multiple, short scripts, we also recommend writing atomic scripts. These also allow you more flexibility when defining the test scenarios. For example, don't log in at the beginning of each script and log out at the end. Instead, write separate login and logout functions, and remove these activities from the individual scripts.

Atomic scripts allow you to more readily build new scenarios from existing scripts. For example, using the Pet Store application, you might define a scenario by stringing together the following scripts:

Sign-in + Browse + Purchase + Search + Purchase + Sign-out

However, Pet Store only requires a user to sign in just before they purchase something. In this case, atomic scripts allow you to rearrange the scenario as follows:

Browse + Sign-in + Purchase + Search + Purchase + Sign-out

If the individual scripts include Sign-in and Sign-out, we cannot rearrange the scenario. When pulling together scripts in this manner, be extra careful about how your load driver handles cookies. Another advantage of keeping the logout script separate is that many customers do not log out of web sites. Creating a separate logout function allows you to build different larger scripts accurately reflecting the actual logout rate of your users.

Develop Primitive Scripts

Use primitive test scripts to exercise different primitive functions of your web site. Primitives start with the simplest path through your web site and become increasingly complex. They allow you to test the paths through each layer of your web site's architecture. For example, start with a simple primitive "pingHTML" script to test your HTTP server performance and a simple "pingServlet" script to test the most basic web application path. If you choose to write primitives, build them to exercise round-trip times to each of your back-end systems, such as servlet to database, servlet to LDAP directory, servlet to Session Bean to Entity Bean, and the like. Figure 7.3 shows an example subset of primitives.

In developing the primitive scripts, you use subsets of your web application, with perhaps a few special functions added to support primitive testing. For example, the WebSphere Performance Benchmark Sample (Trade2)[5] includes a set of web primitives in addition to the application.

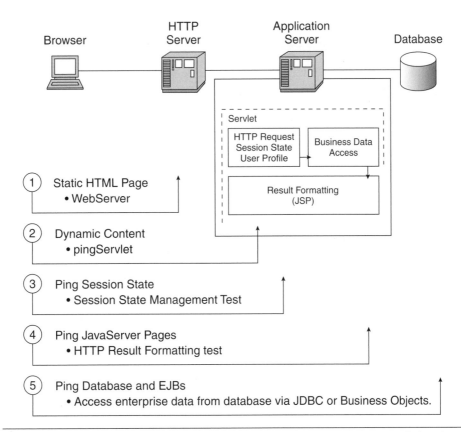

Figure 7.3 Example of primitive scripts. From an IBM internal presentation entitled, "Characterizing WebSphere Performance," by Gennaro Cuomo and Ruth Willenborg.©IBM Corp. 1999. Reprinted with permission from IBM Corp.

Primitives prove extremely useful in debugging problems in your web site and isolating performance problems to a particular layer. For example, if pingHTML fails to perform up to expectations, you quickly isolate your performance issues to the HTTP server or preceding web site components (router, network, and so on). Also use primitives when the site is in production to test the health of different components of the web site.

Test primitives prove useful, but they are not mandatory for good testing. You probably don't want to invest in writing these scripts unless you find a need for them.

---

5. WebSphere Performance Benchmark Sample is available at <http://www14.software.ibm.com/ webapp/download/search.jsp?go=y&rs=benchmark>. The package includes application code, primitives, design documentation, and source code.

Also, not every web application supports the development of primitives. For example, some web applications use their back-end EJB or database functions to generate each dynamic page. In this case, you cannot use a test case to isolate problems at the servlet level or the EJB/database level without adding primitive function support to your web application.

Making Test Scripts Dynamic

Test scripts represent the activities of a typical user. However, during the performance tests, multiple virtual users execute the same test script. Obviously, we cannot build a different script for each user when we potentially simulate hundreds or thousands of users. Instead, we parameterize one script to represent multiple users. For example, if your users log on using their account numbers, make the account number a parameter in the test script. Most test tools allow you to correlate this parameter with a list of potential values. The tool then inserts these values into the script automatically at run time. If the tool inserts a different value for each simulation of the script's login, it simulates multiple user logins with just one script. Parameters require sufficient variation to successfully reproduce user activity. Always buying or selling the same stock does not accurately represent typical user activity. Provide a sufficient pool of test data to simulate production usage.

Identifying script parameters is sometimes difficult. To more easily identify dynamic data in a script, we often record two scripts and make comparisons between them. This comparison allows us to identify the script portions that are common across multiple user requests, as well as the portions differing between requests. For example, we might record the following Browse script in Pet Store:

1. Go to home page.
2. Select category Fish.
3. A list of Fish is returned by the server.
4. Select the first fish, Angelfish, on the returned page.

After completing this script, create a new script, repeating the same steps with only minor changes in the entered data. For example:

1. Go to home page.
2. Select category Reptiles.
3. A list of Reptiles is returned by the server.
4. Select the second reptile, Rattlesnake, on the returned page.

Now you have two scripts of the same steps but using different data inputs. The differences between these two scripts give you the dynamic data to modify for each simulated user iteration. Listing 7.3 shows the two Pet Store scripts, Browse1 and Browse2, recorded from the two scenarios listed above.

Listing 7.3   Example scripts with dynamic data. © 2002 Mercury Interactive Corporation.

```
Browse1()
{
//subset of Pet Store browse script (first browse recording)
//first URL request to Pet Store home page
   web_url("language",
      "URL=http://ruthless/estore/control/language?language=English",
      "TargetFrame=",
      "Resource=0",
      "RecContentType=text/html",
      "Referer=",
      "Snapshot=t1.inf",
      "Mode=URL",
      LAST);

//browse for fish
   web_url("nav-fish.gif",
      "URL=http://ruthless/estore/control/category?category_id=FISH",
      "TargetFrame=",
      "Resource=0",
      "RecContentType=text/html",
      "Referer=http://ruthless:80/estore/control/language?language=English",
      "Snapshot=t2.inf",
      "Mode=URL",
      LAST);

//browse for Angelfish
   web_url("Angelfish",
      "URL=http://ruthless/estore/control/product?product_id=FI-SW-01",
      "TargetFrame=",
      "Resource=0",
      "RecContentType=text/html",
      "Referer=http://ruthless:80/estore/control/category?category_id=FISH",
      "Snapshot=t3.inf",
      "Mode=URL",
      LAST);

   return 0;

Browse2()
{
//subset of Pet Store browse script (second browse recording)
//first URL request to Pet Store home page
   web_url("language",
      "URL=http://ruthless/estore/control/language?language=English",
      "TargetFrame=",
      "Resource=0",
      "RecContentType=text/html",
```

```
        "Referer=",
        "Snapshot=t1.inf",
        "Mode=URL",
        LAST);

//browse for reptiles
    web_url("nav-reptiles.gif",
        "URL=http://ruthless/estore/control/category?category_id=REPTILES",
        "TargetFrame=",
        "Resource=0",
        "RecContentType=text/html",
        "Referer=http://ruthless:80/estore/control/language?language=English",
        "Snapshot=t2.inf",
        "Mode=URL",
        LAST);

//browse for rattlesnakes
    web_url("Rattlesnake",
        "URL=http://ruthless/estore/control/product?product_id=RP-SN-01",
        "TargetFrame=",
        "Resource=0",
        "RecContentType=text/html",
        "Referer=http://ruthless:80/estore/control/category?category_id
➥=REPTILES",
        "Snapshot=t3.inf",
        "Mode=URL",
        LAST);

    return 0;
```

As you can see, these scripts differ in their web_url parameters. Specifically, the first script uses category_id=FISH and product_id=FI-SW-01 (Angelfish). The second script uses category_id=REPTILES and product_id=RP-SN-01 (Rattlesnake). Parameterizing category_id and product_id gives us a general script suitable for simulating multiple users.

This simple example demonstrates the fundamental concepts behind making your test scripts more dynamic. Let's further examine some of the different types of dynamic data your scripts might need to support.

Support Dynamic Decisions

Your customers do not always perform the same actions in every interaction with your application. You don't want every virtual client to execute exactly the same selections. In the Pet Store example, you don't want all users to select Fish from the home page. This does not represent real user activity from a database caching and locking perspective. You want the simulated users to follow different paths and access different data. For example, on the Pet Store home page, you want users to dynamically choose between Fish, Dogs, Reptiles, Cats, and Birds.

Select from File

Many test tools make it easy to identify the dynamic data and replace it with parameters. Instead of hard-coding the category name in the browse script, we replace it with a variable. For example, Listing 7.4 shows a subset of the LoadRunner script with the `category_id` replaced with a parameter named `Category`. Pet Store contains five fixed categories. If we provide these category values in a file, LoadRunner replaces the `Category` parameter with a value from the file at runtime.

Listing 7.4   Example script with parameters. © 2002 Mercury Interactive Corporation.

```
web_url("nav-fish.gif",
    "URL=http://ruthless/estore/control/category?category_id={Category}",
    "TargetFrame=",
    "Resource=0",
    "RecContentType=text/html",
    "Referer=http://ruthless:80/estore/control/language?language=English",
    "Snapshot=t2.inf",
    "Mode=URL",
    LAST);
```

Figure 7.4 shows an example of associating the `Category` parameter with a file containing the five valid categories within the LoadRunner GUI. When this browse script runs, the tool selects the category sequentially from the five pet categories for each different user simulated during the run. LoadRunner optionally selects the category at random from those provided, if specified. Figure 7.4 shows file `category.dat`, containing the categories Fish, Dogs, Reptiles, and Cats. In this case, as shown at the bottom of the screen capture, we choose `Sequential` as our parameter value selection strategy.

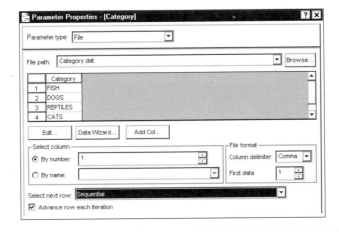

Figure 7.4   LoadRunner parameter properties GUI. © 2002 Mercury Interactive Corporation.

Select Link by Random Number

We also may insert dynamic behavior into our scripts by dynamically selecting links within a page. For example, Segue SilkPerformer assigns a number corresponding to each link in the script.[6] In the Pet Store demo Browse script, Fish corresponds to Link 5, Dogs corresponds to Link 6, and so forth. This allows the tool to select links using random numbers. In the subset of the Pet Store script shown below, the hard-coded link to Fish is replaced with a random number between 5 and 9 corresponding to one of the five valid links on the page.

```
dclrand
//random variable
   rNcategory : RndUniN(5..9);
dcltrans
   transaction TMain
   begin
//original browse link
//WebPageLink("nav-fish", "Product Category"); // Link 5
//replace hard-coded link with random number between 5 and 9
   WebPageLink(NULL, "Product Category", rNcategory);
```

In this case, both the selection of the link randomly by number or by using a parameter from a file yield the same desired result: The first selection from the home page exercises all five options with just one script.

Dynamically Created Web Pages

In the Pet Store demo, the home page contains a predefined set of five categories, and our script dynamically selects one. However, not every page request returns a known set of options. Test scripts must also address pages containing data dynamically created by the web application. For example, Figure 7.5 shows the results from a Browse for Fish. The web application creates a web page with four links for Angelfish, Goldfish, Koi, and Tiger Shark. Looking at the hierarchy from Figure 7.2, every Browse operation within the web application returns different data and often different quantities of data. For example, the Browse operation for Fish returns four fish, while a Browse request for Reptiles returns only two reptiles, Iguana and Rattlesnake.

In the previous section, we parameterized the Browse script to dynamically select a different category. Therefore, when the script runs, the number and list of pets returned differs depending on the category. To properly use one script to simulate a user who has selected Reptiles and also a different user who has selected Fish, the script needs to know the valid choices that the application generates. A simple parameter replacement approach no longer works. This is the trickiest part of writing good test scripts for highly dynamic sites.

---

6. Thanks to Stephan Asboeck for his help with all the SilkPerformer example scripts.

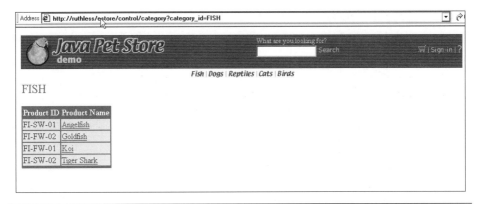

Figure 7.5   Result of Browse for Fish. ©Sun Microsystems. Reprinted by permission of Sun Microsystems.

Adding this type of intelligence to a script typically requires custom programming of the script. A common technique uses a function provided by your load driver to read the links on a returned web page. (Expect this level of functionality only in the better load drivers.) The script then selects one of these links at random as the next step in the script. This technique generally requires multiple steps, including the following:

1. Reading the returned page
2. Determining the number of links on the page
3. Randomly choosing one of the links

Because this requires custom programming, implementations vary between load tools. Let's look at two of the different ways to accomplish dynamic selection.

Using Link Numbers

Our first solution uses SilkPerformer to demonstrate dynamic selection. As shown earlier, SilkPerformer numbers each link on a page. (The numbering starts from the beginning of a recorded script.) Silk provides a special function, `WebPageQueryLink`, to parse a web page. In the example below, the script parses the web page for all the links containing `product_id` and records this count in a variable, `nLinks`. When this section of the script runs after selecting the category Fish, `nLinks` is 4; however, when this script runs after selecting the category Reptiles, `nLinks` is only 2.

```
nLinks:=0;
while WebPageQueryLink("product_id", nLinks+1) > 0 do nLinks := nLinks + 1
➥end;
```

Looking at the link number SilkPerformer placed in the recorded script comments (see the following code segment), note that the first link on the Product page is Link

10. If our number of available links, nLinks, is 4 (indicating a Fish selection), Links 10, 11, 12, and 13 contain product links (our four Fish choices). Therefore, we want to randomly select a link between 10 and 13. However, if nLinks is 2 (indicating a Reptile selection), we only select from Link 10 or 11 (our two reptile choices). As shown in the script below, we accomplish this by replacing the hard-coded link with a random unique number between 10 and (10 + nLinks − 1).

```
//original link
//WebPageLink("Angelfish", "Product Category (#1)"); // Link 10
//replace with random number
WebPageLink(NULL, "Product Category(#1)", RndUniN(10..10+nLinks-1));
```

It's also straightforward to save the link counts from previous pages rather than hard-coding link numbers. Use the SilkPerformer WebPageQueryLink function to save the actual link names in a similar fashion to the LoadRunner example discussed next.

Using Link Names

Another solution involves reading the links from the returned web page into an array and then replacing the hard-coded link with a randomly selected link from the array. Let's look at an example of this technique using LoadRunner. First, add a call to the web_reg_save_param inside the script. This is LoadRunner's command to parse the returned web page, and save an array of values matching a left boundary (LB) and right boundary (RB) specified. (These boundaries act as parsing delimiters.) For example, the following command triggers a parse of the web page returned after selecting a category:

```
web_reg_save_param("sub_pet","LB=\">\n      ","RB=\n\t   </a>",
    "Search=body","Ord=all",LAST);
```

After reading and parsing the links into an array, the script uses LoadRunner functions combined with standard C programming to randomly select one of the links. This section of script below demonstrates this.

```
{        //determine number of links
         Count = atoi(lr_eval_string("{sub_pet_count}"));

         //randomly pick a url link
         sprintf(Param,"{sub_pet_%d}",atoi(lr_eval_string("{Num}")) %
➡Count + 1);

         //assign the link to the Text of the LoadRunner statement
         sprintf(Link,"Text=%s",lr_eval_string(Param));
}
```

In this case, the first command finds the number of elements in the array (the number of links on the page). The second command randomly picks one of these links, and the third command puts this link into a string. The final script step actually invokes the randomly selected link, using the `web_link` command, as shown below:

```
web_link("Select_Pet_Submanual",
        Link,
        "Snapshot=t3.inf",
        LAST);
```

As you can see, this is a little more complicated than simple parameter substitution, but it provides a very powerful and flexible technique to exercise many different selections. In addition, this technique keeps your scripts independent from the content of your test database. In fact, this technique works on our home page as well. Instead of choosing Fish, Dogs, and so forth from a file, we select the category at random. This gives us more flexibility to select new items as the web site changes without modifying our scripts.

Of course, this technique also allows us to test the search function of the web site (the number of links returned are not known beforehand). This also works well for web sites inserting dynamic information into their links (such as object IDs and the like). As we cannot predict the format of the link during scripting, we use dynamic link resolution to pick a link at random during runtime.

Just as with any part of performance testing, consider the trade-offs when using dynamic selection functionality from any vendor. While dynamic selection gives the scripts more flexibility, parsing each page returned may generate more overhead than a hard-coded URL strategy. However, keep in mind that dynamic data selection often provides the only viable alternative for performance testing complex web sites.

Dynamic Data Entry

We parameterized the Pet Store script for dynamic selections of links. Web sites often contain additional dynamic elements, most notably data values entered by the user. When developing a script, consider how to simulate this dynamic data entry. For example, common dynamic data entries often include the following:

1. User identifier—a name or account ID
2. User-entered data—an address information, shipping information, etc.
3. Search parameters—the item to search for, matches to display, and so on.
4. Order quantities—how many of a particular item to buy

Many test tools simplify dynamic data entry simulation. Typically, the test tool accomplishes this by automatically generating random data. Earlier, we showed dynamic selection using random data from a file as well as using a random number. For dynamic data entry, the following types of values make good candidates:

1. Current date/time
2. Random numbers
3. Unique numbers
4. Virtual user IDs
5. Data from a file

For example, the Pet Store application contains a parameter for "Quantity". Rather than hard-coding this value, many test tools support supplying a range of random numbers (perhaps between 1 and 5 in this case) to use during the test run. The user ID also makes a good candidate for dynamic entry inside Pet Store. Several options exist for managing this variable, including generating a unique user ID from a bounded range, selecting the number from a file, or matching the user ID to the simulated virtual user ID. Whichever technique you use to generate user IDs, make sure your test database contains valid data matching these user IDs. (See Appendix C for examples of dynamic data entry in the Pet Store scripts.)

Provide Sufficient Data

As we mentioned earlier, if your web site uses a large database (containing accounts or catalog items, for example), exercise significant portions of this data within your performance test. For example, if an e-Commerce site contains 100,000 products, sample hundreds or thousands of these items in the test scripts. Otherwise, the database cache might satisfy an unusually high number of requests and skew the test with a much lower average response time. Of course, some web sites might receive a significant volume of requests for just a few items (such as a hit CD or a best-selling book) even though they carry a large database of other selections. Consider simulating these conditions in your performance tests as well.

If you need to exercise large volumes of data, keep the following considerations in mind:

- Exercise a reasonable percentage of the possible dynamic selections.
- Choose from a wide selection of dynamic data entry values.

Let's discuss each of these considerations in more detail.

Exercise a Reasonable Percentage of the Dynamic Selections

Sometimes the web site returns the database items as dynamic selections (for example, a search returning a link to each matching item). The random selection technique we discussed earlier provides an excellent solution for obtaining good coverage of these items. This technique works well because it both exercises all the links on the page and does not tie the script directly to the test data.

The LoadRunner and SilkPerformer scripts using this technique do *not* use the actual `product_ids` such as `FI-xx-xx` and link names such as `Angelfish`. This practice allows you to develop scripts with a small set of data, and yet later use these same scripts against large databases or even against the production site, all without having to change the script.

Choose from a Wide Selection of Dynamic Data Entry Values

Randomly selecting links on pages covers browse paths, but users exercise other code paths by entering data. For example, the Search function requires the test script to choose a search value from a wide selection of search attributes (such as book titles or ticker symbols). Because of caching concerns, every virtual user cannot search for the same thing. For example, we wouldn't want to test the Pet Store search feature by only looking for Angelfish.

In most cases, however, we want the value entered to match items in the database. Often, if the script provides an invalid value, the web application generates errors. (Actually, we may provide a few bad searches to test our error path performance, but these usually account for only a few of our test iterations.) Selecting this data from a file generated directly from the database usually works best. Some tools actually allow you to import valid parameter values directly from a database.

Building Test Scenarios

After completing the individual test scripts, put them together to build the test scenarios. Building a test scenario usually involves two steps:

1. Putting together shorter scripts into larger, representative user scripts
2. Defining a set of larger user scripts to represent a typical workload mix

First, take the short scripts, and string them together to represent meaningful single-user paths through your site. For example, in an e-Commerce site, each user does *not* log on, search for one item, put it in the shopping cart, and check out. Instead, some users log on, do a few searches, and then leave the web site. Others make purchases after completing some searches, and still others check the shipping status of outstanding orders.

After establishing the various paths the users execute through the web site, you next establish how frequently each path executes relative to the overall web site traffic. For example, if the test plan specifies that 95% of the users browse on the web site but only 3% actually make purchases, use this weighting when you assign scripts to your virtual users. In this case, 95% of the virtual users execute the Browse script, but only 3% execute the Purchase script.

Putting Scripts Together

User execution paths typically consist of several smaller scripts bundled into larger scripts, which actually model typical usage patterns at your web site. These scripts often resemble programs themselves, with "initialization" steps executed just once, followed by programming logic (including loops and conditional statements), with a clean-up step at the end. Remember, a single script executes multiple times and represents many users; thus, the script requires variation to be realistic.

As an example, let's consider a Browse and Purchase script. This script needs variety in the number of browses, the number of items selected for purchase, and the browse-to-purchase ratio. In building a Browse and Purchase script, the first step might be a login, which occurs only once in the script's initialization section. The main body of the script contains the smaller, atomic Browse, Add-to-Cart, and Checkout scripts. Test tools differ in how they generate variation within these larger scripts. For example, you might create a simple loop around the small Browse script with the tool's scripting language and use a random number to control the loop's iterations. If the average user browses for five items, choose a random loop control variable between 3 and 7 to provide variation.

To simulate a higher percentage of browsers than purchasers, place the small Add-to-Cart script inside a conditional block, and use a random number to trigger the conditional. For example, if the only 25% of users browsing actually add items to the cart, test for a match with a random number between 1 and 4.

Finally, execute the small, atomic Checkout script once at the end of the larger script. Of course, few customers actually make purchases, even if they've placed items in the cart. So, we place the small, atomic Checkout script inside a conditional and execute it randomly about 5% of the time if the user places items in the cart. The checkout occurs outside the browse loop because the user buys stuff just once per visit. Here's some pseudo-code for the logic behind a Browse and Purchase script consisting of several smaller atomic scripts.

```
//initialization-do once
Login;

//body
   cartItems = false;
   numofbrowses = random number(3..7) //pick random # of times to execute
➥browse script
   For i=1 to numofbrowses
      Do
         Browse;
         toCart = random number (1..4) //for placing in the cart 25% of the
➥time
            If toCart = 1 //place item in cart
               Add-to-Cart;
               cartItems=true;
      End;
   toPurchase = random number (1..20) //for purchasing 5% of the time
   If toPurchase = 3 and cartItems=true // buy this item
   Checkout;  //purchase all items in cart
//cleanup-do once
   Logout;  //note- you may want to leave this out since customers
➥frequently skip the logout
```

Use Weighted Testing

We discussed weighted testing in the previous section, but given the importance of this topic, let's discuss it in a bit more detail here. Weighted testing tries to duplicate the normal usage patterns of web site visitors. This helps us properly weight the influence of each function's performance in overall web site performance.

As discussed in Chapter 6, use data from your existing web site or from your marketing and usability studies to define the appropriate weighting for your scenarios. Pull this information together during the test planning phase, and refer to it as you build your scripts and scenarios. For example, let's assume that studies show 80% of our e-Commerce site visitors browse the on-line catalog, and each of these browsing users visits an average of five pages. We need a performance test to simulate these users.

You also want a set of scripts to represent different types of users. While one set of users might browse through categories, another set of users might fast track by using search. Represent each major user path as a separate major script. When you execute the test, run an appropriately weighted mix of these scripts. If you expect the majority of your users to browse, give this script a higher weighting by assigning more simulated users to execute it. For example, the home page for Pet Store allows you to browse from one of five main categories (Fish, Dogs, Reptiles, Cats, and Birds) or to initiate a search. If 80% of your users browse, while 20% use the search function, set up your test runs so that 80% of your virtual users run the Browse script, and 20% run the Search script.

But what about users who are actually making purchases? Don't they normally browse or search before buying something? To handle these cases, create two purchase scripts: Browse and Purchase and Search and Purchase. These scripts combine the smaller, atomic Sign-in and Purchase scripts with Browse and Search. Counting our new Purchase scripts, our web site performance test uses four test scripts to simulate user behavior. Based on the browse, search, and buy data provided in the test plan, you define the weightings for each script as shown in Table 7.1.

Since only 5% of our users actually make purchases, we pull these numbers out of the total browsing and searching users. This is somewhat arbitrary in this example, but easy to change if we obtain more detailed purchase patterns. The test scenario proportions the virtual users in accordance to this weighting. For example, in a test for 100 virtual users, you specify 77 virtual users to perform the Browse script, three virtual users for the Browse and Purchase script, and so forth. Getting the scenario proportions correct is very important. Test teams occasionally build a test to stress only one function, such as the item purchase function. Such tests often result in a web site poorly tuned for its production usage patterns.

Table 7.1 Example Weighting for Pet Store Scripts

Script	Weighting
Browse	77%
Browse and Purchase	3%
Search	18%
Search and Purchase	2%

Exercise the Whole Web Site

Of course, time and money always limit the scope of the your test, but often the infrequently accessed features dramatically impact the performance of the entire web site. Try to test computationally expensive paths, such as search functions. Your site's search function might not frequently entertain visitors, but when it does, it might bog down the site. In general, the more test coverage, the better. Start with your most frequently accessed web site functions, and work your way down to those seldom used. If you run out of time or money, at least your coverage extends to the most traveled areas of the site. However, over time, you probably want to accumulate tests to cover the entire web site. For example, in our examples, we discussed the Browse, Search, and Purchase paths through Pet Store. Other paths include MyAccount, New User, and Help functions.

Common Pitfalls

The success of the performance test hangs on the test scripts. As we've mentioned several times already in this chapter, the scripts must represent a user's activities accurately, or the test provides no bearing on the production web site. Often test teams create the scripts in haste and with little input from the marketing team or the existing web sites on how the users actually use the site. Test accuracy also frequently suffers from simple test script mistakes. Use this list of common test script errors to avoid simple but expensive scripting mistakes.

Inaccuracies

Scripts frequently contain incorrect or extraneous URLs, or they specify the URLs in the wrong sequence. In one case, a script writer forgot to hit the pause button on the script recorder before visiting a popular external news site. For a while, the team inadvertently tested how quickly this external site returned a page! Always read the scripts after recording them, or use your test tool's "playback" feature to confirm what the script actually does.

Hard-Coded Cookies

If the web site under test sets cookies, these cookies may appear in the recorded scripts. Some test tools require the test writer to prepare a variable to explicitly replace the cookie captured in the recording session. The variable allows the script to receive a different cookie value during the test, rather than using the recorded value. If the site uses HTTP session cookies from an application server, cookie substitution is a must. Many test tools now handle cookies automatically, but this is a very important function to verify.

Unsuitable Think Times

If the person recording the script gets a phone call or goes for a cup of coffee while recording the script, expect to see a very long delay in the test script. Conversely, the person recording the script may be so familiar with the test scenario she clicks along much faster than a normal user would. Always check the think times in the script.

As we discussed in a previous section, some of the better test tools allow you to remove the think times or to randomize their values via the test console without explicitly changing the think time values in the script. For example, Figure 7.6 shows the capabilities LoadRunner provides. At runtime, you choose whether to use or ignore think times in the script. The tool also allows you to reduce or increase the think times recorded in the script, or to set think time boundaries. Even if your tool provides this level of flexibility, you need to read your scripts carefully to understand the recorded think time. Of course, if you plan to ignore think times, this becomes less critical. However, few tests run exclusively without think times because they provide a more accurate representation of a user's interaction with the web site.

No Parameterization

We still find examples where teams fail to parameterize their scripts to support dynamic data. Of course, when this happens, every simulated user exercises the exact same path. This does not properly exercise the site, particularly the database interactions. As we discussed earlier, use dynamic data in your scripts to fully exercise your web site.

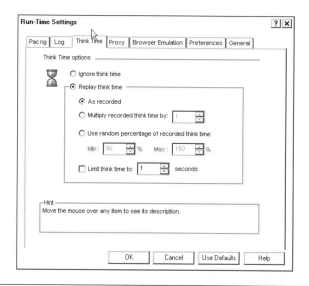

Figure 7.6 Example of customizing think times. © 2002 Mercury Interactive Corporation.

Idealized Users

Do not fall into the trap of assuming that users interact with the site just as the designers intended. As we mentioned before, users rarely log out of a web site; they just move on to the next site. However, almost every performance test we've ever seen includes the lowly logout function as part of the most heavily weighted script. Not only does this put improper emphasis on the performance of the logout function in your testing, but it may also lead to a gross underestimation of user pressure on your web site. Take the time to learn how users interact with your web site, and build your scripts to reflect this.

Oversimplified Scripts

Typically you produce an oversimplified script when you don't have any real data from your existing web site, so you implement some of the use cases generated from your earliest application designs. These make for easy scripts to create, but they provide very limited performance value. For example, if you test only those user interactions that execute simple reads from the underlying database, they tend to execute more quickly than updates or creates, and skew the numbers for how your web application performs in production. If you execute only specific reads instead of commonly used searches returning several hundred database records, again the site appears to execute more quickly, and handle more interactions than will actually be possible under production conditions.

Use your simple scripts to build more complex scripts and scenarios, as we discussed earlier. These more complex interactions give you a better understanding of your web site's production behavior.

Myopic Scripts

Likewise, if you test *only* the complex portions of the application, or test *only* the trivial portions of the application, your performance test won't give you an accurate representation of production behavior. For instance, don't just test the easy stuff like the static data. But on the other hand, don't just test the hard stuff like the dynamic content. Too much static content testing gives you an overinflated sense of the web site's capacity. Conversely, testing only dynamic elements might lead you to build too much capacity for the site.

Summary

Test scripts require a significant investment in planning and development. Good scripts exercise your web site as your users do, and allow you to accurately measure your application's performance. They also give you the basis for web site capacity planning. Conversely, bad scripts often generate inaccurate capacity data or, even worse, leave serious performance problems undetected until the web site enters production. Create scripts that test through the various layers within your application so you know which operations require the most time.

Script writing requires some planning. Write small, atomic scripts for easy insertion in a variety of scenarios. Use your knowledge of typical usage patterns to develop relevant test cases. Also, begin your testing with the most frequently visited areas of your web site, and add scripts to cover the less-traveled areas as time permits. Your scripts need lots of variation to simulate the breadth of requests the site receives and to avoid skewing the performance by using cached items. Finally, use the appropriate weighting to realistically reproduce the distribution of traffic on your web site.

Building test scripts and selecting a test tool need to be taken seriously. In the next chapter, we discuss test tool selection in detail.

Chapter 8

SELECTING THE
RIGHT TEST TOOLS

Selecting the right test tools is critical to the success of your performance test. You depend on performance tools to capture reliable and repeatable data during testing. However, not all testing tools prove suitable for all testing situations. In fact, we occasionally encounter obscure tools that actually *generate* performance problems! In this chapter, we discuss selection criteria for performance test tools. As we discussed in Chapter 7, most performance tools come with a recording tool and often their own scripting language. Therefore, selecting a tool implies an investment not only in the tool software, but also in the test scripts you generate using the tool. Selecting a good, robust tool saves money in replacement costs later, and also in the time required to build your test script library.

As we'll discuss in Chapter 11, successful tests depend on two critical elements:

- Simulating the anticipated production environment
- Obtaining reliable and repeatable measurements

You need a test tool to support these success criteria. Unless your tests adequately simulate the anticipated production environment, problems resulting in significant production issues often go undetected. Likewise, reliable and repeatable measurements allow you to correlate tuning changes with improvements rather than measurement error.

Test tools continue to rapidly improve their capabilities. For this reason, we do not include a feature-to-feature comparison between different tools. Instead, we provide a requirements framework for assessing performance tools, and discuss some of the key feature differentiators. Appendix C includes a checklist summarizing these requirements.

In general, the Internet and the market place both contain plenty of low-end, free, or shareware load drivers, as well as high-end load drivers. Some of the low-end drivers include tools such as Apache Bench, Apache Flood, Jmeter, or Microsoft Web Capacity Analysis Tool (WCAT). These tools typically work best to test static web sites or simple dynamic sites. High-end load drivers come from the leading automated software quality tool vendors, including Mercury Interactive, Rational, Segue, Compuware, Empirix, and RadView.[1] Tools at this end of the market generally work best for large or complex web sites.

Appendix C includes a list of vendors of performance testing or monitoring products. Of course, this is only a partial list and does not contain every tool available. Also, we do not endorse, recommend, or guarantee the tools listed, but merely provide these names for your convenience.

Production Simulation Requirements

A performance tool simulates user load against your web site or test system. These automated performance tools work better than human testers in almost all cases. First of all, you cannot round up a thousand or so humans to run test scenarios against a large web site. Secondly, even if your web site supports significantly smaller user loads (20 or 30 concurrent users, for example), live testers typically do not simulate real world users well. Live testers tend to get "click-happy" and move through the web site very quickly. Thus, they usually generate much shorter think times than found in production. An automated tool gives you more control over the simulation, and allows you to test larger loads with fewer resources.

A performance test tool (sometimes also called a *load driver*) executes your test scripts. As discussed in Chapter 7, most load drivers provide capture and replay capabilities to partially automate the creation of test scripts. This technology allows you to "record" a typical browser interaction with your web site and then automatically replay this same interaction. As shown in Figure 8.1, the tool typically sits between the browser and the server and "listens" to the traffic flow to create the initial script. Most tools provide some type of recording capability to initially create the scripts. However, recorded scripts usually need additional customization to adequately simulate real users. Making these changes requires programming skill as well as time.

---

1. See Richard V. Heiman, "The Distributed Automated Software Quality Tools Market Forecast and Analysis, 2001–2005," IDC Bulletin 25176–July 2001. Retrieved December 27, 2001, from the World Wide Web: <http://www-heva.mercuryinteractive.com/company/pr/idcreport/25176.htm>. Table 1 lists Mercury Interactive Corp, Rational, Segue Software, Compuware Corp, Empirix, and RadView Software as the top six vendors of distributed automated software quality tools by 2000 revenue.

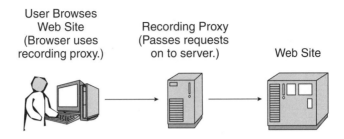

User Browses
Web Site
(Browser uses
recording proxy.)

Recording Proxy
(Passes requests
on to server.)

Web Site

Figure 8.1   Script recording

Performance test tools vary significantly in capability and price. To choose the right tool, begin by understanding the key features of your site and the goals of your test. For example, let's think back to Chapter 5 and the distinguishing features for some of the different types of web sites, as summarized in Table 8.1. Let's map some of the differences to test tool requirements for each major web site type.

Table 8.1   Some Performance Characteristics of Common Web Site Types

Web Site Type	User Pressure	Throughput Dependent	Response Time Requirements	Caching Potential
Financial	High	High	High	Medium
B2B	High	Medium	Medium	Low
e-Commerce	High	High	High	High

Financial Web Site   A financial web site experiences high user pressure and high throughput. These web sites receive large numbers of users, some of whom stay on the site all day, as well as large transaction volumes. Security plays a large role in these sites. Therefore, a tool simulating load for a financial web site must support the following requirements:

1. Simulates many concurrent users
2. Simulates both long user sessions and a large number of short, frequent visits
3. Simulates a mixed workload of many queries and a smaller number of buy/sell transactions
4. Simulates secure transactions
5. Supports high transaction throughput
6. Simulates spikes in traffic

B2B Web Site   A B2B web site experiences high user pressure but typically lower throughput dependencies. Users on a B2B site frequently stay on all day, with multiple, but infrequent, query and update interactions. The web site secures transaction traffic. To simulate a B2B workload, look for a tool satisfying these requirements:

1. Simulates many logged-on users
2. Simulates very long user sessions
3. Simulates few transactions with long wait times
4. Simulates secure transactions

e-Commerce Web Site   An e-Commerce site receives more concurrent users and must support a high transaction rate. Users typically visit the site briefly and consider site response time of paramount importance. Browse ratios significantly outnumber actual purchase transactions. These sites require security only for purchase and account related transactions. A tool needs to support the following to simulate an e-Commerce workload:

1. Simulates many users
2. Simulates a mix of short and long user sessions
3. Simulates a mixed workload of queries and buy/sell transactions
4. Simulates secure transactions
5. Simulates browsing/searching large catalog databases of items

The web site types discussed here share some common workload simulation requirements: All the sites require a way to simulate logged-on user sessions, a mixed workload of read and update transactions, and security.

However, not every site listed here shares every requirement. Your site may also need special performance test features to meet its requirements. For example, if you performance test an e-Commerce site with a large database, you may need a tool that supports easily importing selections from this database into your scripts. Let's take an in-depth look at some of these different tool considerations for workload simulation.

Users

User simulation is paramount to a successful performance test. Every load driver tool claims the ability to simulate many users. However, some tools may simulate only a limited number of unique users. Based on your test plan, determine how many users you need to simulate, and also consider the users you need for future growth of the web site. (Remember, your test scripts represent an investment. Make sure your tool satisfies your projected load testing needs for some time to come.)

For example, an e-Commerce site typically needs more simulated users than a B2B site. *The number of virtual users required contributes significantly to the overall cost of test hardware and software.* Clearly, the more realistic the test, the better; however, simulating all of the expected users may simply cost too much.

The key differentiators between tools regarding user simulation include

- Think time support
- User ramp-up and load control
- Accurate browser simulation, including browser caching
- Accurate cookie support, including the ability to dump the cookie cache between script iterations
- Hardware requirements and platform support
- Multiple driver machine support

Think Time

The most realistic user simulations include think time simulation. Some basic load driver tools, such as Apache Bench, do not provide the ability to simulate think time. However, almost all high-end tools provide think time support, although they differ in the flexibility they provide for adjusting these times. If simulating think time is a high-priority requirement for your site, look for a tool that allows you to change think times without manually updating your scripts.

In order to lower test costs, you may simulate your load by using fewer simulated users with little or no think time. This often generates the desired throughput with fewer user licenses. For example, if your market research projects 1,000 concurrent users, and your usability testing shows an average think time of 10 seconds, this equates to 100 active users at any point in time.

```
1 request/10 seconds/user * 1,000 concurrent users
= 100 user requests/second
```

In this case, using 100 simulated clients without think time produces the same active load as 1,000 users with think time.

Important! This technique proves ineffective for many web sites using HTTP sessions in their web applications. In the first test, your application accesses 1,000 HTTP sessions in memory, whereas in the second test, it accesses only 100 HTTP sessions. Also, the HTTP sessions time out faster using this technique than in a full user test. The case study in Chapter 14 provides an example of testing with reduced think time. Of course, if you use this technique, look for a test tool that allows you to easily reduce or eliminate think times during test execution.

Ability to Control User Load and Ramp-Up

Beyond how many users the tool supports, also consider if the tool allows you to add simulated users during a test run. Adding users to a running test helps simulate spikes in user loading as well as patterns of increasing load. Most high-end performance test tools allow you to specify how many users to start and when to add additional users. For example, when running a 1,000-user test, you might start 100 users and add another 100 users every minute until reaching 1,000 users. This gives your site a gradual "warm-up" period.

Figure 8.2 shows a sample LoadRunner controller screen. In this example, we defined LoadRunner to run a "Ramp Up" schedule, adding 10 virtual users every minute until reaching a total of 100 users. (LoadRunner allows customization of these ramp-up steps and durations.) Of course, if your load driver tool does not provide this kind of user management flexibility, consider simulating ramp-up or spike patterns by using multiple load driver instances. For example, simulate a "spike" against a financial site by starting up another test system late in the test to generate additional load. However, using this approach requires manual collation of the data returned from the test tool instances. Do not underestimate the difficulty of this task.

Browser Simulation and Caching

During your comparison shopping, consider whether the tools correctly simulate typical browser behaviors, including the ability to clear cached items between script

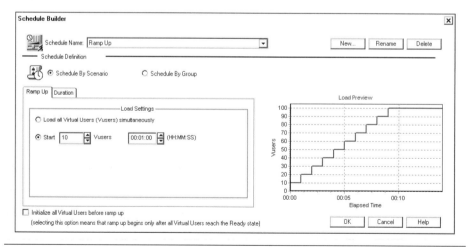

Figure 8.2 Example LoadRunner ramp-up. © 2002 Mercury Interactive Corporation.

iterations. Some tools use clever strategies to simulate browser caching. For example, SilkPerformer does not actually maintain a browser cache (just think of how much disk space a cache for each simulated user might require), but rather the tool remembers each user's "cached" items by name, and does not request them again.

Usually, high-end tools provide several cache clearing options for different simulated users. If your web site focuses on support for a specific browser, check for the proper simulation support for this browser.

Network Address Management

If your web site uses load balancing, look for a tool compatible with your load balancer. As discussed in Chapter 3, some load balancing solutions rely on the client's IP address. During load tests, a single load generator may simulate hundreds of different clients. If each of these clients receives the same IP address, you defeat the load balancer's routing scheme, and all your traffic goes to the same server machine within your test cluster.

To work around this problem, some test teams use multiple test client machines, each with a unique IP address. Also, many performance tools manage simulated users across multiple client machines automatically and provide consolidated reporting in this configuration. However, other tools do not, leaving you to manually consolidate reports from each client machine.

If you test IP address load balancing for your site, give careful consideration to purchasing a load driver with IP address simulation capabilities or with the ability to spread simulated users over multiple client machines.

Cookie Support

If your web application uses cookies to associate users with HTTP session data, select a test tool that handles cookies for each simulated user.[2] Also, make sure the tool allows you to dump the user's cookie cache after each script iteration. (This allows you to simulate a new user for each iteration.)

The current editions of most test tools support cookies in some fashion. Make sure the support meets your needs and requires little or no customization on your part to function properly.

---

2. See Stephan Asboeck, *Load Testing for eConfidence.*

Hardware and Platform Support

Don't overlook the hardware requirements for your planned simulated user load. Many tools require lots of hardware capacity, especially memory. As a rule of thumb, plan a comparable client driver to match every system under test (SUT) in your environment. For example, if your test cluster contains two four-way application server machines, plan to include two four-way performance test client machines in your configuration. Of course, use this as a general rule, but confirm these estimates with the actual recommendations published by your performance test tool vendor. Also, keep in mind that these guidelines vary depending on the complexity of the test, the data returned, the degree of error checking performed by the test tool, and other factors. Ask your tool provider for assistance with hardware recommendations.

Surprisingly, simple tests with high transaction throughput often require more client hardware capacity than the more complex tests (tests generating more server processing per request). A workload of primarily static content generates a higher throughput rate than a complex, transaction-oriented workload, which puts more stress on the test client machines. For example, a mostly static based workload may generate 2,000 transactions per second, while a complex, transaction-oriented workload running on the same hardware may generate only 100 transaction per second. The same client simulator works harder handling 2,000 transactions per second then it does with only 100.

For this reason, the client hardware requirements often increase if you test *less* complex web site logic. For example, if you test an e-Commerce site with lots of static element caching, you may need more client hardware than when testing a B2B site with the same simulated user load. The rapid request and return rate of the static data from the e-Commerce site stands to overwhelm the test client machines.

Also, as you shop for a performance tool, consider the hardware platforms it supports. Performance test tools typically execute against web sites on any hardware platform, just as a browser interacts with web sites deployed on multiple hardware platforms. For example, if your web site uses a UNIX-based platform, you don't necessarily need to limit your performance tool to this platform as well. Most likely, a performance tool running a Microsoft Windows–based system works just as well as one running on a UNIX platform to test your web site.

Many load drivers use test controllers and agent systems to simulate the user load. Many vendors only support a Microsoft Windows–based test controller while supporting the agent simulator on many different platforms, including Microsoft and UNIX systems. For example, Mercury LoadRunner requires a Microsoft Windows platform for their controller, but the controller manages test agents running on Microsoft Windows or several UNIX variants. Keep these important platform requirements in mind as you plan the hardware and skills required for your load tests.

Scripts

As we mentioned earlier, your test scripts represent a significant investment. When you select a test tool, consider how the tool supports script development, customization, and maintenance as part of your selection criteria. Remember, no standard exists for test scripts, so scripts *do not port* between different performance test tools. Once you make an investment in recording and customizing test scripts, switching test tools becomes difficult.

The key differentiators between tools' script support include

- Dynamic data support
  - Parameter substitution
  - Dynamic web page parsing
- Scripting language (learning curve and skill levels required for use)
- Ability to build a scenario from individual scripts and to specify their weighting
- Ability to reuse scripts in production monitoring

Dynamic Data Support

Going back to one of our Chapter 7 discussions, well-written test scripts simulate a typical user's selection process. The script also incorporates enough variation and dynamic data selection to simulate a breadth of interaction consistent with large user volumes. Repetitive scripts (for example, a script driving a single, unchanging URL request over and over again) often miss out on the most important aspects of performance testing. For example, multiple users reading and writing different records from the same tables sometimes cause database contention. Repetitive scripts never generate this level of contention, so they never reveal this potentially serious problem during the test. Also, realistic scripts properly exercise the various caches throughout the system.

Look at the tool's capability to add parameters based on random numbers or file input. Low-end script drivers typically drive the same sequence of URLs over and over again, but frequently lack the support required for highly dynamic, HTTP session driven sites. Dynamic data handling marks one of the key differentiators between low-end and high-end performance test tools. A free tool such as Apache Bench, which excels at driving a sequence of URLs, is easy to use, and requires minimal hardware. Many "shareware" load drivers exhibit similar characteristics. However, the free tools quickly lose their appeal when seriously testing dynamic applications. For example, if your site supports a user login, look for a load driver that simulates different user IDs.

If you plan to use a low-end driver, consider developing custom application logic for better dynamic user simulation. IBM uses this approach with the WebSphere Performance Benchmark Sample (Trade2). IBM developed the `TradeScenarioServlet` to front-end the actual application processing. This scenario servlet actually performs the random user generation and dynamically generates the workload mix. This approach requires additional programming resources to develop the equivalent of the scenario servlet, but simplifies the load generation tool requirements. (Also, this approach requires server-side resources to drive the test load.) The load generation tool needs to handle cookies, but does not need sophisticated dynamic data handling capabilities. IBM took this approach in order to easily share the benchmark with customers using different load generators.

Of course, high-end performance tools support sophisticated dynamic data handling capabilities. The high-end tools perform the same function as the scenario servlet within their client-side processing. In general, we recommend finding a performance test tool that handles your dynamic data requirements as opposed to writing your own. Developing test scripts with a reputable performance test tool usually requires less resource investment in the long run and allows you to more easily manage and change the test scripts over time.

Most high-end load driver tools provide the capabilities required to script web applications like Pet Store or Trade2. However, the scripts normally require customization in order to adequately test the dynamic capabilities. During your tool selection process, we recommend actually prototyping scripts with the different tools under consideration to determine if they support your needs.

Parsing Dynamic Web Pages

Dynamic web pages often vary in content and length depending on the request parameters. For example, just like Pet Store, many web sites include a search function. The search function returns a dynamically generated page (usually of web links) based on the search value submitted by the users. Every search potentially generates a different results page with a different number of results links. These pages often require customized scripts to process and select from the dynamic links returned. In fact, in Chapter 7 we showed you two examples of dynamic link processing using both SilkPerformer and LoadRunner.

If you require dynamic link processing, confirm the performance tools you're considering support this feature. In our experience, each vendor provides a range of capabilities in this area, and often the support involves complex and highly skilled script programming. Regardless of the tool you select, take a class or use consulting resources to assist in the initial development of scripts using this function. (In fact, to produce the scripts for our examples, we received help from both Mercury Interactive and Segue to exploit their advanced features.)

Scripting Language and Skills

In addition to script recording, most performance tools offer test script customization support. However, the level of skill required to accomplish the customization varies among the tool vendors. Some tools support simple application customization using the tool's GUIs; more sophisticated application scripting frequently requires custom script programming. The scripting language used by the tools varies from proprietary scripting languages to JavaScript or C.

As we mentioned earlier, no test script standards exist. This leaves the tool vendors free to select or build any scripting language for their scripts. Before you purchase a performance test tool, understand the effort and skills required to create and maintain test scripts.

Building and Weighting Scenarios

As we discussed in Chapter 7, during runtime your test scripts must represent the actual production usage patterns of your web site. For an e-Commerce web site, the workload mix usually consists of far more browsing users than users making purchases. We reflect this same workload mix when we test the e-Commerce site. Simulating different workload mixes is important, especially for larger web sites. Low-end tools typically execute a single workload for all users. Most high-end tools allow you to assign different scripts to different users. For example, if you run a 1,000-user test, use these tools to specify 300 of the users to run a search scenario, 750 of the users to run a browse scenario, and 50 to run a purchase scenario. Figure 8.3 gives an example of defining a weighted test run using SilkPerformer.

Many of the test tools also provide capabilities to build more complex scripts from smaller, individual scripts. For example, some tools allow you to define a series of scripts to log on, perform a random (or specified) number of browses, and purchase a random selection of items. The ability to isolate function into separate scripts makes it easier to optimize critical paths. For an e-Commerce site, the buy path may constitute a small percentage of the overall workload, but the test plan usually specifies an aggressive response time target for this path. Isolating the buy path to a small, atomic script gives you better control over its execution in the overall workload mix, and, depending on the tool, tighter monitoring of its performance.

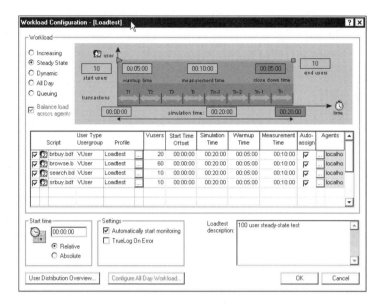

Figure 8.3   Example of SilkPerformer V workload configuration. © 2002 Segue Software, Inc.

Reusing Test Scripts in Production

Frequently, the same scripts used to performance test your web site also come in handy for monitoring and troubleshooting your production site. Periodically, you might run the Search script against your production site under limited load to check the search path's production performance. Several test tool vendors now offer production monitoring tools that use the same scripts developed for load testing. See Appendix C for more information on production monitoring offerings.

Automation and Centralized Control

Consider how well the test tool manages the test execution and results collection. How much of this process does the tool automate, and how much does it require you to do manually?

The key differentiators for automated and central control include

- Controlling multiple client drivers from a central location or machine
- Consolidating results from multiple clients into a single report
- Command line or remote test control

While these differentiators do not actually influence your test results, they make a big difference in the effort required to run your tests. If your test tool requires lots of manual intervention to execute and collect results, the added manual overhead reduces the number of tests you execute every day. The more work you do, the longer it takes to complete the performance tests. Small performance tests (defined by a small test environment, few test scripts, and few simulated users) generally do not require highly automated test runtime management.

Controlling Multiple Client Drivers

If you need multiple test client machines to simulate the user load, consider test tools with support for managing the simulated users distributed over these machines. Figure 8.4 shows a test environment using four client machines to generate the test load. The load generators send requests on an isolated network to the systems under test. The performance test tool provides a central controller to manage the four client machines. The communications between the controller and the load generators traverse a separate network from the actual performance test traffic so as not to interfere with test performance.

Typically, a controller assigns a set of test scripts to a set of virtual users, starts these virtual users on distributed client machines, and monitors the users as the test executes. After the test completes, the controller consolidates the data from all the simulated users. Centralized control is common in the high-end load drivers; most

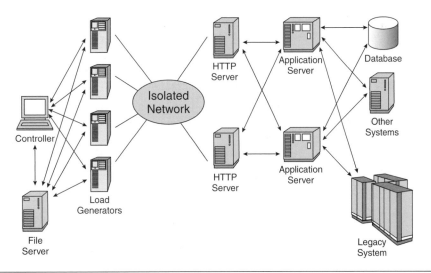

Figure 8.4   Testing environment

low-end tools do not provide this function. If one test machine suffices for your test-ing in the foreseeable future, this function is not a requirement. However, most large web sites require multiple test clients and a test controller to manage their test runs.

Running Tests via Command Line or Remotely

Some organizations run their performance tests from remote locations. Often the performance tests run from labs miles away from the actual test servers. Also, many organizations write automated test control scripts using the test tool's command line interface to control remote or off-shift test runs. If you need these capabilities, check carefully with the performance tool vendor. Many high-end test tools support remote execution but do not provide a command line interface. (High-end tools use sophisticated GUIs to support their functionality. These functions do not translate easily into a command line interface.)

Conversely, many of the low-end tools provide command line access. However, make sure the tool provides *all* the functions you need to support the test.

Pricing and Licensing

The price for load driver tools ranges from no cost (such as for the Apache tool) to hundreds of thousands of dollars. You may be in for a shock at the price demanded for high-end load generation tools. A July 2001[3] study comparing prices for tools from Quest, RadView, Segue, Mercury Interactive, Empirix, and Compuware found that the entry level price for 50 or 100 virtual users is between \$7,500 and \$33,075, plus additional costs to simulate more users.

The base costs and licensing terms quickly become significant considerations when evaluating test tools.

Key differentiators for pricing and licensing include

- Licensing costs (flat fees or based on per simulated user)
- Group sharing of users across multiple controller machines
- Short-term client licenses
- Existing vendor relationship

---

3. Web Testing tools pricing comparison for the big six suppliers. Retrieved December 27, 2001, from the World Wide Web: <http://www.red-gate.com/web_testing_tool_prices.htm>.

Licensing Costs

Many of the high-end load driver products charge a flat fee for each controller installed, which includes a small number of virtual users. Increasing the number of virtual users beyond the base amount usually generates additional "per virtual user" licensing fees. *Large tests with many virtual users often require very expensive licenses.*

In pricing tools, consider the number of users you need to simulate and the cost of simulating these users with the various available tools. Some vendors also offer "unlimited user" licenses. While typically quite expensive, these unlimited licenses may be a good solution for some organizations.

Ability to Share Users across Multiple Controller Machines

Some tools allow you to buy a large number of users and share them as needed across a set of controllers on a "check-out/check-in" basis. Consider this flexible licensing option if your organization supports many test environments and test teams. Of course, for smaller organizations, this licensing option may provide little benefit.

Short-Term Licenses

Several vendors offer short-term licenses (sometimes known as "per day" licenses). These licenses allow you to pay for more virtual users only as you need them over a limited period of time. Early in your testing, you only need a few virtual users to begin tuning a subset of your test environment. Also, early in your testing, you may cut the think time in your test scripts to generate request pressure with fewer virtual users. However, after a time, you may require significantly more users for a scalability test. Also, some organizations insist on a full user test using realistic think times before approving the web site for production release. During these times, you require more virtual users.

Short-term licenses allow you to purchase virtual users for exactly the time you need them. Often this strategy proves more cost effective than buying licenses for virtual users you seldom use. Just be sure to adequately test the environment and scripts beforehand, so as not to waste the short-term license in debugging and setup issues.

Existing Vendor Relationships

Before you purchase a performance test tool, check with your company's software acquisition group. Some organizations enter into agreements with performance tool vendors to provide tools or virtual users at a negotiated cost. Using these agreements usually saves money over purchasing the tool through regular channels.

Also, avoid conflicts with products already approved by your organization. For example, if your company uses functional test or production monitoring tools from another vendor, make sure your performance test tool selection works with these other tools.

Tool Requirements for Reproducible Results

Performance testing demands repeatable and reliable run measurements. Your test procedures and setup play a major role in the repeatability and reliability of the results. Likewise, the test tool also influences your ability to generate these results. If your tool does not produce reliable and repeatable results, you *cannot* determine if your tuning adjustments actually improve performance. Beyond a shadow of a doubt, this is *the most critical* factor in performance tool selection.

Some of the key tool requirements for supporting reproducible results include the following: The tool

- Provides a warm-up period to initialize the environment
- Obtains measurements within a steady-state period
- Verifies error-free test execution
- Drives the same workload between runs
- Captures measurements without impacting performance

The performance tools collect the measurements for your analysis. At a minimum, insist on average throughput and response time measurements from your tool. Many tools provide the minimums and maximums for each data point reported as well as standard deviations.

Also, look for measurement granularity. The better tools break down measurements by script to help you better determine the performance of various functions during the run. This level of analysis shows you how the function performs under load and with other key web site functions in use. This gives you a more realistic systemic analysis of individual web site functions.

Some tools collect key measurements from the machines under test as well as the test client machines themselves. Usually this requires installing small monitors from the tool vendor on the systems under test. These monitors report measurements back to the test controller. Of course, there's nothing preventing you from collecting these measurements yourself (as we'll discuss in Chapter 12). However, using the test tool to collect and collate these measurements usually makes for easier analysis.

Capturing any errors during the test is critical. This includes error pages returned or logged application errors. Tests requesting a few thousand pages over the course of the run normally experience a handful of page errors. However, significant numbers of page or application errors invalidate a performance run. Page errors often artificially inflate throughput results, as error pages require less processing and embed fewer static elements. Therefore, web sites return error pages significantly faster than other dynamic pages. Conversely, web application errors lower performance, as these tend to require more processing.

Reporting

As we mentioned above, select a test tool with the reporting capabilities you need. The high-end performance test tool vendors differ significantly in their test reports. In many cases, this becomes one of the key differentiators in performance tool selection. Even though the tool provides terrific test runtime support, it must capture and deliver relevant information after the test finishes. Often, test teams purchase a tool without realizing it cannot generate the reports they need.

Key reporting differentiators:

- Summary reports containing the key results you want
- Summary reports for the steady-state time period
- Collated reports from multiple runs
- Real-time reporting during test execution

Key Results

As part of your tool selection process, review each tool's generated reports, and identify data interesting for your particular web site. Remember, you want the tool to work for you. Poor or insufficient reporting usually requires significant manual data manipulation by your test team. This makes for longer analysis on each test run and reduces the "tune and test" iterations accomplished by the team each day. Good reporting makes for faster test cycles.

Consider how the tool reports data and how well the tool isolates key measurements. More data is not always better. If you must glean two or three data points from seven reports, consider a simpler or more customizable tool. During testing, we always want to see key measurements such as response time and throughput. We also like to select a time range or set of values for the tool to use in its calculations. (If the test performs a ramp-up and ramp-down of users, this feature allows us to eliminate the data collected during those times from our steady-state analysis.)

Figure 8.5 below shows a sample Summary Report from LoadRunner. Notice the summary includes client load levels, throughput in bytes per second, HTTP hits per second, and response time. However, this report does not contain one of our favorite measurements: transactions per second (often different than hits per second). To obtain this data, we use the New Graph option to include this particular detailed graph.

In analyzing reports, also look at the granularity of data returned. Low-end load drivers usually provide only averages. High-end tools often provide more granularity, such as minimum, maximum, and 90th percentile measurements. For example, Figure 8.5 shows a LoadRunner report of this data for the Snoop servlet.[4] This granular data is extremely useful in problem determination and capacity planning.

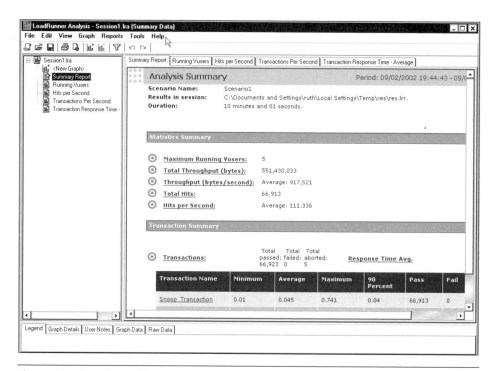

Figure 8.5   Sample LoadRunner Summary Report. © 2002 Mercury Interactive Corporation.

---

4. Snoop Servlet is a sample servlet provided with IBM WebSphere Application Server and is used here with permission from IBM.

Some high-end tools provide automatic charting. The tool generates charts from the collected data and provides them as part of the runtime reports. Charts allow you to easily visualize and analyze the collected measurements.

Finally, if you need special measurements, consider a tool with data export capability. Many tools export data in various spreadsheet data formats. You then pull the data into your favorite spreadsheet and develop your own custom reports and graphs.

Steady-State Measurements

As Chapter 11 discusses in more detail, always try to capture performance measurements during the steady-state period of your test run. Different tools make obtaining steady-state measurements more or less difficult. If you use simple performance tools with no support for user ramp-up or warm-up, run multiple tests or very long tests to obtain valid steady-state measurements. If you run multiple tests, consider the first run a priming run and discard the results. Use the data from subsequent tests in your actual measurements.

High-end test tools make steady-state data capture easier. SilkPerformer, for example, provides steady state as one of its predefined test configurations. When you select this option, the tool automatically discards the warm-up and cool-down periods of the test in its reported measurements. Figure 8.3 shows a screen capture of the SilkPerformer Workload Configuration. Notice the tool contains steady state as a pre-defined workload option, along with selections for the number of virtual users, measurement times, and close down time.

Some high-end load drivers record all their measurements in a database, which you then manipulate to obtain different reports. This approach works well for client ramp-up measurements. For example, you might ramp up a test by adding users every 15 minutes. The post-analysis tool then allows you to examine data specific to these 15-minute periods. This technique takes a little more effort to get the data, but it may work well for your test environment.

Real-Time Reporting

Real-time reporting gives you performance measurements *during* the actual test run. This incredibly useful feature lets you observe the performance characteristics of the system as the test tool ramps up users and runs at steady state. This reporting gives you instant "cause-and-effect" feedback during the test runs. For example, five minutes into the run, the real-time report might indicate a significant performance degradation, followed in a few minutes by a period of normal operation. This report points out a potential problem with web site "burstiness" (discussed more in Chapter 13).

Of course, this detail also appears in the summary reports of many tools, but watching the system behave during a test often makes performance analysis and tuning faster. Also, you receive immediate feedback on serious environment problems, such as a misconfigured router, that are impacting your performance tests. Rather than finding out much later, with real-time reporting you know to halt the test and resolve the problem.

Most high-end monitoring tools now provide real-time charting. At a minimum, make sure any tool you select provides some visible indicator of slowdowns or problems during execution.

Multiple Runs

Controlling the amount of data returned and the number of reports generated becomes especially important if you plan to run a lot of unattended tests. For example, if you typically run a series of tests overnight and analyze the results later, you may want short summary reports from each run, instead of generating many, extremely detailed reports to wade through. In addition, multiple tests producing large reports often overflow the available disk space and disrupt other planned tests. Particularly if your tests run unattended, keep the reports generated to a useful minimum.

This also becomes a differentiating factor among the high-end tools. If your test plans call for unattended testing, explore this feature carefully in the tools under consideration.

Verification of Results

Avoid misleading and worthless test measurements from a web site or performance test generating errors. As we mentioned earlier, tests receiving error pages from the web site often generate better response time and throughput than tests producing correct results. Likewise, a web application producing errors may run more slowly than its healthy counterpart. For example, load-related defects in Java applications often cause exceptions. The exception paths often require more processing in terms of exception handling and logging, causing the application performance to be extremely poor. Collecting performance measurements in either case we've discussed is a waste of time.

Some tools include verification support. At a minimum, many tools look at the incoming HTML pages and check them for errors or unexpected conditions. Most tools readily identify failed or timed out HTTP connections as well.

Key results verification differentiators:

- ■ Automatic data verification
- ■ Log verification

Data Verification

Some test tools verify the data on the incoming pages. Of course, doing this for dynamic pages presents special challenges: What defines a "correct" page when every page request generates a potentially infinite set of response pages? In these cases, consider adding custom code to your performance tool to verify the incoming pages. Perhaps the error pages always contain a special header or other element; use this in the verification script to distinguish the error pages.

If your performance tool does not support customization, consider manual verification of many pages during the test runs. In fact, this proves useful for other reasons apart from simple error verification. As we discussed in Chapter 4, web applications sometimes mismanage variables in the concurrent servlet environment. Checking key dynamic pages, such as customer account information, alerts you to concurrency issues in the web application. (For example, if you want to see customer A's account information, but suddenly find yourself looking at customer B's information instead, the web application has a problem.)

Be careful that the data verification does not interfere with client driver or network performance. Verification usually takes a significant amount of client resources as well and may require additional client hardware to support on a large scale.

Log Verification

In addition to verifying the pages returned, look at the logs from all the test systems, including the HTTP servers, database servers, and application servers *after every test run*. We recommend building scripts to gather up the logs after each test run and to reset them for the next run. After examining the logs for errors, keep them at least until you complete the data analysis for the run.

To our knowledge, no commercial test tool provides log analysis and collection for you. However, you *must* perform this manual verification after each run to truly validate your results.

Real-Time Server Machine Test Monitoring

Earlier we described monitoring test results in real time. Those results included performance metrics such as throughput and response time. Other real-time monitors also provide useful information during the test run. In particular, some test tools allow you to monitor the remote systems under test during the test runs. These tools report key server machine metrics, such as CPU utilization, as the run progresses. The tool usually displays this information on one panel, as demonstrated using the LoadRunner run-time monitor in Figure 8.6. Seeing all of your performance data on one screen helps you understand the relationship between your performance numbers and the state of the systems monitored. Also, machine monitor data provides information about machine capacity, and helps you identify resource bottlenecks during testing.

Chapter 4 discussed the typical components in a web site. You need a way to monitor all the components in your test environment:

- Network
- System
- HTTP server
- Application server
- Database
- Additional back-end systems

Just as performance test tools vary in price and effectiveness, test system monitoring tools vary significantly depending on the level of functionality you want. However, you need at least some basic tools, and you may want to consider purchasing better tools for specialized analysis. *Key differentiators in real-time server machine test monitoring products are the following:*

- Integration with performance test reporting
- Price
- Detailed analysis and problem isolation
- Reusable in the production environment

Integration with Performance Test Reporting

The performance test tool monitors throughput and response time data at the test client. However, for a full understanding of the test environment, we also need measurements from the servers and test client machines themselves. Of course, we usually consider each machine's CPU utilization the most critical of these measurements, but other information, such as paging rates and disk I/O, prove useful as well.

We monitor CPU to detect systems with overutilized or underutilized CPUs, which may indicate a bottleneck (either at the machine itself or elsewhere in the environment) or available capacity. For example, if we drive the test client machines to 100% CPU utilization, the other machines in the system may present low CPU utilization

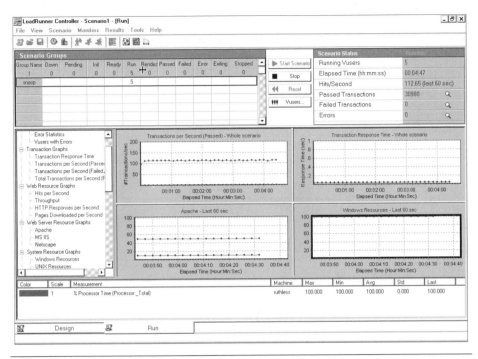

Figure 8.6   Sample LoadRunner monitor © 2002 Mercury Interactive Corporation.

because the test client cannot generate sufficient load. (Test client capacity is one of the most frequently overlooked test bottlenecks we encounter.)

In addition to system statistics, we often need middleware statistics such as the number of HTTP server processes, application server threads, and database locks to resolve performance problems. Monitoring these key tuning and analysis elements is important. Low-end drivers rarely contain any monitoring capabilities. High-end load driver tools typically support basic system monitoring. For example, these tools capture CPU metrics from remote servers and graph these statistics during the test run. Your test controller assembles the statistics from multiple systems and reports them real-time with other data. This capability is extremely useful. For example, when troubleshooting a "burstiness bottleneck," watch the CPU on the application and database servers in conjunction with the overall test throughput and response times to find a correlation between the burstiness patterns and the CPU utilization of these machines.

Additionally, some vendors provide middleware metrics. For example, Mercury Interactive provides performance data from middleware systems such as HTTP servers, system resources, networks, web application servers, and database servers. Figure 8.6 provides an example from a LoadRunner test. On the left-hand side, you see the selection of monitors available. In the center, you see real-time charts display-ing the client-side results for transactions per second and response time. Along with this data, you see monitor data about the Apache Web Server busy processes as well as data on the Windows resource which tracks CPU utilization on the application server. LoadRunner allows you to select different graphs and different servers to monitor. It also allows you to customize test reports with your desired metrics.

Price

If your load driver tool does not provide integrated monitors, or does not provide the depth of monitors required for your analysis, other monitors exist to help you collect data during your test. Most operating systems provide some degree of machine mon-itoring. Depending on the platform, these monitors range from detailed and elabo-rate to very basic. As with any tool, understand how these monitors impact your performance before you use them. Even some operating system monitors use signifi-cant resources, robbing your test of valuable capacity. Of course, operating systems provide some level of monitoring for free, and may offer other, more sophisticated monitors for a relatively small upgrade charge.

On the downside, you must manually control and monitor these tools apart from your performance test tool. Again, writing scripts to start these monitors and save their data often makes coordinating the data they produce much simpler. Regardless, after collecting this data, you must manually coordinate the performance test results with the data captured by these monitors. Appendix C provides a list of common, free monitoring tools. Chapter 12 also provides example data generated from some of these tools.

Detailed Analysis and Problem Isolation

For many customers, the tools described above provide sufficient monitoring for their performance testing and analysis requirements. However, some sites may require more data and analysis. In these cases, consider purchasing a high-end moni-toring tool to complement your performance test tools.

The design of most high-end monitoring tools focuses on production monitoring and warning. These tools normally watch production systems and issue warnings to a system operator when the machines fail or reach some critical threshold. Not sur-prisingly, these tools usually come with a significant price tag, but if you need advanced monitoring data, you might consider using them to augment your test environment.

These tools provide specialized monitors and allow centralized control of data capture. They also support reporting data from multiple systems. Because they specialize in system monitoring, they frequently provide data not available through the traditional monitoring products and interfaces. Specialized monitoring tools simplify the troubleshooting portion of your test by quickly pinpointing system problems. They also provide useful information for network diagnosis, application server problems, and database issues.

Appendix C provides a list of specialized monitoring tools such as Wily Introscope and Precise Indepth. Both of these vendors provide specialized tools for application servers. These products leverage "byte-code" insertion technology to capture detailed information about the running web applications. They also provide response time data, which allows you to see if a specific EJB or JDBC call invoked by a servlet actually takes most of the overall servlet response time. Such data simplifies problem isolation.

Price and learning curve become limiting factors for monitoring tools. For many test environments, the runtime monitoring provided by a high-end performance test tool provides sufficient information to tune the web site. However, in many cases using the right tool (particularly for very large or complex tests) shortens your test and tuning process, and contributes to significant performance improvements. Before introducing specialized monitoring tools into your test environment, validate that they do not cause a significant performance degradation to your overall system.

Reusability in the Production Environment

When evaluating the monitoring tools for your performance testing, think ahead to the tools and processes planned for your production environment. Your operations team may already use tools to monitor servers. Consider using the same tools for your testing. Conversely, the operations team may rely on you to recommend monitoring products. Having the same capabilities in both environments helps you to establish initial baseline behavior and thresholds for production monitoring.

Buy versus Build

In the early years of web site testing, many organizations often resorted to writing their own test tools. However, a wide variety of excellent free and licensed performance test tools exist today. If the free tools do not meet your needs, we strongly suggest purchasing the level of performance test tool support you require rather than writing your own. If you can't afford these tools, consider leveraging some of the low-cost or free tools with some additional custom code.

However, as your site grows and testing requirements become more sophisticated, you may quickly need the capabilities of a high-end load driver. Your test scripts, automation, and customization represent a significant investment, and switching test tools comes with a much higher price tag than just the cost of the software. Pick a tool that meets your needs for awhile.

In the monitoring space, you need the capabilities that come with the operating system and applications to gather data. Your choice is whether to gather this data manually, through your load driver, or with custom tooling. For simple tests, using the free system and application tools to gather metrics and manually watching and recording the monitoring data typically suffices. If you have many systems under tests or long-running tests, look for a load driver that captures this data across the set of servers, or develop custom tools (usually scripts) to collect and correlate the data.

If you struggle with performance problems in a complex environment, consider investing in specialized monitoring tools, especially for application servers and data-bases. Be sure to invest in training to make the most of these tools. In general, purchasing test tools and investing programming time and resources in your business applications is the right trade-off. However, if you run a lot of tests, consider applying some resource to test automation to simplify execution and analysis.

In the end, select a performance test tool for your budget, but be prepared for a higher price tag than expected, especially if you need advanced runtime or reporting features. Spending in the neighborhood of $100,000 on testing tools seems excessive, but if your production site does not perform under load conditions, the loss of customers and revenue quickly justifies the expense of adequate testing.

Summary

Many people find test tool selection a daunting process. The market contains a variety of excellent tools in a wide range of prices. In this chapter, we covered some of the major selection criteria for performance test tools. We've discussed features such as multiple client controllers, real-time monitoring, and automatic charting. However, the most important consideration is how the tool meets the needs of your test.

Give your tool selection some forethought. Whatever tool you pick represents a significant investment to your organization. Beyond the often considerable price of the tool, your team must devote time to gain skill in using the tool and in building scripts. Pick a tool that will meet your needs as the web site continues to grow.

In Appendix C, we provide a requirements summary chart to help you organize your tool evaluation criteria. After you've narrowed your search, consider evaluating several tools in your test environment to get a better feel for their operation and the reports they produce. In the next chapter, we discuss how to build a good environment for executing your performance test.

Chapter 9
TEST ENVIRONMENT CONSTRUCTION AND TUNING

A good stress test uncovers any problem areas before deploying the web site to production. The time and expense of performance tests pays off in the gains realized in customer satisfaction and overall site reliability. So far, we've discussed building good performance tests for your web site. Now let's cover building a realistic environment in which to run these tests.

In short, you cannot go cheap in building your test environment. Poor infrastructure impacts performance and stress tests more than any other type of tests you'll run against your web site. Don't expect to meet your web site performance goals if you build the test environment with cheap cable, underpowered client machines, and low-bandwidth networks. To get the most out of your performance test efforts, the test environment must mimic the production environment as closely as possible, given the ever-present constraints of time and expense. Obviously, if the web site contains hundreds of servers, you cannot recreate a huge server farm for a performance and stress test. In these cases, scale down the test to a few machines, keeping the scale proportional to the production system. Figure 9.1 shows a typical small test cluster with peripheral systems.

Proportion remains important in "scale environments" in other ways as well. Again, if the 20 machines in the production cluster use 200 database connections, assume that the small cluster of two machines needs 20. The same goes for network bandwidth, test clients, and other resources you might need for the test. Also, when using a smaller environment, keep in mind the behavior of the system at two servers might be drastically different than with twenty. The web site team must test scalability in a small-scale environment.

Of course, the reduced costs of small-scale environments lead to reduced coverage of all the situations your large-scale web site faces in production. If you test with a small-scale environment, you may encounter undiscovered problems when you move to production. In fact, you may encounter problems you can *only* recreate on

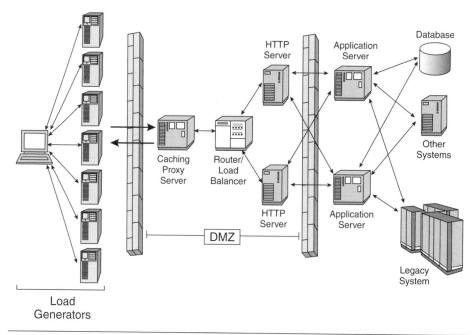

Figure 9.1   An example test environment

the production web site. The best test environment remains a full-scale reproduction of the production web site, whenever possible.

The Network

The network plays an enormous role in performance and stress testing, yet it rarely receives the attention it requires. The network often becomes a hidden source of problems and limitations during the test. Only after days or weeks of fruitless testing and problem resolution of higher-level components does the network come under scrutiny. Consider the network before testing begins. Estimate the amount of data the network must carry and plan sufficient network capacity for testing.

Network Isolation

As always, we want the test network as close as possible to the production setup. However, even if the production environment shares its network with other systems, build an isolated network for the stress and performance testing. Some companies balk at the expense and time that building an isolated network requires. However, without an isolated network, you cannot control the traffic volumes on the network during testing. We're often amazed at some of the traffic moving across an internal network, even during normal business hours. A few of the things we've seen in the field include

- Heavy network traffic from employees connecting to a company-sponsored gaming server
- Network "storms" created by a faulty network card somewhere on the network
- Massive system backups moving across the network for hours at a time.

In short, if you don't control the network, you don't control its traffic, either. Figure 9.2 shows some of the daily network traffic fluctuation factors. Some test teams try to work around this problem by running their tests at night or early in the morning. Sometimes this works, but often they discover their company uses the network 24 hours a day. As mentioned earlier, the networks might be in use at night for large data transfers and backups.

If you must use a non-isolated network, try to set up a network protocol analyzer (more on how these work below) to monitor network traffic volumes. *Before you do this*, check with your corporate network team. Many companies restrict or forbid the use of network protocol analyzers on their networks. And, yes, they can find out if you install one anyway. The best solution remains building an isolated network.

Remember, you need *repeatability* to perform an effective performance and stress test. Some test teams, however, cannot get the same results twice from the same performance test, even if they don't make any adjustments to the system under test. In such an environment, you cannot effectively tune the system. If you make a change, and see better performance, you cannot know if you've found a legitimate improvement or if the environment actually factors in the solution. Testing on an open network introduces more environment variability than you can ever hope to control.

Network isolation is probably one of the most overlooked issues in performance testing, and yet it is one of the most important. If you can't know from one run to the next whether a change made improved things or not, your test dissolves into an exercise in dart-throwing as you struggle to understand your web site bottlenecks and optimal tuning.

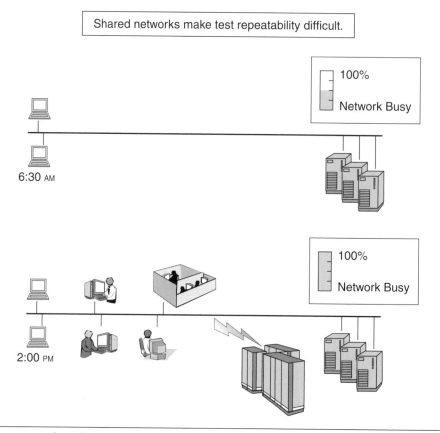

Figure 9.2   Shared network impact

Network Capacity

The network carries all the data for the test (and subsequently for the production environment). You need to do some network capacity planning prior to building the network, and certainly before beginning any tests. The network needs enough capacity to carry the data generated by the test. This begs the question: What data does the test generate, exactly? Here's a list of some common data packages the network handles during a performance test:

- User/server communications
  - User HTTP requests
  - Server HTML responses
  - Embedded HTML page elements, such as *gifs*, *jpegs*, and JavaScript
  - Embedded frame elements (usually resulting in additional page requests)

- Mid-tier (server-to-server) communications
  - HTTP session data sharing within a cluster
  - Application database transfers
  - Traffic to services servers (for example, a stock quote server)
  - Traffic to mail/messaging services
  - LDAP requests/responses
  - DNS requests/responses
- Back-end (server-to-host) communications
  - Host databases transfers
  - Host application communications

Usually the largest network impact comes from a few major sources:

- HTML responses
- Embedded elements such as *gifs* and *jpegs*
- HTTP session data sharing within a cluster
- Application database transfers

However, as we've discussed before, every web site and web application differ. A good understanding of your particular web application, the kinds of pages it returns, and its interactions with other systems helps you put together a reasonable network traffic estimate.

e-Commerce Network Capacity Planning Example

e-Commerce web sites require lots of network bandwidth. As we discussed in Chapter 5, the pages returned by these sites usually contain lots of embedded pictures in the form of *gifs* and *jpegs*. Users browse the pages of the e-Commerce web site and perhaps search for groups of items ("Show me a selection of coffee pots," for example). Because these pages return items the customer probably hasn't seen before, the user's browser does not contain cached copies of the images. To build a network estimate, figure out the average and maximum page size returned to the users. Decide how frequently the maximum page size might go out to the users, and whether it merits special calculation as a worse case scenario. Again, this exercise results in estimates. Use the performance test to validate these estimates.

Let's make the following assumptions about our e-Commerce site:

- Average page size: 45KB
- Maximum page size: 70KB

Let's also assume you want to use a 100Mbps Ethernet network to support the web site. If the web site team hopes to move 100 pages per second through the site at peak (remember, we *always* plan for peak loading), the network receives *sustained* traffic of 4.5MBps.

```
45,000 bytes per page * 100 pages per second = 4.5MBps
```

Note that 4.5MB approaches the upper bound of sustained traffic we consider acceptable for a 100Mbps Ethernet web site. Under ideal conditions, a 100Mbps network could potentially handle 12.5MB of sustained traffic:

```
100Mbps / 8 bits per byte = 12.5MBps
```

However, Ethernet networks lose efficiency because of traffic collisions and retransmissions. Academics tell us to expect an Ethernet to support 66% of its potential capacity, or about 8.3MBps of sustained traffic. For planning purposes, we prefer to use a more conservative estimate of 5MBps of sustained traffic.[1] This allows the network to absorb unexpected traffic spikes. Web sites operating through a switched network are the exception to this rule. A switched network acts as a point-to-point network, which makes it more efficient. When dealing with switched networks, we raise the planning estimate to 8MBps.

The 4.5MBps we estimated above tells us the peak *outbound* traffic on the web site. How much *inbound* traffic does the web site carry? Inbound traffic consists of HTTP requests, which we usually measure in terms of a few bytes. For example, if the average HTTP request requires 100 bytes, the network load generated at peak is

```
100 bytes/request * 100 requests/second = 10KB/second
```

This is less than 1% of the outbound HTML content traffic. Keep in mind that TCP/IP generates lots of overhead packets to support "guaranteed delivery" (a hallmark of the TCP/IP protocol). So, as a rule of thumb, we estimate inbound traffic at about 20% of outbound traffic.[2] In this case, we'll use a planning estimate of

```
4.5MBps * 20% = 900KBps
```

Now, let's consider the transfer of data between the application servers and the application database on the network. Let's assume each user request requires the transfer of 10KB of data from the database. At peak, this gives us the following traffic:

```
10,000 bytes per request * 100 requests per second = 1MBps
```

---

1. Thanks to Carolyn Norton for sharing her expertise in this area.
2. Thanks to Susan Hanis for sharing her TCP/IP expertise here.

If the web site uses HTTP session persistence, we need to account for this traffic as well. If each request generates 1KB of HTTP session traffic, we estimate the following HTTP session burden:

```
1,000 bytes per request * 100 requests per second = 100KBps
```

Lots of installations grossly underestimate the size of the HTTP session data they maintain for each user. Check the HTTP session database, and check the size of the data stored for your users to properly size the average HTTP session. See Chapter 2 for more details on HTTP session management.

Other factors also influence the amount of HTTP session data on your network. HTTP session caching combined with affinity routing reduces the data read from a persistent HTTP session store. On the other hand, if your application server vendor supports a distributed HTTP session scheme, this sometimes generates more network traffic, depending on the implementation.

The network burden estimates so far add up to the following, as shown in Table 9.1.

Table 9.1   Estimated Network Traffic Burden

Data	Network Burden
Outbound HTML/static elements	4.5MBps
Inbound HTTP requests	900KBps
Application data transfer	1MBps
HTTP session data transfer	100KBps
Total	6.5MBps

At 6.5MBps of sustained traffic, this web site exceeds our planning limit of 5MBps for the 100Mbps Ethernet. The web site needs a more sophisticated network plan. We might consider a switched 100Mbps network rated at 8MBps, but this doesn't give the web site a lot of room for growth or for unexpected load peaks. A gigabit network might be a better fit for this web site.

Network Components

Networks consist of more than cable. Any number of switches, routers, load balancers, and other equipment make up the test environment network. The brands and types used largely depend on what's available for the test, as well as company standards. Frequently the test team reuses network equipment from other test projects or receives the equipment as a loan from a production group. Often, the equipment becomes a part of the test network without anyone really understanding how it works or how to configure it properly. The end result is a piece of equipment that may impact web site performance in ways difficult to detect without specialized monitoring equipment and skills.

Keep in mind the following questions when dealing with network components:

- Is the component rated for this network? We regularly find customers trying to use network equipment rated for a 100Mbps network on a gigabit network. Also, your diagnostic equipment, such as network protocol analyzers, may not work with ultra-high-speed networks.
- How was the equipment used previously? Borrowed equipment often contains filters, limits, and other settings still in place from a previous assignment. For example, if you borrow a router previously used in a production web site, its current settings may intentionally limit HTTP connections to a defined maximum. While this protects against denial of service attacks in production, it limits the load you're able to generate against the web site during the test. Review the settings on all equipment to avoid unintentional limitations on performance.
- Does the component support all the features the test environment requires? Routers, load balancers, and other components may or may not have features required by the web site. Know your requirements for key features such as affinity routing and SSL support, and understand how well the equipment supports your desired configuration.

Network Protocol Analyzers and Network Monitoring

A network protocol analyzer monitors traffic flows across a network and allows you to find out exactly how much traffic passes over the network during a test. If permitted, we highly recommend you use a network protocol analyzer to validate the network load during testing. Don't be surprised if your test generates a very different network load than you originally estimated. Often your estimates fail to consider all the factors at play during execution. Also, you may find the page sizes you used for your estimates incorrect.

Network protocol analyzers vary greatly in sophistication and expense. The most expensive network protocol analyzers cost tens of thousands of dollars and work with high-speed networks. These high-end network protocol analyzers usually come with tools for analyzing the network traffic at various levels in the protocol stack. For test teams on a more limited budget, many free or inexpensive network protocol analyzers exist, and they usually run on a machine already connected to the network. They provide limited functionality and don't always work with high-speed networks. However, for providing a gauge of network activity on many classes of networks, these tools work just fine. Just be sure whatever tool you pick works with the network it will monitor. This requires checking the tool's tolerance for network type and network speed. Chapter 12 discusses these tools in more detail, and Appendix C contains a list of some vendors of these products.

Warning: Many companies actively monitor their networks for network protocol analyzer activity. Some companies consider a network protocol analyzer a breech in their security and do not allow them. We've visited companies where using a network protocol analyzer on a company network results in instant job termination. Please take this warning seriously; obtain permission before inserting a network protocol analyzer into a network.

The Servers

The network connects all the components of your web site. Let's next go up a level and consider the server components you need in the test environment.

Application Server Machines

In terms of configuring the web application servers, strive to make the test configuration as close to the deployment configuration as possible. If you're deploying to a farm of four-way Sun machines with 8GB of RAM, you should use the same equipment during your testing, if at all possible.

Even though the Java web application server might port to different platforms, web applications do not perform and scale the same on a one-way NT box as on a four-way Sun box. If you must choose between fewer servers for your test or smaller servers, pick fewer servers. When you use fewer servers, scale the other components of the test (databases, HTTP servers, and so on) proportionally as well.

If you deploy the web application on multiple machines in a cluster, then test on multiple machines in a cluster as well. Get a representative number: If you plan to deploy on more than four machines, test on more than two. If your target environment contains eight application server machines or more, then four application servers in your test environment should suffice, as long as you scale the rest of the test web site proportionally to match.

We often encounter test teams trying to test and tune all the software used in their web site (application servers, databases, HTTP servers, etc.) on a single machine. However, this technique doesn't work if the production web site actually uses multiple machines. For example, many production web sites separate their HTTP servers

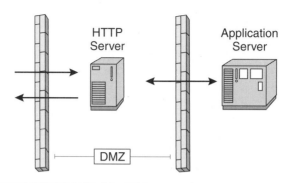

Figure 9.3   Typical DMZ configuration for application servers

from their application servers. Often the production team places the HTTP servers in a DMZ with firewalls in front and behind, as shown in Figure 9.3. It is impossible to successfully performance test for this configuration with a single server machine. If the web site uses SSL, for example, the HTTP server needs so much CPU for encryption/decryption that it chokes the performance of the application server.

Database Servers

Most production web sites use mid-tier database servers to hold application data or data specific to the web site (such as an HTTP session database). Often the web applications access these databases on every user request. Despite their central role in the operation of the web site, the mid-tier databases sometimes receive little or no tuning before the site enters production deployment. Often the test team lacks the database administrator (DBA) skills required to tune the database properly. Thus the team ignores the database unless they stumble across a specific problem in production. The problems we see frequently with databases usually fall into one of two broad categories: Poor software configuration or poor hardware configuration.

Poor Database Software Configuration: Indexing

By far the biggest database tuning problem we encounter is poor table indexing. Usually the problem starts this way: The test team receives a database backup from the production database staff. They dutifully load the database definition and the data itself, but never bother to build indexes for the tables they've just loaded. In fact, they may not even know what an index is, much less how to build one. Chapter 6 discusses how to put together the performance test team, including DBA skills needed to tune environments using databases.

The index allows the database software to find elements in a table without scanning the table repeatedly. This saves tremendous amounts of resource, particularly CPU. Also worth noting, the DBA may build new indexes and remove old ones as usage patterns change over time. New indexes apply even when web applications use existing databases. Often these databases contain indexes tailored for existing applications, but they might require new ones to better support the web application. By monitoring database reports, the DBA determines the web application's usage patterns and makes appropriate adjustments. The DBA may also review the SQL used in the web application to find out where indexes might be most beneficial.

Poor Database Software Configuration: Internal Resources

Web applications receive many simultaneous requests. In turn, they make a proportionally large number of simultaneous requests to the database servers supporting them. These database servers need enough resources to support large volumes of simultaneous requests. These resources include things such as buffer pools, cursors, and sockets to support high-bandwidth operation.

Regrettably, we often see high-concurrency web sites struggling to pull data from databases tuned for small, fat client applications. New applications and usage patterns require a fresh look at the tuning parameters for the database. Do not assume the database is tuned properly because the DBA made a few tweaks some years ago for the usage patterns of a fat client application.

Poor Database Software Configuration: Caching

Particularly for sites with enormous application databases, the database cache becomes very important for optimal site performance. The cache holds the results of the most common queries and makes an impact on sites with large catalogs of items but a few frequently accessed "best sellers." These items return from the cache quickly without an expensive retrieval from the hard disk.

Caching helps some web sites, but a few cannot take advantage of this feature. For example, if every query submitted by the web site is unique (if, say, every query contained the user's account number), the cache may not return a hit even though the query may return items retrieved many times before. The web site team might want to work with the DBA to build queries better able to use the caching mechanisms available.

Poor Database Hardware Configuration: I/O Management

Eventually, all databases interact with the hard disks to read or write data. Database tuning often focuses on the CPU required by the database server without focusing on how to manage the storage required by the same database. We sometimes see very large multiple-processor database machines spending most of their time waiting to access one tiny hard disk. Adding CPU does not solve disk I/O problems.

If the database server spends most of its time waiting to read or write from the disk, tune the I/O resources. If the database supports it, try adding a multiplatter disk array to the database server. By using multiple disks, the database spreads out the read and write operations for better simultaneous access. The database reads and writes spread out across multiple points rather than queuing up on a single disk. Figure 9.4 shows an example using multiple disk platters.

Likewise, the hard disks themselves often contain tunable features. Some disks allow the system administrator to specify buffering to the disk, which may also improve

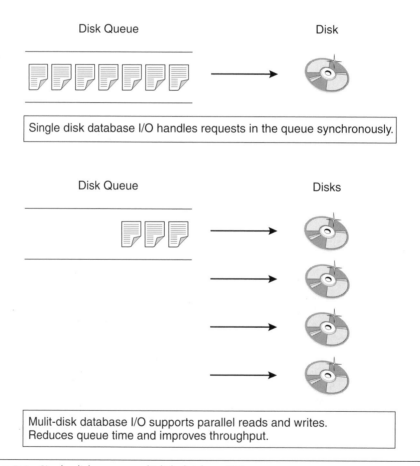

Figure 9.4   Single-disk versus multidisk database I/O

performance. Some databases write more efficiently to disk than even the native file system itself. For example, IBM's DB2® database product provides mechanisms for "raw" I/O management (DB2 bypasses the file system to write directly to the disk) and for multidisk data writing.

Finally, when spreading the data to multiple hard disks, don't forget about the database logs. Databases keep detailed logs for rollback and recovery purposes. Every action taken by the database must be logged, and this requires a write to the hard disk. "Striping" these logs across multiple hard disks, if supported by the database, often improves disk I/O wait times.

Legacy Servers

Legacy servers and their applications present daunting challenges to web site test teams. First, the legacy system usually resides beyond the control of your test team, on a host machine somewhere. (The system may not even reside in the same state as the test team!) Secondly, customers and internal user applications run against the legacy systems during the day and sometimes even during nighttime hours. Finally, these systems require tuning, just like the web application and web site, particularly if the system doesn't currently support a high-volume, multi-threaded application.

The first issue, *access*, requires teamwork to resolve. You need help from the teams supporting the legacy systems to collect performance statistics during the test runs. Also, since the test team usually does not have the skills necessary to tune the legacy systems, you need the legacy support team available to make any tuning adjustments on these systems. We frequently encounter teams attempting a test using legacy systems without assistance from the legacy support team. Invariably, these tests fail because the test team cannot on their own find and resolve bottlenecks on these systems.

The support teams also come in handy to resolve the next issue: *scheduling*. Do not run performance tests against a legacy system in use by customers or in-house applications. Performance tests, by their nature, attempt to drive resources involved in the test to their full utilization. For example, if the web site makes use of a host database shared by multiple applications, the performance test might drive the database to 100% utilization, effectively locking the other applications out of the database. Figure 9.5 illustrates this point.

The legacy system, however, might be available in the evenings or late at night. Many test teams use these off-shift hours to run performance tests against web sites using these systems. This solution works well if you keep a couple of points in mind.

- The tests cannot run unattended. Despite the impact on your social life, performance testing requires many, small iterations to obtain measurements and make tuning adjustments. You also need assistance during these runs from the legacy support team to monitor their systems and make necessary performance adjustments. Later, after finalizing the key performance adjustments, the subsequent long run and stability tests, happily, run overnight with little human intervention.
- Know your legacy system backup and maintenance schedules. Again, the support teams for the legacy system play a big role in obtaining this information. The legacy systems frequently use the nighttime hours for system maintenance and backups. The performance test cannot run during these operations: Backups and maintenance take lots of system resource and result in abnormal readings for the performance test.

  Before scheduling an off-shift test, discuss the maintenance schedule with the legacy support team to either fit the test into an existing schedule or to modify the schedule to fit the test. Also, be aware of maintenance on other systems with the potential to impact the test environment. For example, a system backup crossing the network might disrupt your testing.
- Sometimes you cannot run tests against the production legacy system at any time. If this is the case, consider rebuilding the legacy system inside a test system.

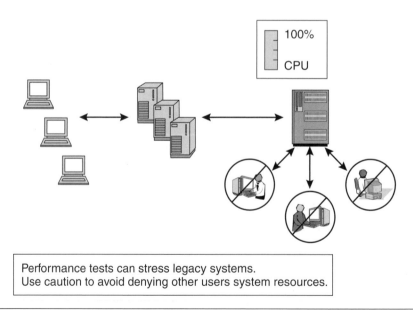

Performance tests can stress legacy systems.
Use caution to avoid denying other users system resources.

Figure 9.5   Testing live legacy systems

Finally, tuning the web application requires tuning the legacy system to which it connects. When visiting web site teams testing web applications using legacy systems, we commonly encounter the following problems:

- The web site generates more traffic than ever seen before at the legacy system. Remember, a lot of legacy systems exist to support fat client applications. These applications generate less traffic than a popular public web site. The legacy system needs tuning to support such a site, and a good performance test normally brings this issue to light. Legacy application tuning tasks fall into the following general areas:
  - Adding connections to handle the large number of simultaneous requests from the web applications.
  - Providing a larger region for the legacy application to execute.
  - Increasing memory buffers for the internals of the applications (particularly important for database applications).
  - Adding processing capacity. Sometimes the increased burden on the host system warrants additional processing capacity.
- The connection software used by the web application also frequently requires tuning. Here's a list of some of the problems we run into regularly with connection software:
  - The connection software needs more bandwidth. The software often requires adjustment to support the large number of simultaneous connections the web application requires.
  - Home-grown connection software designed for a fat client application does not usually work for a web application. Most web applications run as multi-threaded applications. They need the ability to send multiple, simultaneous requests to the back-end legacy host system, something most fat client applications don't require. Often the web site team discovers too late that their custom connection software isn't thread safe for multi-threaded access. Whenever possible, we recommend using commercially available connection software. Otherwise, check the connection software early on for thread safeness.

Production web sites often use back-end legacy systems. Most of the problems we encounter with these systems during performance tests find their roots in a lack of communication between the web site team and the legacy support teams. The legacy support team belongs in the planning and tuning effort for every web site using the resources under their care.

Host Database

Host databases share all the problems of other common legacy systems, as well as a few unique issues. Many host databases contain huge amounts of data and support multiple applications. The company cannot afford to use these production databases to support a performance test. This leaves you with the problem of replicating a massive database for performance testing. Of course, the performance test works best when it runs against the full database. Some databases, however, contain terabytes of data and use many, massive disk farms to contain everything. You cannot afford to move the full contents of these databases to the test environment.

For extremely large databases, you require a working subset of the data in the test environment. Taking a meaningful subset of a monster database requires skill, as the data tends to be intertwined with cross-references. Taking a sample indiscriminately often results in data the web application cannot use: The cross-references the web application seeks in the data do not exist in the sample. The sample must also be large enough to generate the proper behavior from the database. An undersized sample, for instance, might be largely held in the database's cache, resulting in overly optimistic database response times.

Also, coordinate your test scripts with the sample data. If you create the scripts using the full database, make sure the data referenced by these scripts exists in the sample as well. For example, if the script tries to purchase a toaster not available in the test database, the script fails.

Finally, apply the key tuning parameters of the production database to your test database, as appropriate. These include things like buffer sizes, indexes, and connection settings. Since your sample database represents a scaled-down model of the production database, scale the tuning parameters as appropriate for the sample.

The Load Generators

Load generators (part of a performance test tool, as discussed in Chapter 8) generate the test environment "traffic." A performance test requires hundreds or thousands of users to simulate production conditions. The load generator uses prewritten test scripts to simulate the users and their activities at the web site. Generating large numbers of "virtual users" requires the right supporting equipment. In the field, we often find test teams running expensive, state-of-the-art performance test tools on old, underpowered PCs retrieved from storage. Without sufficient supporting equipment, the best tools on the market cannot generate sufficient load to properly test the web site. If the load generator cannot provide sufficient load to the web site, the web site never achieves the target throughput. Often the test team misreads the symptoms of this condition and spends weeks tuning the web site when, in fact, they need to add capacity to the load generator machines.

Likewise, the test team needs a network analysis of the traffic generated by each client machine. This includes inbound and outbound requests, just as we discussed earlier in this chapter. The traffic generated by the test tools sometimes overloads the network subnet supporting the client machines. Also, the traffic burden sometimes overloads the network cards in individual client machines.

In short, take the load generator environment seriously. The load generator requires more capacity than most teams originally estimate. If the client machines reach 75% CPU utilization or the network traffic passes the safety threshold, increase capacity on these devices. You cannot drive load against your web site if the load cannot make it to the intended servers.

Master/Slave Configurations

Many industrial performance tools use the master-slave test configuration, shown in Figure 9.6. The "master" machine manages each test and collects data. The "slaves" actually manage the threads and sockets representing the virtual users, and run the corresponding test scripts. For extremely small configurations (10 to 20 virtual users), the master and slave both run on the same machine. However, for larger tests, the master runs on a different machine, with one or more slaves also running on different boxes.

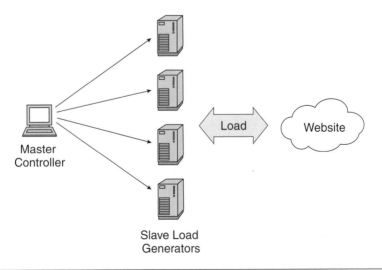

Figure 9.6   Master/slave load generator configuration

The best practices to remember with a master/slave configuration include the following:

- Keep traffic between the master and slaves to a minimum. Many performance test tools allow the test manager to define the frequency with which updates and status travel between the slave and the master. If you're using a new performance test tool for this first time, use a protocol analyzer to determine the actual network burden on the client subnet.
- The master (also known as the "controller" or "coordinator" machine) often requires less CPU capacity than the slave machines. Conversely, if it stores reports for the test cluster, it may require a larger hard drive than a slave machine.
- Watch the CPU on *all* test machines during the performance test. If CPU utilization exceeds 75%, the machine needs more capacity.
- Watch the logs and hard disk on the client machines. Often the clients accumulate large log files and pass these logs back to the master after the test completes. Frequent logging, of course, increases the disk I/O burden for the client machine and impacts testing. Likewise, if these logs accumulate over time, the client machines may not have enough room for subsequent runs. Before starting a run, make sure the client machines contain sufficient free disk space for any logging they may perform.
- Recycle the machines frequently. The slaves and the controller sometimes throw odd errors or stop responding after several testing cycles. In general, we find it best to recycle the test machines once or twice a day during periods of extended testing.
- Try to keep the test slave hardware homogenous. Often, because of load balancing techniques, one or two client machines may drive all the load a server in a clustered environment receives. If the test cluster contains one machine significantly more powerful than the others, some servers in the web site cluster may not achieve full loading.
- It's often useful to simulate traffic from a number of different client IP addresses, especially when performing a test that utilizes an IP sprayer in front of several HTTP servers. Web sites often configure IP sprayers for affinity routing between the incoming user and a particular sever in the cluster.

    You need sufficient test client machines, NICs, and supporting performance test software to make IP affinity work during your testing. See Chapter 8 for more details.

After the Performance Test

Many companies treat the performance test environment as a transient entity. The environment exists for a few weeks to test the performance and scalability of the web site. Afterward, the team pulls the test environment apart and uses the components to build other test environments or sends the equipment to production. This works well for most test scenarios, but major production web sites often require a permanent, separate test environment. A permanent test environment allows you to

- Safely test new features and bug fixes prior to their introduction into the production web site.
- Recreate problems seen on the production site without using production resources. Because of the multi-threaded nature of web applications, some problems only appear under load conditions. You need a reliable test environment to find these problems.

At a minimum, keep enough test client capacity to stress at least one production server. These clients may reside either with the test environment, if one exists, or may be a part of the production environment. Ideally, configure these clients to drive load in either the production or test environment, if needed.

Few companies dedicate test machines to a particular web site or web application, but this increases another risk: If you run into a problem in production, you don't have machines set aside where you can immediately try to reproduce the situation. The problem determination cycle often takes much longer when you can only work with the problem in production. Having available machines dedicated to testing and problem determination often makes it simpler and cheaper to recreate and debug production problems.

Hardware and Test Planning

Many teams bring all of their hardware online and start testing. Invariably, they experience performance problems and spend lots of time trying to isolate the components or applications contributing to the bottleneck. A better approach calls for bringing hardware components into the test systematically to gauge the performance impact of each piece of equipment.

We recommend limiting the hardware involved in early phases of testing. The first step in the test might be a network performance test, as shown in Figure 9.7. If the tester sends a file from the HTTP server to the application server via FTP, does it take more or less time than sending it from the application server to a legacy system? This simple test validates the network across multiple points, and it can be very important if multiple network segments are engaged in your environment.[3]

---

3. Thanks again to Susan Hanis for her networking expertise.

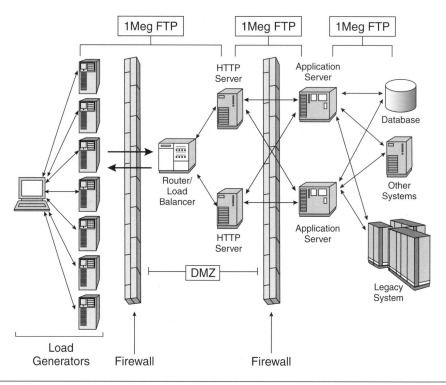

Figure 9.7   Testing the networks with FTP

Next, bring an HTTP server and an application server on-line for testing. Initially, consider stubbing out calls to mid-tier and legacy databases, or use test script primitives (as discussed in Chapter 7) to test only HTTP and servlet function without exercising the back-end systems. (Figure 9.8 outlines a progressive performance test strategy using a typical test environment.)

Add these systems into the mix only when you're certain of the soundness of the HTTP server and application server configuration. After successfully testing and tuning a single HTTP server and application server with the back-end systems, add multiple HTTP servers and application servers to the cluster to test scalability. Next, increase the complexity of the test by turning on the firewalls and, later, the reverse proxy server. At this point, you might decide to exercise the SSL portions of the web application using test scripts.

This approach allows you to bring hardware into the test in a layered fashion. Key components come into the test, receive intense test scrutiny and tuning, and, as a result, stabilize. Of course, this technique requires planning. Plan the network

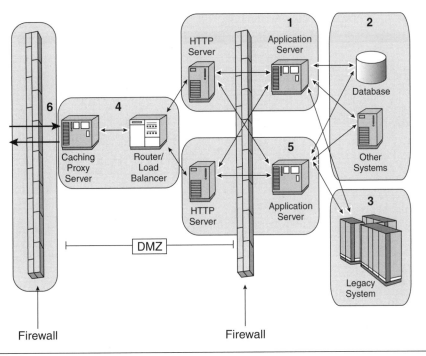

Figure 9.8   One possible test ordering for a large test environment

topology carefully to support easy removal and addition of key components. In the long run, you benefit by understanding the performance impact of each piece of hardware used in the web site.

Summary

This chapter covered some test environment planning basics like using an isolated network to ensure repeatability. We walked through an example of how to develop network capacity estimates for your web site and test environment, and how to scale a test and still accurately predict how your production web site will behave. We also discussed hardware and software tuning issues common to database servers, test clients, application servers and other key web site components. This chapter also recommended a strategy for progressively performance testing these components.

All the setup in the world won't help you if you schedule your test while some of your legacy or database systems are under load or offline for maintenance. Be alert to the production and maintenance schedules of the components of your test environment. In addition to systems, you need to make sure that the right people are available to assist with monitoring and tuning during the test.

The next chapter marks the beginning of a three-part case study. The example in this study combines many of the topics covered so far and provides concrete examples for their application.

Chapter 10

CASE STUDY: PREPARING TO TEST

Case Study Assumptions

This case study examines a portion of the performance test cycle for a fictitious e-Commerce company. We decided to use an e-Commerce web site for several reasons.

- The high graphical content of their pages tends to stress the network.
- Many retail sites receive sustained bursts of traffic at the holiday season, which requires us to plan for these peak load periods.
- These sites tend toward higher complexity with various databases on the back end and some special servers to assist with graphic content on the front end.

In short, e-Commerce web sites give us the broadest demonstration of the concepts we discuss in the book.

We decided to make our fictional e-Commerce company fairly large. As you'll notice when you read the case study, our fictional retailer receives 100,000 users per day during the peak season. That's a significant amount of traffic for an e-Commerce retailer, and does not apply to most of the e-Commerce sites we see. On the other hand, 100,000 user visits per day is not the largest site we've ever encountered, and certainly does not put our fictional web site among the Internet's heavy hitters.

A large web site allows us to better demonstrate some of the techniques of test planning more thoroughly (and on a grand scale). It also allows us to illustrate a very important point: Don't be afraid of large numbers. You can develop manageable and correct performance tests, even for large web sites. This case study addresses the highlights of a performance test cycle. Obviously, we can't cover every potential issue, or even address in depth some of the issues our fictional team uncovers. However the case study gives you a feel for an actual test cycle.

Fictional Customer: TriMont Mountain Outfitters

TriMont Mountain Outfitters operates the premiere whitewater supply company in the southeastern United States. The company owns a dozen or so retail outlets, but the bulk of their sales comes from catalog orders. In recent years, TriMont expanded their product offerings to include men and women's outdoor clothing, camping supplies, and, oddly enough, a range of gourmet cookware.

TriMont ventured into e-Commerce two years ago with a CGI-based web site. Sadly, this site often experienced outages and unacceptable response times during the peak shopping season. They've decided to move to a Java application server and give their site a fresh look. The IT shop wrote the servlets and JSPs for the web site, and now they're ready to begin their performance testing.

Given their history with the old web site, they want to put the new site through a rigorous performance test before releasing the site to the public. Because the TriMont Mountain web site team lacks strong testing skills, they asked you to act as their performance consultant during the testing. They need help throughout the performance testing life cycle: planning, setting up the environment, and testing. Also, when they find performance issues during the testing, they anticipate requiring your help to resolve them. They've done very little at this point, except buy an introductory copy of a test tool with a 500 virtual user license.

An Introduction to the TriMont Web Site

The new Java-based web site contains basic e-Commerce features such as the following:

- View items by category
- Various search functions
- Shopping cart
- Order status
- Account information

The new site has some features the TriMont team hopes will give them an edge over their competition:

- Boat Selector—Select your favorite river, and this feature shows you a selection of boats suited for that river's specific conditions.

- River Conditions applet—Viewer specifies a list of rivers, and the applet displays the current conditions at those locations (river height, temperature, wind speed, and so on).

Site Requirements

Here are a few site requirements the TriMont team shares on your first consulting visit:

- Based on the traffic to their existing web site, they expect the new site to get about 100,000 users per day (the clothing and gourmet cookware generate a lot of interest in the site) during the peak days of the Christmas shopping season.
- They estimate the user visit to last seven minutes.
- TriMont hopes 5% of users actually make purchases.
- Response time for any page must be under five seconds, even at peak.
- They expect significant activity on the new site 24 hours a day.

Initial Assessment

What do you know about the site at this point, and what do you need to create a more complete plan? Surprisingly, even at this point, you know a great deal about the site's key performance stress points.

The e-Commerce Profile

The TriMont Mountain site fits the pattern of the classic e-Commerce site covered in Chapter 5. You assume the TriMont performance test needs to focus on the following performance pressure points:

- *Concurrent users*: Notice that TriMont expects the average user to remain on the site seven minutes. Again, e-Commerce sites often experience user visits of several minutes as users look at items in the online catalog. This is an average, and some of their users visit for much longer. The company plans to keep its HTTP session timeout at 30 minutes, allowing customers to browse leisurely without risking session loss.
- *Transaction rate*: During peak season, e-Commerce sites serve up lots of pages to their visitors. The site needs to support this high transaction rate while satisfying the maximum response time requirement. (The TriMont

team, as we know, expects 100,000 user visits per day. This results, as we'll see later, in many more page requests during the peak day.)

- *Response time:* As with all web sites, response time is critical for e-Commerce sites. If visitors become frustrated by slow response time, they leave. This costs the company business and goodwill with their customers. Again, Tri-Mont wants to keep response time under five seconds, even during peak loading.

Also, as we discussed in Chapter 5, e-Commerce sites typically generate large pages, which usually contain lots of *gifs, jpegs,* and other static elements.

Peak Site Users

TriMont doesn't provide much detailed information about its peak loading. At this point, we recommend using the information you have to generate some rough estimates. This first estimate gives you a frame of reference for any other numbers you might receive during the planning phase. For example, you often receive peak load estimates from different sources inside the company. The marketing team might develop one projection for the peak hour, while the web master for the existing CGI web site might produce completely different numbers. A rough estimate gives you a starting point for comparing disparate requirements.

We'll fill in the Capacity Sizing worksheet from Appendix A as we go along. Table 10.1 shows the data that is currently available.

Begin by obtaining a rough estimate of the peak load relative to the average daily load. For example, you might estimate the user arrival rate in the peak hour at five times the rate in an average hour:

```
100,000 users/day / 8-hour day ➔ 3.5 users/second (average load)

3.5 users/sec * 5 (peak versus average load)
= 17.5 users/second (peak adjusted)
```

Normally we'd recommend a "three times" estimate for an e-Commerce peak hour. However, the previous TriMont web site experienced serious performance problems. The company wants to be very conservative with its estimates because of these problems and allow plenty of what seems to be excess capacity.

Notice also that the example uses 8 hours for the load distribution, not 24, despite the customer's stated expectations. Few web sites actually receive large volumes of

Table 10.1 Capacity Sizing Worksheet, Initial Input Data

	Input Data (estimates)	Source of Data	Your Data
1.	Number of user visits (day)	Marketing team	100,000

Note, if you cannot estimate 2, provide estimates for 3 and 4 below.

	Input Data (estimates)	Source of Data	Your Data
2.	Percentage of daily users arriving in peak hour	Estimate	Unknown

Note, provide 3 and 4 below only if you did not know 2.

	Input Data (estimates)	Source of Data	Your Data
3.	Number of hours per day site is actively used (load distribution time)	Estimate provided by marketing team (when in doubt use 8 hours)	8 hr
4.	Peak load increase over normal hour	Estimate (typically between 3 and 5)	5

5–7 must be provided to calculate throughput from user visits. (Items 6 and 7 appear in Table 10.3.)

	Input Data (estimates)	Source of Data	Your Data
5.	Average user visit time	Marketing team	7 min

traffic overnight. You need to confirm this with the customer at your planning meeting, but 8 hours results in a more conservative estimate. Given these assumptions, the example leads you to the following peak hour traffic:

```
17.5 users/second * 60 seconds/minute * 60 minutes/hour
= 63,000 users/hour
```

In other words, almost two-thirds of the daily traffic arrives during the peak hour. In our experience, this seems high for this type of site, but again, given the problems with the old site, this might be a reasonable peak estimate.

Using the peak users per hour, you next determine how many users are on the system during any seven-minute interval (this is the average user visit):

```
17.5 users/second * 60 seconds/minute * 7 minutes (average user visit)
= 7,350 users
```

At the peak hour, you estimate the site contains about 7,350 concurrent users. Note this number does not account for HTTP session timeout. This merely tells us how many people interact with the system during the time of an average user visit. Table 10.2 shows the peak calculations using the worksheet.

Table 10.2   Capacity Sizing Worksheet, Peak Load Calculations

	Calculated Data	Equation	Total (per hr)	Total (per min)	Total (per sec)
If you have data for 3 and 4, use the following calculations					
9.	Number of user visits adjusted for length of day	Number of user visits/Web site day Line 1 / Line 3	100,000 visits/day / 8 hr = 12,500 visits/hr	12,500 visits hr / 60 min = 210 visits/min	210 visits/min / 60 sec = 3.5 visits/sec
10.	Number of user visits adjusted for peak load	Number of user visits/day * Peak load factor Line 9 * Line 4	12,500 visits/hr * 5 peak adjustment = 63,000 visits/hr (peak)	1,050 visits/min (peak)	17.5 visits/sec (peak)
Do the following calculations. Use the value from line 8 (optional) or line 10.					
11.	User arrival rate (new users per time unit)	User arrival rate = Line 8 or Line 10	63,000 visits/hr (peak)	1,050 visits/min (peak)	17.5 visits/sec (peak)
12.	Concurrent users	User arrival rate * User visit time Line 11 * Line 5	Not typically used	1,050 visits/min* 7 min = 7,350 concurrent users (peak)	Not typically used

Next Steps

You need additional information to build a good performance test with this customer. You make plans to visit the customer again to discuss the test plan with the team leaders and their management. Prior to your visit, you request the following information from the customer:

- The data you need for a network analysis
  - Typical outbound page size.
  - How many pages does the average user visit in seven minutes?
  - How big are other elements such as applets and JavaScript?
  - How frequently are these elements accessed?
  - Size of any other data moving across the network (for example, database transfers).
- Components
  - Does the application server vendor have any capacity estimates to help the customer select a server for the test?
  - A list of other components involved in the test (databases, HTTP servers, weather servers, shipping company servers, and so on).
  - How big are the databases involved? Where are they located? Is this a production database?

- Visit patterns
  - What do the users do on the site?
  - Can the customer provide a breakdown of the frequency of certain activities (for example, 75% browse, 2% check their order status, and so on).
  - How frequently is the applet requested? How much traffic does it generate?
- Miscellaneous
  - Do they use HTTP sessions? How big are they?
  - Does the site use SSL? If so, list the functions covered by SSL.
  - What security functions does the site use? If they call an LDAP server on every request, this adds time and network traffic to our totals. (For the sake of simplicity, we did not add any security issues to the numbers in the case study.)

Also, now is a good time to discuss issues like high availability for the web site. Should you plan for session failover? What about redundant hardware and networks?

Detailed TriMont Web Site Planning Estimates

The TriMont web site team reviewed your list of questions, and provided additional information prior to your second visit.

- A user averages five pages per visit.
- The average page size is about 60KB and contains 15 static elements.
- The catalog database contains about 1M items and is located on a mainframe.
  - The average catalog database request returns 2KB of data.
  - Ninety percent of page hits touch the catalog data.
- The order system contains about 50,000 active orders during the peak shopping season (it takes about a week to ship the order and have it delivered to the customer). The order system database is on a mid-tier UNIX machine.
  - The team expects about 3% of a day's users to check order status.
  - The order system also connects to the shipping company's site via a URL link on TriMont's site.
- The account database contains 17M accounts and is located on the mainframe.
  - The team expects 2% of a day's users to check their accounts.
- The River Conditions applet updates its condition information every 15 minutes. The condition information is only a few hundred bytes, at most, so we consider its overall effect on the traffic negligible. Other applet information of interest:
  - The applet is 750K.
  - The team guesses about 10% of the daily users load the applet.
  - The traffic from the applet to the server is included in the daily figures.

- TriMont's Boat Selector function uses a special local application database kept on a mid-tier UNIX system. The database is about 20KB in size, and it references catalog items kept in the host catalog database.
  - Boat Selector receives about 15% of the day's user traffic.
  - Each query returns an average of 1K.
- The site only uses SSL if the user does one of the following:
  - The user enters the Purchase sequence.
  - The user checks private information, such as his account.
- The average HTTP session size is 2K per user.
  - User sessions time out after 30 minutes.
  - Users have a logout function that immediately destroys the HTTP session object.
- Your question about failover struck a chord with the TriMont team.
  - They are very interested in setting up the site for failover.
  - Their application server shares HTTP session data between servers by using a common HTTP session database.
  - They want a minimum of two servers to provide failover capability, whether or not the expected load actually requires multiple servers.

Now that you have some more information about the site, you may run some additional estimates prior to your follow-up visit with the customer. Let's begin with the throughput calculations to complete the Capacity Sizing worksheet, and then we'll move on to the network analysis. Table 10.3 shows the remaining input data for the Capacity Sizing worksheet.

Table 10.3 Capacity Sizing Worksheet, Remaining Input Data

6.	Average pages per visit	Marketing team	5
7.	Average static elements per page	Web site application architect	15

Calculating Throughput (Page Rate and Request Rate)

Page Rate

The customer tells us the average user views five pages during her visit. Let's use this number to determine how many pages per second the site must serve at peak. The peak page rate calculation looks like this:

```
Users arriving/hour * Pages each user requests / minutes/hour /
seconds/hour = Page arrival rate/second

63,000 users/hour * 5 pages/user visit ➔ 87.5 pages/second
```

Network Traffic Mix

TriMont told you something very interesting about its web pages: Each page contains 15 static elements, on average. So, for every page the site returns, the browser asks for 15 static elements from the site to complete the page. At peak, the site receives the following request burden:

```
87.5 pages/second * 15 static requests/page
= 1,312.5 static requests/second
```

Assuming the pages don't contain framesets (which might result in multiple dynamic calls), each page request results in a call to one dynamic element, such as a servlet or JSP. This means the site takes the following total request rate during peak:

```
1,312.5 static requests/second + 87.5 dynamic requests/second
= 1,400 total requests/second
```

You might encourage this customer to consider a caching proxy server for the static content, as we discussed in Chapter 3. Such a server might improve the overall performance of the web site by returning static elements more quickly to the users.

Table 10.4 shows the completed throughput section of the Capacity Sizing worksheet.

Table 10.4 Capacity Sizing Worksheet, Throughput

	Calculated Data	Equation	Total (per hr)	Total (per min)	Total (per sec)
13.	Throughput: page rate	User arrival rate * Average pages/visit Line 11 * Line 6	63,000 visitors/hr * 5 pages/visit = 315,000 pages/hr	5,250 pages/min	87.5 pages/sec
14.	Throughput: requests	Dynamic page rate + Average static elements/dynamic page * Page rate Line13 + (Line7 * Line13)	Not typically used	Not typically used	87.5 dynamic page/sec + 87.5 pages/sec * 15 static elements/page = 1,400 total hits/sec

Network Analysis

Now let's complete a rough network analysis as described in Chapter 9. For this example, we'll go through the steps; later we'll show you how to use the Network Capacity worksheet in Appendix A to build the estimate. This example assumes that all of the components of network traffic (outbound, inbound, database transfers, and so on) share the same network at some point. Some web sites use different networks for inbound versus outbound traffic. Likewise, database traffic sometimes moves on a separate network as well. In practice, you need to consider the size of data elements sharing the same network in order to size the network in question.

Always use peak load for your estimates. You must build a site capable of handling the largest anticipated traffic volume.

Calculating Network Analysis Components

Most networks rate their transmission capabilities in terms of the bits or bytes per second they transmit. Therefore, we need to break our data into bytes and focus on reducing our data to the peak second.

User Arrival Rate

A key estimate required for subsequent network analysis calculations is the user arrival rate. This estimate tells us how many users come onto the site during any given second in the peak hour. On some sites, the user's first page request "weighs" more than subsequent visits. For example, the user might trigger a download of a frameset, JavaScript, or graphics on her first visit. The browser caches this information for subsequent requests, so the subsequent requests generate less network traffic. In addition, the server sets up HTTP session data and perhaps retrieves preference data from a database on the first viewed page.

For this site, we know some users make use of a heavyweight applet. We need the user arrival rate for later estimates involving the impact of this applet on the network traffic. If you didn't do this calculation before, the user arrival rate in seconds is

```
Users arriving at the peak hour / Minutes/hour / Seconds/minute
= User arrival rate/second

63,000 users at peak/hour ➔ 17.5 users/second
```

The input data for the Network Capacity Sizing worksheet is shown in Table 10.5.

Table 10.5   Network Capacity Worksheet, Input Data

	Input Data	Source of Data	Your Data
1.	Average page size (bytes)	Web application architect	60KB
2.	Maximum page size (bytes)	Web application architect	(NA)
3.	Requests per second	Appendix A: Capacity Sizing worksheet	87.5
4.	User arrival rate per second	Appendix A: Capacity Sizing worksheet	17.5
5.	Average bytes of application data transfer per request (i.e., from database)	Web application architect	2KB for catalog; 1K for Boat Selector data

Table 10.5 Network Capacity Worksheet, Input Data (Continued)

	Input Data	Source of Data	Your Data
6.	Percent of requests requiring data transfer	Web application	90%
7.	HTTP session size (only if shared session is used)	Web application architect	2KB
8.	Size of applets	Web application architect	750KB
9.	Percentage of user requests requiring applet download	Web application architect/marketing	10%

Outbound Sustained Traffic

First, let's look at the traffic generated by the page requests. As we discussed in Chapter 5, e-Commerce sites typically do not benefit significantly from browser caching. Thus, let's assume most of the data on each page requires loading on each request. The calculation in this case looks as follows:

```
Page rate * Average page size = Bytes/second

87.5 pages/second * 60KB/page = 5.25MB/second
```

Inbound Sustained Traffic

Outbound traffic is always larger than the inbound request traffic. As a generalization, we assume inbound traffic at 20% of the outbound traffic. For an e-Commerce web site, this might be a bit generous, given the overall size of the pages, but we *always* prefer to overestimate rather than underestimate. (Slightly too much capacity is less problematic than slightly insufficient capacity.) This is our estimate for inbound traffic in this case:

```
Outbound sustained traffic * 20% = Inbound traffic/second

5.25MB/second * 20% = 1.05MB/second
```

Database Transfer

We must consider other data moving in the network as well, such as data returned from application databases, in our calculations. The customer tells us the database returns about 2KB of data. About 90% of the site's requests generate a database call. The database transfer calculation looks like this:

```
Page rate * Data retrieved/page * Weighting factors = Bytes from db/second

87.5 pages/second * 2KB/page * 90% = 157.5KB/second
```

Notice that TriMont did not provide any information about the database transfers from the account and order databases. These data transfers may be very small relative to other traffic (such as the outbound HTML pages), but you need to verify this with the customer at your next meeting.

HTTP Session Transfer

The customer wants to use a database for HTTP session failover purposes. For this calculation, we like to assume the full contents of the HTTP session transfers between the application server and the persistent HTTP session database. This transfer occurs on every request, depending on the customer's application's characteristics.

We also assume some type of caching mechanism at the server, so we do not consider a round trip for this information in our calculations. This means that the session database is not read on every request, but is updated on every request, at a minimum to update the *last access* timestamp. If the caching scheme is not in place or does not work effectively, you must account for this in your calculation. The HTTP session transfer calculation looks like this:

```
Page rate * Average HTTP session data transferred/page
= Bytes to the HTTP session db/second

87.5 page requests/second * 2KB/request = 175KB/second
```

Applet Transfer

This web site contains a large applet (750KB). Depending on the frequency of the applet's download, the applet might impact the network capacity significantly. The customer tells us that about 10% of the site's users access this applet, so let's use the user arrival rate to give us a feel for the impact of the applet at any given second. The applet transfer calculation looks like this:

```
User arrival rate * Applet size * Weighting factors = Applet bytes
transferred/second

17.5 users/second * 750KB/user transfer * 10% = 1.313MB/sec
```

Total Transfers

Now we add up all of the elements of the network traffic to get a rough total of sustained network traffic:

```
Outbound traffic + Inbound traffic + Database transfer + HTTP session
database transfer + Applet transfer = Total known data transferred/second
```

```
5.25MB/second + 1.05MB/second + 157.5KB/second + 175KB/second +
1.313MB/second = 7.946MB/second total known data transfer
```

In Chapter 9, we estimate how much sustained traffic three popular network types support. These estimates include some allowance for protocol overhead (packet headers, connection "handshaking," and so on).

This web site probably needs a Gigabit network to give us a comfortable operating margin in production. If we use a switched Ethernet, we might experience a site slowdown if our estimates prove even just a little too low. Also, the switched network does not give us a lot of room for future web site growth.

Using the Network Planning Worksheet

Let's complete the calculations in the worksheet from Appendix A in Table 10.6.

Table 10.6   Determining a Minimum Network Requirement of 1Gb

	Network Data	**Equation**	**Total**
10.	Outbound HTML / static elements	Average page size * Requests/sec Line 1 * Line 3	60KB * 87.5 pages/sec = **5.25MB/sec**
11.	Inbound HTTP requests (estimate)	20% * Outbound data 20% * Line 10	5.25MB/sec * 20% = **1.05MB/sec**
12.	Application data transfer	Average bytes/request * Requests/sec * % request requiring data Line 4 * Line 3 * Line 6	(Catalog) 2KB * 87.5 pages/sec * 90% = **157.5KB/sec**
		Average bytes/request * Requests/sec * % requiring data	(Boat Selector) 1KB * 87.5 pages/sec * 15% = **13KB/sec**
13.	HTTP session data transfer	HTTP session size * Requests/sec Line 7 * Line 3	2KB * 87.5 pages/sec = **175KB/sec**
14.	Applet transfer	Applet size * User arrival rate/sec * % requests using applet Line 8 * Line 4 * Line 9	750KB * 17.5 users/sec * 10% utilization = **1.313MB/sec**
	Total		**7.959MB/sec**

Table 10.6   Determining a Minimum Network Requirement of 1Gb (Continued)

Network Sizing			
Network Speed (bits)	**Estimated Bytes Supported (Planning)**	**Equation**	**Yes/No**
100Mbps Ethernet	5MBps	5MBps > 7.959?	No
100Mbps Switched Ethernet	8MBps	8MBps > 7.959?	Yes (but really, really close)
1Gbps Ethernet	50MBps	50MBps > 7.959?	Yes

Dial-up User Considerations

If TriMont receives a lot of dial-up traffic, the page sizes might become a factor over slow phone lines. The average page size is 60KB. Over a 24.4Kbps phone line, this requires at least

```
24,400 bits/second / 8 bits/byte = 3,050 bytes/second
```

```
60,000 bytes / 3,050 bytes/second = 19.6 seconds!
```

This well exceeds the five-second response time threshold the TriMont team set for themselves.

You discuss this with the TriMont team. They believe most of their traffic comes from high-speed connections or users equipped with 56Kps modems. This brings the transfer time on the large pages to the sub-10-second threshold. They believe this is a reasonable response time expectation for people using this level of equipment. You consider the TriMont team's attitude a bit optimistic. In case they change their minds in the future, you give them the following suggestions to consider:

- They could give users a choice of "low-resolution" pages returning fewer or no graphics.
- The pages might return fewer search items by default. For example, if the TriMont site normally returns a maximum of 15 items per user catalog search, they might instead return only the top 3 (with a link to view all the search results) to reduce transfer size. Users with higher bandwidth connections could choose to see more items per page on their search results.
- They might consider using different compression techniques to reduce the graphical element sizes.

It is also worth mentioning to the customer that the applet requires very long download times over a 24.4Kbps modem (more than four minutes). Even doubling the modem speed does not move the applet into the desired response time range.

HTTP Session Pressure

After completing the network analysis, you turn your attention to memory issues. Since the TriMont site uses HTTP sessions, you need an estimate for how much memory the HTTP sessions require during the peak period. As we discussed in Chapter 4, you need to make sure the Java application server has enough memory to operate. The TriMont site removes the user's HTTP session when the user logs out. *Do not count on this in your estimations of HTTP session pressure!* Most users do not log out at the end of their visits; they just move on to another web site. So, when you calculate HTTP sessions, do not assume the web site gets significant benefit from the logout function. (Likewise, do not write your test scripts so that each virtual user dutifully logs out of the test case.) See Chapter 7 for further information.

TriMont's HTTP session timeout is 30 minutes. Given that the average user visit is 7 minutes, let's assume the user's session lasts 37 minutes (7 minutes for the actual visit and 30 minutes for HTTP session timeout). Given our previous user arrival rate estimate of 17.5 users per second, the web site might have the following simultaneous HTTP session in memory during the peak:

```
User arrival rate (seconds) * 60 seconds/minute * Number of minutes user's
session lasts = Maximum HTTP sessions

17.5 users/second * 60 seconds/minute * 37 minutes = 38,850 HTTP sessions
```

TriMont HTTP sessions average 2KB of data in size. At peak load, the web site requires the following memory to hold the HTTP sessions:

```
38,850 simultaneous HTTP sessions * 2KB/HTTP session = 77.7MB
```

Using the JVM Sizing Worksheet

Let's put all of the HTTP session sizing into the worksheet from Appendix A in Table 10.7.

Table 10.7   HTTP Session Impact Worksheet

	Input Data	Source of Data	Your Data
1.	User arrival rate (per minute)	Appendix A: Capacity Sizing worksheet	1,050 visits/min
2.	Average user visit time (minutes)	Appendix A: Capacity Sizing worksheet	7
3.	Planned HTTP session timeout interval (in minutes)	System Administrator	30
4.	HTTP session size (per user)	Appendix A: Network Capacity Sizing input	2K

Table 10.7   HTTP Session Impact Worksheet (Continued)

Calculating HTTP Session Memory Requirement			
	Calculated Data	**Calculation**	**Total**
5.	Average time HTTP session stays resident in memory (in minutes)	Average user visit time + HTTP session timeout Line 2 + Line 3	7-min visits + 30 min timeout = 37 min
6.	Number of HTTP sessions in memory	User arrival rate * Average time session in memory Line 1 * Line 5	17.5 users/sec * 37 min = 38,850 max HTTP sessions in memory
7.	HTTP session memory required	Number of user sessions in memory * HTTP session size Line 6 * Line 4	38,850 HTTP sessions in memory * 2KB/session = 77.7MB

Given the number of users on the web site during the peak time, this is a very reasonable HTTP session footprint. In fact, the HTTP sessions for all these users could, depending on the web application footprint, fit inside a single JVM. Keep in mind that a small increase in the average HTTP session on this site means a significantly larger HTTP session footprint. If the session size grows to 10K (still not very much data), we'd need 385MB just for session data at peak usage. Your JVM might not have enough heapsize to handle this. Make a note to recheck the average HTTP session size with the TriMont development team before the testing begins.

The TriMont team's usage of HTTP sessions puts them in a great position regarding their memory footprint. Of course, not every customer manages their HTTP session footprint as well as TriMont apparently has. See our discussion in Chapter 2 for more details on techniques to reduce HTTP session pressure if you find yourself working with a web site with large HTTP sessions.

Test Scenarios

The customer gave you a lot of information about visitor usage patterns. You can use this information to develop a rough breakout of the test scenarios you need to test the web site.

Potential Test Scripts

We know of the following scripts and their relative weighting:

- Browse (90%)
- Check Order (3%)
- Check Account (2%)

We also know of some special functions of the web site:

- Purchase (5% of Browse traffic)
- Boat Selector (15% of all customers)
- River Conditions applet (10% of all traffic)

Notice our "bread and butter" functions of Browse, Check Order, and Check Account do not add up to 100% of the traffic. Maybe the TriMont team left some buffer for users of Boat Selector function and River Conditions applet who do not go further into the site to use other features such as Browse. You need to double-check this with the TriMont team (we don't want to miss a significant function).

Also, you might want to request a further breakdown of the Browse activity. Do most users take advantage of the Search functionality discussed earlier while browsing, or do most users browse by category rather than searching? Finally, will it make a significant difference in our performance test if the users search versus walking through a series of categories? Again, clarification on small details might make a significant difference in the success of the test.

Test Scenario Considerations

You need a very large shopping list. The catalog database contains one million items. Avoid reusing the same items repeatedly in your scripts, or the items you use repeatedly might be cached at the host database. This results in a lower response time for the test than you will see in the field. See Chapter 7 for details.

You also need to interact with a production account and order system. TriMont plans to exercise the site fully, including placing orders and checking on their status. However, you *don't* want to trigger delivery of merchandise to the test lab! You want to operate outside the order and delivery system, but keep the shopping experience as authentic as possible for the performance tests.

In these cases, you need to work closely with the TriMont team. As we discussed in Chapter 9, the customer has probably resolved this problem at some time in the past. TriMont may use a special set of account numbers to generate test orders. The order system recognizes these special accounts and does not reduce or ship inventory. Other options include building a special order database just for the test that bypasses the standard order and inventory system. (You also need a set of order numbers for the Check Order function. Again, the customer might generate a set of dummy orders just for this part of the test.)

Moving Ahead

The Java application server vendor probably provides some capacity planning information to customers. Now that you know more about the TriMont application, you should consult the vendor's web site for white papers to help you pick the server capacity the application needs. The test needs hardware. TriMont needs to pick a hardware vendor for their new site, if they haven't already. They also need to pick machines for testing that match the eventual production configuration.

Capacity planning at this stage is only an educated guess. The vendor's guidance probably narrows the range of possible servers. For example, the application might require something in an 8–12 CPU configuration, but it definitely needs more than a 4 CPU server provides. However, the estimates give you a starting point for machine sizing, which you will confirm as part of the performance test. (See Chapter 15 for more details on determining machine capacity.)

Summary

In this chapter we began our progressive case study of a fictional e-Commerce web site. We demonstrated some of the calculations for network capacity estimates. We also took an initial pass at HTTP session memory requirements based on information from the customer. After generating these estimates, it's time to talk over the initial findings with the customer. As with all estimates, they're only useful if they match reality on the production web site.

The next part of the book focuses on actually running a performance test against a web site, obtaining useful results, and making appropriate tuning adjustments. We begin in the next chapter by discussing the test process. Also, we continue this case study in Chapters 14 and 15 after we further develop some more testing concepts.

Chapter 11

EXECUTING A
SUCCESSFUL TEST

After completing your preparation work and building a test environment, it's time to begin testing. In this chapter, we discuss how to run a performance test. We begin by discussing the basic iterative tuning process we use to gather data, perform analysis, and make tuning adjustments. Next, we examine the progressive phases of the test. Finally, we discuss the best approach for testing and tuning all the components in your web site.

Testing Overview

Let's step back for a moment and consider what you want to accomplish with your test. Ultimately, you want to achieve the performance goals in the test plan. By reaching these goals, you demonstrate sufficient performance to support production traffic. Many test teams begin by enabling *all* the features and components of the web site, and running the performance test against them. We've never witnessed a successful test using this "all or nothing" strategy. Instead, we use a more systematic approach to testing.

First, start with a simple system. Begin testing and tuning a basic hardware configuration and add more components and features systematically. As you'll see in the section entitled Test Environment Configurations below, we recommend starting with the simplest form of your test environment possible: one HTTP server and a single application server instance interacting with minimal remote back-end systems.

Second, find the baseline of this simple system. How well does it perform *now*? A surprising number of people start tuning without knowing where the system stands initially. Always find the throughput plateau and response time of the system *before* beginning the tuning process described in the next section. We cover how to do this in the Test Phases section of this chapter. Now you're ready to begin tuning if your system falls short of your performance goals. In the next section, we discuss the basic iterative process for tuning a system.

After you finish tuning your basic system, add other key parts of the web site, such as load balancers, to the test and tune them, using the performance of the simple system as a gauge. When you're satisfied with these components, it's time to begin scaling your system.

Remember, the key to a successful test is simplicity. Start with a simple system, tune it, and use this as a gauge as you increase the complexity of the test. Add components individually beyond the baseline and retest to determine their impact on performance. By adding components slowly and systematically, you quickly identify any performance problems introduced by these components and resolve them before moving on.

Whether your web site requires five application servers or fifty, the performance test always starts with the basics and walks toward the ultimate system. By resolving performance problems before adding the next level of complexity, you save time. This approach also allows you to collect capacity data for the basic components of the web site. The rest of this chapter covers our recommended test approach in more detail.

Test Analysis and Tuning Process

The success of the test depends on your ability to accurately collect data, analyze performance measurements, and make tuning changes. Each step in this iterative process follows the same basic flow shown in Figure 11.1. The first step in the process is executing a performance test. For example, run a test scenario against your web application simulating 100 clients against a single four-way server. During this test, capture data about your test clients, application servers, and other components used in the test. After completing the test run, analyze the data collected before proceeding to the next test.

Here's where your performance preparation pays off: After obtaining run data, review the objectives for this part of your test. If the test shows you've met the performance criteria for that test, move on to other tests. If not, it's time to analyze the results more carefully and make tuning adjustments. Keep in mind that all systems contain bottlenecks. However, you only need to address bottlenecks if they prevent you from reaching your targets. As we said earlier, without targets, you never know when to stop tuning. You may iterate through the test, measure, and tune process many times per test until you reach your performance goals. Let's discuss the steps of this process in more detail.

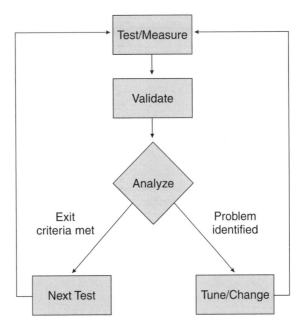

Figure 11.1   Iterative test and tuning process

Test and Measure

Throughout the first portion of the book, we have emphasized the importance of reliable, reproducible results. Now it's time to determine if your system really generates repeatable results. Especially during your initial testing, never take a single test run at face value. Instead, run the same test at least three times *without making any changes*, and compare the results.

Before the run, reset the environment to the same state. After the test begins, let it run for 10–15 minutes at steady state before stopping. Later you may want to run longer tests to simulate a full day's activities against the web site, but for now use shorter tests as you tune the various parts of the web site.

After you perform multiple runs, look at the results: Did each run produce roughly the same results? If the answer is yes, proceed with tuning if required. If not, check the validation section below for some guidelines on resolving run variation.

Most test tools generate a report after each test run, giving you information on throughput and response time achieved by the test. The size and complexity of the report usually depends on the sophistication of the tool and the size of the test (number of virtual users, test iterations, test machines, and so on). Appendix D provides a sample worksheet to record key data reported by your performance test tool. Keep this data at least until you complete your performance testing. You need this data for comparison against future tests and to establish trends in your testing. Designate an archive machine with sufficient disk space to hold the data generated by your test, and use a naming convention to coordinate this data with the appropriate test run.

As we discussed in Chapter 8, test tools differ in how they measure a given test run. Some tools include the entire test run in their calculation of throughput and response time. Other tools allow you to pick an interval during the run for your measurements. If your tool allows you to pick, choose an interval during the test's steady state. As shown in Figure 11.2, omit any ramp-up or ramp-down of users, as these tend to skew the response time and throughput of the system. Instead, pick the interval after ramp-up when all virtual users are running against the system.

Less sophisticated test tools use all data points in their calculations of throughput and response time for the run. If you cannot control how the tool measures the run, shift your focus to modifying the run to give you better data. For these tools, increase the duration of your test run. By increasing the length of the run relative to the ramp-up and ramp-down time, as shown in Figure 11.3, you reduce the impact of these phases of the test on your results.

In addition to the throughput and response time measurements collected by the test tool, also record CPU utilization from each of the servers, as well as all the tuning

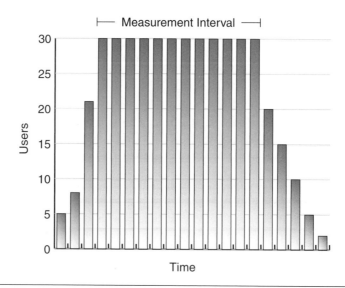

Figure 11.2   Test run measurement interval

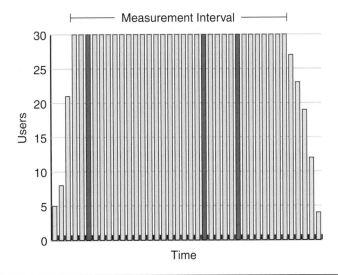

Figure 11.3 Measuring over long runs to simulate steady state

parameters adjusted for the run. Appendix D includes a worksheet for common tuning parameters. See Chapter 12 for information on collecting and interpreting CPU utilization data.

Validate

Another aspect of a successful test process is the results validation step. This includes checking whether measurements make sense, as well as checking that no errors occurred. Develop a checklist to use for validation (a sample validation checklist is provided in Appendix D). To ensure accurate tests, use both the tester and an independent test team member to validate the results. Make sure that at least two team members review all measurements.

Do not expect exactly the same throughput and response time for each test. Some run-to-run variation is normal. In Chapter 7, we expended a lot of effort on making our test scripts somewhat random to avoid artificial caching situations. This means each run executes a slightly different path through the code, and hits different rows of the database. Also, because the web application runs inside a JVM, garbage collection also slightly impacts our run-to-run data.

We look for excessive variation between test runs. As a rule of thumb, we expect run-to-run variation to remain less than 4%.[1] Remember, if you experience high variation

---

1. The 4% target is based on collective experiences in performance analysis of web and Java applications. Highly repetitive tests or true performance benchmarks have even less variation.

between runs, you cannot establish a cause-and-effect relationship between tuning changes and your test results. For example, Figure 11.4 shows the results of three test runs. Notice that the second run produced 13% higher throughput than the first run and 22% higher throughput than the third run. Assume we make a tuning change and take a fourth test run. If the results show a 22% improvement, we cannot fully attribute this to the tuning change. After all, without the change, we saw the same throughput during our second run.

Instead, your test needs to produce results closer to those shown in Figure 11.5. In Figure 11.5, the second run still produces the best results; however, the difference between runs falls in the 2%–4% range. Also, we don't see a *trend* in these numbers. The second run gave us the best throughput; the third run produces the worst. From just these three figures, we don't see the three tests becoming progressively faster or slower.

In contrast, Figure 11.6 shows a set of three runs with a downward trend. As this figure also shows, additional runs continue the trend, requiring additional investigation. See the subsection entitled What Can Go Wrong? later in this section for possible causes. If additional runs do not continue the trend, the variance is most likely just normal environmental variation.

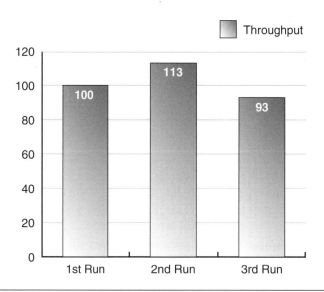

Figure 11.4   Example of high run-to-run variation

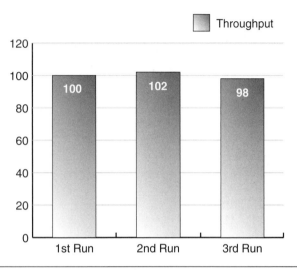

Figure 11.5 Example of acceptable run-to-run variation

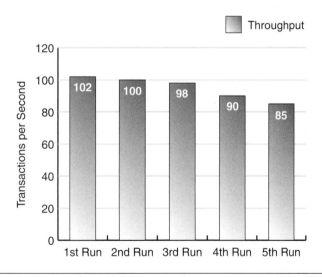

Figure 11.6 Example of run variation with a downward trend

Beyond run consistency, check the following items after every test:

- The measurements reflect three or more runs (especially during initial testing).
- Run-to-run variation falls within 4%.
- Successive runs do not show an upward or downward trend.

- All measurement data recorded.
- All tuning parameters recorded.
- No errors reported from the test tool.
- No errors in the various logs (application server, web application, and so on).

What Can Go Wrong?

If your test environment produces too much variation, correct this before beginning your performance tests. Some common contributors to run-to-run variation include the following.

Shared Environment   Other activity on your servers or the network often impacts the results of your test. Two examples of this are the following:

- *Shared Network:* As we discussed in Chapter 9, traffic fluctuates dramatically on public networks during a workday. Depending on when you take your measurements, you may get very different results.
- *Shared Back-End Resource:* Similarly, if your test environment shares a back-end system with other users or applications, their activities may impact your performance results.

Short Runs   Despite time pressures, give your tests sufficient runtime to smooth out variance. For example, if you only run your test for a minute, the results might vary significantly if a garbage collection cycle starts during the second run but not the first. Experiment with your test runs to find your best runtime. As we mentioned before, 10 to 15 minutes of steady-state runtime usually suffices.

Database Growth   Your application probably creates and updates rows in a database during the test. The web application may register new users, thereby creating new rows in the user table. As database tables grow significantly, database queries take longer. In addition, a database query, such as a search, might return more data as the table size increases. (For example, the database processing and network transfer time for 500 database records exceeds that of only 50 records.) Database growth sometimes causes performance to degrade over a series of runs.

If your test artificially inflates the new records created in the database, consider using a script to reset the database between performance runs. This allows you to take consistent measurements across multiple tests.

However, if your test mimics production conditions, work with the DBA to manage the data growth over time. Since the web site faces the same problem in production, you need a solution to the larger problem, not a quick fix to make your testing neater. Tuning the database or changing the application is in order.

Too Much Variation in Workload Simulation   As we discussed in Chapter 7, your performance scripts need dynamic data and a certain amount of random variation to effectively test your site. However, extreme random simulation in your scripts makes it difficult to obtain consistent test runs.

If you set up your workload simulation for a target mix of 90% browse and 10% buy, you get approximately 90% browse and 10% buy on each run, but not *exactly this mix*. You might get 89% browse and 11% buy on one run, and slightly more browse than buy on the run after that. This is probably an acceptable variation on the mix. However, too much variability gives you wide swings in your results. For example, 20% buy on the first run and 10% buy on the second run most likely leads to incomparable results.

Double-check that your test scripts generate the correct activity mix and random data selection. Also, running your scripts for several minutes usually results in more consistent activity mixes between tests.

Analyze

After confirming the consistency of your measurements, it's time to analyze the data captured during the test. This may seem a little obvious, but nevertheless it bears saying: *Look at the data before tuning the system.* As part of your analysis, review the data against the test plan targets. If the performance meets your targets, move on to the next test. Otherwise, look further at the data to identify your bottlenecks, and make tuning adjustments accordingly. After making the adjustments, run the test again, and repeat the analysis process.

The specifics of the analyses performed change depending on the phase of your test plan being executed, but the basic process for successful analysis does not change. These steps include comparing your results to

- Expectations based on previous or historical results
- Projected throughput and response time curves
- The test plan exit criteria

Chapter 1 discussed the expected relationships between load, throughput, and response time. In the analysis step, compare the throughput and response time results from the new runs with previous results at different client loads.

As an example, let's assume you hit a throughput plateau at 100 users. You've tested 150 users, and saw response time increase, but throughput remains constant, which confirms your conclusion about the plateau. Now you've run a 200 user test. If you've reached a "throughput plateau," the throughput doesn't vary significantly between the 100 and 200 user load test, but the response time probably doubled.

Of course, look for inconsistencies. If the throughput suddenly increased, or the response time improved between the 100 and 200 user test, you might want to run your 100 user test again. Perhaps the test ran in error originally. Or maybe something changed during the 200 user test. In any case, look for predictable patterns in your data.

In the analysis step, also compare the results to exit criteria from your test plan (more discussion on exit criteria appears in the Test Phases section later). When the analysis indicates you're not getting the desired performance results, you apply the steps to identify and correct any performance bottlenecks, introduce the required change, and repeat the test measurements.

Tune

Ideally, when you tune, you should make only one tuning adjustment per test iteration. That is, make a tuning adjustment, run another complete test iteration, and analyze the data before making another adjustment. This allows you to isolate which tuning adjustments actually improved performance, as well as which changes made little difference or actually made things worse.

The success of the tuning process is very dependent on your measurement process. Figure 11.7 shows the "before and after" results of applying tuning changes to a system. The first set of runs (1a, 1b, 1c) all show throughput between 98 and 102 transactions per second. After tuning, the second set of runs (2a, 2b, 2c) all show throughput between 114 and 117 transactions per second. Because the run variation remains low, the results clearly show that the tuning changes resulted in positive performance improvements.

Again, keep your tuning changes between runs to a minimum. Make only one tuning adjustment per test iteration; otherwise you encounter one of the following situations:

- You see a measurable performance difference, but you do not know which tuning adjustment brought it about. In this case, you gained performance, but not knowledge. If you need to adjust similar systems in the future, you cannot give specific guidance on optimal tuning parameters.
- You do not see a measurable performance difference because one adjustment actually improved performance, but the other change hindered performance, so that they cancel each other out.
- You do not see a measurable difference because the changes did not have an impact, but you can't be sure the changes (as mentioned above) aren't just canceling each other out.

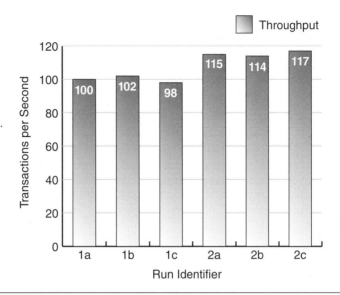

Figure 11.7   Results after introducing a change

Clearly, you need to understand the impact of each change, so take your time, introduce a change, and complete an iteration to measure and analyze the change's impact.

Test Phases

Now that we've covered the basic test process, let's discuss the order for each test. Before diving into full load tests, we suggest starting with simple, single-user tests. After successfully completing these, move ahead with testing under load. Finally, after tuning the system under load, consider testing the system under load for extended periods (known as *long-run* testing). Let's discuss each of these test phases in more detail.

Phase 1: Simple, Single-User Paths

First, understand the performance of the individual script paths through your application. Begin the testing by running each major test script individually. This ensures that scripts run correctly and sometimes gives you surprisingly early insights into major performance issues.

When you run a script with only one simulated user, focus on the response time. At this stage, the response time should easily fall within plan requirements for the functions tested. However, if you see large response times (say your Browse script shows consistent ten-second response times), don't go any further. Delay load testing until single-user performance falls well within acceptable response time limits.

Even when you do simple-path, single-user runs, the basic concept of steady-state, repeatable measurements applies. For example, the first time you exercise a JSP, you may experience a significant compile time. Make sure to prime the environment before taking these measurements, usually by running a test once, throwing away the results, and then running the test and recording the results.

Exit Criteria

If you don't see good response time with one user, adding more load doesn't make sense, as more users only increase response times. Exit single-user testing only after the response time falls well within your planning ranges for this function. Obviously, if you want five-second response time for 1,000 users, and you're only getting four seconds for one user, the load test won't go very far before you find yourself addressing response time issues again. Before you leave this phase of testing, obtain a response time with a reasonable cushion for the projected load.

What Can Go Wrong?

Usually single-path runs go quite well. The application development team normally tests their code during development with these types of runs, so they generally deliver code in reasonable condition for the single user. However, occasionally problems arise during these tests. Here's a list of the more common single-user test issues.

- *DNS and network configuration issues:* Single-user testing often uncovers network configuration issues within the test environment. Happily, testing with only one user makes solving network problems easier. Reading a trace of one user's network traffic proves much easier than reading a trace of hundreds of conversations.
- *Too many graphics:* Applications returning pages stuffed with graphics usually show poor response times even in the single-user case. Large graphics files and/or many graphics files experience lots of network latency. Again, a network trace allows you to break down the time spent loading various elements of each page in the scenario (some test tools provide this level of detail as well).
- *Classpath configuration issues:* Not surprisingly, sometimes the single-user test uncovers a misconfiguration in the web application's classpath. In addition to

producing errors, this also creates a longer execution path for the application, resulting in poor response time.

On a related topic, also use the single-user tests to look for misconfigured embedded HTML elements. Consider turning on your HTTP server's full access logging to check for 404 errors. Often the test scripts try to retrieve static elements not present in the test environment. Remove these elements, or configure the environment correctly to include them.

Use the single-user test to flush out any problems in your test scripts or the test environment. A little time spent in the beginning often saves hours of analysis work later in the testing. Resolve these performance issues now before they amplify under load.

Phase 2: User Ramp-Up

Once your single-user paths perform, begin testing the system under load. Of course, do not do this with *all* of your planned load right way; begin by gradually introducing load to your test environment. We recommend incrementally increasing load to establish the initial throughput plateau for your environment. After establishing this baseline, analyze your system for bottlenecks and make tuning adjustments to raise the plateau.

Start with one user and increase your user load by small increments until you find the throughput plateau. At this point, run additional measurements by successively doubling the load. Use these measurements to confirm the plateau and to find the point on the plateau where response time no longer becomes acceptable for your environment. For example, if you run measurements at 1, 2, 5, 10, 15, and 20 users, you might obtain the results shown in Table 11.1 (note, "tps" means "transactions per second"). On the basis of these results, you conclude that the saturation point occurs at ten users, with a throughput plateau of 29 transactions per second.

At this point, run additional measurements, doubling the client load each time until throughput really falls off or the response time is well above an acceptable threshold. Figure 11.8 shows the throughput from tests of 40, 80, 160, 320, and 640 virtual users against our system. Notice that we enter the buckle zone at around 160 users.

After establishing a baseline for your system, decide whether you need more performance from the areas of your web site under test. If your test plan calls for better

Table 11.1 Throughput for Progressive Test Runs

1 User	2 Users	5 Users	10 Users	15 Users	20 Users
5 tps	8 tps	20 tps	30 tps	29 tps	29 tps

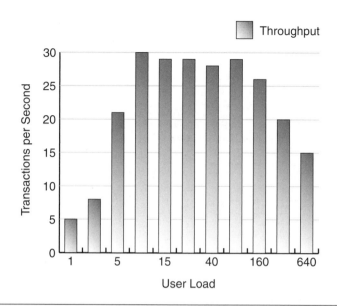

Figure 11.8   Throughput curve to determine saturation point

performance, it's time to analyze the data further and make tuning adjustments (the goal being to move the plateau higher and/or to decrease the response time). Otherwise, if you find the performance acceptable, move on to your next set of tests.

Exit Criteria

OK, in reality almost no one "moves on" after establishing the first load test plateau. Typically, the initial user ramp-up delivers disappointing performance results because of bottlenecks in the system. The user ramp-up phase often takes the bulk of your test time. After establishing a throughput plateau, you spend additional time improving the performance of the systems to increase throughput and lower response time to meet your goals. Also, you may find that, even after meeting your goals, additional tuning might squeeze additional capacity from your test systems. Determining when to leave this phase of testing requires some skill.

While analyzing your data from a user ramp-up test, consider the following questions:

- Are you able to generate the load, throughput, and response time required by your test plan for this configuration?
- What are the load, throughput, and response time at the saturation point?
- Does the saturation point drive the CPU to 100% utilization?
- How much load does it take to reach the throughput "buckle zone"?
- Is the increase in response time linear at loads beyond the saturation point?

Of course, the first question is the most important: Do these results meet your test plan's exit criteria? If you answer yes to this question, you're probably ready to move to your next test.

However, keep in mind that you might reach your goals without getting the most out of your systems. If your test reaches the saturation point without driving the CPU on your primary systems (normally the application servers) close to 100% utilization, you have a bottleneck in the system. Large, multi-CPU, symmetric multiprocessing (SMP) machines are an exception to this rule. A single application server instance rarely drives very large machines to 100% CPU utilization.

Before you leave this phase, try to tune the systems to meet your performance goals. If you've met your goals, but you believe you're leaving lots of system capacity on the table, it's probably worthwhile to remove any major bottlenecks preventing full utilization of your systems. In the end, you decide when you've reached the point of diminishing returns in tuning and bottleneck removal. The following section discusses the process for removing bottlenecks in more detail, and Chapter 13 provides specific guidance on bottleneck symptoms and solutions.

What Can Go Wrong?

Early load testing usually uncovers load-related failures in the application. Remember, the developers test in single-user mode throughout development, but rarely (if ever) put their code under load. As you run your tests, don't forget the validation steps described earlier. Make sure the system runs correctly before diving into performance analysis, and check the logs for errors under load. Also, use a browser to run a few manual tests while load testing to check for multi-threading problems.

The major activity for load testing, however, is bottleneck resolution. Chapter 13 describes the symptoms and possible resolutions of the bottlenecks we commonly encounter in the field. Please refer to this chapter for more details on identifying and resolving bottlenecks. For now, however, let's discuss how to prioritize the bottlenecks you find in load testing.

Removing Bottlenecks

We recommend beginning your bottleneck removal by focusing on CPU utilization. As we mentioned earlier, until you drive the CPU utilization of the application server(s) to near 100%, one or more bottlenecks exist in your system. Remove the bottlenecks hindering your CPU utilization first.

Your saturation point often provides clues to the source of the bottleneck. The saturation point defines the lowest user load constrained by a limitation in the system. Either by using monitoring tools (discussed more in the next chapter), thread dumps, or the process of elimination, try to find the resource (connection pool, database, security server, and so on) that is constraining the system's performance.

Consider the example from Chapter 1, where we initially saw a saturation point of five customers in the brick and mortar bookstore. The store's five checkout lines became a limiting factor for us after five customers began to check out. This prevented our throughput from exceeding five customers per minute. Likewise, in your web site, look for the constrained resource.

Remember: Try to remove your bottlenecks in order of severity. If you devote resources to tuning your application database, but it's not the largest bottleneck in the system, you see little (if any) performance gains from this activity. Take the bottlenecks as they come, resolve them, and decide if the system requires further tuning.

Reaching 100% CPU utilization does not guarantee optimal performance, however. After driving your systems to their capacity, focus on using the systems more efficiently. Usually this involves an examination of the web application code for poor programming practices; sometimes it involves fine-tuning resources such as container threads.

System Resources

Often your web site waits for external resources such as databases or security servers. While your servlet threads wait, they do no work, so the CPU utilization of your server remains low. Check the system usage statistics of your peripheral systems and suspect any system that is running near 100% CPU utilization.

Never rely on external analysis alone. Combine external analysis with a thread dump of the application server, if at all possible. Remember, you want the most severe bottlenecks first, and although your database server needs a CPU upgrade, it may not be the biggest bottleneck in your web site. A thread dump shows you servlet, JSP, and even EJB activity during the test and helps you identify with great clarity the most significant bottleneck encountered during the run.

Middleware and Application Resources

Some bottlenecks originate in application resources such as queues and pools. If you see threads in your thread dump waiting for these resources, check their settings. Perhaps they're simply set too low, or perhaps an external system accessed via the pooled resources is not keeping pace with demand. Sometimes resources *in front* of the application servers restrict traffic flows. If all HTTP server threads become fully engaged serving static content, for example, the application servers become underutilized.

Keep an eye on your middleware and application resources as you increase the load and test complexity. Referring back to the HTTP server again, it usually requires additional tuning if you enable security or if you add more application servers to the cluster it serves.

Application Implementation

Frequently the bottleneck lies within the web application itself. Poorly written logging routines, bad string management, or excessive synchronization, among other things, often become the most performance-expensive elements of your system. Employing a code-profiling tool on the web application before testing begins eliminates some types of application problems. Others only appear under load testing, so don't be surprised to find you still require application tuning after completing a profiling exercise. Obtain and use programming skill to resolve these bottlenecks.

After you have completed these steps, your system under test should run at close to 100% CPU utilization. Hopefully, the throughput of your site also increases, and you require more virtual users to reach your throughput saturation point. Again, 100% CPU utilization makes for a good start in your tuning, but it rarely marks the end of your efforts. After fully utilizing your CPU resources, focus on how to use them more efficiently. Efficiency also improves performance by reducing response times and increasing throughput.

Regardless, avoid making your tuning exercise a "fine-tuning" experiment. Keep focused on meeting the objectives of your web site rather than squeezing the last bit of capacity out of your test environment. Any system contains a near infinite number of bottlenecks. Removing a few of these usually provides the largest benefits, while resolving the rest provides very little performance gain. Meet your goals, obtain good machine utilization, and move on.

If you cannot meet your targets, or you cannot get past a utilization threshold, reconsider your test plan. Particularly if you cannot control parts of your environment (such as remote resources), or if you do not have code access to the web application, you may reach a point where further meaningful tuning is not possible. Consider moving on with scalability testing to compensate for poor individual server performance.

Test Environment Configurations

Your test not only exercises the web application, but it also stresses the entire test environment. Just as we recommend starting with single-user testing before moving to user ramp-up testing, we also recommend starting your tests with a simple environment. As you better understand the performance of the simple environment, add complexity until your full environment comes under test.

A simple-to-complex strategy allows you to find problems in a manageable environment and to introduce complexity systematically to understand each component's performance impact. Do not add more complexity until you reach an acceptable performance baseline on your current configuration.

Start Simple

Start your tests with a single application server. Place any databases on one or more remote machines. Usually, we recommend putting the HTTP server on its own machine as well, depending on your ultimate production configuration. Of course, always use separate machines for the test clients. We recommend starting with this basic setup because it is easy to configure, allows you to identify most major application performance issues, and provides an excellent baseline of your core web site components.

Also, keep the component features used at this point to a minimum. Do not introduce complex features such as security and shared HTTP session management yet. Use only those features essential to correct application execution to establish your initial baselines.

Add Complexity

After removing the major bottlenecks and achieving acceptable performance with a simplified test environment, begin introducing real-world complexity to your test web site. Systematically add more components and more features to the site, establish a new baseline for each, tune as necessary, add the next component or feature, and repeat. Not only does this approach help you resolve system bottlenecks in a more ordered fashion, but it also provides critical information for web site capacity planning. By understanding the capacity of each hardware and software component of your site, you develop a good idea of how large your site needs to be to support your expected user loads.

As you add components to your test system, repeat the baseline and tuning processes to resolve any newly introduced bottlenecks. We recommend introducing complexity into your site in the following order:

1. Core web site features (HTTP session sharing, SSL, and so on)
2. Vertical scaling
3. Horizontal scaling

Let's discuss each of these steps in more detail.

Core Web Site Features

Many web sites use the HTTP session sharing features of their application servers and the SSL security features of their HTTP servers. These two elements frequently introduce significant performance issues, so understanding the impact of each of these elements is important for capacity planning. If you use these features in your web site, introduce them into your test individually *after* tuning your basic web application.

HTTP Session Sharing

As we discussed in Chapter 3, many application server vendors provide some means for sharing HTTP session data among clustered application server instances. This allows the instances to share session data, which proves very useful for failover. (If one instance fails, the web site routes the user to another available instance, which retrieves the user's session information from the shared datastore.)

As with other aspects of your web site, begin testing shared HTTP sessions with only one application server instance. After you baseline and tune your single application server instance, turn on session sharing, and measure the performance impact. (Note: This only works if you use a persistent HTTP session database to share session information. Distributed session sharing schemes require two or more application server instances.)

For example, if you get 100 transactions per second throughput with a single application server instance without HTTP session sharing, you might only reach 85 transactions per second after enabling this feature. (HTTP session sharing often produces a 10%–15% performance degradation.)[2] We also recommend testing your hardware cluster without HTTP session sharing enabled at first. This gives you a baseline for measuring the impact of session sharing across the cluster. Also, it makes it somewhat easier to find and resolve other cluster bottlenecks.

Security

Most production web sites require encryption for some pages. Using SSL carries a significant performance overhead. The impact depends on how many pages the site encrypts, the size of the pages returned, and the number of pages accessed after initiating an SSL session. Depending on the site and the age of the HTTP server involved, the SSL degradation varies widely. Of course, the initial handshake protocol

---

2. The range of 10%–15% is based on performance benchmark experience with applications following best practices for HTTP session. Large session objects may cause a more significant performance impact.

requires a significant portion of this time. Using HTTP affinity routing to eliminate repeated handshaking improves overall SSL performance.

Again, test the site without SSL, if possible, before enabling this feature, so that you can gauge the performance impact. SSL requires lots of CPU for the encryption and decryption of requests and pages. See Chapter 3 for details on tuning your server for SSL.

Vertical Scaling

We discussed vertical scaling in Chapters 2 and 4. As you may recall, vertical scaling refers to adding application server instances to a single server, increasing the physical capacity of the server (memory, CPU, and so on), or doing both. However, as we warned you earlier, not all platforms and JVMs benefit from vertical scaling. Before you develop capacity plans based on this technique, use your performance test to determine if this actually works for you.

Analyze this scaling from both a hardware and JVM perspective. If you are running on a four-way server (a machine with four CPUs) in your test lab, try booting your server in one-way, two-way, and four-way configurations. Many operating system and server vendors give you control of the number of CPUs enabled on a boot. This allows you to find the best processor configuration for your application.

For each configuration, perform a series of measurements and compare performance. Is the two-way configuration throughput close to two times the performance of the one-way configuration? Likewise, is the four-way performance close to four times the one-way throughput? If the answer to these questions is yes, your application, JVM, and operating system exhibit good SMP scaling characteristics at this level.

Figure 11.9 shows the SMP scaling results of two operating system platforms. The first platform shows good SMP scaling as we move from a one-way to a two-way configuration (the two-way throughput is 1.8 times greater than one-way throughput). However, when we move to a four-way configuration, the throughput only reached 2.6 times that of the one-way system. (We see these same scaling patterns frequently on some PC-based and Linux systems, even for well-written applications.)

Naturally, you cannot expect perfect scaling from a multiprocessor box. As you add processors, the box becomes less efficient in terms of throughput. Referring again to Figure 11.9, notice the scaling factors for the second platform. With four CPUs enabled, the throughput reaches 3.7 times that of the one-way configuration. Expect roughly this level of scale with well-behaved applications on traditional UNIX-based platforms with most JVMs.

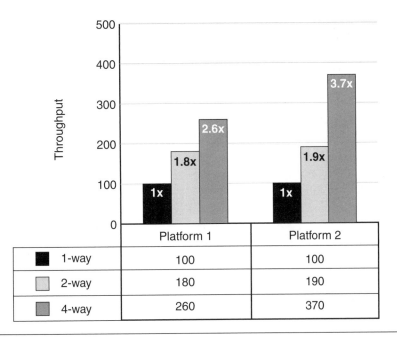

Figure 11.9 SMP scaling comparisons

Also, look at the CPU utilization for these systems. As you add processors, does the application take advantage of them? Particularly on larger systems, a single application server instance often cannot utilize all the processing capacity of the box. In these cases, adding another application server instance often improves CPU utilization and throughput (assuming the machine contains enough memory to support another JVM). Of course, if the CPU utilization already comes close to 100%, adding another application server instance does not increase throughput.

However, if you believe another application instance might help, add just one new instance and run additional measurements. If throughput increases but you're still not fully utilizing the CPU, consider adding another if the machine's memory supports it. Continue this process until

- Throughput remains constant.
- The CPUs run at 100% utilization (or very close to it).
- The machine memory cannot support another instance.

For example, Figure 11.10 shows a maximum throughput of 372 transactions per second with one JVM but only 54% CPU utilization. After exhausting standard attempts to remove any single application server bottlenecks, try additional instances (JVMs) to increase throughput. In this example, a second JVM increased throughput to 549 transactions per second, a third JVM to 628 transactions per second, and a fourth to 720 transactions per seconds. At this point the CPUs became saturated, and more JVMs provided no additional throughput. In this case, vertical scaling effectively doubled the overall throughput.

Keep in mind: *This technique only works if the low CPU utilization is not caused by a bottleneck.* If your single instance can't use all of the CPU because it's waiting for a poorly tuned remote database, adding another instance usually makes the situation worse. If you add instances, but don't see throughput improvements, go back and examine the single-instance environment for bottlenecks.

Also, as you use vertical scaling, be realistic about the instances you require each server to support. We've encountered many grotesque misapplications of vertical scaling in the field. A four-way server typically supports 1 or 2 application server instances well; however, don't expect it to support 80. Keep your expectations realistic and validate them during testing.

As you add instances, be careful to gauge the impact of this extra capacity on the rest of the environment. Adding more instances often requires capacity increases in remote systems, such as databases, and may also impact your network resources.

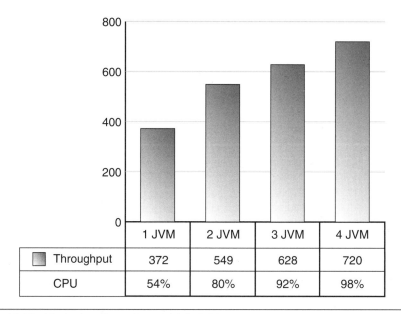

	1 JVM	2 JVM	3 JVM	4 JVM
Throughput	372	549	628	720
CPU	54%	80%	92%	98%

Figure 11.10 Vertical scaling using multiple JVMs

Monitor the entire test environment as you progressively add instances to avoid overwhelming components.

Finally, vertical scaling requires some type of routing mechanism to distribute load to the application server instances. Because the instances normally share the same IP address behind an HTTP server, the application server vendor usually provides a software balancer to handle request distribution. As we'll discuss further in the following section on horizontal scaling, understanding the overhead of this mechanism may be important to your overall performance.

Horizontal Scaling

Beyond vertical scaling, we look at increasing web site resources by adding more servers and placing application server instances (including EJB servers) on these instances. In this step, we duplicate the successful single-server pattern we developed through our performance testing and vertical scaling techniques discussed earlier, and form a machine cluster.

To accomplish this, use load balancing techniques to distribute requests across duplicate servers. Horizontal scaling techniques apply to multiple points in your architecture. For example, if your architecture separates the HTTP servers from the application server, you might apply load balancing techniques in front of the HTTP servers as well as between the HTTP server and the web container. Similarly, if your architecture separates servlets from EJB business logic, you might apply load balancing between the web containers and the EJB containers. Figure 11.11 illustrates some common web site load balancing points.

The common load balancing points exist between the

- Load balancer and HTTP server
- HTTP server and web container
- Servlet or other Java client and EJBs

Your architecture probably requires one or more points of load distribution. Referring back to Figure 11.11, almost all web sites use Type 1 load balancing. Many sites also use Type 2 balancing to support both vertical and horizontal scaling of an application server domain. This distribution type also works across a firewall. Type 3 load balancing comes into play for sites using EJBs in their web applications and/or supporting thick clients.

You perform load balancing tests in a similar manner to previous tests: Start simple, and grow incrementally. Systematically add machines and repeat tests to fully

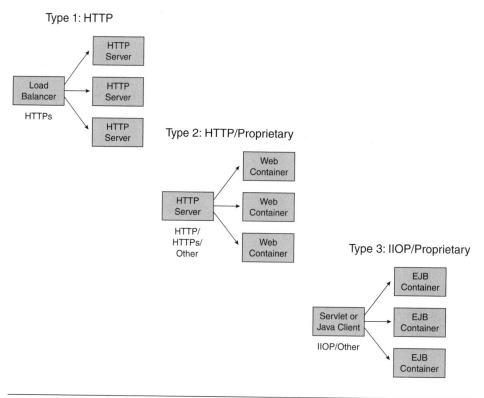

Figure 11.11   Load balancing architecture options

understand the scaling characteristics at each point along the way. In this phase, it is important to understand the capacity ratio required between the servers. For example, if your architecture separates the web containers from the EJB containers, use scalability testing to find out if you need one EJB container per web container (a 1:1 ratio), or more in one tier than another. For complex business logic, you may require for every web container two EJB containers (a 1:2 ratio). More likely, however, the overhead of presentation logic in the web container may mean you use three web containers for every EJB container in the web site (a 3:1 ratio).

During scaling tests, check for linear scalability as you increase the size of the cluster. Just as with vertical testing, as you double your cluster resources, expect throughput to nearly double as well. Make sure your cluster handles proportionally more load than a single server. For example, let's assume a single-server configuration performs

100 transactions per second with one second response time at a concurrent load of 1,000 users. As we increase the servers in our cluster, what kind of performance do we see relative to our single-server baseline? If you add a second identical configuration with a load balancer in front of the servers, does this cluster now support close to 2,000 users and 200 transactions per second, while maintaining one second response time?

The test process for clustering requires multiple, iterative steps:

1. Test each server individually.
2. Quantify load balancing overhead.
3. Test cluster performance and analysis.
4. Add another server and repeat step 3.

These steps are discussed in order in the following subsections.

Test Each Server Individually

First, you need to understand the performance of the individual servers used in your clusters. Although we recommend using identical servers, if possible, in your cluster, do not assume even identical servers produce the same results. Before you run the servers as a cluster, run each individually to determine its behavior.

If two "identical" servers don't perform within 5% of each other, this indicates a configuration problem or an error in your testing of the other machine. For example, we've seen cases where supposedly identical machines performed differently because someone enabled tracing on one of the machines, or because the machines differed in maintenance levels. Figure 11.12 illustrates a successful test of individual server performance.

In this step, also consider the performance and utilization of resources shared by the cluster. As we mentioned in the vertical scaling section, keep in mind your test environment as a system. Adding capacity at the application server level may drive other resources such as the network and remote databases beyond their capacity. Therefore, monitor these devices as you begin ramping up your cluster.

As you leave this step, hopefully you've answered the following questions:

1. Does the cluster use identical machines?
2. Do each of these machines produce similar results?
3. What is the performance of other shared resources at this point?

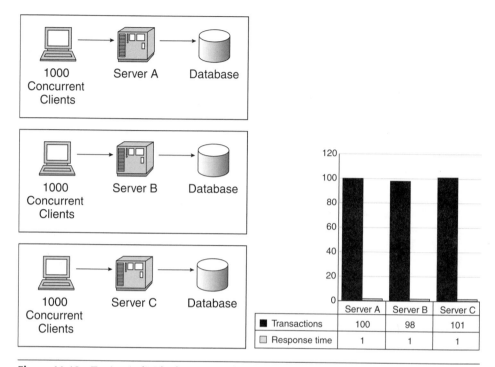

Figure 11.12   Testing individual server performance

Quantify Load Balancing Overhead

Most load balancing technology operates in a nonintrusive manner, but we recommend verifying this before beginning a scalability test. As we discussed in Chapter 3, some special configurations of load balancing software and hardware require more overhead than "vanilla" balancing. For example, if your load balancer makes processing decisions based on inspecting a cookie, this adds path length and slows down overall transaction rates. Now's the time to measure for any unexpected load balancing overhead.

To accomplish this, measure the performance of a single server or web application instance *with the load balancer included*. While this seems counterintuitive (you don't need the balancer for a single resource), the balancing algorithm typically runs through the same steps with one server or ten. By comparing these results with your single-server baseline test (without the balancer), you obtain the impact, if any, of the balancer on the test.

Figure 11.13 shows the performance of Server A with the addition of the load balancer. In this step, the client driver points to the load balancer rather than the individual

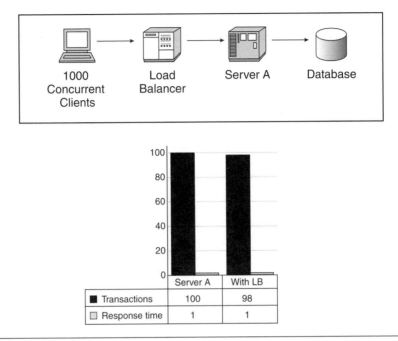

Figure 11.13 Quantifying load balancer overhead

server. (We used the same test here as shown with a single client in Figure 11.5). Note negligible load balancer overhead in this case (less than 2%). However, this technique does not always work for software load balancing (Types 2 and 3 as shown in Figure 11.11). These balancers often contain enough intelligence to optimize their "routing" in a single-instance case.

Try to determine the answers to the following questions during this test step.

1. How much overhead does the load balancer introduce?
2. Is the additional load balancer path length influencing performance?
3. How much machine resource does the load balancer use?

Cluster Performance and Analysis

In this step, you actually put your load balancer to work distributing requests across two servers. Just as with the single-server tests, you run client ramp-ups to understand the throughput and response time dynamics. Plan to run twice the load you ran against the individual servers. Figure 11.14 shows a typical two-server cluster configuration.

To compare a single-server test done with 1,000 concurrent users, drive 2,000 concurrent user requests to the load balancer. This equates to 1,000 concurrent users per server.

As discussed in Chapter 7, if you use IP affinity, make sure your load driver simulates multiple IP addresses, or be sure to use multiple client driver machines. Otherwise, all the simulated users come from the same IP address, and IP-based affinity will route all the users to the same server, resulting in no load balancing.

In this step, you look for linear scaling dynamics. A two-server cluster should typically provide almost two times the throughput (the sum of each individual server) with the same response time as a single server. Figure 11.15 shows the performance results for a 2,000 concurrent user run. As you can see, the total throughput of 196 transactions per second is nearly double the throughput of a single server. Also note that the response time remains at one second (an important point). This tells us the two-sever cluster supports linear scalability. Doubling the hardware capacity doubled the capacity of the web site without impacting the response times.

If your results are not similar to those shown in Figure 11.15, follow the techniques we described earlier to look for bottlenecks. Cluster scaling usually shows linear scale unless the cluster exhausts shared resources, such as the network or remote systems. Remember, your cluster now serves twice as many user requests, which means a shared application or HTTP session database also receives twice the traffic. Scale shared resources as you scale the servers on your web site.

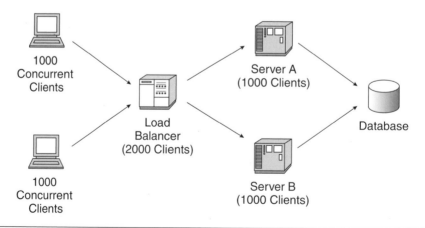

Figure 11.14   Testing a two-server cluster

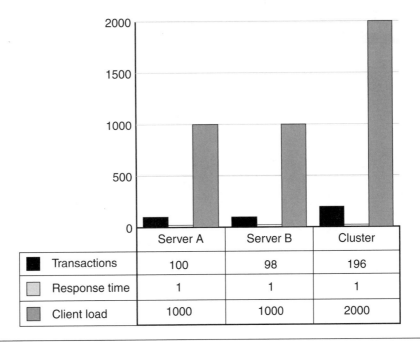

Figure 11.15   Two-server cluster scalability results

Resolve the following questions during this step:

1. Is the cluster throughput linear in relation to the single-server baseline?
2. Is the cluster response time similar to the individual server baseline?
3. At what point does the cluster exhaust shared resources?
4. Is each individual server contributing the same level of performance?

Add Another Server and Repeat Step 3

Continue to add additional servers until you verify that the site supports your peak loads. Remember as you add each server to check for new bottlenecks, particularly in shared resources.

Summary

A successful performance test requires disciplined execution. A staged approach starting with a simple configuration and adding complexity at each stage works best. Run sufficient test iterations to understand the performance characteristics of your application and the impact as you add load. Use these tests to remove bottlenecks and lay the foundation for successful production performance and capacity planning. Although you may be tempted to test all your web site components at once, a more measured approach always saves time and helps you readily identify bottlenecks.

Also, just as you bring equipment into the test in a controlled manner, so you should validate your web application software in a similar fashion. Begin with simple, single-user tests of your code paths to find any errors or missing static components. As you increase load, validate your environment by observing the results variance between runs. Excessive variance usually indicates problems with the environment you must resolve before you can conduct a meaningful test.

This chapter covered the basic processes and stages of a good performance test. In the next chapter, we discuss capturing key measurements as the tests run.

Chapter 12

COLLECTING USEFUL DATA

Y our performance test is only as good as the data it produces. We often find customers with excellent performance tests in place but no clear plan for gathering data. Without good data from each test run, you cannot know if the changes you make between runs have the desired impact on your site's performance.

In our experience, customers either capture too much or too little data during their test runs. Not surprisingly, a large, multi-tiered web site generates lots of data. Some customers capture so much data that they actually impact the performance of the test environment. Excessive data logging and data capture often take away significant resources from the test systems. At the other extreme, some customers fail to capture even the most fundamental data points for each run.

CPU Utilization

The CPU provides the processing capability for the various machines involved in your testing. Measuring *CPU utilization* throughout your system gives you a tremendous amount of information about the effectiveness of your test and any tuning adjustments you've made. CPU utilization measures how much of the CPU (or CPUs) available are actually engaged in work. A fully engaged CPU (a CPU running at 100% busy) cannot process more work, so giving the CPU additional work does not result in increased throughput. Likewise, a CPU running at low utilization indicates a system not working as hard as it might. (See Chapter 15 for more details on correlating CPU utilization to system performance.)

During your testing, capture CPU utilization *on all systems involved in the testing.* This includes test clients, HTTP servers, Java application servers, and database machines. Don't forget any mid-tier systems or host systems involved in the test as well. CPU utilization is a cheap thing to measure; it gives you a lot of information about the remaining capacity of the equipment involved in the testing. Also, comparing CPU usage among the systems involved in the test gives you insight into potential bottlenecks.

Monitoring CPU on UNIX Systems

UNIX systems provide some simple tools for measuring the different components of CPU utilization along with some other metrics. The most familiar UNIX-based monitoring tool is vmstat. To run vmstat, simply type in vmstat followed by the refresh interval (in seconds). For example, typing

vmstat 5

tells the system to sample the system every five seconds. The resulting output is shown in Figure 12.1.

Notice the last three columns, where vmstat breaks the CPU down into multiple components: *user* (us), *system* (sy), and *idle* (id).[1] In rough terms, *user* CPU indicates the amount of CPU utilized by an application running on the server. *System* CPU indicates the CPU used by lower-level processes. For example, excessive HTTP listeners sometimes push up the system component of CPU. Also, all Java virtual machines we've seen tend to drive up the system component of CPU slightly (usually under 15%–20%) while the application executes. Add the user and system components to determine total CPU utilization.

The *idle* component indicates how much of the CPU capacity is going unused. Idle indicates the machine capacity still available to handle processing. In this Linux vmstat, CPU wait time is not explicitly broken out. Here, *wait* is detected by using the process stats on the left, indicating running (r), blocked (b), and waiting (w). Nonzero wait values indicate the CPU wants to work but is waiting for some unavailable resource. As discussed in Chapter 13, high wait usually appears when the system experiences excessive disk I/O. Also, we sometimes see this condition during network or remote system failures. Some systems provide an iowait component of CPU time in their vmstat reports. This also gives you an indication of how much time the CPU spends waiting for unavailable resources.

The vmstat report also provides information on paging and disk I/O for the system. These statistics sometimes provide insight into excessive paging or I/O problems within the system. Watching the cs column monitors context switching, and monitoring the swpd column shows system swapping statistics. As we've mentioned before, if you find your JVM paging, reduce the JVM's heapsize or add more memory to your machine. A paging JVM does not give acceptable performance.

Vmstat sends results to stdout by default. To capture the results to a file, redirect them via the command line. We strongly recommend capturing this data to a file for

---

1. A definition of each field shown in Figure 12.1 is found at <http://www.uwsg.iu.edu/usail/man/linux/vmstat.8.html> retrieved from the World Wide Web March 15, 2002.

procs			memory			swap		io		system		cpu		
r	b	w	swpd	free	buff	cache	si	so	bi	bo	in	cs	us	sy	id
0	0	0	0	775344	80060	235576	0	0	0	2	9	32	1	1	16
1	0	0	0	768216	80060	235576	0	0	0	0	111	656	24	1	75
2	0	0	0	763964	80064	235576	0	0	0	70	123	908	56	4	40
2	0	0	0	757760	80064	235576	0	0	0	51	234	1334	47	4	49
0	0	0	0	756128	80064	235576	0	0	0	0	266	2961	16	2	82

FIELD DESCRIPTIONS

Procs

   r: The number of processes waiting for run time.
   b: The number of processes in uninterruptable sleep.
   w: The number of processes swapped out but otherwise runnable.
   This field is calculated, but Linux never desperation swaps.

Memory

   swpd: The amount of virtual memory used (kB).
   free: The amount of idle memory (kB).
   buff: The amount of memory used as buffers (kB).

Swap

   si: Amount of memory swapped in from disk (kB/s).
   so: Amount of memory swapped to disk (kB/s).

IO

   bi: Blocks sent to a block device (blocks/s).
   cs: The number of context switched per second.

CPU

   These are percentages of total CPU time.
   us: User time
   sy: System time
   id: Idle time

Figure 12.1   Sample `vmstat` output

future inspection. We also suggest developing a naming convention to coordinate this information with reports from other systems. Usually a naming convention incorporating the name of the machine, the date, and a test run identifier allows you to associate all of the files for a given test.

Vmstat is a tool supplied by nearly every UNIX operating system, so it's generally available, easy to use, and very understandable. However, if you have multiple components of your web site installed on the same machine, say an HTTP server and an application server, it's difficult to isolate the CPU consumption of each process using `vmstat`. This is one reason why we recommend only deploying one major process to each machine while you're testing, so that you can clearly understand the performance characteristics of each component, and quickly determine which is causing a bottleneck. Some UNIX systems also provide more sophisticated analysis tools such as top and monitor, which help you to understand the CPU utilization of different processes on the same box.

Monitoring CPU on Windows Systems

Microsoft provides the *System Monitor* as part of the Microsoft Management Console. On Microsoft Windows 2000, the function is located under the Administrative Tools → Performance menu structure. The System Monitor provides a dizzying array of information about your system. We suggest starting with simple measurements such as your CPU. (If you use multiprocessor systems, make sure you are getting cumulative reports for all your CPUs.)

Figure 12.2 shows a sample output from the System Monitor. This shows CPU utilization fluctuating as high as 100% with an average of approximately 21%. System Monitor, like many monitoring tools, requires some care. Some measurements require significant resources to obtain, and obtaining them may impact the performance of the system you're measuring. Also, monitoring systems remotely with System Monitor tends to require significant resources.

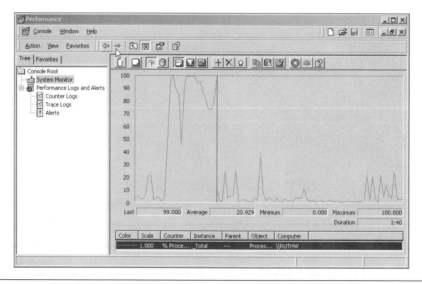

Figure 12.2   Sample Microsoft Windows 2000 System Monitor. ©Microsoft Corporation 2002. Screen shot reprinted by permission from Microsoft Corporation.

Monitoring CPU with a Test Tool

Some test tools allow you to monitor the CPU of the system under test (SUT) along with other measurements such as throughput, user load, and the like. If your test tool provides this feature, you might find it easier to coordinate CPU utilization with certain phases of your test. Do not forget to take CPU measurements on the database, HTTP server, and other systems. Some tests tools make this easy by allowing you to collect statistics from multiple servers.

Java Monitoring

Many operating systems provide a large array of tools to monitor running applications. Sadly, Java applications rarely benefit from these tools because they run inside yet another "machine"—the Java Virtual Machine process running on the system. The JVM remains impenetrable to most operating system level tools. So we look to other tools to help us look inside the JVM.

Verbose Garbage Collection

At least at the early phases of your testing, monitor your JVM heapsize carefully. Also take note of how frequently the JVM garbage collects and how many objects it frees during each collection. As we discussed earlier, constant heap growth indicates a memory leak. Likewise, frequent garbage collections involving the recovery of lots of objects point to poor object management within the application.

Some web application server vendors, as well as some test tool vendors, provide graphical tools for monitoring the JVM during your performance test. For example, Figure 12.3 shows JVM heap dynamics using IBM's WebSphere Application Server Resource Analyzer tool. This figure shows garbage collection dynamics on a run with a 512MB heap. As the chart shows, garbage collection reclaims most of the heap memory, and there is no increasing memory acquisition trend to indicate a memory leak.

Graphical tools are useful for identifying problems. However, the –verbosegc JVM option provides the most detailed information available on garbage collection. The trace produced by this option gives you details about each garbage collection generally not available through a graphical interface.

Verbosegc causes the JVM to write out statistics on each garbage collection to stderr. (Many application server vendors capture stderr in a file.) These stats give you the details as to the frequency and duration of the garbage collection. They also

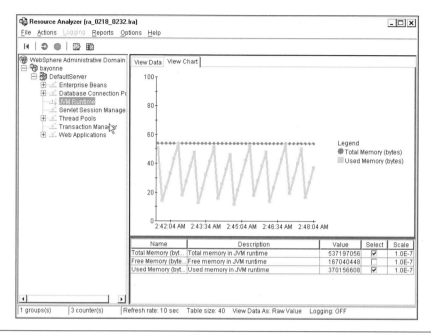

Figure 12.3   Sample JVM heap monitor. ©IBM Corp. 2002. Reprinted by permission of IBM Corp.

tell you how much memory the garbage collection recovered and how many objects it reclaimed. By analyzing the garbage collections over the course of a test run, you get insight into how well the application manages memory.

Listing 12.1 contains a subset of a **verbosegc** output.[2] This particular snippet comes from the fourth garbage collection during a test run. The first line shows the previous allocation failure was 37 seconds prior; also you see this garbage collection cycle completed in just over 1 second. We conclude from this snippet that garbage collection does not present a problem at this point in the test run. (Garbage collection takes a very small percentage of the overall test time.) The log also contains detailed data on the bytes freed and the percentage of the heap free.

Listing 12.1   Sample **verbosegc** output (highlighting provided for readability)

```
<AF[4]: Allocation Failure. need 8208 bytes, 37063 ms since last AF>
<AF[4]: managing allocation failure, action=1 (81352/533723648)
(3145728/3145728)>
```

---

2. Thanks to Harvey Gunther for providing the IBM WebSphere Resource Analyzer data and −verbosegc data for these examples.

```
<GC(4): mark stack overflow>
<GC(4): GC cycle started Mon Feb 04 11:47:06 2002
<GC(4): freed 378953424 bytes, 71% free (382180504/536869376), in 1261 ms>
<GC(4): mark: 1192 ms, sweep: 69 ms, compact: 0 ms>
<GC(4): refs: soft 0 (age >= 32), weak 0, final 17027, phantom 0>
<AF[4]: completed in 1263 ms>
```

By contrast, Listing 12.2 shows the garbage collection behavior much later in the same run. In this log, we find that the time between memory allocation failures falls from 37 seconds to just 3 seconds. (A memory allocation failure indicates no more memory available in the heap and triggers a garbage collection.) In addition, the garbage collection cycle takes longer and frees far less memory.

Listing 12.2 Sample verbosegc output with memory leak occurring (highlighting added for readability)

```
<AF[331]: Allocation Failure. need 8208 bytes, 3391 ms since last AF>
<AF[331]: managing allocation failure, action=2 (356680/536869376)>
<GC(473): mark stack overflow>
<GC(473): GC cycle started Mon Feb 04 13:19:01 2002
<GC(473): freed 34127696 bytes, 6% free (34484376/536869376), in 3155 ms>
<GC(473): mark: 3109 ms, sweep: 46 ms, compact: 0 ms>
<GC(473): refs: soft 0 (age >= 32), weak 0, final 1556, phantom 0>
<AF[331]: managing allocation failure, action=3 (34484376/536869376)>
<AF[331]: managing allocation failure, action=4 (34484376/536869376)>
<AF[331]: clearing all remaining soft refs>
<GC(474): mark stack overflow>
<GC(474): GC cycle started Mon Feb 04 13:19:04 2002
<GC(474): freed 311384 bytes, 6% free (34795760/536869376), in 3101 ms>
<GC(474): mark: 3055 ms, sweep: 46 ms, compact: 0 ms>
<GC(474): refs: soft 9 (age >= 32), weak 0, final 2, phantom 0>
<GC(475): mark stack overflow>
<GC(475): GC cycle started Mon Feb 04 13:19:07 2002
<GC(475): freed 120 bytes, 6% free (34795880/536869376), in 3103 ms>
<GC(475): mark: 3056 ms, sweep: 47 ms, compact: 0 ms>
<GC(475): refs: soft 0 (age >= 32), weak 0, final 0, phantom 0>
<AF[331]: completed in 9368 ms>
```

This listing shows us either an application with a woefully insufficient heap setting or an application with a memory leak. In this case, a memory leak actually caused the memory problems in the test run. After you reach steady state, if verbosegc output shows a pattern of more frequent garbage collections, with less memory being freed in each GC cycle and a smaller percentage of free heap, profile your application for memory leaks.

Verbosegc generates little additional performance overhead. Many customers choose to enable verbosegc throughout their test phase with little impact to their systems. We do, however, recommend running with and without this feature enabled to verify its benign nature in your test environment. We also recommend removing it in production.

Thread Trace

Thread traces give you a snapshot of thread activity inside the JVM. We use these all the time on systems with potential bottlenecks. The snapshot shows us all of the servlet threads waiting inside the JVM for a slow remote system or queuing for a synchronization point. The thread trace provides valuable information about the work occurring inside a JVM.

The thread trace, however, impacts system performance. Obtaining a trace slows the JVM to a crawl, so do not use the performance measurements from the run you used to generate the trace. If you suspect an application bottleneck, setting up a run to obtain one or more thread traces often helps you find the problem.

To obtain a thread trace, issue the following command from a UNIX command prompt:

```
kill -3 <pid>
```

where `pid` is the process ID of the JVM you want to analyze. (Some web application servers run multiple JVMs, so make sure you select the correct JVM!) The resulting trace may wind up in a variety of places depending on the operating system: in the current directory, inside the `stderr` or `stdout` files, or in a working directory. (On Windows systems, use Dr. Watson to trigger the thread dump.)

The resulting file contains a series of thread traces like the one shown in Listing 12.3.

Listing 12.3   Sample thread trace output

```
2: "Servlet.Engine.Transports:75" daemon prio=5 tid=0x5b3a50 nid=0x1f1
waiting for monitor entry [0xebb80000..0xebb819e0]
3: at BadLogger.println(BadLogger.java:61)
4: at BadLogger.printlnDetail(BadLogger.java:36)
5: at HitCount.service(HitCount.java:107)
6: at javax.servlet.http.HttpServlet.service(HttpServlet.java:853)
7: at com.ibm.servlet.engine.webapp.StrictServletInstance.doService
(ServletManager.java:827)
8: at com.ibm.servlet.engine.webapp.StrictLifecycleServlet._service
(StrictLifecycleServlet.java:159)
9: at com.ibm.servlet.engine.webapp.ServicingServletState.service
(StrictLifecycleServlet.java:306)
10:at com.ibm.servlet.engine.webapp.StrictLifecycleServlet.service
(StrictLifecycleServlet.java:106)
11:at com.ibm.servlet.engine.webapp.ServletInstance.service
(ServletManager.java:472)
12:at com.ibm.servlet.engine.webapp.ValidServletReferenceState.dispatch
(ServletManager.java:1012)
13:at com.ibm.servlet.engine.webapp.ServletInstanceReference.dispatch
(ServletManager.java:913)
```

```
14:at com.ibm.servlet.engine.webapp.WebAppRequestDispatcher.handleWebApp-
Dispatch (WebAppRequestDispatcher.java:499)
15:at com.ibm.servlet.engine.webapp.WebAppRequestDispatcher.dispatch
(WebAppRequestDispatcher.java:278)
16:at com.ibm.servlet.engine.webapp.WebAppRequestDispatcher.forward
(WebAppRequestDispatcher.java:105)
17:at com.ibm.servlet.engine.srt.WebAppInvoker.doForward
(WebAppInvoker.java:67)
18:at com.ibm.servlet.engine.srt.WebAppInvoker.handleInvocationHook
(WebAppInvoker.java:123)
19:at com.ibm.servlet.engine.invocation.CachedInvocation.handleInvocation
(CachedInvocation.java:67)
20:at com.ibm.servlet.engine.invocation.CacheableInvocationContext.invoke
(CacheableInvocationContext.java:106)
21:at com.ibm.servlet.engine.srp.ServletRequestProcessor.dispatchByURI
(ServletRequestProcessor.java:125)
22:at com.ibm.servlet.engine.oselistener.OSEListenerDispatcher.service
(OSEListener.java:315)
23:at com.ibm.servlet.engine.http11.HttpConnection.handleRequest
(HttpConnection.java:60)
24:at com.ibm.ws.http.HttpConnection.readAndHandleRequest
(HttpConnection.java:313)
25:at com.ibm.ws.http.HttpConnection.run(HttpConnection.java:242)
26:at com.ibm.ws.util.CachedThread.run(ThreadPool.java:122)
```

In this version of the IBM WebSphere Application Server, the application server names threads available for running servlets or JSPs as follows:

```
"Servlet.Engine.Transports"
```

Notice that the trace associated with the thread gives the code statement executing on the thread at the time we took the trace.

The thread dump contains a trace like the one in Listing 12.3 for each thread executing in the JVM. (We've included only a snippet here for the sake of brevity. An actual thread trace usually includes hundreds of lines.) Review the dump for activity patterns, such as many threads executing the same code statement. Another common bottleneck pattern shows multiple threads waiting for an SQL statement to finish executing, thus indicating a poorly tuned database or a network problem.

Sometimes a thread trace shows us what's *not* happening in your JVM. If you consistently see underutilization of your application server, the thread trace sometimes shows many idle threads! This indicates a bottleneck *before* the application server rather than behind it. In these cases, look at the test clients, HTTP servers, routers, networks, and other equipment preceding the application server in the test environment. You cannot expect the application server to function at full capacity if you cannot deliver requests to it.

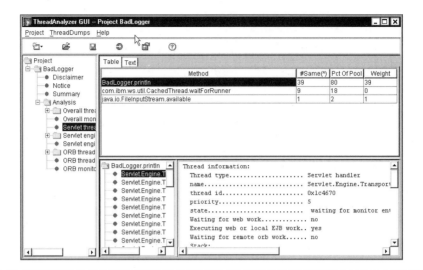

Figure 12.4   Sample Thread Analyzer screen capture. ©IBM Corp. 2002. Reprinted by permission of IBM Corp.

The IBM WebSphere Application Server provides the Thread Analyzer tool to assist in viewing thread dumps. Figure 12.4 shows an example thread dump using this tool. In this example, the dump shows 39 threads, all in the same `BadLogger.println()` method.[3] This indicates a likely bottleneck caused by over-synchronization in the application logging routine. Chapter 13 provides examples of when to use thread dumps to help resolve bottlenecks. Keep in mind that the trace is a snapshot. You might require several traces to give you a feel for any trends in the data. However, for each snapshot you take, restart your JVM and restart your test.

Warning: We recommend using great care when obtaining a thread trace against a production system. Sometimes taking the trace causes the JVM to fail. In all cases, the trace slows the JVM, and it may leave some applications in an uncertain state after it completes. If at all possible, avoid taking a production thread trace; instead, use a test environment .

Other Performance Monitors

Earlier we discussed CPU utilization as one of the key measurements of your web site. Now let's consider some other key measurements to help you better understand the performance of your web application.

---

3. Thanks to Erik Daughtrey for writing the `BadLogger` example and providing the thread trace.

Network Monitoring

We discussed in Chapter 9 how to estimate network capacity for your web site. During the test, however, you need to validate these estimates, particularly if your web site demonstrates bottleneck symptoms such as underutilization. Regrettably, networks don't come equipped with a handy external gauge to report how much traffic they're handling. Instead, you must rely on a variety of tools to tell you how much traffic goes through your network.

On some systems, you may use the `netstat` command to monitor network traffic from a machine attached to an Ethernet network. The machine "sees" all of the traffic passing across the network from its network interface card and tells you how many packets passed through the NIC. Take the netstat measurement before starting the test and after it completes. The difference is the amount of traffic moved across your network during the test. Confirm that the number of packets sent and received looks somewhat reasonable. Also notice whether you're losing a relatively large number of packets over the course of the run.

For Windows systems, use the following command to obtain network statistics:

`netstat -e`

For Solaris and AIX systems, use this command:

`netstat -in`

Some sample output from the `netstat -e` command is shown in Listing 12.4. If you see a proportionally large number of errors or discards in the Received or Sent columns, check your network as well as the sending/receiving machine. Discards indicate dropped packets and point to either network congestion, problems with a specific sending/receiving machine, or a poorly configured network. We cannot emphasize this enough: *You cannot start testing until you successfully analyze and fix any network issues.*

Listing 12.4   Sample `netstat` output

```
C:\>netstat -e
Interface Statistics

                          Received            Sent

Bytes                  354827077         7435073
Unicast packets           239280          126297
Non-unicast packets        31895             127
Discards                       0               0
Errors                         0               0
Unknown protocols          12062
```

If you need more detailed network utilization, consider using a *network protocol analyzer* to analyze your network. The functionality of these tools increases proportionally with price, of course. Some network protocol analyzers exist as freeware software programs and provide some basic information on network capacity, but usually not detailed traffic breakdowns. Also, these inexpensive or free software tools tend to support the slower networks rather than the newer, faster networks.

If you really need detailed information about your network, or you're using a high-speed network, you might require a dedicated network analyzer. These specialized pieces of equipment usually cost thousands of dollars, but they make it much easier to diagnose tricky network problems. Appendix C provides a list of some network protocol analyzer vendors.

These tools examine the packets as they travel across the network and formulate average response times for each component in the test environment. For instance, if the packets for a database request all enter the database server, but the first response packet returns several seconds later, consider tuning the database server. Almost all protocol analyzers provide some analysis of network congestion. Many also help in tracking down misconfigurations, such as DNS problems.

Warning: Check with your network security office before using a network protocol analyzer on your company's network. Many companies actively monitor for network protocol analyzers and consider them a security risk. Also, some companies immediately terminate any employees using these devices on an internal network. Please take this warning seriously, and ask before you use one of these devices.

Software Logs

Several times a year, we receive a call from a customer with a potential performance problem. The customer has tuned a variety of things in the system but can't resolve the bottleneck. Frequently, after examining the log files from the systems involved, we find application errors contributing to the bottleneck condition.

Monitor the logs from your system during each run. As we discussed earlier, the performance test might be the first true, multi-threaded test for a given application. Errors under load occur frequently and usually show up in the logs. Also, the logs sometimes reflect problems due to outages or errors from remote systems. Review the logs after each run, even if things seem to be going well. (Remember, some errors artificially improve test performance.)

Save the logs using a naming convention to distinguish the logs from each run (as discussed earlier in the section on CPU utilization). Keep at least a few days' worth of logs around in case you need to review them later. Of course, watch your hard disk space, particularly on the systems under test. If necessary, archive the logs to a system not actually involved in the testing.

Finally, set your logging to production levels unless you're chasing a problem. We often find customers using verbose logging during their performance testing, which skews their performance numbers. After your initial runs, turn the logging down to the levels you plan to use in production. Otherwise, you impact your performance with excessive disk I/O.

Java Application Server Monitors

Some Java application servers allow you to monitor key measurements as the application server executes. For example, the IBM WebSphere Application Server Resource Analyzer tool allows you to monitor the resources inside the running JVM.

Using the Resource Analyzer, you specify the items of interest, such as a connection pool, or the size of a Bean pool inside an EJB container. The Resource Analyzer allows you to watch these items using a graphical interface. Figure 12.5 shows a Resource Analyzer screen capture for the database connection pool. In this time slice, you see that the pool's utilization hovers in the 40%–70% range. In addition, the data shows connections available immediately for threads (concurrent waiters and average wait time both at zero). The database connection pool appears to be behaving well and does not indicate a bottleneck. (If anything it might even be a little too big.)

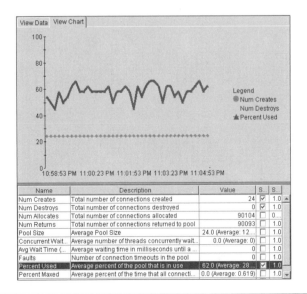

Figure 12.5   Sample Resource Analyzer output. ©IBM Corp. 2002. Reprinted by permission of IBM Corp.

If your Java application server provides a runtime monitoring tool, consider using it as part of your testing. These monitors allow you to observe the internals of your web application server during the test. However, keep in mind that some items might be "performance expensive" to monitor. IBM's Resource Analyzer, for example, gives you the relative "weight" of each item you choose to monitor. During performance runs, try to avoid the expensive measurements unless you're trying to obtain more details for problem resolution. You might consider turning off the monitoring tools periodically to make sure they're not impacting your performance.

Summary

Collect test data throughout your system while testing. Knowing the behavior of as many components as possible helps you identify and resolve performance issues quickly. Also, look at the data you collect from a system perspective. Look for cause-and-effect relationships between the systems under test. If your application server suddenly goes quiet, look for a corresponding activity spike on another system indicating a bottleneck. Remember, the test environment (and the production web site it represents) acts as a system. Measure the entire environment rather than just the web components.

In the next chapter, we explore how to use the data you collect to find bottlenecks. We describe a series of common bottleneck symptoms and walk you through the analysis steps required to pinpoint the actual problem.

Chapter 13

COMMON BOTTLENECK SYMPTOMS

A performance test uncovers performance problems. The tougher task is solving the problems the test uncovers. This chapter discusses how to recognize and eliminate common bottlenecks you might encounter in your testing or even in production. We describe the common patterns of underutilization, bursty utilization, high utilization, and uneven cluster loading. For each pattern, we discuss the symptoms, as well how to diagnose and resolve the problem behind them.

Underutilization

Underutilization describes a system unable to reach full CPU utilization. Let's review the common symptoms of this problem.

- Client and server machines in your test systems never reach their full CPU utilization, regardless of how much you increase the user load.
- The response time increases as you add users, while the throughput remains the same or maybe even starts to decrease.

For example, Figure 13.1 shows Test Run #1 with CPU utilization on the client, application server, and database server all under 50% utilization. In Test Run #2, the client load doubles; however, CPU utilization remains low on all the systems, throughput remains unchanged, but response time increases significantly.

Underutilization appears frequently in performance testing, and indicates one of two problems:

- A bottleneck due to an overloaded resource elsewhere in the system (network, database, test driver, and so on)
- Serialization within the system or the application

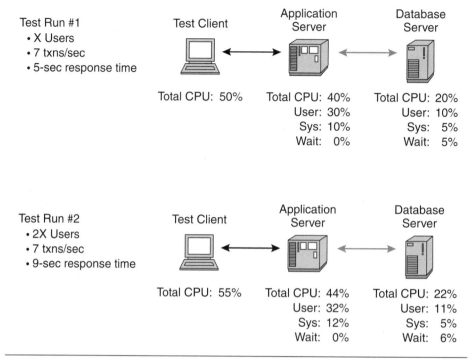

Figure 13.1 Underutilization example. From "Experiences with Successful Website Performance Testing," presented by Stacy Joines at the Solutions 2001 conference, San Francisco, CA. © IBM Corp. 2001. Reprinted by permission of IBM Corp.

Let's examine some of the more common causes of underutilization.

Insufficient Network Capacity

The network acts as a synchronization point if it cannot transfer the full volume of traffic generated by the load. We see this problem frequently if the web site returns much larger pages than originally anticipated during the network design phase.

How to Diagnose

- First, get a feel for the actual page sizes the web site returns. Review the calculations in Chapter 9, and verify (on paper, at least) the traffic volumes moving over the web site.
- If you have a network protocol analyzer, place it on the network to verify the data volumes during the test. (Remember to verify permission to do so first.)

- If a network protocol analyzer is not an option, use the `netstat` command described in Chapter 12 to estimate the data carried by the network.

How to Resolve

- If your network is overwhelmed, you need to increase network capacity. Upgrade the network to support the traffic volume.
- Reduce the amount of data moved across the network. This might include reducing large static elements such as *gifs* and *jpegs* on your pages. However, this usually only provides temporary relief. As your traffic volumes increase, you'll need more network volume.
- Modifying the test scripts sometimes provides another temporary solution. If you want to keep testing while waiting for your network upgrade, you might remove large static elements from your test scripts and only interact with the dynamic portions of the web site. Again, this provides limited, temporary value for your overall testing. Do not apply the results from this type of testing to your production web site.

Application Serialization

We discussed in Chapter 4 some of the synchronization points you might find in your application. Web application synchronization forces the multiple threads running the web application to wait in line to enter the synchronization block. Depending on the size of the synchronization block, this might effectively force a multi-threaded web site into single-threaded operation.

How to Diagnose

Obtain a thread trace of the running web application under load.[1] The thread trace allows you to view what each thread in the web application is doing. Use the thread trace to determine if your applications threads are stalled. See Chapter 12 for more details.

How to Resolve

Remove the synchronization point or reduce the size of the synchronized block in your application.

---

1. On some JVMs, obtaining a thread trace might cause the JVM to fail. Obtaining a thread trace almost always results in a noticeable degradation in system performance. Use this technique with great caution on production systems.

Insufficient Resources

Is your application starving? We discussed above how an overloaded network "starves" your system of incoming load. Likewise, back-end serialization starves your system of data needed to satisfy user requests. Poorly tuned back-end resources, or insufficient resource pools, often cause underutilization.

How to Diagnose

- A thread dump gives the best information about this condition. The threads in the application server appear in the thread dump waiting for a back-end resource. They may be stalled inside an LDAP call, for example, or waiting for a database connection.
- Use analysis tools to help you see the state of the web application server. As we discussed in Chapter 12, the IBM WebSphere Application Server provides a Resource Analyzer tool to help administrators monitor key resources like database connection pools. Key indicators include observing all of a pooled resource in use or threads waiting to obtain a resource.
- Observe the performance of remote resources and capture trace data for your application. How long does it take for the host database to respond to a query? Is a mid-tier database running at 100% CPU? Does the DBA see excessive table scans in the application database? As we discussed in Chapter 9, poor performance on a back-end server impacts the entire web site. Make sure you monitor *all* of the servers and systems involved in your web site. You may find one or more suffering from unnoticed *overutilization*.

How to Resolve

- Fix any performance problems at back-end systems. If your database requires better indices, more CPU, or extra disk platters, add them.

   After resolving a back-end bottleneck, retest the system *without* adding more pooled resource (such as database connections). If the back-end system speeds up, the resources return to the pool more quickly. This makes them available more quickly for the next requestor. For example, we've seen database connection usage drop from 20 simultaneous connections to 2 simultaneous connections after tuning the database.
- If the back-end system seems to be tuned properly, try increasing the pooled resource available. Again, if your back-end system is *not* tuned properly, adding more access points to this resource only makes things worse.

Insufficient Test Client Resource

Insufficient test client hardware cannot drive your test environment to full utilization. That's why we strongly recommend monitoring your test client hardware throughout the testing.

How to Diagnose

- Check your test clients for high CPU utilization. If utilization on any client exceeds 75%, you probably need more client hardware.
- Review the access logs on your HTTP servers or a thread trace from your application server. If the logs show a low number of incoming requests, this also indicates a potential test client problem. This is also true if the thread trace shows few active threads.

How to Resolve

Fix any performance problems with the test clients. Add additional test client hardware as required. Look for options to reduce the test client CPU requirements such as performing less verification or less logging.

Scalability Problem

If you use very large multiprocessor boxes, underutilization, rather than being a symptom of a problem, might be normal behavior, given the current configuration. As we discussed in detail earlier, in some cases a single JVM cannot use all of the CPU capacity of a large multiprocessor box. In this case, you might require more than one JVM to take advantage of most of the processing power of the server.

How to Diagnose

- Only consider scalability as the cause of an underutilization problem if the server contains many processors (at least 12 CPUs). Small to mid-sized servers do not suffer from significant underutilization problems.
- Perform a vertical scalability test on your server, as described in Chapter 11. If your server reaches full utilization with fewer processors, but is underutilized with many processors, you may have a scalability problem.

How to Resolve

Try adding more JVMs to run your web application. Many application servers support starting additional instances of the application server on the same machine, or across multiple machines. See your application server documentation for specific information on configuring multiple instances.

Bursty Utilization

Bursty utilization (also known as *burstiness*) represents a special case of underutilization. The web site runs at high utilization for part of the test, but at other points goes quiet. During these quiet periods, throughput drops as well.

Burstiness occurs for many of the same reasons as underutilization. A synchronization point in a web site component stalls the site for some period of time. After the congestion clears, the site continues with normal operation until a backlog forms again at the synchronization point.

Figure 13.2 shows bursty behavior ten minutes into a test run. The application server and database server CPU utilization drops to only 5% and 2% respectively. Several minutes later, the application server CPU utilization rises to 80%, and the database server CPU utilization goes up to 22%.

Bursty behavior is probably the most challenging performance issue to resolve. Let's look at a few of the more common causes of bursty behavior.

Application Synchronization

Application synchronization sometimes triggers burstiness. The application might contain an infrequently accessed section of code that contains a severe synchronization point. As requests hit this point, they stall until they clear the synchronized block.

How to Diagnose

- A thread trace gives you detailed information on what your threads are actually doing. If your threads are waiting to clear a synchronization block, the thread trace makes this clear.
    In bursty situations, obtain the thread dump during the *idle phase* of the bursty behavior, because any wait occurs during the idle cycles.
- If you cannot obtain a thread trace, try observing the response time of individual servlets and EJBs, if possible. During the idle phase, look for response time spikes on specific paths through your web site. Considering adding traces to your code to analyze the performance of specific methods. Finally, look for timeouts and other error conditions in your logs.

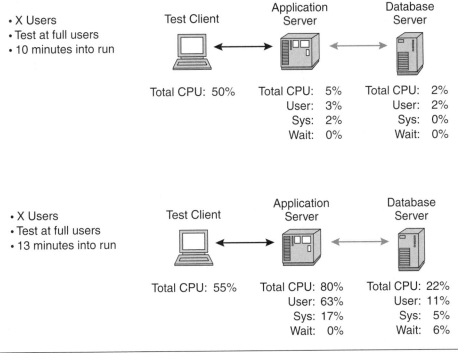

- X Users
- Test at full users
- 10 minutes into run

Test Client

Application Server

Database Server

Total CPU: 50%

Total CPU:	5%	Total CPU:	2%
User:	3%	User:	2%
Sys:	2%	Sys:	0%
Wait:	0%	Wait:	0%

- X Users
- Test at full users
- 13 minutes into run

Test Client

Application Server

Database Server

Total CPU: 55%

Total CPU:	80%	Total CPU:	22%
User:	63%	User:	11%
Sys:	17%	Sys:	5%
Wait:	0%	Wait:	6%

Figure 13.2   Example of bursty behavior. From IBM AIM Services Performance Workshop presented by Stacy Joines, 2001, Hursley, U.K. © IBM Corp. 2001. Reprinted by permission of IBM Corp.

How to Resolve

- If you find that the thread trace shows threads waiting for a serialized resource, remove the synchronization point, or reduce the size of the synchronized code block. If you choose to remove a synchronization point, make sure the code inside the block is threadsafe.
- Resolve any stalled back-end systems impacting your web application. For example, if the thread trace shows all of your threads waiting for responses to JDBC queries, improving the responsiveness of the database involved should resolve the wait condition.

Client Synchronization

The test client is a surprisingly frequent cause of burstiness. Sometimes the test team inadvertently sets up the test tool to feed the web site traffic in bursts. Usually this occurs when the test scripts include think time. The test client software synchronizes these think times, resulting in bursty traffic.

How to Diagnose

- Use your HTTP server and application server monitors to see if work is reaching the servers. For example, look at the active thread count in your application server. If the processes and threads in your server are waiting for work during the idle period, this indicates an upstream problem such as client synchronization.
- Obtain a thread trace. In these cases, the application server doesn't contain any running threads! The system is idle because it doesn't have anything to do.
- Look at the minimum, maximum, and average response times at the test client. Are the response times shorter than the burstiness period? If so, this indicates test clients are not waiting on requests to return during the slow period.
- Check the network with a network protocol analyzer. This diagnosis requires more skill than network capacity analysis; you need the inbound and outbound traffic analyzed. Has the web site responded to the inbound requests, but not received additional requests in a while? This is usually a good indication of test client synchronization.

How to Resolve

Better quality test client software usually allows you to randomize the virtual client think times. You provide a range of acceptable think time values, and the test client software randomly picks a think time within the range. Random think times provide a more even loading of the web site and more realistically represent production traffic.

Back-End Systems

We discussed earlier the impact of stalled back-end systems. Frequently these show up in a thread trace, but you may detect these issues without obtaining a trace. A periodic back-end system stall occurs for a number of reasons. For databases, the system may stall while resolving a deadlock. Other stalls might result from network issues or disk I/O. Once the bottleneck clears, the system runs at capacity until the condition leading to the bottleneck occurs again.

Figure 13.3 shows a misbehaved back-end system where the database CPU jumps to 100% CPU utilization 10 minutes into the run and then returns to 22% at 13 minutes.

How to Diagnose

Observe the CPUs and disk I/O of your back-end systems. Does the CPU stay busy on one of your systems while the other systems are idle? The system still busy probably contains the source of the bottleneck.

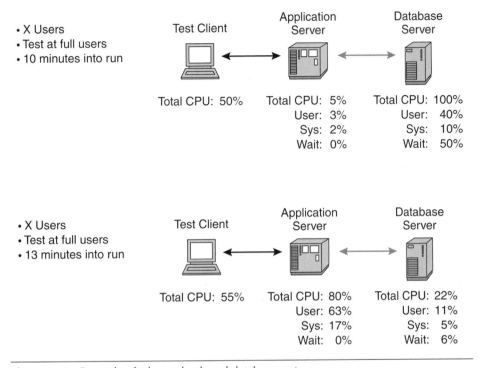

- X Users
- Test at full users
- 10 minutes into run

Test Client

Application Server

Database Server

Total CPU: 50%

Total CPU: 5%
User: 3%
Sys: 2%
Wait: 0%

Total CPU: 100%
User: 40%
Sys: 10%
Wait: 50%

- X Users
- Test at full users
- 13 minutes into run

Test Client

Application Server

Database Server

Total CPU: 55%

Total CPU: 80%
User: 63%
Sys: 17%
Wait: 0%

Total CPU: 22%
User: 11%
Sys: 5%
Wait: 6%

Figure 13.3 Example of a bursty back-end database system

How to Resolve

You need assistance from the administrator of the system in question. Use your DBAs or host specialists to find the cause of the bottleneck on the remote system and help you resolve it.

Garbage Collection

During normal operation, the application server stops servicing requests during the synchronized parts of the garbage collection cycle. As JVM garbage collection technology continues to improve, the synchronized portion of the cycle shortens; however, all other JVM work still ceases for a period of time during garbage collection. This especially applies during compaction cycles. Usually, garbage collection does not produce prolonged periods of burstiness. However, very large JVM heaps often require long garbage collection cycles and cause noticeable burstiness.

How to Diagnose

- Using CPU monitoring techniques described in Chapter 12, look for the CPU percentage utilized on the application server box dropping to 1/number of processors. This behavior occurs during the single-threaded portions of the garbage collection cycle. (in this part of the cycle, only one processor is busy.) Also, look for reduced utilization of back-end systems during this time period.
- Use your application server JVM monitors or `verbosegc`, as described in Chapter 12, to determine if the idle period on the web site corresponds to garbage collection cycles. Also, check the `verbosegc` log for the length of the garbage collection cycles.

How to Resolve

- Reducing the maximum heap setting on your JVM shortens the duration of garbage collection. The JVM garbage collects more often but for shorter periods of time, minimizing the bursty behavior. Refer to Chapter 4 for more discussion on garbage collection dynamics.
- Reduce the amount of garbage created by your application. Use this technique in conjunction with reducing the maximum heap size.

Timeout Issues

Abnormal timeout values often trigger bursty behavior. In these cases, the test system may wait for an unusually long period until the timeout associated with some resource expires. Solaris, for example, defaults the timeout for TCP/IP connections to four minutes. A test generating heavy load against these systems may suddenly encounter a four-minute idle period while waiting for a TCP/IP connection to come available on the servers. Lowering the timeout interval (`tcp_time_wait`) resolves this problem.

How to Diagnose

Look for a consistent pattern or interval in the idle period. (Use your monitoring tools to closely measure the burstiness pattern.) If the idle period lasts roughly three minutes, for example, then look for a corresponding configuration setting set to approximately three minutes in the test environment.

How to Resolve

- Adjust the configuration setting and retest.
- If you cannot adjust the setting, consider adding more of the constrained resource to work around the problem.

Network Issues

Finally, if all else fails, look at the network involved. Check the settings on your firewalls and any other intervening hardware. Network-induced burstiness occurs less frequently than the other causes we've discussed, but sometimes improper network configuration leads to burstiness under load. Even if the network isn't at fault, it usually holds clues to help you resolve the problem.

How to Diagnose

- Use a network protocol analyzer. Plug it into all the segments of your network in a systematic manner. Where does the traffic go before the idle phase of the burst hits? Are you seeing network timeouts during the idle phase? Try to determine if the traffic flows through all components and segments of the network.

  This requires some skill in network analysis. You need experience with following network "conversations" at a low level inside your network. Some tools support HTTP protocol diagnosis, while others only support analysis at the IP level. Of course, if you use SSL, obtaining detailed conversation information may be difficult because of encryption of the packets. Turn off SSL, if possible, to make analysis possible.
- Eliminate unnecessary components. Take firewalls, routers, switches, and load balancers out of the equation. If the burstiness goes away, add the equipment back to the network one component at a time. Once you find the offending component, check its settings and operation to uncover the source of the problem.

How to Resolve

Obviously, you need help from your network team. Once you isolate the problem component, you need someone who is knowledgeable about the offending equipment to resolve the issue.

High CPU Utilization

During your testing, the CPU utilization of one of your servers may reach high levels (95% or above). High CPU utilization indicates CPU saturation. You have exhausted the processing capacity of this computer.

What are your options after the application server CPU reaches full utilization? Is this the maximum load for your server, or can you add more load to this server? To answer these questions, we explore the components of the burdened CPU. We also look at the throughput plateau and corresponding response times of the busy system.

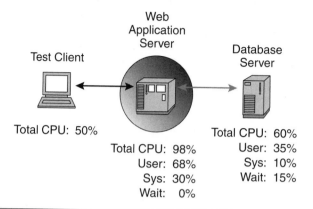

Figure 13.4 Example of high CPU utilization. From "Experiences with Successful Website Performance Testing," presented by Stacy Joines at the Solutions 2001 conference, San Francisco, CA.© IBM Corp. 2001. Reprinted by permission of IBM Corp.

High User CPU

In Figure 13.4, the total CPU contains a high amount of user CPU (68% in this case). High user CPU means the server is very busy handling requests from the web application. Also, notice that the system component of CPU in our example is at 30%. For Java applications, the system component of CPU normally tends to be somewhat high.

If the application uses most of the CPU, consider these choices before continuing with your testing. First, consider your response time. For a reasonably tuned application, the CPU saturation indicates a throughput plateau for your testing on this server. In other words, you cannot continue to increase throughput on this server regardless of how much additional load you apply.

However, the CPU saturation does not necessarily mean the server cannot support additional load. Users only know response time. A saturated server may continue to support increasing load as long as the response time remains acceptable. Of course, the server queues the arriving load once the server becomes saturated. However, if the wait in the queue remains short, the overall response time remains acceptable as well. (See Chapter 1 for more discussion on throughput, load, and response time dynamics.)

Under normal conditions, we don't recommend increasing the load on a saturated CPU. The additional load waits for CPU resources to free. If load increases on this server, the wait time grows linearly for all users. As a general rule, try to keep queues in front of your HTTP server to allow optimal load balancing. Minimizing queues within your application and database server provides the optimal performance. However, your test results may show that the high user CPU does not prevent you from achieving your performance objectives.

Let's assume you anticipated getting better throughput or response time through the server than you're currently achieving. Let's look at some of the common causes of high CPU utilization during a test run.

How to Diagnose

During your tests, the CPU utilization reaches 100%. If the user component of CPU exceeds 75%, with little or no utilization in the wait component, the system runs with high user CPU utilization.

How to Resolve

- Tune the application. Make the application more efficient so it requires less CPU to perform the tasks you're requesting of it. Use a code profiler to uncover inefficiencies in the application and make improvements.

    To help focus on the critical paths to profile, look at a "runtime profile" of your application. When your system is running under load, which areas of the web application does the profiler identify as being slow? Focus your tuning efforts on the slow but frequently called areas of your application.

    After completing your profiling exercise, consider using thread traces to further remove bottlenecks in the application. The thread trace shows the thread activity under load, unlike many code profilers, which show only a single execution path.

    Application tuning makes a lot of sense when you reach CPU saturation. You might find opportunities for significant performance improvements and reduce the CPU burden of your application. This increases the capacity of each of your servers and reduces the equipment you need for your web site.
- Add processing capacity. At some point, additional application tuning begins to provide diminishing benefits. If you need to support additional load, you need additional processing capacity. Try adding servers to the web site cluster or increasing the CPUs in the server. You might also try increasing the speed of your CPUs by updating the web site hardware. Refer to Chapters 1 and 3 for more discussion on scaling a web site.

High System CPU

As mentioned in the previous section, the system component of CPU tends to run somewhat high with Java applications. However, other factors influence system

CPU. Too much time devoted to this component impacts the CPU capacity available to run the web application. Figure 13.5 shows the application server at 80% CPU utilization. Of this, the system component absorbs 45% of the utilization.

How to Diagnose

Observe the CPUs on your application server. If your CPU is near 100%, look at the breakdown between user, system, and wait time. Check to see if the system component is using more than 30% of the total CPU, and there is little to no wait time.

How to Resolve

- Check the HTTP server. If the HTTP server runs on the same machine as the application server, the listeners started by the HTTP server impact the CPU of the machine. This impact usually appears in the system component of the CPU utilization. To resolve this problem, reduce the number of listeners started by the HTTP server or move the HTTP server onto its own machine.

  Excessive listeners (over a few hundred, for example) usually indicate a performance problem within the web application. If the application responds quickly, the web site usually requires fewer listeners.
- Check other processes running on the box. These processes sometimes run at a low level in the system and impact system CPU. Eliminate unnecessary processes on your application server boxes.

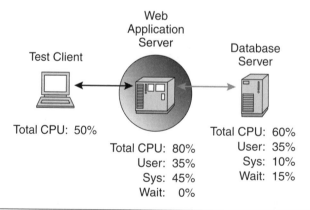

Test Client

Web Application Server

Database Server

Total CPU: 50%

Total CPU: 80%
User: 35%
Sys: 45%
Wait: 0%

Total CPU: 60%
User: 35%
Sys: 10%
Wait: 15%

Figure 13.5 Example of high system CPU utilization. From "Experiences with Successful Website Performance Testing," presented by Stacy Joines at the Solutions 2001 conference, San Francisco, CA.© IBM Corp. 2001. Reprinted by permission of IBM Corp.

High Wait CPU

Excessive wait CPU indicates a serious performance problem, and it usually occurs when the CPU interacts with a slower resource. Usually the high wait cycle problem emerges when the server spends a proportionally large amount time interacting with the hard disk. However, occasionally high I/O wait times result from network problems or other issues.

Any machine is prone to high wait CPU, although it most commonly occurs on database and web application servers. Figure 13.6 shows the database server at 75% CPU utilization, with 50% of this devoted to wait time.

Note that all database servers usually show some amount of CPU wait. However, if this component becomes too high, it shows that the CPU accomplishes very little aside from waiting on the hard disk. In these cases, tuning is usually appropriate.

How to Diagnose

- Observe the CPUs on all your servers. Look for any database or other server performing extensive I/O with more than 30% wait time, and any less I/O intensive server with greater than 3% wait time.
- Use a thread trace at the application server to determine if the I/O really represents a bottleneck. If you see threads waiting for logging to complete or waiting for a database with high wait CPU, you need to begin tuning.

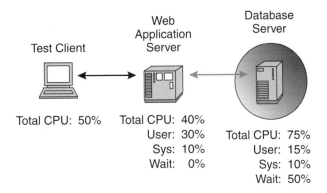

Figure 13.6   Example of high CPU wait on a database server

How to Resolve

- Check application logging. Excessive application logging requires the system to interact with the hard drive more frequently, which triggers abnormally high CPU wait.

  We've discussed effective logging strategies for various components throughout the book and won't repeat them here. However, review these sections to develop a better logging strategy. (In case you've forgotten, Chapter 9 discusses database logging, Chapter 2 covers web application logging, and Chapter 3 discusses the HTTP server logs.)

  Test clients also succumb to excessive logging problems, so keep your logging at the test client to a minimum (particularly if your test requires hundreds or thousands of virtual users).

- Check disk space availability on the server. If the server doesn't have enough room to write the logs, you might see CPU wait problems. You might also see application errors. Add disk space, reduce logging, or clean out some space on the existing drives.

- Check database efficiency. If the system in question is a database server, try some of the tuning tips for databases mentioned in Chapter 9. Consult your DBA for detailed reports on database performance and consider tuning the database to make its disk I/O more efficient.

- Check remote systems and the network. In rare cases, sluggish remote systems trigger high wait CPU. After you eliminate other causes, check the performance of the remote systems and the network connected to your web site.

Uneven Cluster Loading

Multiple server clusters sometimes exhibit *uneven cluster loading*. One or more machines in the cluster receive a disproportionate amount of traffic compared to the other servers in the cluster. Figure 13.7 shows a cluster of two application servers, where one application server's CPU is at 90% utilization, while the other server is only 5% busy.

Uneven cluster loading prevents your site from utilizing all of its potential capacity. As traffic increases, a few servers bear the brunt of the load, while other servers in the cluster remain idle. Let's examine some of the common causes behind this symptom.

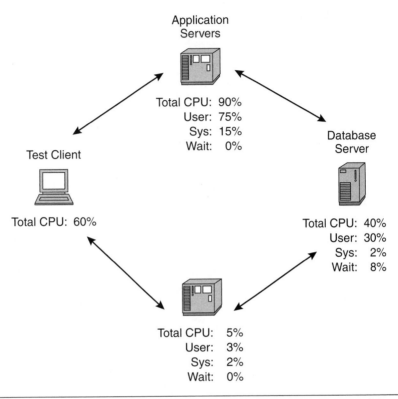

Figure 13.7 Uneven cluster loading. From IBM AIM Services Performance Workshop presented by Stacy Joines, 2001, Hursley, U.K. © IBM Corp. 2001. Reprinted by permission of IBM Corp.

Network Issues

How to Diagnose

Check your network hardware. Load balancers and firewalls involved in your website's construction, in particular, are likely to contribute to this problem. Check for improper configuration of these devices that is potentially contributing to this problem. For example, your firewall might limit traffic flow to some addresses to prevent denial of service attacks. If these limits are misconfigured, the firewall might starve some servers.

How to Resolve

- Simplify your environment and retest. If the problem goes away, systematically add components back into the environment, retesting after each addition. After you pinpoint the offending equipment, work with your network team to reconfigure the equipment in question.

- Use a network protocol analyzer to isolate any component that is sending uneven traffic levels to your servers. This requires detailed analysis of network conversation traffic, which requires a skilled network person.

Routing Issues

How to Diagnose

Look at the CPU utilization on each application server. If CPU utilization is unbalanced, look at the number of requests handled by the HTTP server and the application server. Is the number of incoming requests unbalanced? Check the routing policy for the load balancer.

How to Resolve

Avoid IP affinity routing. Some load balancers allow you to route users repeatedly to a given server based on the user's IP address. Affinity routing allows users to complete their visits without changing servers and improves performance if the web site uses SSL. Affinity also improves performance if the web application uses HTTP sessions.

However, IP affinity causes uneven loading on large, public web sites. Public web site traffic often comes from large ISPs. Large ISP users interact with public web sites through one or more of the ISP's proxy servers. Any user going through the proxy server interacts with the internet using the proxy's IP address. For large ISPs, potentially thousands of users could appear on the internet with the same IP address.

Replace IP affinity routing with user-based routing, as shown in Figure 13.8. For example, the IBM WebSphere Application Server provides an affinity routing mechanism to route users to specific web application server clones. The IBM WebSphere Application Server uses proprietary software in the HTTP server plug-in to support the affinity routing. This software does not rely on an IP address, but uses other means to uniquely identify each incoming user, regardless of whether she enters the site via a proxy. Refer to Chapter 3 for more information on load balancing techniques.

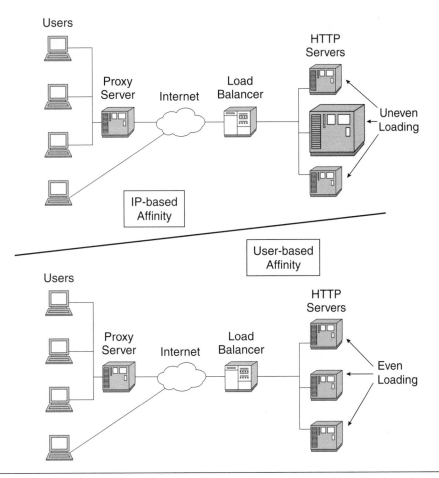

Figure 13.8   IP-based versus user-based affinity

Summary

Bottlenecks are inevitable during performance testing. There are several common patterns easily distinguished by observing the CPU utilization on the different servers during the test. Each of these patterns (underutilization, bursty utilization, high utilization, and uneven cluster loading) potentially results from a number of different causes. Performance testing requires recognizing and resolving each of these bottlenecks in order to meet your performance objectives. We apply some of these techniques in the next chapter as we continue our case study.

Chapter 14

CASE STUDY: DURING THE TEST

Update

During the last case study, the TriMont team sent you some early data on their new web site, and we worked through a preliminary analysis of this data. Now the TriMont team is ready to begin their performance testing in earnest.

Test Environment

Many things, of course, happened to move the test forward to this point. Let's review some of the activity at TriMont since the initial case study.

Hardware Configuration

The TriMont team reviewed your initial network analysis and agreed to the assumptions you made. The web site manager became somewhat alarmed at the traffic volumes expected at peak loading (the potential for 1,400 requests/second in the peak hour). The TriMont team decided to use a caching proxy server for their static content.

TriMont representatives also spoke with their web application server vendor and came up with some rough sizing estimates for their web site. The site receives, at peak, 87.5 dynamic requests/second. The TriMont team wants to give the web site a margin of safety for unexpected traffic (for more details on headroom estimates, see Chapter 6), so they actually use 120 dynamic requests/second as their planning number. This provides a little over 25% headroom for the web site, which they consider sufficient.

```
87.5 requests/sec / 120 requests/sec = 73%
```

The application server vendor publishes capacity planning data for its customers. TriMont estimates an eight-CPU UNIX server should support 40 requests per second given their particular application. Using this estimate, the web site requires three eight-CPU UNIX servers to support 120 requests per second. To handle site capacity if one server fails, the team plans for four eight-CPU servers.

Input Data

Tables 14.1 and 14.2 show the calculations using the Hardware Sizing worksheet from Appendix A.

Table 14.1   Hardware Sizing Worksheet, Lines 1–6

	Input Data	Source	Your Data
1.	Concurrent users	Appendix A: Capacity Sizing worksheet	7,350 users
2.	Throughput: page rate	Appendix A: Capacity Sizing worksheet	87.5 pages/sec
3.	Throughput: requests	Appendix A: Capacity Sizing worksheet	1,400 requests/sec (87.5 dynamic)
4.	Response time	Marketing	5 sec
5.	Headroom factor	Marketing/planning	25%
6.	Estimated throughput supported on your selected hardware	Hardware/application server vendor	40 requests/sec (dynamic)

Calculating Hardware Requirement Estimate (Pre-Test)

Table 14.2   Hardware Sizing Worksheet, Lines 7–10

	Calculated Data	Equation	Total
7.	Concurrent users (with headroom)	Concurrent users + Concurrent users / (100 / Headroom − 1) Line 1 + Line 1 / (100 / Line 5 −1)	7,350 + 7,350/3 = 9,800 users Round to 10,000 users
8.	Throughput requirement (with headroom): page rate	Throughput + Throughput / (100 / Headroom − 1) Line 2 + Line 2 / (100 / Line 5 − 1)	87.5 + 87.5 / 3 = 117 pages Round to 120 pages/sec

Table 14.2   Hardware Sizing Worksheet, Lines 7–10 (Continued)

	Calculated Data	Equation	Total
9.	Throughput requirement (with headroom): requests	Throughput + Throughput / (100 / Headroom – 1) Line 3 + Line 3 / (100 / Line 5 – 1)	1,400 + 1,400 / 3 = 1866 requests/sec
10.	Application servers required	Throughput requirement / Estimated throughput for your hardware + 1 Maintenance) Line 8 / Line 6 + 1	120 / 40 + 1 = 4 servers

TriMont wants a basic DMZ configuration, as discussed in Chapter 3. They put together the list of equipment shown in Table 14.3.

Table 14.3   Production Equipment List

Equipment	Quantity
Router	1
Caching proxy server	2
HTTP server machines	4
Java Web Application Server machines	4
Firewall servers	2
Persistent HTTP session database servers	1
Boat Selector DB server	1

At your urging, TriMont agrees to performance test at least half of the production configuration. The actual performance test environment uses two Java web application servers, two HTTP servers, and one caching proxy server (the other hardware remains the same). Figure 14.1 shows the resulting test environment configuration.

Note the following things in this configuration:

- In the test-planning phase, you approached TriMont about their Orders database. Since the performance tests actually place orders, you wondered if TriMont might use special account numbers to test their systems.
- Actually, TriMont doesn't use special account number to test their system. Instead, they build a special Orders test database for testing purposes. This database lives outside their business infrastructure, so they can run tests without impacting their inventory, shipping, or accounting systems.
- This system should work just fine for the performance test. The test scripts just require an order to check, which this provides. The URL link to the shipping company's web site is not part of the TriMont performance test, so integration of order numbers between TriMont and the shipper is not important for performance testing.

- As discussed in Chapter 11, TriMont does not plan to throw the switch on all this equipment on the first day of performance testing. This means they will use just an HTTP Server/application server pair (and backend databases) for the first week or so. All of the intervening equipment (firewalls, routers, caching proxy servers) remain inactive during this initial testing.
- Next, they plan to double the load on the web site and add the second HTTP Server and application server to the mix, along with the router and perhaps the caching proxy server. Finally, in the last days of the test, they plan to turn on the firewalls to assure they do not significantly impact the performance of the web site.

We know more about the TriMont test than we did in the initial assessment. For example,

- The site must support 120 pages per second.
- Three servers should handle all of this traffic.

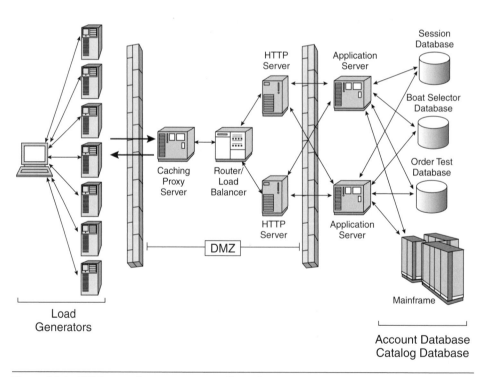

Figure 14.1   TriMont performance test configuration

120 pages per second translates to the following number of concurrent users:

```
120 pages/sec / 5 pages/user = 24 users/sec
```

```
24 users/sec * 7 min/visit * 60 sec/min = 10,080 concurrent users
```

Since we are estimating anyway, let's round to 10,000 concurrent users for simplicity's sake. (We'll do this throughout this section.) Note that this number corresponds to the Hardware Planning Worksheet, line 7 (Table 14.2), give or take a little for rounding order.

The test environment only uses two servers, whereas we expect to fully engage three servers in the production environment. (The fourth production server is spare capacity for failover). Since we're using two-thirds of our production capacity in the test environment, we need to generate two-thirds of the production users:

```
10,000 concurrent users * 2/3 = 6,700 concurrent users
```

As we discussed in Chapter 8, most major commercial performance test tool vendors charge on a "per virtual user" basis. A 7,000 user license represents a significant investment when dealing with most major testing client vendors. Not surprisingly, TriMont does not want to spend potentially tens of thousands of dollars on virtual user licensing.

Instead, TriMont decides to try a different testing technique. They want to reduce the duration of each virtual user's visit by reducing each virtual user's think time. For example, if the average user visit becomes 45 seconds instead of seven minutes, the number of virtual users required by the test drops dramatically:

```
120 pages/sec / 5 pages/user = 24 users/sec
```

```
24 users/sec * 45 sec = 1,080 simultaneous users
```

The test environment requires two-thirds of these users to drive the two boxes:

```
1,080 users * 2/3 = 720 simultaneous users
```

Of course, we need to be sure 45 seconds is a reasonable amount of time for a user visit to complete:

```
45 sec/visit / 5 pages/visit = 9 sec/page
```

TriMont wanted 5 second response time or better, even at peak loading. Nine seconds per page allows us to meet this response time with a small margin for think time. Therefore, 45 seconds should work for the test.

HTTP Session Pressure

So, TriMont uses fewer virtual users but requires them to interact with the site faster. This gives the same traffic rates as a larger number of users with longer think times. This technique works well in many situations, but may lead to problems if the web site software caches or uses HTTP sessions (which TriMont's does). For example, a TriMont user stays on the site an average of 7 minutes in production usage. The HTTP session stays in memory until the timeout period for the HTTP session completes (currently, TriMont's is set at 30 minutes). This means each HTTP session stays active for an average of 37 minutes. If the user visit lasts only 45 seconds, the HTTP session active time becomes approximately 31 minutes. This reduces the number of HTTP sessions in memory, and gives an overly optimistic view of memory requirements.

Let's do some calculations to work out the impact of fewer users on the TriMont performance test. Remember, we calculated 10,000 concurrent users for the entire web site, given our new requirements for additional headroom. Since we're only testing two-thirds of the web site's capacity, we estimate 6,700 concurrent users for our two test servers (10,000 concurrent users * 2/3). In a full test, 6,700 concurrent users generate the following number of HTTP sessions within 37 minutes (the production HTTP session timeout period):

```
37 min / 7 min/visit * 6,700 users = 35,500 simultaneous HTTP sessions
(for two-thirds of the web site traffic)
```

Note this only represents two-thirds of the simultaneous HTTP sessions for the full web site. For the full web site, the simultaneous HTTP sessions would be higher:

```
37 min / 7 min/visit * 10,000 users = 53,000 simultaneous HTTP sessions
(for the full web site traffic)
```

Also, notice the slightly *different* way we calculated the maximum HTTP sessions in this exercise. We're trying to measure how many visits or iterations each virtual user makes during the test. At the end of each visit, the virtual user starts a new visit as a new customer. As a new customer, the virtual user triggers a new HTTP session at the web site. So, if the virtual user requires 7 minutes to complete a visit under one user identity, the virtual user only assumes about 5 different customer identities during a 37-minute test (37 minutes / 7 minutes per visit = 5 different customer visits). We multiply this by the total virtual users involved in the test to determine how many HTTP sessions we generate during the test period.

Continuing our example, we only use 720 users in the reduced virtual user test, and we reduce their visit time to 45 seconds. This results in the following HTTP session pressure within 31 minutes (the reduced average HTTP session timeout period):

```
31 min / 45 sec/visit * 720 users = 29,760 simultaneous HTTP sessions
```

Of course, as discussed in Chapter 11, iterations of the initial performance tests only last a few minutes (at most 15 or 20 minutes in the beginning). This further reduces the difference in the HTTP session memory footprint. For example, both styles of testing (full virtual users versus recycled virtual users) generate the following number of HTTP sessions during a 20-minute test:

```
20 min / 7 min/visit * 6,700 users = 19,143 HTTP sessions
```

```
20 min / 45 sec/visit * 720 users = 19,200 HTTP sessions
```

Therefore, the shorter test actually generates

```
19,200 HTTP sessions - 19,143 HTTP sessions = 57 more HTTP sessions
```

Compare this to the difference in HTTP sessions in a *longer test* spanning a full timeout range:

```
35,500 HTTP sessions - 29,760 HTTP sessions = 5,740 fewer HTTP sessions
```

TriMont decides to continue with a reduced number of virtual users for their initial performance testing. They plan to keep their 500 user license until they reach capacity on the first machine. Depending on the results of that test, they will upgrade the license when they add another server to the mix. However, they want to exert more pressure in their post-performance test work. They may buy the much larger 7,000 virtual user license for a limited time (maybe two or three weeks). Using this license, they plan some long-run stress testing before they enter production. This approach not only reduces their expenses in regard to virtual user licensing, but also gives them a realistic long-run test of the environment prior to entering production.

Testing Underway

In this part of our case study, we'll look at some potential problems the TriMont team might encounter while conducting the performance test. In Chapter 13, we covered some of the common performance symptoms and causes we encounter frequently in the field. We try to apply some of those lessons in this case study. Of course, for any given performance test, you may encounter a completely different set of problems. Likewise, for any given performance problem symptom (burstiness, underutilization, and so on), a variety of solutions exist. Please do not assume that the solutions we present in this case study are the only solutions for the symptoms discussed.

Burstiness

As planned, the TriMont team begins the testing with only one Java web application server machine and one HTTP server machine. They set up a small cluster of test client machines and plan to start the test with 100 virtual users. Remember, we expect 720 virtual users to drive both our systems to full utilization. Testing only one web application server and HTTP server pair, we expect we'll need half that number (360 virtual users); thus, 100 users represent about 27% of the load we expect these servers to handle.

Symptoms

The TriMont test team starts the 100 user test and brings the virtual users on-line over the course of 5 minutes (20 users per minute). The team lets the test run for 10 minutes *after* all the users log on. Then the virtual users finish the test over a period of 2 minutes. This gives us a total test time of 17 minutes, 10 minutes of which actually generates usable data. (Remember: don't use the ramp-up or ramp-down time in your results; see Chapter 11 for details.)

Unfortunately, the initial data doesn't look good at all. Here's a sample of the CPU data captured during the testing:

Table 14.4   TriMont Initial Test Results

Time (from test start)	HTTP Server	Java Web App Server	Catalog Database Server
6 minutes	20%	20%	5%
8 minutes	0%	0%	0%
10 minutes	21%	21%	5%
12 minutes	0%	0%	0%

The team repeated the test several times, but got similar results for each run attempted. They even tried adding more users to the test, but continued to see similar results (with higher CPU utilization before the CPU went to 0% busy).

Problem Isolation

This is a classic presentation of the *burstiness* performance problem. For some reason, our servers (and database, in this case) do no work at intervals during the test. As we discussed in Chapter 13, this could be because no work is arriving at the servers or because some back-end resource (such as a database) is not providing needed information in a timely manner to the servers. You ask a few questions of the TriMont test team to try to isolate the problem. Here's the dialog with the test team.

What is the response time during the lulls?

The team has not isolated the response times during the lulls in the test. However, the overall response time remains acceptable (under three seconds).

What type of scripts does the test run?

The test only runs the browse script at this point. This limits the systems involved in the testing to the following:

- HTTP server machine
- Application server machine
- Catalog database server machine
- HTTP session database server machine

Do you have any CPU data for the HTTP session database server?

Yes. The HTTP session database server exhibits the same pattern of bursty activity as the catalog database.

This exchange tells you that none of the servers involved in the testing have an overwhelmed CPU. Theoretically, all servers involved in the test have enough capacity to support the traffic. Also, you learned that the response time during the test remains good despite the "dead spots" in the test. This raises your suspicions about the test client's role in the burstiness. If the clients waited during the "dead spots," you would expect a high overall response time. Granted, you don't have a good run as a basis for comparison at this point, but still this data puts the test client high on your list of suspects. Also, it's early in the test, and TriMont lacks experience with test tools. You want a closer look at the test client setup.

Problem Resolution

You examine the test client settings and discover a few problems:

- The think times in the scripts are too long. The team forgot to reduce the times from the 7-minute visit to think times more appropriate to a 45-second visit.
- The test team did not randomize the think times in the script. All of the virtual users in the test wait exactly the same amount of time after they finish a task.
- The test does not gradually increase the active virtual users in groups of 20 over a 5-minute period. Instead, the team configured (accidentally, of course) *all* of the virtual users to start making requests *simultaneously* after a 5-minute wake-up period. (The virtual users start in groups of 20 every minute (they

"wake up"), but they don't actually start sending requests until all 100 users are "awake.")

Overall, TriMont took several shortcuts that made problem resolution more difficult. As discussed in Chapter 7, always take the time to read the generated scripts (Appendix B, Pretest Checklists, Test Simulation and Tooling). Reviewing the scripts identifies the think time issues. In addition, the team started testing with a 100 client simulation. As described in Chapter 11, a good practice is to start with a single user run as this makes problems easier to identify and diagnose.

Also, the team never caught the last problem (the synchronized start) because they didn't capture data during the start-up period. Of course, you don't want to use this data in your final analysis, but it's a good idea to watch the systems during all parts of the testing for unusual behavior. If the TriMont team had followed this advice, they would have noticed that none of the servers were active during the start-up time.

The TriMont team addresses each of these problems. They reduce the think times in their scripts and randomize them within an upper and lower bound. They also fix the start-up to provide the staggered start they always intended. After they make these changes, the burstiness goes away. They see CPU utilization remain steady throughout the testing.

Other Considerations

The test client headed our list of suspects and actually turned out to be the source of the problem. However, if we had pursued the test client angle but found everything in order, the next step might be a closer examination of the network. A network protocol analyzer always proves useful in these cases, as it allows us to see which component in the test system has stopped sending or receiving traffic. Also, a thread trace might help by telling us if the application servers are active, or if they're waiting on a back-end resource.

Also, we recommend watching the test run and collecting real-time data. This allows you to double-check the information you receive from third parties (in this case, the TriMont test team). In fact, if you had watched the test run in this case, you might have noticed right away that the remote systems showed no activity during test startup.

Bad information costs lots of time in bottleneck resolution. The data points you to potential problem areas. A bad data point may lead you to waste lots of time examining systems that are not involved in the bottleneck. Nothing replaces watching the test run for yourself and collecting key data points.

Underutilization

After resolving the burstiness problem, the performance test moves ahead. Using the corrected test client setup, the performance team successfully runs 100 virtual users against the HTTP server and application server setup. Table 14.5 contains the recorded system metrics for the test. The test team arrived at these numbers by obtaining measurements at steady state. These represent maximum usage for the systems (discounting garbage collection cycles on the application server).

Table 14.5   One Hundred Virtual Users Test Results

Measurement	Value
CPU utilization	
■ HTTP server	20%
■ Web application server	22%
■ Catalog database server	5%
■ HTTP session database server	25%
■ Order test database server	7%
■ Boat Selector database server	3%
■ Account database server	5%
Response time	**2 sec**
Throughput	**11 pages/sec**

The systems look terrific at this point. The CPU values indicate that our projections regarding the capacity of the key servers seem just about right (with one exception, but more on that in a moment). The response time remains well under our five-second target for this machine, and the actual throughput is right on target with our projections:

```
45 sec/visit / 5 pages per visit = 9 sec/page or 1/9 page/sec

1/9 page/sec * 100 users = 11 pages/sec (projected throughput)
```

The only point of concern right now is the HTTP session database server. This server uses more CPU than we anticipated. Remember, the test team only ran 100 virtual users to get these numbers. The HTTP session database must support over *seven times* this load eventually, but already requires 25% of its available CPU to support our 100 users. The DBA for the HTTP session database agrees to take a look at the server. In particular, he's very interested in whether the database server might write more efficiently to the hard disk space available. In the meantime, the TriMont team rightly decides to proceed with more testing. They want to try doubling the test load to 200 virtual users, and you agree they have enough capacity on the system to do this (and hopefully more!).

Symptoms

The team runs the 200 virtual user test a few times and comes up with some unexpected results, as shown in Table 14.6. Basically, the team adds more load, but the systems do not respond in kind. The CPU utilization remains at about the same levels seen during the 100 user test. The throughput does not increase, although the response time doubles.

Table 14.6   Two Hundred Virtual Users Test Results

Measurement	Value
CPU utilization	
▪ HTTP server	22%
▪ Web application server	25%
▪ Catalog database server	5%
▪ HTTP session database server	27%
▪ Order test database server	7%
▪ Boat Selector database server	3%
▪ Account database server	5%
Response time	**4 sec**
Throughput	**13 pages/sec**

Problem Isolation

This is a presentation of an *underutilization* problem. As we discussed in Chapter 13, underutilization occurs when the system lacks resources other than CPU to support the additional load. Underutilization results from a variety of causes, including insufficient network capacity, synchronization inside the web application code, and poor resource management (connection pools, and so on). In TriMont's case, the team successfully ramped up to 100 users before the problem appeared. This seems to point to something other than the web application software, although that software certainly is not completely in the clear just yet.

You decide to take a multipronged approach to resolving the problem, and you make the following requests of the TriMont team.

- Run the 200 user test again while monitoring key resource pools:
  - Database connection pools
  - Connection requests at the host database servers
  - Application server threads
  - HTTP server listeners

- Try walking the test up from 100 users more slowly to see if they can find a threshold. (Try 110 users, 120 users, and so on, until the response time begins to increase.)
- Collect all logs from the 200 user runs on the various servers.

Problem Resolution

Based on your request, the TriMont team runs additional tests to collect more information. In the meantime, you look at the logs they captured on the first runs at 200 users. The logs from the application server show several database errors. The logs show the application server software attempting to establish more connections to the mainframe account and catalog databases, but these attempts to establish new connections with the mainframe fail. Remember, as discussed in Chapter 11, always check the server logs as part of the measurement validation process (also, see Appendix D: Results Verification Checklist).

The resource tool provided by the application server vendor also reports some unusual behavior inside the connection pools for the account and catalog databases. While the pools each allow a maximum of 20 database connections, the resource tool shows a maximum of 5 connections in the pool at any given time. Furthermore, when the test runs more than 110 users, the resource tool shows many requests "waiting" to obtain a database connection from the pools for these two databases.

The account and catalog databases reside at the mainframe. The DBA for the mainframe databases runs some reports during a subsequent 200 user test. The reports show the host databases in question only have five connections available each for the Java web application server machines to use. (The DBA also reports all of these connections in use during the 200 user run she observes.)

The DBA bumps the available connections to 60 each for these mainframe databases. Although the maximum connection pool for the server currently under test is only 20, she gives us three times the capacity to support our other two servers when they come on line. In return, we agree to let her know if we raise or lower the individual connection pools based on our testing so she can make similar adjustments. After the DBA makes her changes, the test team runs the 200 user test again. After a few runs, they show the results given in Table 14.7.

These figures look much better and fall in line with expectations. The CPU on the system involved increases pretty much proportionally with the increase in load. The response time remains low, although it begins to increase a bit as the CPU becomes more engaged on the system involved. The system still keeps up well with the throughput demands.

Table 14.7   Two Hundred Virtual Users Test Results (after DBA Changes)

Measurement	Value
CPU utilization	
■ HTTP server	41%
■ Web application server	43%
■ Catalog database server	8%
■ HTTP session database server	49%
■ Order test database server	15%
■ Boat Selector database server	6%
■ Account database server	8%
Response time	**2.5 sec**
Throughput	**22 pages/sec**

Also, the HTTP session database remains disproportionately pressured given the level of load. Also notice the burden on the HTTP server. Keep in mind the tests move a lot of static content, so the HTTP server stays very busy during the test. The team may decide to add the caching proxy server to the test a bit sooner than originally planned to remove some of this burden from the HTTP server and improve response time. However, given the linear scalability demonstrated so far by the systems, the web application itself shows good performance characteristics at this point. The system handles 22 pages per second (or about 352 total hits per second) with a very acceptable response time.

Of course, the web application may still hold some surprises for us. Remember, the HTTP session database is surprisingly busy at this point. The web application might actually generate much larger HTTP sessions than we originally estimated. If this is the case, we may need to revisit our network and database capacity estimates (or ask the web application team to reduce the HTTP session size). However, we need the DBA's analysis before we proceed further along those lines.

Next Steps

What next? The test team really needs to figure out the solution to the HTTP session database problem next. This is most likely the next major system bottleneck, and it must be resolved before the test proceeds much further.

After resolving the HTTP session database issue, the team should continue the test-analyze-solve cycle we've demonstrated in the two problems we examined in detail. As outlined in Chapter 11, the team will continue this process until they reach the capacity of this server. Following this, they will add the next HTTP server/application server pair and continue increasing the load. After they're satisfied with the performance of these systems, they will begin adding the firewalls and other components to the tests to gauge their impact on performance.

Summary

In this part of the case study, we started our testing and resolved a few initial performance problems. Again, a performance test is an iterative process. The test, measure, verify, analyze, and tune process continues repeatedly until you reach your performance goals.

The next chapter discusses how to apply the lessons learned from your performance test. In particular, it looks at capacity planning and site growth based on your test results.

Chapter 15

CAPACITY PLANNING AND SITE GROWTH

In this chapter, we discuss how to use the results of your performance test to plan for site capacity and growth. This involves comparing your original performance test plan objectives with the results of the test and extrapolating to develop your production hardware and software needs.

Capacity planning tells you how much hardware and software you need to dedicate to the production web site. It gives you the best production deployment configuration to use based on the performance results. Also, it provides a growth plan for your web site to help you plan the growth of equipment, software, and expense over a defined period of time.

Review Plan Requirements

In the planning step, you estimated your average and peak loads. *Always base capacity plans on peak usage projections.* This provides you with the capacity for peak loads and, of course, also supports your average needs. During the planning phase, in addition to estimating your peak load, you specified a target objective for response time. In this capacity planning exercise, you take the site usage projections and plan requirements and map them to the performance test results.

Review Load, Throughput, and Response Time Objectives

Begin the capacity planning phase by revisiting the requirements specified in your test plan. You want to understand the load, throughput, and response time requirements you specified in this plan. Response time is a critical objective for your capacity planning and usually becomes the limiting factor in your capacity planning. Your web site may support a large number of users without failure on a relatively small system; however, if this configuration produces poor response time, you must upgrade the hardware. Be prepared to spend to support good response times.

Start your capacity plan by filling out a Hardware Sizing worksheet from Appendix A if you haven't already. Capacity planning also requires some of the calculations from this worksheet. We'll use the same test plan data discussed in the example in Chapter 6. Table 15.1 shows the first part of the worksheet.

Table 15.1   Hardware Sizing Worksheet: Initial Input Data

	Input Data	Source	Your Data
1.	Concurrent users	Line 12, Capacity Sizing worksheet	5,000
2.	Throughput: page rate	Line 13, Capacity Sizing worksheet	42 pages/sec
3.	Throughput: requests	Line 14, Capacity Sizing worksheet	252 requests/sec
4.	Response time	Marketing	2 sec

Incorporate Headroom

Next, decide how much headroom you want in case you misjudged the load or to allow for future growth. How much headroom to use depends on how confident you are in your performance test requirements and performance test results. If your usage projections came from your existing web site, you might choose a low buffer factor. Also, if you expect your user community to start small, you may use less headroom and rely on collecting actual production performance data to adjust capacity planning targets. However, if you anticipate an aggressive web site launch, you need to incorporate a significant amount of headroom.

For example, say you want to allow for 50% headroom. This means at peak load, you use only 50% of the capacity of your systems, or, if your estimates are incorrect, your systems should be able to accommodate twice the estimated load. Headroom also gives your web site capacity for expected growth. For example, if you plan based on needs for the first three months, but you expect a steep ramp-up in site usage, incorporate headroom into your calculations to meet these near-term requirements.

To incorporate a headroom buffer into capacity planning, proportionally increase the number of concurrent users and the requests per second required. Keep your response time objective the same. To support 50% headroom for the example shown in Table 15.1, double the requirements to 10,000 concurrent users and 500 requests/sec with the same two-second response time. Table 15.2, a continuation of the Hardware Sizing worksheet, shows the specific calculations.

Table 15.2 Hardware Capacity Worksheet: Headroom Objectives

	Input Data	Source	Your Data
5.	Headroom factor	Marketing/planning	50%
	Calculated Data	**Equation**	**Total**
6.	Concurrent user requirement (with headroom)	5,000 users + 5,000/(100/50-1)	10,000
7.	Throughput requirement (with headroom): page rate	42 pages/sec + 42 / (100 / 50 – 1)	84 pages/sec
8.	Throughput requirement (with headroom): requests	252 requests/sec + 252 / (100 / 50 – 1)	504 requests/sec
9.	Response time (with headroom)	Response time = Response time	2 sec

The planning objectives from lines 6, 8, and 9 in the Hardware Capacity worksheet transfer directly to Part 1 of the Capacity Sizing worksheet, also found in Appendix A. Now, let's continue on to Part 2 of the Capacity Sizing worksheet.

Review Performance Test Results

In order to turn the test objectives into a capacity plan, we map the performance tests results to the objectives. For capacity planning purposes, the most critical performance test results are the following:

1. User ramp-up (load, throughput, response time)
2. Scalability results
3. Server CPU utilization data
4. Network utilization data

Let's look at some sample performance test results and see how to use them to build a capacity plan.

Single-Server User Ramp-Up

Earlier, when we suggested that you should start with a simple configuration and work your way up to a more complex environment, we mentioned that the information you gleaned from your simple tests would help with capacity planning. Now we've arrived at the point where we use the simple configuration data to help us build a capacity plan for the web site.

We also suggested doing a user ramp-up test on this simple configuration. This test gives us the load, throughput, and response time plateaus for this simple case. For this exercise, use a ramp-up test performed against the final, tuned version of the system to obtain the best possible numbers for your planning.

If you haven't already filled out a Summary Test Results graph (from Appendix D), do this now. On this graph, chart the client ramp-up results for throughput and response time. Using this graph, locate your response time objective, and find the corresponding load and throughput values. Sample performance results are shown in Figure 15.1.

Using the data shown in Figure 15.1, the response time goal of two seconds (2,000 milliseconds) corresponds to a 2,000 user load with a transaction rate of almost 100 transactions per second. Notice that if instead your response time goal was 500 milliseconds, the system would reach this point with only a 500 user load. Record the load and throughput at your response time objective in Part 2 of the Capacity Planning worksheet, as shown in Table 15.3.

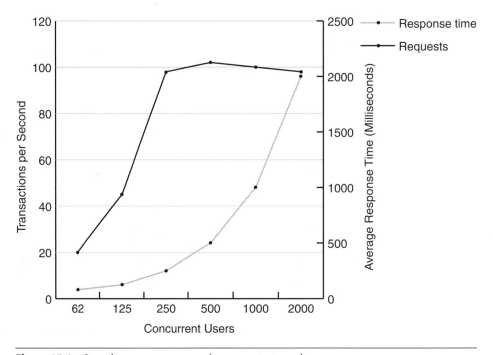

Figure 15.1   Sample user ramp-up performance test results

Table 15.3 Capacity Planning Worksheet, Line 4

	Response Time (Line 2 Above)	Simulated Load (from Performance Results)	Measured Throughput (from Performance Results)
4.	2 sec	2,000 users	100 requests/sec

The results in the table tell us that a simple configuration supports 2,000 concurrent users with acceptable throughput and response time. These numbers tell us at an "atomic" level what the basic configurations inside our web site support. However, we cannot assume that adding ten of these simple systems gives us ten times the capacity of the single system. Instead, we must consult the scalability data from our performance test to determine how the atomic components of our web site scale.

Scalability Data

The most important information to consider here is the fundamental scalability characteristics demonstrated in your tests. These characteristics dictate the scalability assumptions to make for your web site. For example, did your cluster tests demonstrate near linear scalability? Linear scalability (or close to it) allows us to estimate that, indeed, ten times the current resources gives us ten times the capacity. We look to our performance testing to validate this assumption and to show us any factors that might limit our scale. (See Chapter 11 for more details.)

In this step, take your cluster test results and summarize them in the Cluster Scalability section of the Capacity Planning worksheet, using the cluster test results that correspond to the web site response time objective. Table 15.4 provides an example. In this case, the data shows near linear scalability. Two servers handle nearly twice the transactions while maintaining two-second response time, and three servers support almost triple the transactions.

Table 15.4 Capacity Planning Worksheet: Scalability Data, Lines 5–7

	Number of Application Servers	Response Time	Simulated Load	Measured Throughput
5.	1	2	2,000	100 requests/sec
6.	2	2	4,000	196 requests/sec
7.	3	2	6,000	295 requests/sec

Processor Utilization

Beyond the raw test data, we also look at the data collected from the machines during the test runs as we work through a capacity plan. The CPU utilization plays an important role in capacity planning and helps us extrapolate beyond the data collected during performance testing.

For capacity planning, capture the processor utilization data from the cluster test work performed in your production configuration. For example, if your production configuration separates HTTP servers, application servers, and database servers, as shown earlier in Figure 3.13, then you need the processor utilization for each of these servers. Fill in the processor utilization data in lines 8–10 of the worksheet. Make sure to use only the data corresponding to the target response time. Table 15.5 contains data we'll use in the next section on estimating performance.

Table 15.5   Capacity Planning Worksheet: Processor Utilization Data, Lines 8–10

	Number of Application Servers	Application Server CPU	HTTP Server CPU	Load Balancer CPU	Database 1 CPU	Database 2 CPU	Other CPU
8.	1	75%	20%	10%	15%	n/a	n/a
9.	2	75%	40%	15%	30%	n/a	n/a
10.	3	75%	60%	20%	45%	n/a	n/a

Projecting Performance

In order to do a capacity plan, you sometimes must estimate performance beyond the actual results measured in your lab tests. In this section, we work through an example of capacity extrapolation. While this procedure is never ideal, many web sites use extrapolation to cover gaps in their performance testing.

Projecting Application Server Requirements

As in the previous steps, start with the client load and throughput at your response time objective. As shown earlier in Table 15.3, the site response time objective of two seconds occurs at 2,000 users and 100 transactions per second. A cluster of three application servers with 6,000 concurrent users achieved 295 transactions per second and a two-second response time. This also represents the highest user load achieved in the lab.

However, we really want to support 10,000 concurrent users, 500 requests per second, and a two-second response time. So we extrapolate our performance test results across additional servers to meet the plan requirements for concurrent users and the throughput objectives. Start by calculating the scaling ratio from the cluster tests (lines 11–13), and then estimate the scaling ratio across additional servers (lines 14–16), as shown in Table 15.6.

Table 15.6   Capacity Planning Worksheet: Scaling Ratio Calculations, Lines 11–16

	Number of Application Servers	Measured Throughput	Scaling Ratio Calculation	Scaling Ratio
11.	1	100 requests/sec	Throughput (1) / Throughput (1)	1×
12.	2	196 requests/sec	Throughput (2) / Throughput (1)	1.96×
13.	3	295 requests/sec	Throughput (3) / Throughput (1)	2.95×
	Number of Application Servers (projected)		Scaling Ratio Calculation	Scaling Ratio Estimate
14.	4		2.95 + (2.95 – 1.96)	3.94×
15.	5		3.94 + (3.94 – 2.95)	4.93×
16.	6		4.93 + (4.93 – 3.94)	5.92×

Now use the scaling ratio calculations to estimate the throughput supported by additional servers. Table 15.7 shows the estimated performance through a five-server cluster. We estimate that five servers will support the 10,000 client requirement (2,000 clients per server) with two-second response time. Using the five-server scaling ratio of 4.93 calculated earlier, the estimated throughput is 493 transactions per second. This is just short of the 502 transactions per second requirement in our test plan, and considering the headroom factors built into the estimates, it is probably close enough. There is no need to plan on a sixth application server at this time.

Table 15.7   Capacity Planning Worksheet: Estimated Servers, Lines 17–19

	Number of Application Servers	Estimated Load (Number of Application Servers * Load, Line 5)	Meets Requirement? (Line 1)	Scaling Ratio	Estimated Throughput (Scaling Ratio * Throughput, Line 5)	Meets Requirement? (Line 3)
17.	4	8,000	no	3.94×	394 requests/sec	no
18.	5	10,000	yes	4.93×	493 requests/sec	yes
19.	6	—	—	5.92×	—	—

This simple example assumes five servers exhibit the same scaling proportions as your three-server test results. As a general capacity planning rule, do not extrapolate beyond twice the performance limits measured in your test environment. Extrapolating within double capacity generally presents manageable risk.

Projecting Hardware Capacity

Completing a capacity plan requires an in-depth look not only at application server requirements, but also at the other servers and application factors that affect scaling. Limiting your estimates just to your HTTP or application server does not give you a sufficient capacity for your web site as a whole. Let's now look at the hardware requirements across all the servers.

We use CPU utilization in this step as a gauge of server capacity. By measuring the increase in CPU utilization on the servers during scalability testing, we obtain a key indicator of how increasing the application server capacity impacts other parts of the web site.

Projecting Processor Utilization

In this step, you look for the pattern of processor utilization demonstrated by each of the servers during the cluster tests. For example, the CPU utilization results from Table 15.5 show that as load increases from 2,000 to 4,000 users, the HTTP server, database server, and load balancer CPU utilization all increase. During the test runs, the HTTP server and database CPU utilization doubled as the client load doubled. The load balancer CPU, on the other hand, did not significantly increase. The doubling of resources on the HTTP server and database is not surprising, given that both these servers handled twice the transactions; however, we need to factor these increases into our planning estimates.

For hardware planning purposes, extrapolate the processor utilization for each server using the same relative increase shown in the performance tests. Table 15.8 shows the relative increase for the HTTP server, load balancer, and database CPU utilization as we added application servers and load to the cluster.

Table 15.8   Capacity Planning Worksheet: CPU Utilization Delta, Lines 20–23

	Number of Application Servers	Application Server CPU	HTTP Server CPU	Load Balancer CPU	Database 1 CPU
20.	1	75%	20%	10%	15%
21.	2	75%	40%	15%	30%
22.	3	75%	60%	20%	45%
23.	Delta	n/a	+20%	+5%	+15%

Using the delta, project the processor utilizations for all the servers when adding more application servers. Table 15.9 shows these projections for our example. These projections point out a significant issue. As you can see in Table 15.9, we project the processor utilization for the system running the HTTP server to be at 100% CPU utilization with five application servers. Remember, once a server is running near 100% utilization, wait time increases for resources (a bottleneck), which also results in longer response times. Therefore, at five servers, we project that the HTTP server becomes a bottleneck for our system. Also, note the estimates for database processor utilization. While they still fall within acceptable ranges, you may want to consider an upgrade for this system as well.

Table 15.9 Capacity Planning Worksheet: CPU Utilization Projections, Lines 24–25

	Number of Clients	Number of Application Servers	Application Server CPU	HTTP Server CPU	Load Balancer CPU	Database CPU
24.	8,000	4	75%	80%	25%	60%
25.	10,000	5	75%	100%	30%	75%

Based on the processor utilization projections, the application server performance projections done earlier in Table 15.7 are most likely invalid (HTTP server capacity needs adjusting). Let's look at how to do this next.

Identify Server Ratios

Good capacity planning determines the resources needed throughout the web site to handle projected user loads. This means carrying your scalability extrapolations to the rest of the equipment in your web site as well. The scaling alternatives for other systems are similar to those discussed in Chapter 11 for the application server: Employ additional hardware resources on a single server or use some type of cluster configuration.

Many production sites deploy multiple HTTP servers and use a centralized database. Many web sites also devote separate servers to each database used by the web applications. For example, they place the persistent HTTP session database on one server and the application databases on another server. Also, as we've discussed previously, if the HTTP servers and database receive lots of traffic, consider caching techniques to reduce the stress on these systems.

To continue our web site projections, we try to develop capacity ratios between the various components in the web site. For example, a single HTTP server requires only 20% CPU utilization to support one application server operating at almost maximum CPU utilization. Therefore, a ratio of approximately three or four application servers for each HTTP server is appropriate for this web site. So, for five application servers, we need two HTTP servers.

The Capacity Sizing worksheet assists with this calculation, as shown in Table 15.10. Configurations with significant static content and high security needs may actually invert these ratios (they require more HTTP servers than application servers).

Table 15.10   Capacity Planning Worksheet: HTTP Server Projections

	Number of Application Servers	Projected HTTP Server CPU CPU ($n - 1$) + Delta	Additional Server (If CPU 80% or Higher)	New Projected Server CPU (If New Server Added)
27.	4	60% + 20% = 80%	+1	40% each
28.	5	40% + (20% / 2) = 50%	+1	n/a
29.	6	—	—	—

Similarly, the test results show that one application server only requires 15% of the database CPU capacity, so a single database probably supports five application servers. However, as a rule of thumb, assume no more than 80% CPU utilization on a database server before impacting overall application response time. On the basis of these results, we develop the following planning ratios:

```
1 HTTP server : 4 application servers
5 application servers : 1 database server
```

Now, let's reapply these ratios to our earlier projections. In our example, we estimated requiring five application servers to handle the web site's load. Using our newly developed ratios, we plan for two HTTP servers, five application servers, and one database server to support the web site's load. Table 15.11 contains the completed projections.

Table 15.11   Final Hardware Projections

	Number of Application Servers	Number of Times to Scale HTTP Servers	Number of Times to Scale Databases	HTTP Server	Database Server
36.	5 at 75%	1	0	2 at 40%	1 at 75%

At this point, if you've never tested with multiple HTTP servers, it might be worthwhile to set up a small test in your lab with two HTTP servers and two application servers. Through this test, you establish that the HTTP servers do not impact vertical scalability. While we feel very confident that this is true for most commercial

HTTP servers, any time you develop a plan with an untested configuration, consider testing this setup briefly to confirm your assumptions about its performance.

In this example, we've discussed *horizontal scaling* for this web site and how to develop estimates for a cluster of machines. Of course, if you prefer, you might apply your *vertical scaling* test results in the capacity planning phase and develop a plan for growing your existing hardware rather than acquiring more machines. In fact, depending on the headroom in your calculations, consider vertically scaling the database server. We currently project 75% utilization for this component, which nears its maximum useful capacity. Placing it on a larger machine gives you a wider margin of comfort.

Scaling Assumptions

As the previous exercise demonstrated, capacity planning involves a certain amount of guesswork. The closer your tests come to simulating production conditions and loads, the better your capacity projections. Once you deploy your application, monitor its performance and validate the assumptions you made about load and usage patterns. Often, things don't quite operate as planned, and you must readjust your web site accordingly.

Before you have production data, what are reasonable assumptions to make based on test hardware configuration and test results? If your tests were comprehensive enough to actually meet your user load and response time goals, start by assuming that your production application performs comparably to your test application. It bears repeating: This assumption is only as good as the test plan behind it, as well as your ability to simulate the production environment and user patterns. Having performance data that covers your expected load makes your capacity planning much easier. Use the test numbers directly, apply a headroom factor to account for any estimation errors or unexpected conditions, and complete the planning exercise.

Looking back to our example, if we really required only 1,000 users and a one-second response time, the test data shows us directly that we can support this with one server. If you want significant headroom in this case, use a two-server cluster (also included in our tests). Your test data gives you a higher level of confidence that the two-server cluster meets your capacity requirements. Sometimes it's impossible to test the full load of the web site in your test lab. In these cases, the extrapolations we just covered provide the best planning data available.

In general, making any scalability assumptions implies risk. A web site contains many components, and any one these may become a bottleneck under the right conditions. Often, adding resources in one area of the web site produces a bottleneck in another area. If possible, prove scalability beyond two servers during your testing in order to confidently project near linear scalability. In general, web applications typically show good "near linear" horizontal scalability, assuming the absence of application bottlenecks or other infrastructure issues.

As a general rule, we recommend running your tests with at least three servers in a cluster configuration. Also, try to test at least half of the performance your production web site requires. This lowers the extrapolation risk in your production performance.

Case Study: Capacity Planning

We left the TriMont team in Chapter 14 working in their test phase. Now let's build a capacity plan based on the results of their test. Since the capacity planning task is relatively short, we'll complete it here, rather than devoting an entire chapter. This part of the case study looks at the three phases of capacity planning just outlined in this chapter: Review plan requirements, review performance test results, and project capacity.

Review Plan Requirements

In Chapter 14, the case study testing phase, TriMont estimated load and throughput requirements. They also decided on 25% headroom. Based on the work in Chapter 14, the first part of the Capacity Planning worksheet is completed as shown in Table 15.12.

Table 15.12 TriMont Capacity Planning Worksheet, Part 1

	Input Data	Source of Data	Your Requirement
1.	Concurrent users (with headroom)	Appendix A, Hardware Sizing worksheet, line 7	10,000 concurrent users
2.	Response time	Appendix A, Hardware Sizing worksheet, line 2	5 sec
3.	Throughput (with headroom)	Appendix A, Hardware Sizing worksheet, line 9	120 pages/sec

Review Performance Test Results

We left Chapter 14 without developing any final test results, so before going any further, let's look at some performance results achieved during the TriMont tests. After the DBA investigated and corrected the HTTP session database CPU utilization problem by adding additional disk drives to the database to reduce I/O contention,

TriMont completed single-server ramp-ups, with the results shown in Figure 15.2. As you see from the data shown in the figure, the test reached the target response time of five seconds with 400 concurrent users. At this point, we also reach a throughput plateau of 41 pages per second.

TriMont also set up a two system cluster and, as expected, worked through some issues; eventually, however, the team produced good cluster scalability, as shown in Figure 15.3.

Let's fill in Part 2 of the Capacity Planning worksheet with the TriMont test results. Remember, in order to reduce the load driver virtual user costs, the team ran the tests with reduced think time. Based on the calculations in the testing phase, 1 user with a 45-second average user visit time is approximately equivalent to 10 users with the full 7-minute average user visit. Therefore, the 400 client test load corresponds to 4,000 concurrent users with the full 7-minute user visit time.

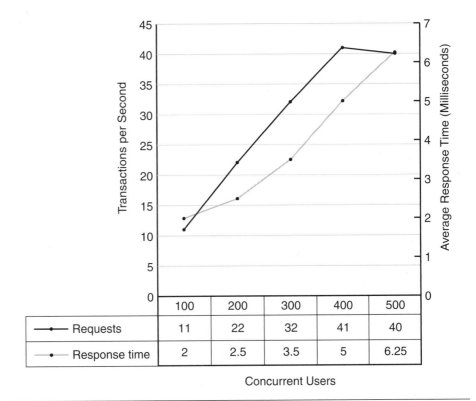

	100	200	300	400	500
Requests	11	22	32	41	40
Response time	2	2.5	3.5	5	6.25

Concurrent Users

Figure 15.2 User ramp-up performance test results

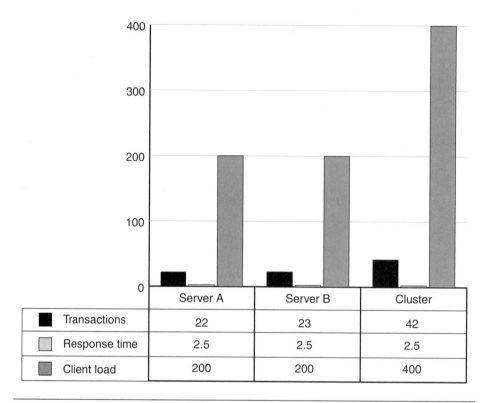

	Server A	Server B	Cluster
■ Transactions	22	23	42
▨ Response time	2.5	2.5	2.5
▨ Client load	200	200	400

Figure 15.3 TriMont scalability results

To fill out the cluster scalability section of the worksheet, we need the cluster load and throughput corresponding to 5-second response time results. However, Tri-Mont's cluster tests only went up to a 2.5-second response time because they did not simulate enough client load to reach the 5-second mark. If you recall, TriMont only purchased a 500 user license for this phase of testing. For now, let's use the cluster results TriMont achieved at 400 users, and decide later if the capacity plan contains too much risk and requires more testing.

Similarly, the CPU utilization collected for the cluster run does not represent the 5-second response time objective. However, single-server CPU utilization results do exist for response times at both 2.5 seconds and 5 seconds. We document all this data for Part 2 of the Capacity Planning worksheet in Tables 15.13, 15.14, and 15.15.

Table 15.13 TriMont Capacity Planning Worksheet, Part 2: Single-Server Results

	Response Time (Line 2 Above)	Simulated Load (from Performance Results)	Measured Throughput (from Performance Results)
4.	5	4,000 concurrent users	41 pages/sec

Table 15.14 TriMont Capacity Planning Worksheet, Part 2: Cluster Scalability Results

	Number of Application Servers	Response Time	Simulated Load	Measured Throughput
5.	1	2.5 sec	2,000	22 pages/sec
6.	2	2.5 sec	4,000	42 pages/sec
7.	3 (not done)			

Table 15.15 TriMont Capacity Planning Worksheet, Part 2: CPU Utilization Data

Measurement	200 Clients	400 Clients (1 Application Server)	400 Clients (Cluster)
CPU Utilization			
▪ HTTP server	41%	80%	41%/40%
▪ Web application server	43%	86%	43%/43%
▪ Catalog database server	8%	15%	15%
▪ HTTP session database server	20% (after DBA)	38%	38%
▪ Order test database server	15%	30%	30%
▪ Boat Selector database server	6%	12%	12%
▪ Account database server	8%	16%	16%
Response time	**2.5 sec**	**5 sec**	**2.5 sec**
Throughput	**22 pages/sec**	**41 pages/sec**	**42 pages/sec**

Project Capacity

Though TriMont only tested a two-server cluster, the scaling ratio data is still useful to the capacity plan. The cluster results of 42 pages per second with a 400-client load against two servers makes for an excellent 1.9× scaling ratio, as shown in line 12 of Table 15.16. Using this scaling ratio, we estimate the three- and four-server cluster scaling ratios at 2.8× and 3.7× respectively, as shown in Table 15.17. Remember, we do not recommend projecting beyond double the cluster size tested; therefore, we do not include estimates for a five- or six-machine cluster.

Now we must estimate the load and throughput even though the cluster results did not reach a five-second response time. Based on the single-server ramp-up results and the cluster results, we assume their two-server cluster reaches five-second response time with approximately 800 test clients and a throughput of approximately 42 pages per second. This closely matches the single-server results shown earlier for 400 users: a five-second response time and 41 pages per second.

Using this data, TriMont estimates that a three-server cluster supports 12,000 concurrent users and 118 pages per second. This matches nicely with the test plan estimate of three application servers to support the web site's peak load.

TriMont is relatively confident that a cluster of three application servers supports the load and dynamic page requests for the site. Now, to complete the capacity planning exercise, we need to consider the processor utilization data across all the servers in

Table 15.16   TriMont Capacity Planning, Part 3: Cluster Scaling Ratio

	Number of Application Servers	Measured Throughput	Scaling Ratio Calculation	Scaling Ratio
11.	1	22 pages/sec	Throughput (1) / Throughput (1)	1×
12.	2	42 pages/sec	Throughput(2)/Throughput(1)	1.9×
13.	3	n/a	Throughput(3)/Throughput(1)	

Table 15.17   TriMont Capacity Planning Worksheet, Part 3: Estimate Scaling Ratio

	Number of Application Servers (Projected)	Scaling Ratio Calculation	Scaling Ratio Estimate
13.	3	Line 12 + (Line 12 – Line 11)	2.8×
14.	4	Line 13 + (Line 13 – Line 12)	3.7×
15.	5	Line 14 + (Line 14 – Line 13)	n/a
16.	6	Line 15 + (Line 15 – Line 14)	n/a

Table 15.18   TriMont Capacity Planning Worksheet, Part 3: Estimate Throughput and Load

	Number of Application Servers	Estimated Load (Number of Application Servers * Load, Line 5)	Meets Requirement? (Line 1) [10,800]	Scaling Ratio	Estimated Throughput (Scaling Ratio * Throughput, Line 5)	Meets Requirement? (Line 3) [120]
17.	3	12,000	yes	2.8	118 pages/sec	close
18.	4	16,000	yes	3.7	156 pages/sec	yes

Total number of application servers required: 3

the web site. As you can see from the CPU utilization results in Table 15.15, at 400 clients none of the servers in the cluster goes beyond 50% utilization. As mentioned, the DBA solved the original problem of high utilization on the HTTP session database, bringing it down to only 38% at 400 clients.

Now let's estimate the CPU utilization for a three-server cluster supporting 10,080 users and 120 pages per second in Table 15.18. First, we double the projections for 800 users. Then, as shown in Table 15.19, we use these results to estimate the CPU utilization on each server at 1,200 test clients. The last column meets the plan objectives for load, throughput, and response time.

Table 15.19   TriMont Processor Utilization Projections

Measurement	400 Clients (2-Server Cluster)	800 Clients (2-Server Cluster)	1,200 Clients (3-Server Cluster)
Projected user load	4,000	8,000	12,000
CPU utilization			
■ HTTP server	41%/40%	82%/80%	80%/80%/80%
■ Web application server	43%/43%	86%/87%	87%/87%/87%
■ Catalog database server	15%	30%	45%
■ HTTP session database server	38%	76%	100%+ [!!]
■ Order test database server	30%	60%	90%
■ Boat Selector database server	12%	24%	48%
■ Account database server	16%	32%	48%

Based on these projections, our original estimate of a 1:1 ratio between the HTTP server and the application server looks good. The addition of the caching proxy servers also lowers the HTTP server processor requirements. However, based on these numbers, the HTTP session database server looks like a potential bottleneck at peak load. At a minimum, the HTTP session database requires a larger server.

The Order test database server processor utilization projection of 90% doesn't really concern us, since this is not the production database. Of course, we recommend that TriMont monitor the additional load against the real production Order database to make sure that it is sufficiently sized.

Once TriMont resizes the HTTP session database, they begin their production deployment of their web site. Just like any other web site, the TriMont site needs an ongoing capacity plan, as we'll discuss in the next section.

Ongoing Capacity Planning

Continuous web site monitoring makes for successful long-term capacity planning. By continually monitoring your web site against your plans and projections, you develop more accurate estimates for the site, and better understand how to develop future test plans as well. We recommend two analysis perspectives for your ongoing monitoring:

- Is the performance similar to the test performance?
- Is the actual usage similar to your plan expectations?

An error in either of these projections often spells disaster for your web site. Sometimes your actual site does not perform as it does in your tests. If your test scripts and environment did not accurately simulate your production environment, the performance numbers you obtained in your test will not apply to the real site. For example, if your usage patterns actually result in more "buy" traffic than your test scripts simulated, your web site contains application servers improperly sized for the amount of purchasing business logic that "buy" generates. In addition, "buy" uses more SSL processing to support the higher percentage of purchases.

On the other hand, you often find that your tests actually simulated your production performance quite well, but the actual number of users visiting your site differs from your original sizing. If you receive significantly more users than planned, this raises the overall response times beyond your objectives.

Collecting Production Data

For your production site, monitor the same data captured during load testing on your production machines. We recommend capturing at least the following data:

- Client load
- Throughput (requests per second)
- Response time
- CPU utilization on all machines

Many additional metrics come in handy for tuning and troubleshooting problems, but these four metrics give you the essentials for comparing the actual performance of your site against capacity planning projections.

Analyzing Production Data

Let's return to our example from Chapter 6 (rather than continuing with the case study at this point), and compare some actual usage data against the capacity plan. Table 15.20 shows the capacity plan projections and the actual web site performance results.

Table 15.20 Production Performance Results

	Number of Users	Response Time	Transactions/Sec
Plan requirement	5,000	2 sec	250
With headroom	10,000	2 sec	500
Actual peak performance	2,500	2 sec	350

The original example required 250 transactions per second and a two-second response time. On the surface, the production results of 350 transactions per second and a two-second response time look great! The web site meets the established response time criteria and actually serves more transactions than planned. The web site gets more orders than expected, and everyone is happy. Hopefully, you don't bask in the site's success for too long, but take this opportunity to study the actual web site performance data against your plan and test results. There may be serious discrepancies here that spell disaster in the future. Remember to look at the results against both your test performance and the expected usage patterns of your site.

First, how does the actual performance compare to your test results? Remember you built this site for peak load requirements and with a significant 50% headroom buffer. If your site performance actually mirrors the test environment, the peak performance of the site should match the test plan *before* including the headroom estimate. Table 15.21 shows the expected peak performance versus the actual production web site results.

Actually, we expected a *one-second* peak response time at this point, not two seconds. By looking just at this statistic, you already see a potential problem looming. Next,

Table 15.21 Expected versus Actual Production Results

	Users	Response Time	Transaction Rate	Application Server CPU Utilization
"Expected" based on plan/test results	5,000	1 sec	500 requests/sec	75%
Actual	2,500	2 sec	350 requests/sec	80%
Delta	−2,500	+1 sec	−150 requests/sec	+5%

let's consider the transaction rate. At first, getting 350 transactions per second seemed like a great thing; however, based on the buffered capacity of the server, we really expected 500 transactions per second at this point. Given your peak load of only 2,500 users, not 5,000 users, you realize that your site does not match the test results.

With discrepancies like this, we recommend digging deeper into the web site's performance. Today the site operates just fine, but clearly if the user load increases to the original projections, we can expect the web site to miss its performance objectives. For example, the application server uses a lot of CPU capacity at this point; therefore, if the user load doubles to the originally expected 5,000 users, response time will probably increase significantly and is likely to reach almost four seconds.

At this stage, look at both comparisons to the test performance and to the plan. The first difference is the user load of 2,500, half of the planned load. Looking into this, you find that the advertising campaign for your web site is running behind. The marketing team is just getting the word out, and expects the load to meet the planned projections within the next month!

The next difference is the lower transaction rate and higher response time exhibited by the site. To understand the cause behind the lower throughput, look at the actual transactions to see how they match your tests by comparing the HTTP server access logs to your test scripts. For example, you might find that the actual visits to the site consist of a much higher percentage of "buy" requests than the test scripts simulated. While a lot more purchases explain the excitement with the web site's success, capacity becomes a concern: "Buy" transactions use significantly more application server processing. They also use more HTTP server resources for SSL support, and they allow less caching. This taxes the HTTP server, application server, and database more heavily, which results in lower throughput and correspondingly higher response times per user.

At this point, you should adjust your capacity plan requirements. Plan to increase the amount of HTTP server and application server processing power in time to meet the increased load coming your way. Also, check CPU consumption on your database systems and upgrade them as necessary. Finally, feed this information back to the test team. The next time they test new function for the web site, this information provides them with the correct mix of test scripts to simulate production behavior.

This type of analysis and adjustment needs to be ongoing. Use the actual production site statistics to readjust your capacity planning and to change any future test scripts. Be sure to monitor and compare all the key metrics—user load, throughput, response time, and CPU utilization—so you do not miss major trends. In addition, keep abreast of any marketing initiatives or new applications that might significantly increase the user load against your site.

Summary

The capacity planning exercise combines your test plan objectives with your test data to determine the appropriate combination and number of servers. By focusing on the scalability data and CPU utilization, you build initial capacity plans. Later, after deploying the web site, compare the actual site performance to the plans. You may find inaccuracies in your initial projections or discover that the test cases did not match your actual production site usage patterns. If either of these is true, adjust your capacity plans accordingly.

Appendix A
PLANNING WORKSHEETS

This appendix includes a collection of worksheets to help with your planning work. Each worksheet corresponds to processes and data discussed in the book. Use the first five worksheets during the test planning stages. Use the final worksheet, the Capacity Planning worksheet, at the conclusion of your tests for the final production capacity planning.

1. Capacity Sizing worksheet
2. Network Capacity Sizing worksheet
3. JVM Memory HTTP Session Sizing worksheet
4. Hardware Sizing worksheet
5. Capacity Planning worksheet

Capacity Sizing Worksheet

Use the Capacity Sizing worksheet to prepare your test plan and to derive your *peak* usage projections for *load* and *throughput*. Please refer to Chapter 6 for a complete description of the data and calculations in the worksheet. Also Chapter 10, the first part of the case study, provides an example using this worksheet.

Input Data

In order to estimate concurrent users and throughput, you need data provided by your marketing team and web site architect. The data includes expected user visits (per day), average user visit time, and pages per visit. Since you base all planning work on peak usage, you need a factor for estimating peak load over daily average load. The worksheets provide two methods to estimate peak load, as described in Chapters 6 and 10.

	Input Data (Estimates)	**Source of Data**	**Your Data**
1.	Number of user visits (day)	Marketing team	

If you cannot estimate 2, provide estimates for 3 and 4 below.

	Input Data (Estimates)	**Source of Data**	**Your Data**
2.	Percent of daily users arriving in peak hour	Estimate	

Provide 3 and 4 below only if you did not know 2.

3.	Number of hours per day site is actively used	Estimate provided by marketing team (when in doubt, use 8 hours)	
4.	Peak load increase over normal hour	Estimate (typically between 3 and 5)	

Items 5–7 must be provided to calculate throughput from user visits.

5.	Average user visit time	Marketing team	
6.	Average pages per visit	Marketing team	
7.	Average static elements per page	Web site application architect	

Calculating Peak Load (Concurrent Users)

For convenience, the worksheet provides space for all calculations in hours, minutes, and seconds. Obviously, multiplying the hours by 60 to get minutes, and by 60 again to get seconds derives these calculations. Express later calculations in hours, minutes or seconds, depending on your preference.

	Calculated Data	**Equation**	**Total (hr)**	**Total (min)**	**Total (sec)**

If you have data for 2, use the following calculation, otherwise skip to 9.

	Calculated Data	**Equation**	**Total (hr)**	**Total (min)**	**Total (sec)**
8.	Number of user visits adjusted for peak load	Number of user visits * Percentage of users arriving at peak Line 1 * Line 2			

If you have data for 3 and 4, use the following calculations.

	Calculated Data	**Equation**	**Total (hr)**	**Total (min)**	**Total (sec)**
9.	Number of user visits adjusted for length of day	Number of user visits / Hours in web site day Line 1 / Line 3			

	Calculated Data	Equation	Total (hr)	Total (min)	Total (sec)
10.	Number of user visits adjusted for peak load	Number of user visits adjusted for day * Peak load increase factor Line 9 * Line 4			

Do the following calculations (use the value from line 8 or line 10).

11.	User arrival rate (new users per second)	User arrival rate = Line 8 or line 10			
12.	Concurrent users	User arrival rate * User visit time Line 11 * Line 5			

Calculating Throughput (Page Rate and Request Rate)

	Calculated Data	Equation	Total (hrs)	Total (min)	Total (sec)
13.	Throughput: page rate	User arrival rate * Average pages per visit Line 11 * Line 6			
14.	Throughput: requests	Page rate + (Average static elements * Page rate) Line 13 + (Line 7 * Line 13)			

Network Capacity Sizing Worksheet

Use the Network Capacity Sizing worksheet to estimate the size of the network required to support your web site. Choose between an estimated network size of 100 Mbps Ethernet, 100 Mbps switched Ethernet, or 1Gbps Ethernet. Please see Chapter 9 for a complete description of the data and calculations in the worksheet. Also, see Chapter 10, Case Study: Preparing to Test, for an example using this worksheet. The worksheet calculates in seconds, so please use the "per second" data from the Capacity Sizing worksheet.

Input Data

	Input Data	Source of Data	Your Data
1.	Average page size (bytes)	Web application architect	
2.	Maximum page size (bytes)	Web application architect	
3.	Requests per second	Capacity Sizing worksheet, line 14	
4.	User arrival rate per second	Capacity Sizing worksheet, line 11	
5.	Average bytes of application data transferred per request (i.e., from database)	Web application architect	
6.	Percentage of requests requiring data transfer	Web application architect/marketing	
7.	HTTP session size (only if shared session is used)	Web application architect	
8.	Size of applets	Web application architect	
9.	Percentage of user requests requiring applet download	Web application architect/marketing	

Calculating Network Requirements

	Network Data	Equation	Total
10.	Outbound HTML / static elements	Average page size * Requests/sec Line 1 * Line 3	
11.	Inbound HTTP requests (estimate)	20% * Outbound data 20% * Line 10	
12.	Application data transfer	Average bytes/request * Requests/sec * % requests requiring data Line 5 * Line 3 * Line 6	
13.	HTTP session data transfer	HTTP session size * Requests/sec Line 7 * Line 3	
14.	Applet transfer	Applet size * User arrival rate/sec * % requests using applet Line 8 * Line 4 * Line 9	
	Total		

Network Sizing

Network Speed (Bits)	Estimated Bytes Supported (Planning)	Equation	Yes/No
100Mbps Ethernet	5MBps	5MBps > Total?	
100Mbps switched Ethernet	8MBps	8MBps > Total?	
1Gbps Ethernet	50MBps	50MBps > Total?	

The Minimum Network Requirement is _____.

JVM Memory HTTP Session Sizing Worksheet

Use the HTTP Session Sizing worksheet to estimate the JVM memory required to support HTTP sessions. Please see Chapter 6 for a complete description of the data and calculations in the worksheet. Also, see Chapter 10, Case Study: Preparing to Test, for an example using this worksheet.

Input Data

	Input Data	Source of Data	Your Data
1.	User arrival rate (in seconds)	Capacity Sizing worksheet, line 11	
2.	Average user visit time	Capacity Sizing worksheet, line 5	
3.	Planned HTTP session timeout interval (in minutes)	System administrator	
4.	HTTP session size (per user)	Network Capacity Sizing worksheet, line 7	

Calculating HTTP Session Memory Requirement

	Calculated Data	Calculation	Total
5.	Average time user session stays resident in memory (in minutes)	Average user visit time + Session timeout Line 2 + Line 3	
6.	Number of user sessions in memory	User arrival rate * Average time session in memory Line 1 * Line 5	
7.	HTTP session memory required	Number of user sessions in memory * HTTP session size Line 6 * Line 4	

Hardware Sizing Worksheet

Use the Hardware Sizing worksheet prior to testing in order to estimate the hardware requirements for a production web site. After completing the test, use this worksheet as input to the Capacity Planning worksheet, which is included in this appendix. See the case study in Chapter 14, as well as Chapter 15, for examples using this worksheet.

Input Data

	Input Data	Source	Your Data
1.	Concurrent users	Capacity Sizing worksheet, line 12	
2.	Throughput: page rate	Capacity Sizing worksheet, line 13	
3.	Throughput: requests	Capacity Sizing worksheet, line 14	
4.	Response time	Marketing	
5.	Headroom factor	Marketing/planning	
6.	Estimated throughput supported on your selected hardware	Hardware/application server vendor	

Calculating Hardware Requirement Estimate (Pre-Test)

	Calculated Data	Calculation	Total
7.	Concurrent users (with headroom)	Concurrent users + Concurrent users / (100 / Headroom – 1) Line 1 + Line 1 / (100 / Line 5 – 1)	
8.	Throughput requirement (with headroom): page rate	Throughput + Throughput / (100 / Headroom – 1) Line 2 + Line 2 / (100 / Line 5 – 1)	
9.	Throughput requirement (with headroom): requests	Throughput + Throughput / (100 / Headroom – 1) Line 3 + Line 3 / (100 / Line 5 – 1)	
10.	Application servers required	Throughput requirement (dynamic requests) / Estimated throughput for your hardware + 1 (for maintenance) Line 8 / Line 6 + 1	

Capacity Planning Worksheet

Use the Capacity Planning worksheet to do your production capacity planning. This worksheet requires information from the initial requirements plan and your actual performance test results. For more information on capacity planning and examples using this worksheet, please refer to Chapter 15.

Part 1: Requirements Summary

Part 1 of the Capacity Planning worksheet contains a summary of the key requirements for your web site: load, throughput, and response time. Use this data to help determine your hardware needs.

	Input Data	Source of Data	Your Requirement
1.	Concurrent users (with headroom)	Hardware Sizing worksheet, line 7	
2.	Response time	Hardware Sizing worksheet, line 4	
3.	Throughput (with headroom)	Hardware Sizing worksheet, line 9	

Part 2: Performance Results Summary

Part 2 contains a summary of the final performance test results. Use the final, tuned results from the performance worksheets recorded during the test. Appendix D provides example performance worksheets.

Single-Server Result

Using the performance worksheet or graphs of your test results, locate the performance of a single server corresponding to your response time objective, as specified in line 2 above.

	Response Time (Line 2 Above)	Simulated Load (from Performance Results)	Measured Throughput (from Performance Results)
4.			

Cluster Scalability Results

Using the performance worksheet or graphs of your cluster test results, locate the performance of the cluster corresponding to your response time objective, as specified in line 2 above. We recommend doing at least a three-server cluster test. Add more rows to this table for larger tests.

	Number of Application Servers	Response Time (Line 2)	Simulated Loads	Measured Throughput
5.	1			
6.	2			
7.	3			

CPU Utilization Data

From the performance worksheet, locate the CPU utilization for each of the servers during your cluster runs. Make sure to record the CPU utilization for all servers in the test bed. Add more columns for additional servers and more rows for larger cluster tests.

	Number of Application Servers	Application Server CPU	HTTP Server CPU	Load Balancer CPU	Database 1 CPU	Database 2 CPU	Other CPU
8.	1						
9.	2						
10.	3						

Part 3: Capacity Planning Estimates

This section estimates hardware requirements for your web site using the data from Parts 1 and 2.

Cluster Scaling Ratio

Calculate the scaling achieved during your cluster runs. You do this by calculating the ratio between the throughput of the cluster and the individual server's performance.

	Number of Application Servers	Measured Throughput	Scaling Ratio Calculation	Scaling Ratio
11.	1		Throughput (1) / Throughput (1) Line 5 / Line 5	1×
12.	2		Throughput (2) / Throughput (1) Line 6 / Line 5	
13.	3		Throughput (3) / Throughput (1) Line 7 / Line 5	

Estimate Scaling Ratio

This step estimates the scaling ratio as we add additional servers to the cluster. This section of the worksheet assumes that additional servers follow the same scaling pattern measured in the lab. We *do not* recommend estimating beyond twice the tested performance.

For example, to calculate the scaling ratio for four application servers, take the scaling ratio for three application servers plus the delta between the ratio at three application servers and two application servers. This sum gives us the projected scaling for four servers. Generally, the calculation for the scaling ratio for n number of servers is ratio $(n-1)$ + (ratio $(n-1)$ – ratio $(n-2)$).

	Number of Application Servers (Projected)	Scaling Ratio Calculations	Scaling Ratio Estimate
14.	4	Line 13 + (Line 13 – Line 12)	
15.	5	Line 14 + (Line 14 – Line 13)	
16.	6	Line 15 + (Line 15 – Line 14)	

Estimate Throughput and Load

This step estimates the concurrent users and throughput as you add additional servers to a cluster. The estimated load is a pure linear projection. Derive the estimated throughput using the scaling ratio calculated above. Continue adding servers to your estimate until you meet both the load and throughput requirements.

	Number of Application Servers	Estimated Load (Number of Application Servers * Load, Line 5)	Meets Requirement? (Line 1)	Scaling Ratio	Estimated Throughput (Scaling Ratio * Throughput, Line 5)	Meets Requirement? (Line 3)
17.	4			Line 14		
18.	5			Line 15		
19.	6			Line 16		

The total number of application servers to meet the estimated load and throughput requirement is _____.

Estimate CPU Utilization

To complete the hardware estimates, consider CPU utilization on all the servers included in your web site. You cannot achieve the application server scaling estimates if other servers' CPU utilization becomes a bottleneck.

CPU Utilization per Additional Server

Calculate the increase in CPU utilization for each type of server as you add more application servers to the test cluster.

	Number of Application Servers	Application Server CPU	HTTP Server CPU	Load Balancer CPU	Database 1 CPU	Database 2 CPU	Other CPU
20.	1						
21.	2						
22.	3						
23.	Delta						
24.	4						
25.	5						
26.	6						

HTTP Server CPU Utilization Projections

Estimate the number of HTTP servers required to support the projected load and throughput. This calculation takes the CPU utilization of the preceding cluster run and adds the delta CPU utilization increase anticipated as both the load increases and the cluster adds an additional application server. Once the CPU utilization projections reach 80% or higher, plan to add an additional HTTP server, or to add additional processing power to existing server(s).

	Number of Application Servers	Projected HTTP Server CPU CPU ($n - 1$) + Delta	Add Server (If CPU at 80% or Higher) Yes/No	New Projected Server CPU (If New Server Added)
27.	4			
28.	5			
29.	6			

Database Server CPU Utilization Projections

Estimate the number of database servers required to support the projected load and throughput. This calculation takes the CPU utilization of the preceding cluster runs and adds the delta CPU utilization increase anticipated as the load increases and the cluster adds an application server. Once the projected CPU utilization reaches 80% or higher, plan to split your databases across additional servers or add more processing power to the existing server.

	Number of Application Servers	Projected Database Server CPU CPU ($n - 1$) + Delta	Need to Scale Server (If CPU at 80% or Higher) Yes/No	New Projected Server CPU (If New Server or More Hardware Added)
30.				
31.				
32.				

Other Server Utilization Projections

Follow the same methodology used above for all other servers in your environment.

	Number of Application Servers	Projected Other Server CPU CPU ($n - 1$) + Delta	Need to Scale Server (If CPU at 80% or Higher) Yes/No	New Other Server CPU (If New Server or More Hardware Added)
33.				
34.				
35.				

Summary CPU Utilization Data

	Number of Application Servers	Number of Times to Scale HTTP Servers	Number of Times to Scale Databases	Number of HTTP Servers and CPU Utilization	Number of Database Servers and CPU Utilization
36.					

Appendix B
PRE-TEST CHECKLISTS

This appendix contains a set of checklists to use prior to beginning your tests. These checklists include best practices for the web application and test environment.

1. Web Application checklist
2. Component checklist
3. Test Team checklist
4. Test Environment checklist
5. Test Simulation and Tooling checklist

Web Application Checklist

The actual web application design and implementation play the most critical performance role for a high-performance web site. You cannot overcome a poor application with hardware tuning. Here is a checklist containing the critical do's and don'ts for the web application. Please refer to Chapters 2 and 3 for more information on each of these elements.

Servlets

- ❑ Short code paths.
- ❑ Each servlet returns a few basic page choices.
- ❑ Multi-threaded model (don't implement `SingleThreadModel`).
- ❑ Acquire static resources at initialization (JNDI lookup for datasource, and so on).
- ❑ Check for unnecessary "synchronized" statements.
- ❑ Synchronization used only for *small*, rapidly executing sections of code.

Java Server Pages

❑ Use JSPs for output. (Don't use servlets to create HTML or XML.)
❑ Turn off reload interval (or at least make it infrequent).
❑ Remove default HTTP session object creation (`<% page session= "false"%>`).[1]
❑ Pre-compile or pre-click JSPs.

JavaBeans

❑ Avoid the `bean.instantiate()` method.
❑ Use a database to persist data.

XML/XSL

❑ Use JSPs to generate XML.
❑ Be aware of server cost for parsing XML.
❑ Offload page assembly to client machine if possible.

Static Content

❑ Use HTTP server.
❑ Avoid file-serving servlet.

Logging

❑ Support and use logging levels.
❑ Reduce production logging.
❑ Make logging runtime configurable.
❑ Consider buffered writing.
❑ Limit memory requirements of buffer.
❑ Avoid the `servlet.log()` method.
❑ Avoid the `System.out.println()` method.

---

1. This assumes that automatic HTTP session creation is not required by your application.

HTTP Session

❑ Keep session objects small.
❑ Persist data that needs to be persisted (keep HTTP sessions small).
❑ Reduce HTTP session timeout.
❑ Support a logout function.
❑ Keep HTTP session working set in memory.
❑ Make HTTP session data serializable.
❑ Avoid nontransferable data.

Enterprise JavaBeans

❑ Use Stateless Session Beans as façades (avoid direct servlet interaction with Entity Bean).
❑ Avoid fine-grained EJB data models.
❑ Mark methods as read-only.
❑ Use local interfaces for co-located beans.
❑ Use lowest acceptable transaction isolation level.
❑ Consider scalability issues of Stateful Session Beans and Entity Beans.
❑ Cache Bean content in custom finders.
❑ Cache homes.
❑ Remove unused Stateful Session Beans (avoid EJB passivation).

Web Services

❑ Use UDDI with care.
❑ Minimize SOAP data transfers.
❑ Monitor changing web site usage patterns.

Database Connection

❑ Use vendor-supplied database connection pool capabilities.
❑ Return database connections to the pool quickly.
❑ Close all connections.
❑ Check exception paths to avoid connection leaks.

Object Pools

❑ Create custom object pools if your application launches threads.
❑ Use configurable limits.
❑ Never wait indefinitely within pool (avoid freezing the web site).
    ❑ Plan for back-end outages.
    ❑ Be especially careful with asynchronous MOM access.
❑ Set pool "hard maximums."
❑ Set timeouts for retrieving connections.

Garbage Collection

❑ Minimize garbage collection.
❑ Check for memory leaks (especially from hash tables).
❑ Minimize object creation.
    ❑ Use `StringBuffer` objects for concatenation.
    ❑ Use `ResourceBundle` or `Singleton` object for `String` literals.
    ❑ Avoid dynamic allocation (use static final whenever possible).
    ❑ Check for unused local variables.
    ❑ Pool and reuse objects.

Component Checklist

Performance problems may originate with any of the components in your web site. Use the checklist below to check component tuning and potential problems. See Chapter 2, Chapter 4, and Chapter 9 for a complete description of these concepts.

Routers

❑ Configured for full bandwidth.

Firewalls

❑ Properly configured.
❑ No TCP/IP timeouts.

Proxy Servers

- ❑ Check for bottlenecks.
- ❑ Use to cache content.

Network Interface Cards

- ❑ Check that processes are bound to correct NIC.
- ❑ Check for bottleneck.
- ❑ Check that NIC speed matches network speed.

Operating System

- ❑ Set TCP/IP timeout low.
- ❑ File descriptors increased if necessary.

HTTP Servers

- ❑ Appropriate number of threads or processes configured.
- ❑ Timeouts correct.
- ❑ Check logging level.
  - ❑ No date conversion.
  - ❑ No DNS look-ups.
- ❑ Keep-alive set appropriately.
- ❑ SSL only used when necessary.

Web Container

- ❑ Load servlets at startup.
- ❑ Precompile or preclick JSPs.
- ❑ Turn off reload interval.
  - ❑ Servlets
  - ❑ JSPs

Thread Pools

❑ Keep thread pools small (more is not always better).
❑ Establish thread pool "funnel".
   ❑ HTTP listeners
   ❑ Web container
   ❑ EJB container
   ❑ Database connection pools

Enterprise JavaBean Container

❑ Configure the pool size large enough to contain the working set.
❑ Find the right balance on cleanup interval.
❑ Use local interfaces when possible.
   ❑ Application server configuration settings
   ❑ EJB 2.0 capabilities (beware of future scalability considerations)

JVM Heap

❑ Maximum heap big enough to handle spikes.
❑ Maximum heap not so big that garbage collection takes too long.
❑ Minimum heap 25%–50% of maximum heap.
❑ Total of all JVM heaps on server less than physical memory.

Application Server Clones

❑ Do not clone servers already at capacity (near 100% CPU utilization).
❑ Scale resources as you add clones.

Database Server

❑ Correct indices.
   ❑ Indices copied to test database.
   ❑ New indices added for new applications.
❑ Resources tuned for web application (not fat-client).
   ❑ Bufferpools
   ❑ Cursors
   ❑ Sockets

❑ Caching used
❑ Multiple disks used
❑ Stripe logs

Legacy Systems

❑ Add connections to handle web application user requests.
❑ Provide larger region for the legacy application.
❑ Increase memory buffers.
❑ Add processing capacity.
❑ Tune connection software bandwidth.
❑ Multi-threaded connection software.

Test Team Checklist

A successful performance test requires participation from many people within the organization. Use this checklist to identify the skills required during your test. Please refer to Chapter 6 for more details.

Test Team

❑ Load driver skills
❑ Performance analysis skills
❑ Performance tuning expertise
   ❑ Java
   ❑ Application server
   ❑ Network
   ❑ Database

Support Team

❑ Network administrators
❑ Systems administrators
❑ Database administrators
❑ Systems analysts
❑ Legacy application programmers

Web Application Developers

❑ Application architect
❑ Application developers

Leadership and Management Team

❑ Quality assurance manager
❑ Performance test lead
❑ Marketing

Test Environment Checklist

Successful test environments make for successful tests. Solve test environment problems prior to capturing meaningful measurements. Chapter 9 provides more details on setting up the environment.

Controlled Environment

❑ No other load running on your server(s)
❑ No other load running on any component of your test (i.e., back-end systems)
❑ Private network
❑ Servers all ready (not still initializing)
❑ Host files instead of DNS name server

Network

❑ Understand required network capacity (i.e., 100Mbps, gigabit, and so on).
❑ Understand network capabilities.
❑ Sufficient network capacity between client and HTTP servers.
❑ Sufficient network capacity between application servers and back-end systems.
❑ Connectivity tested between all systems, including client drivers and back-end systems.

Hardware

- ❏ Representative of production environment
- ❏ Installed and configured
- ❏ Rated for use in your network
- ❏ Clean configurations (beware of settings on borrowed hardware)

Prerequisite Software

- ❏ Supported levels
- ❏ Configuration as expected in production environment
- ❏ Clean installs

Application Code

- ❏ Single path performance optimizations completed.
- ❏ No memory leaks.
- ❏ Individual paths tested.
- ❏ Stress testing successful.

Back-End

- ❏ Reasonable simulations for back-end systems in place and tested.
- ❏ Enough data in the back-end to eliminate unrealistic caching.
- ❏ Queries to back-end exhibit performance characteristics similar to those of production environment.
- ❏ Similar tuning applied as that found in production.
- ❏ Data matches test scripts.

Test Simulation and Tooling Checklist

The test tools simulate the production users; they make up a critical part of your test. Please see Chapters 7, 8, and 9 for more details.

Performance Test Tool Resources

If you don't provide enough capacity for your performance test tool, you may introduce a bottleneck into the system at your test client machines. Typically, you need as much hardware resource dedicated to the client driver(s) as to your application server(s).

❑ Client driver on separate machine(s)
❑ Enough client driver machines
❑ Client driver CPU utilization not at maximum
❑ Client network card not at maximum capacity
❑ Client drivers dedicated to test

Test Scripts and Scenarios

The test scripts simulate your target users. If these scripts do not represent your web site usage, you cannot rely on the results of your performance tests. Before beginning your tests, make sure your scripts work. Consider building scripts for the primitive paths for easy troubleshooting and optimization.

❑ Scripts representative of actual user activities
   ❑ Not too simple
   ❑ Not too focused
❑ Multiple, short scripts
❑ Atomic scripts
❑ Exercise whole web site
❑ Weighted testing
❑ Access sufficient backend data
❑ Use dynamic decisions
❑ Scripts tested
   ❑ No wrong or extraneous URLs
   ❑ No hard-coded cookies
   ❑ Correct think times
❑ Scripts for primitive paths

Tools

Before beginning, install all your tools, and train your team to use them. This includes load drivers and monitors, and tools to record your results.

❑ Load driver
❑ Monitors
❑ Recording
❑ Administration

TEST TOOLS

This appendix contains information about several performance test tools, including a list of some tools, and a requirements checklist to help you select the best tool for your needs. Additionally, we include sample test scripts from both LoadRunner and SilkPerformer.

Disclaimer: We list these tools to help you get started with your performance tool selection process. However, we do not endorse, recommend, or guarantee the tools listed in this section. Also, the information provided here comes from generally available marketing materials provided by the vendors. We merely provide this information for your convenience.

1. Performance analysis and test tool sources
2. Load Driver checklist
3. Example LoadRunner script
4. Example SilkPerformer script

Performance Analysis and Test Tool Sources

A wide variety of vendors provides performance testing and analysis tools. Rick Hower's web site, the Software QA/Test Resource Center, provides a listing of tools.[1] In this appendix, we provide a shorter list of common tools.

Java Profilers

Use a Java profiler tool during the development of any Java application to identify performance hot-spots in the application code. Also, the tools prove useful in analyzing

---

1. Software QA/Test Resource Center web site by Rick Hower. Retrieved December 27, 2001, from the World Wide Web: <http://www.softwareqatest.com/qatweb1.html>. This site lists hundreds of products, including load and performance test tools, Java test tools, external site monitoring services, web site management tools, and log analysis tools.

object creation rates, finding memory leaks, and many other important performance analysis tasks. Several companies provide profiling tools. Two widely used profilers are Sitraka JProbe and VMGEAR Optimizeit (recently purchased by Borland). In addition, IBM recently released profiling function in the IBM WebSphere Studio Application Developer.

IBM WebSphere Application Developer Workbench

The WebSphere Application Developer Workbench provides monitoring and profiling tools for recognizing, isolating, and fixing performance problems. You use the tool to view, among other things, object creation and garbage collection, execution sequences, thread interactions, and object references from within the development environment.

Sitraka JProbe Suite

Sitraka JProbe Suite provides performance profiling, memory debugging, code coverage, and thread analysis capabilities in one integrated suite, designed for Java developers. JProbe Suite includes the JProbe Profiler, Threadalyzer, and Coverage.

VMGEAR Optimizeit

The Optimizeit Suite includes three integrated tools for tuning performance throughout the development cycle. Optimizeit also supports tracking down performance bottlenecks, correcting memory leaks, and uncovering thread contention.

Java Profiler Product Summary

Company	Product	Web Site
IBM	WebSphere Application Developer Workbench	\<http://www.ibm.com\>
Sitraka	JProbe	\<http://www.sitraka.com\>
VMGEAR (Borland)	Optimizeit	\<http://www.optimizeit.com\>

Performance Test Tools

At least fifty different performance test tools products exist.[2] In Chapters 7 and 8, we provide examples using two popular tools, Mercury Interactive LoadRunner and Segue SilkPerformer, and provide a more complete listing of available performance test tools here. Many of these companies also provide performance monitoring and functional test products.

Apache's ApacheBench

ApacheBench is an Internet Benchmarking tool that comes (free) with the Apache Web Server. See <http://httpd.apache.org/docs/programs/ab.html>.

Apache Jmeter

Apache Jmeter is a 100% pure Java desktop application designed to load test functional behavior and measure performance. It is part of the Jakarta project at <http://jakarta.apache.org/jmeter/index.html>.

Compuware QALoad

QALoad simulates load generated by many users on your application. The company also provides a Script Development Workbench for developing test scripts, and test results are available in a variety of reports, graphs, and charts. Compuware also provides testing and monitoring products.

Empirix e-Load

The e-Load tool provides a scalability testing solution designed specifically for the web. It provides real-time, detailed performance views for each tier of the system under test, as well as supporting customized reports. Empirix also provides functional testing and monitoring products.

Mercury Interactive Astra LoadTest

Mercury offers Astra LoadTest, a load driver tool for smaller web sites. Astra LoadTest focuses on supporting HTTP-based testing and includes real-time graphing and monitoring of operating systems, HTTP servers, application servers, and databases.

---

2. See Rick Hower's web site, Software QA/Test Resource Center. Retrieved December 27, 2001, from the World Wide Web. This site lists approximately 50 load and performance test tools.

Mercury Interactive LoadRunner

LoadRunner is Mercury's high-end, scalable, automated load testing solution. LoadRunner includes real-time graphing and monitoring of an extensive set of operating systems, web servers, application servers, and databases. Mercury Interactive also provides functional testing and monitoring products.

Quest Benchmark Factory

Benchmark Factory provides a scalable load testing, capacity planning, and performance tuning tool. Benchmark Factory allows you to determine system capacity, pinpoint system bottlenecks, and isolate system stress related problems. Quest also provides performance analysis and monitoring products.

Rational Suite TestStudio

Rational Suite TestStudio supports performance testing via simulating virtual testers. Rational provides support to build complex usage scenarios and produce realistic system loads. They also provide development and testing products.

RadView Software WebLOAD

WebLOAD simulates real-life Internet user behaviors and reports performance issues and bottlenecks within an application to help companies successfully deploy high-performing e-business applications. RadView also provides functional testing tools.

Segue SilkPerformer

Segue's SilkPerformer lets you simulate the fluctuating demands of a live e-business environment. SilkPerformer can predict the scalability and performance of your web application, ensuring its reliability before it goes live. Segue also provides functional test and monitoring products.

Load Driver Summary

Company	Product	Web Site
Apache	ApacheBench	<www.apache.org>
Apache	JMeter	<Jakarta.apache.org>
Compuware	QALoad	<www.compuware.com>
Empirix	e-Load	<www.empirix.com>

Company	Product	Web Site
Mercury Interactive	Astra LoadTest	<www.mercuryinteractive.com>
Mercury Interactive	LoadRunner	<www.mercuryinteractive.com>
Quest	Benchmark Factory	<www.quest.com>
Rational	Performance Studio	<www.rational.com>
Segue	SilkPerformer	<www.segue.com>
RadView Software	WebLOAD	<www.radview.com>

Java Application Performance Monitoring

Many of the load driver tools listed above provide integrated performance monitors to collect data during testing. In addition, we'd like to mention a new class of product for Java applications: performance monitoring tools. Consider using these products to provide in-depth information on the web application that is executing during the load test. Unlike Java profilers, these tools are less intrusive and typically do not significantly alter the application's performance, which allows you to analyze performance issues under load conditions. While these tools focus on production monitoring, they sometimes come in handy for testing high-performance web sites, or if you cannot isolate a performance problem with your existing tool set.

Precise Indepth for J2EE

Precise Indepth for J2EE collects detailed application response time data, as well as JVM and system performance data. Though sold as a production monitoring product, Precise provides an HTML interface displaying HTTP or EJB entry points sorted by response time, with drill-down capabilities. These features also make it easy to see performance problems during load testing. Precise also provides Indepth products for other web site components, such as databases, as well as a monitoring framework.

Sitraka PerformaSure

PerformaSure targets the performance testing environment specifically by using a combination of lightweight instrumentation to provide high-level performance data across web server, application server, and database. The company also provides more performance intrusive drill-down capabilities.

Wily Technologies Introscope

Introscope provides monitoring for a wide range of Java applications. Introscope specifically monitors EJB and servlet performance, JVM memory, JDBC connections, CPU utilization, and network socket traffic. Introscope is customizable to add other monitoring points. Introscope provides a set of tailorable dashboards to monitor key components of your choice.

Java Application Performance Monitoring Summary

Company	Product	Web Site
Precise Software Solutions	Indepth for the J2EE platform	<www.precise.com>
Sitraka	PerformaSure	<www.sitraka.com>
Wily Technology	Introscope	<www.wilytech.com>

Database Performance Analysis

The monitoring tools discussed so far focus on production monitoring for Java web applications or Java applications in general. However, specialized monitors also exist for monitoring databases. Like their Java monitoring cousins, these tools focus on production database monitoring, but they sometimes prove valuable during testing as well. If your web application includes a significant database access component, these tools may aid database optimization.

Database Performance Monitoring Summary

Additional products supporting IBM's DB2 database are listed in the Global Solutions Directory at: <http://www8.software.ibm.com/solutions/isv/igssg.nsf/ searchgui2>.

Company	Product	Web Site
DGI	Flight Deck, SQL-GUY, and other related products	<www.database-guys.com>
Precise Solutions	Indepth for Oracle Indepth for DB2 UDB	<www.precise.com>
Quest	Spotlight on Oracle Spotlight on SQL Server Quest Central for DB2, and other related products	<www.quest.com>

Network Protocol Analyzers

Network protocol analyzers range in price from freeware to more than $100,000. The table below contains a list of some common network analyzers.[3]

Network Protocol Analyzer Summary

Company	Product	Web Site
Ethereal	Ethereal	<www.ethereal.com>
Sniffer Technologies (Network Associates)	Sniffer	<www.sniffer.com>
Wildpackets	Etherpeek	<www.wildpackets.com>

Product Capabilities

In addition to the specialized monitoring products, don't forget the excellent, low impact capabilities packaged with the operating systems and middleware. Frequently, these are the only monitoring products you need during your tests. Chapter 12 contains descriptions and examples using some of these tools.

Product Capabilities Summary

Component	Tool
Network	netstat
System	UNIX: vmstat, iostat, sar
	Microsoft Windows: Performance Monitor
Application Server	WebSphere Resource Analyzer
	WebSphere Thread Analyzer
	WebLogic Administration Console
Java Virtual Machine	Verbosegc
Database Server	DB2 Snapshot
	Oracle Statspack, Oracle Enterprise Manager

---

3. "Selecting a Protocol Analyzer," posted on NetworkWorldFusion, October 8, 2001, by Ron Nutter. Retrieved December 27, 2001, from the World Wide Web: <http://www.nwfusion.com/columnists/ 2001/1008helpdesk.htm>.

Production Monitoring Solutions

Once your site is in production, you'll need to monitor the performance for problem identification and ongoing capacity planning. For completeness, we have included below a list of production monitoring products providing support for IBM's WebSphere Application Server and other leading application servers.[4]

Production Monitoring Summary

Company	Product	Web Site
Altaworks	Panorama	<www.altaworks.com>
BMC Software	Patrol	<www.bmc.com>
Candle	OMEGAMON	<www.candle.com>
Computer Associates	Unicenter	<www.ca.com>
Dirig Software	Fenway	<www.dirig.com>
Empirix	OneSight	<www.empirix.com>
IBM Tivoli	Web Component Manager	<www.tivoli.com>
IBM Tivoli	Tivoli Manager for WebSphere	<www.tivoli.com>
Mercury Interactive	Topaz	<www.mercuryinteractive.com>
Nastel Technologies	AutoPilot	<www.nastel.com>
Precise Software Solutions	Precise Indepth	<www.precise.com>
Wily Technologies	Introscope	<www.wilytech.com>

---

4. For a list of performance monitoring products supporting IBM's WebSphere Application Server, see <http://www-4.ibm.com/software/webservers/pw/dhtml/wsperformance/performance_bpsolutions.html>.

Load Driver Checklist

This checklist corresponds with the requirements covered in Chapter 8. Please refer to the chapter for more detailed descriptions of each requirement.

Website Type: _____

Number of Users: _____

Key Requirements: _____

USER SIMULATION				
	Requirement	**Do you need this capability? How important is it to you?**	**Tool A**	**Tool B**
Think time	Record and play back			
	Customize at runtime			
User load	User ramp-up			
	Simulate spikes			
Browser simulation	Simulate browser caching			
	Simulate clearing cache			
	Simulate specific browsers	Which browsers do you need?		
	Client IP address simulation	Are you testing IP-based load balancing?		
Cookie support	Supports cookies	Does your site use cookies?		
	Automatically records and correlates cookies			
	Dump cookie cache			
Hardware and platform support	Estimated hardware per user	Number of users to simulate		
	Controller platforms			
	User agent platforms			

SCRIPTS				
	Requirement	**Do you need this capability? How important is it to you?**	**Tool A**	**Tool B**
Dynamic data	GUI based interface	What types of dynamic data do you need?		
	User ID substitution			
	Random files			
	Random numbers			
	Import from DB			
Web page parsing	List of links	What support do you need?		
	Other dynamic results			
Scripting and skill	Scripting language			
	Skills needed			
Building and weighing scenarios	Run multiple scripts			
	Random weighting across scripts			
	Combine scripts into longer script			
	Run scripts individually			
Reuse scripts in production	Production monitoring product			

AUTOMATION AND CENTRALIZED CONTROL				
	Requirement	**Do you need this capability? How important is it to you?**	**Tool A**	**Tool B**
Multiple drivers	Support multiple client simulators	Will your site tests need multiple client drivers?		
	Report consolidation			
	Command line	Do you need to drive tests from command line?		
	Remote control	Do you want to drive tests from remote location?		

PRICING AND LICENSING				
	Requirement	**Do you need this capability? How important is it to you?**	**Tool A**	**Tool B**
Licensing terms	Price of controller			
	Number of users needed and price			
	Flat based license			
	Unlimited license			
Share users	Share users across controllers	Do you have a lot of tests and/or controllers?		
Short-term license	License users by day or week			
Existing relationship	Company relationship			
	Test tools in use			
	Production tools in use			

REPORTING				
	Requirement	**Do you need this capability? How important is it to you?**	**Tool A**	**Tool B**
Key results	Average response time			
	Granular response time data			
	Pages per second			
	Transactions per second			
	Summary report			
	Customizable reports			
Steady state	Steady state supported			
	Results automatically subset			
Real-time charts	Results displayed during test			

REPORTING

	Requirement	Do you need this capability? How important is it to you?	Tool A	Tool B
	Transactions per second			
	Response time			
	Schedule multiple runs			
	Amount of data returned customizable			

VERIFICATION OF RESULTS

	Requirement	Do you need this capability? How important is it to you?	Tool A	Tool B
Verification of data	Errors reported			
	Verify data			
	Verify dynamic data			
Verification of logs	Verify web server logs	We haven't found a tool that automatically does this.		
	Verify application server logs			
Monitors	Supported by load test tool	What servers do you need to monitor?		
	Monitor any server			
	Real-time graphing of monitors			
	Reports include monitor data and performance test results			
Operating System	Operating Systems	What operating systems are your servers on?		
	Network			
	HTTP server			
	Application server			
	Database			
	Others	What other applications or middleware do you have?		

Sample LoadRunner Script (© 2002 Mercury Interactive Corporation)

In Chapter 7, we included subsets of a Pet Store test script as examples. This section contains the complete scripts for the application.[5] **Warning:** We do *not* recommend Pet Store as a performance benchmark application for running under load conditions. We provide these scripts merely as examples for building your own test scripts, but we *do not* recommend that you use them for actual performance testing.

LoadRunner Initialization Section

```
#include "as_web.h"
#include "lrw_custom_body.h"
/* This is a LoadRunner sample script using LoadRunner 7.02 against a IBM
   WebSphere Advanced Edition running Sun's Pet Store Sample Application.
   We emulate the shopping activity of a store visitor. First the visitor
   logs in to the store (in the vuser_init session), then the visitor
   browses through the store for different pets (in the Action1 session),
   finally the visitor proceeds to finish the check out procedure and then
   log out (in the vuser_end session).

   Make sure that you go to the parameter file to add the user ID to log
   in to the pet store! */

vuser_init()
{

/* type in the Pet Store url:    */

   web_url("main",
      "URL=http://localhost/estore/control/main",
      "TargetFrame=",
      "Resource=0",
      "RecContentType=text/html",
      "Referer=",
      "Snapshot=t1.inf",
      "Mode=HTML",
      LAST);

   lr_think_time( 2 );

   web_image("sign-in.gif",
      "Src=/estore/images/sign-in.gif",
      "Snapshot=t2.inf",
      LAST);

   lr_think_time( 9 );
```

---

5. Profuse thanks to Leo Cai for his work on this sample script.

```
    /* Sign in to the pet store. */

    lr_think_time( 2 );

    web_submit_form("verifysignin",
       "Snapshot=t3.inf",
       ITEMDATA,
       "Name=j_username", "Value={userid}", ENDITEM,
       "Name=j_password", "Value={Passwd}", ENDITEM,
       "Name=submit.x", "Value=29", ENDITEM,
       "Name=submit.y", "Value=6", ENDITEM,
       LAST);

    lr_think_time( 2 );

    /* Click on store main page   */
web_link("Store Main Page",
   "Text=Store Main Page",
   "Snapshot=t4.inf",
   LAST);

    return 0;
```

LoadRunner Action1 Section

```
#include "as_web.h"

/* This is the section where the visitor will browse through the pet store
   and add the pets to the shopping cart. */

int i,j, Count;// declare the integer used in the script
char Param[256];// declare a character string used in the script
char Link[256];// declare a second character string used in the script
Action1()
{
   /* Click on main page. */
   lr_think_time( 2 );

   /* The following statement captures the array of pet categories and
      saves them as pet_1, pet_2, etc. */
   web_reg_save_param("pet","LB=images/nav-",
➥"RB=.gif\"","Search=body","Ord=all",LAST);

    /* Visit first level of pet store.  */
   web_url("main",
      "URL=http://localhost/estore/control/main",
      "TargetFrame=",
      "Resource=0",
      "RecContentType=text/html",
```

```
    "Referer=",
    "Snapshot=t1.inf",
    "Mode=HTML",
    LAST);
{
```
/* The following statement saves the total number of pet counts to an
   integer Count */
```
    Count = atoi(lr_eval_string("{pet_count}"));
```

/* The following statement does three tasks:
   1. LoadRunner randomly picks a number defined by Num (you can change
   the range from the parameter list. It defaults from 1 to 10000) and
   then Num is modulized by Count. Since the web page numbering starts
   from 1 instead of 0, a 1 is added to the modulized result. Please refer
   to C programming language documentation for an explanation of the modu-
   lus operator.
   2. After a number is randomly picked, the pet category is determined by
   pet_1, etc.,
   3. the category is then assigned to a character string called Param */
```
    sprintf(Param,"{pet_%d}",atoi(lr_eval_string("{Num}")) % Count + 1);
```

/* The following statement constructs a string that can be used in a
   LoadRunner function statement. For example, if pet_1=cat is picked
   from the previous statement, then Link will be assigned
   "Src=/estore/images/nav-cat.gif" */
```
    sprintf(Link,"Src=/estore/images/nav-%s.gif",lr_eval_string(Param));
}
```

/* The following statement will capture the subcategories of the pet store
   and save them as sub_pet_1, sub_pet_2, etc. */
```
  web_reg_save_param("sub_pet","LB=\">\n ","RB=\n\t
</a>","Search=body","Ord=all",LAST);
```

/* This statement will simulate a click on any of the categories dictated
   by Link */
```
  web_image("The first link: species",
    Link,
    "Snapshot=t2.inf",
    LAST);
{
```
/* The following statement saves the total number of subcategories to an
   integer Count*/
```
    Count = atoi(lr_eval_string("{sub_pet_count}"));
```

/* Similar to previous sprintf statement, this statement will accomplish 3
   tasks again:
   LoadRunner randomly picks a number between 1 to 10000 and modulized by
   the total number of counts (plus 1) and then
   assigns the random number to sub_pet_(number) so that Param will be
   assigned sub_pet_1.
   sub_pet_2, etc. sub_pet_1, etc. is captured in the web_image ( )
   LoadRunner function statement. */

```
      sprintf(Param,"{sub_pet_%d}",atoi(lr_eval_string("{Num}")) % Count +
1);

/* The following statement will construct the string Link to be used in
   the subsequent LoadRunner function statement. For example, Link repre-
   sents "Text=Bulldog */
      sprintf(Link,"Text=%s",lr_eval_string(Param));
   }
/* The following statement simulates a click on one of the sub catego-
   ries. */
   web_reg_save_param("sub_pet2","LB=\">\n
","RB=</a>","Search=body","Ord=all",LAST);

   web_link("The second link: sub categories",
      Link,
      "Snapshot=t3.inf",
      LAST);
   {
/* The following statement saves the total number of sub_pet2 categories
   to an integer Count */
      Count = atoi(lr_eval_string("{sub_pet2_count}"));

/* Similar to previous sprintf statement, this statement will accomplish 3
   tasks again:
   LoadRunner randomly picks a number between 1 to 10000 and modularized
   by the total number of counts (plus 1)
   and then assigns the random number to sub_pet_(number) so that Param
   will be assigned sub_pet_1.
   sub_pet_2, etc. sub_pet_1, etc. is captured in the web_image ( )
   LoadRunner function statement. */
      sprintf(Param,"{sub_pet2_%d}",atoi(lr_eval_string("{Num}")) % Count +
1);

/* The following statement will construct the string Link to be used in
   the subsequent LoadRunner function statement. For example, Link repre-
   sents "Text=Bulldog */
      sprintf(Link,"Text=%s",lr_eval_string(Param));
   }
/* The following statement makes a click on the third page of the
   pet site */
   lr_think_time( 2 );
   web_link("The third link: specific pet",
      Link,
      "Snapshot=t4.inf",
      LAST);
   lr_think_time( 2 );
   /* click to add pet to the shopping cart. */
   web_image("Add Item to Your Shopping Cart",
      "Alt=Add Item to Your Shopping Cart",
      "Snapshot=t8.inf",
      LAST);
   lr_think_time( 2 );
   return 0;
```

LoadRunner End Section

```
#include "as_web.h"
vuser_end()
{
/* This is the section where the visitor has finished browsing the pet
   store and is getting ready to check out and leave the pet store. */
   web_url("checkout",
      "URL=http://localhost/estore/control/checkout",
      "TargetFrame=",
      "Resource=0",
      "RecContentType=text/html",
      "Referer=http://localhost/estore/control/cart?action=
      //updateCart&itemQuantity_EST-1=1&update.x=33&update.y=8",
      "Snapshot=t10.inf",
      "Mode=HTML",
      LAST);
   web_image("Continue",
      "Alt=Continue",
      "Snapshot=t11.inf",
      LAST);
   lr_think_time( 2 );
   lr_start_transaction("Process_payment");
   lr_think_time( 2 );
   web_submit_form("validatebillinginformation",
      "Snapshot=t12.inf",
      ITEMDATA,
      "Name=credit_card_type", "Value=Visa", ENDITEM,
      "Name=credit_card_number", "Value=9999 9999 9999 9999", ENDITEM,
      "Name=expiration_month", "Value=01", ENDITEM,
      "Name=expiration_year", "Value=2001", ENDITEM,
      "Name=given_name", "Value=Cai", ENDITEM,
      "Name=family_name", "Value=Leo", ENDITEM,
      "Name=address_1", "Value=1325 Borregas Ave", ENDITEM,
      "Name=address_2", "Value=", ENDITEM,
      "Name=city", "Value=Sunnyvale", ENDITEM,
      "Name=state_or_province", "Value=California", ENDITEM,
      "Name=postal_code", "Value=94089", ENDITEM,
      "Name=country", "Value=USA", ENDITEM,
      "Name=telephone_number", "Value=408-822-5737", ENDITEM,
      "Name=ship_to_billing_address", "Value=on", ENDITEM,
      "Name=x", "Value=66", ENDITEM,
      "Name=y", "Value=9", ENDITEM,
      LAST);
   lr_end_transaction("Process_payment", LR_AUTO);
   lr_think_time( 3 );

   /* Now it is time to leave the store! */
   lr_think_time( 3 );
   web_image("sign-out.gif",
      "Src=/estore/images/sign-out.gif",
      "Snapshot=t13.inf",
      LAST);
   return 0;
```

Sample SilkPerformer Script © 2002 Segue Corporation

In Chapter 7, we included subsets of a Pet Store test script as examples. In this section, we include the complete SilkPerformer script for this example.[6] **Warning:** We do *not* recommend Pet Store as a performance benchmark application for running under load conditions. We provide these scripts merely as examples for building your own test scripts, but we *do not* recommend that you use them for actual performance testing.

Sign-in, Browse, and Purchase Script

```
benchmark SilkPerformerRecorder
use "WebAPI.bdh"

dcluser
 user
   VUser
 transactions
   TInit : begin;
   TMain : 1;

var
 sUsername, sPassword, sCardNumber, sExpirationMonth, sExpirationYear,
➥sTelephone: string;

dclrand
 sCreditCardType   : RndInd("Visa" = 0.3; "Mastercard" = 0.3;
➥"AmericanExpress" = 0.4);
 sThreeDigits      : RndStr("0123456789", 3..3);
 sFourDigits       : RndStr("0123456789", 4..4);
 sGivenName        : RndFile("Efname.rnd", 64);    // random first name
 sFamilyName       : RndFile("Elname.rnd", 64);    // random last name
 sAddress1         : RndFile("Address.rnd", 64);   // random address
 sCity             : RndFile("City.rnd", 64);      // random city
 sStateOrProvince  : RndInd("California" = 0.3; "New York" = 0.3;
➥"Texas" = 0.4);
 sPostalCode       : RndStr("0123456789", 5..5);   // random postal code

dcltrans

transaction TInit
 begin
   WebSetBrowser(WEB_BROWSER_MSIE5);
   WebSetUserBehavior(WEB_USERBEHAVIOR_FIRST_TIME);
```

---

6. Equally profuse thanks to Stephan Asboeck for his work on this sample script.

```
    WebSetDocumentCache(true, WEB_CACHE_CHECK_SESSION);
    sUsername := "user" + string(GetUserId());
    sPassword := "pass" + string(GetUserId());
    sCardNumber := sFourDigits + " " + sFourDigits + " " + sFourDigits +
➡" " + sFourDigits;
    sExpirationMonth := string(RndUniN(1 .. 12));
    if StrLen(sExpirationMonth) < 2 then sExpirationMonth := "0" +
➡sExpirationMonth end;
    sExpirationYear := "200" + string(RndUniN(2..9));
    sTelephone := sThreeDigits + "-" + sThreeDigits + "-" + sFourDigits;
// random phone number
 end TInit;

transaction TMain
 var
   nLinks: number;
 begin
   WebPageUrl("http://ruthless/estore", "Java(TM) Pet Store Demo");
   WebPageAddUrl("../images/helpHL.gif");
   WebPageAddUrl("../images/sign-inHL.gif");
   WebPageAddUrl("../images/sign-out.gif");
   WebPageAddUrl("../images/sign-outHL.gif");
   WebPageAddUrl("../images/searchHL.gif");
   WebPageAddUrl("../images/my_account.gif");
   WebPageAddUrl("../images/my_accountHL.gif");
   WebPageAddUrl("../images/cartHL.gif");
   WebPageAddUrl("../images/fish.gif");
   WebPageAddUrl("../images/fishHL.gif");
   WebPageAddUrl("../images/dogs.gif");
   WebPageAddUrl("../images/dogsHL.gif");
   WebPageAddUrl("../images/reptiles.gif");
   WebPageAddUrl("../images/reptilesHL.gif");
   WebPageAddUrl("../images/cats.gif");
   WebPageAddUrl("../images/catsHL.gif");
   WebPageAddUrl("../images/birds.gif");
   WebPageAddUrl("../images/birdsHL.gif");
   WebPageAddUrl("../images/logo-topbar.gif");
   WebPageAddUrl("../images/splash.gif");
   /* Redirecting http://ruthless/estore/populate?command
      =checkTables&redirect=/control/language%253Flanguage%253DEnglish ->
      http://ruthless/estore/control/language?language=English */
   ThinkTime(2.1);
   WebPageLink("Enter the store", "Welcome to Java Pet Store Demo");
   // Link 4

   ThinkTime(5.1);
   WebPageLink("sign-in", "Sign In"); // Link 3
    ThinkTime(8.2);
   /*Form 2 */
   WebPageSubmit("button_submit", ESTORE_CONTROL_VERIFYSIGNIN001,
➡"Welcome");      WebPageAddUrl("../images/banner_birds.gif");
   ThinkTime(3.0);
```

```
     WebPageLink(NULL, "Welcome to Java Pet Store Demo (#1)"); // Link 1
     /* Randomly select a "category" */
     WebPageLink(NULL, "Product Category", RndUniN(6 ..10));
       nLinks := 0;
     while WebPageQueryLink("product?product_id=", nLinks + 1) > 0 do
➥nLinks := nLinks + 1 end;
     /* Randomly select a "product" */
     WebPageLink(NULL, "Product Category (#1)", 10 + RndUniN(1 .. nLinks));
       nLinks := 0;
     while WebPageQueryLink("productdetails?item_id=", nLinks + 1) > 0 do
➥nLinks := nLinks + 1 end;
     /* Randomly select an "item" */
     WebPageLink(NULL, "Product Information", 10 + RndUniN(1 .. nLinks));
       ThinkTime(2.9);
     WebPageLink("Add Item to Your Shopping Cart", "Cart"); // Link 11
       ThinkTime(6.0);
     WebPageSubmit("cart-update", ESTORE_CONTROL_CART002, "Cart (#1)");
     // Form 2
       WebPageLink("Proceed To Checkout", "Check Out"); // Link 15
       WebPageLink("Continue", "Enter Your Information"); // Link 12
       ThinkTime(3.7);
     WebPageSubmit("button_cont", ESTORE_CONTROL_VALIDATEBILLINGIN003,
➥"Confirm Shipping Data"); // Form 2
       WebPageLink("Continue", "Order Shipped"); // Link 11
       ThinkTime(7.0);
     WebPageLink("sign-out", "Sign Off"); // Link 3
   end TMain;

dclform
   ESTORE_CONTROL_VERIFYSIGNIN001:
     "target_screen"             := "" <USE_HTML_VAL> , // hidden, unchanged
//value: "null"
     "j_username"                := sUsername,
     "j_password"                := sPassword,
     "submit.x"                  := "28", // added
     "submit.y"                  := "9"; // added
   ESTORE_CONTROL_CART002:
     "action"                    := "" <USE_HTML_VAL> , // hidden, unchanged
//value: "updateCart"
     "itemQuantity_EST-1"        := "2", // changed
     "update.x"                  := "25", // added
     "update.y"                  := "4"; // added
   ESTORE_CONTROL_VALIDATEBILLINGIN003:
     "credit_card_type"          := sCreditCardType,
     "credit_card_number"        := sCardNumber,
     "expiration_month"          := sExpirationMonth,
     "expiration_year"           := sExpirationYear,
     "given_name"                := sGivenName,
     "family_name"               := sFamilyName,
     "address_1"                 := sAddress1,
     "address_2"                 := "",
     "city"                      := sCity,
```

```
"state_or_province"       := sStateOrProvince,
"postal_code"             := sPostalCode,
"country"                 := "USA", // changed
"telephone_number"        := sTelephone,
"ship_to_billing_address" := "on", // changed
"x"                       := "74", // added
"y"                       := "8"; // added
```

Search Script

```
benchmark SilkPerformerRecorder
use "WebAPI.bdh"

dcluser
 user
   VUser
 transactions
   TInit           : begin;
   TMain           : 1;

dclrand
 sSearchExpressions: RndFile("SearchExpressions.txt", 64);

dcltrans
 transaction TInit
 begin
   WebSetBrowser(WEB_BROWSER_MSIE5);
   WebSetUserBehavior(WEB_USERBEHAVIOR_FIRST_TIME);
   WebSetDocumentCache(true, WEB_CACHE_CHECK_SESSION);
 end TInit;

 transaction TMain
 var
   nLinks: number;
 begin
   WebPageUrl("http://ruthless/estore", "Java(TM) Pet Store Demo");
   WebPageAddUrl("../images/helpHL.gif");
   WebPageAddUrl("../images/sign-inHL.gif");
   WebPageAddUrl("../images/sign-out.gif");
   WebPageAddUrl("../images/sign-outHL.gif");
   WebPageAddUrl("../images/searchHL.gif");
   WebPageAddUrl("../images/my_account.gif");
   WebPageAddUrl("../images/my_accountHL.gif");
   WebPageAddUrl("../images/cartHL.gif");
   WebPageAddUrl("../images/fish.gif");
   WebPageAddUrl("../images/fishHL.gif");
   WebPageAddUrl("../images/dogs.gif");
   WebPageAddUrl("../images/dogsHL.gif");
   WebPageAddUrl("../images/reptiles.gif");
   WebPageAddUrl("../images/reptilesHL.gif");
```

```
WebPageAddUrl("../images/cats.gif");
WebPageAddUrl("../images/catsHL.gif");
WebPageAddUrl("../images/birds.gif");
WebPageAddUrl("../images/birdsHL.gif");
WebPageAddUrl("../images/logo-topbar.gif");
WebPageAddUrl("../images/splash.gif");
/* Redirecting http://ruthless/estore/populate?command=checkTa-
   bles&redirect=/control/language%253Flanguage%253DEnglish ->
   http://ruthless/estore/control/language?language=English */
ThinkTime(2.5);
WebPageLink("Enter the store", "Welcome to Java Pet Store Demo");
// Link 4
WebPageAddUrl("../images/fish1.jpg");
WebPageAddUrl("../images/cat1.gif");
WebPageAddUrl("../images/bird4.gif");
WebPageAddUrl("../images/fish4.gif");
ThinkTime(8.6);
WebPageSubmit("search", ESTORE_CONTROL_SEARCH001, "Search"); // Form 1
ThinkTime(2.8);
nLinks := 0;
while WebPageQueryLink("product?product_id=", nLinks + 1) > 0 do
➥nLinks := nLinks + 1 end;
if nLinks > 0 then
  WebPageLink(NULL, "Product Category", 9 + RndUniN(1 .. nLinks));
end;
end TMain;

dclform
ESTORE_CONTROL_SEARCH001:
  "search_text"            := sSearchExpressions,
  "search.x"               := "20",
  "search.y"               := "11";
```

New Account Script

```
benchmark SilkPerformerRecorder
use "WebAPI.bdh"

dcluser
 user
   VUser
 transactions
   TInit           : begin;
   TMain           : 1;

var
 sUsername, sPassword, sEMail, sTelephone: string;

dclrand
 sGivenName          : RndFile("Efname.rnd", 64);    // random first name
```

```
sFamilyName        : RndFile("Elname.rnd", 64);    // random last name
sAddress1          : RndFile("Address.rnd", 64);   // random address
sCity              : RndFile("City.rnd", 64);      // random city
sStateOrProvince   : RndInd("California" = 0.3; "New York" = 0.3;
➥"Texas" = 0.4);
sPostalCode        : RndStr("0123456789", 5..5);   // random postal code
sThreeDigits       : RndStr("0123456789", 3..3);
sFourDigits        : RndStr("0123456789", 4..4);
sLanguage          : RndInd("English" = 0.5; "Japanese" = 0.5);
sCategory          : RndInd("Birds" = 0.2; "Cats" = 0.2; "Dogs" = 0.2;
➥"Fish" = 0.2; "Reptiles" = 0.2);

dcltrans
transaction TInit
begin
  WebSetBrowser(WEB_BROWSER_MSIE5);
  WebSetUserBehavior(WEB_USERBEHAVIOR_FIRST_TIME);
  WebSetDocumentCache(true, WEB_CACHE_CHECK_SESSION);
  sUsername  := "user" + string(GetUserId());   // sequential user name
  sPassword  := "pass" + string(GetUserId());   // sequential password
  /* Sequential e-mail address */
  sEMail     := "user" + string(GetUserId()) + "@company.com";
  /* Random phone number */
  sTelephone := sThreeDigits + "-" + sThreeDigits + "-" + sFourDigits;
end TInit;
transaction TMain
begin
  WebPageUrl("http://ruthless/estore", "Java(TM) Pet Store Demo");
  WebPageAddUrl("../images/helpHL.gif");
  WebPageAddUrl("../images/sign-inHL.gif");
  WebPageAddUrl("../images/sign-out.gif");
  WebPageAddUrl("../images/sign-outHL.gif");
  WebPageAddUrl("../images/searchHL.gif");
  WebPageAddUrl("../images/my_account.gif");
  WebPageAddUrl("../images/my_accountHL.gif");
  WebPageAddUrl("../images/cartHL.gif");
  WebPageAddUrl("../images/fish.gif");
  WebPageAddUrl("../images/fishHL.gif");
  WebPageAddUrl("../images/dogs.gif");
  WebPageAddUrl("../images/dogsHL.gif");
  WebPageAddUrl("../images/reptiles.gif");
  WebPageAddUrl("../images/reptilesHL.gif");
  WebPageAddUrl("../images/cats.gif");
  WebPageAddUrl("../images/catsHL.gif");
  WebPageAddUrl("../images/birds.gif");
  WebPageAddUrl("../images/birdsHL.gif");
  WebPageAddUrl("../images/logo-topbar.gif");
  WebPageAddUrl("../images/splash.gif");

  /* Redirecting http://ruthless/estore/populate?command=checkTa-
     bles&redirect=/control/language%253Flanguage%253DEnglish ->
     http://ruthless/estore/control/language?language=English */
```

```
    ThinkTime(2.3);
    WebPageLink("Enter the store", "Welcome to Java Pet Store Demo");
    // Link 4
    ThinkTime(10.1);
    WebPageLink("sign-in", "Sign In"); // Link 3
    WebPageLink("New User", "Create New Account"); // Link 10
    ThinkTime(46.8);
    WebPageSubmit("button_submit", ESTORE_CONTROL_VALIDATENEWACCOUN001,
"Account Created"); // Form 2
    ThinkTime(6.7);
    WebPageLink("sign-out", "Sign Off"); // Link 3
  end TMain;

dclform
  ESTORE_CONTROL_VALIDATENEWACCOUN001:
    "action"                   := "" <USE_HTML_VAL> , // hidden, unchanged
    //value: "createAccount"
    "user_name"                := sUsername,
    "password"                 := sPassword,
    "user_email"               := sEMail,
    "given_name"               := sGivenName,
    "family_name"              := sFamilyName,
    "address_1"                := sAddress1,
    "address_2"                := "",
    "city"                     := sCity,
    "state_or_province"        := sStateOrProvince,
    "postal_code"              := sPostalCode,
    "country"                  := "USA",
    "telephone_number"         := sTelephone,
    "language"                 := sLanguage,
    "favorite_category"        := sCategory,
    "myList_on"                := "on",
    "banners_on"               := "on",
    "Submit.x"                 := "30",
    "Submit.y"                 := "5";
```

Appendix D

PERFORMANCE TEST CHECKLISTS AND WORKSHEETS

T his appendix includes checklists and worksheets for use during your performance testing.

1. Performance Test Results worksheet
2. Results Verification checklist
3. Tuning Settings worksheet
4. Bottleneck Removal checklist
5. Summary Test Results graph

Performance Test Results Worksheet

Use this worksheet to record the results during the tests. Be sure to accurately record all the data for each run, adding additional rows and columns as necessary. See Chapters 1, 11, and 12 for more information on the data you need to collect.

Test Configuration: _____

Date:_____

Hardware and Software:

  HTTP Server: _____

  Application Server:_____

  Database Server:_____

  Other: _____

General Comments:_____

_____

_____

_____

_____

_____

_____

Results:

Number of Clients	Run Length	Number of Requests	Throughput (req/sec)	Response Time (sec/page) avg/min/max	Server CPU HTTP/app/DB	Client CPU	Comments (changes/ errors)

Results Verification Checklist

Use this checklist after each test iteration to verify that the test run followed the recommended testing process. See Chapter 11 for more details on each of these items and their importance.

- ❏ Correct number of iterations run.
- ❏ Runs of sufficient length.
- ❏ Steady-state measurements.
- ❏ Warm-up period to prime caches, compile JSPs, and so on.
- ❏ Run-to-run variation within 4%.
- ❏ Isolated environment.
- ❏ Database or other back-end systems reset between runs.
- ❏ Successive runs do not show a linear pattern of decreasing performance.
- ❏ All measurement data recorded.
- ❏ All tuning parameters recorded.
- ❏ No errors reported from the test tool.
- ❏ No errors in the servers' logs.

Tuning Settings Worksheet

Use this worksheet to record the tuning parameters for your tests. As you change parameter settings between runs, record the changes in the comments section of the Test Results worksheet. This worksheet lists the most common settings influencing Java web site performance. See Chapters 2, 3, 4, and 9 for additional information on each of these settings. If you tune additional settings during your tests, be sure to add them to this worksheet.

Hardware

Parameter	Value
MHz	
Processors	
Memory	

Operating System

Parameter	Value
Tcp_time_wait	
Ulimit	

HTTP Server

Parameter	Value
Number of listeners (processes or threads)	
Keep-alive timeout	

Application Server

Parameter	Value
Web container thread pool	
EJB/ORB thread pool	
EJB pool/cache size	
EJB pool clean-up interval	
Database connection thread pool	
Prepared statement cache	
Servlet reload interval	
JSP reload interval	
HTTP session timeout interval	
HTTP session sharing	

JVM

Parameter	Value
Xms	
Xmx	

Application Parameters

Parameter	Value

Database Server

Parameter	Value
Bufferpool	
Cursors	
Sockets	

Bottleneck Removal Checklist

This checklist helps identify various common bottlenecks and their causes. Please refer to Chapter 13, Common Bottleneck Symptoms, for a complete description of how to diagnose and resolve these bottlenecks.

Underutilization

- ❑ Insufficient network capacity
    - ❑ Check for sufficient network capacity (network protocol analyzer).
    - ❑ Reduce amount of data moved across network.
- ❑ Application serialization
    - ❑ Check for highly synchronized code (thread trace).
- ❑ Insufficient resources
    - ❑ Check system resources (memory, and so on).
    - ❑ Check application resources (thread pools, and so on).
        - ❑ Check remote resources.
        - ❑ Stalled.
        - ❑ Check again for any overutilized back-end resource.
- ❑ Insufficient test client resource
    - ❑ Check for overutilized client CPU resource.
    - ❑ Check client network cards.

❑ Scalability
    ❑ Underutilization on large SMP systems (eight or more processors).
        ❑ Add more HTTP server and application server processes.

Bursty Utilization

❑ Application serialization
    ❑ Check for highly synchronized code (thread trace).
❑ Client synchronization
    ❑ Check for test client traffic "bursts."
    ❑ Verify requests actually reaching the HTTP server and application server (server monitors and thread trace).
    ❑ Compare response time against the length of the slowdown.
    ❑ Review think times in test scripts.
    ❑ Review virtual user test definitions.
❑ Back-end systems
    ❑ Check for deadlocks.
        ❑ Check EJB transaction isolation levels.
❑ Garbage collection
    ❑ Use `verbosegc` to check frequency and length of garbage collection cycles.
    ❑ Check JVM maximum heap size.
❑ Exhausted resources
    ❑ Check for exhausted resources during the idle period.
    ❑ Check for resources that recycle or timeout on the same interval as the length of the slowdown/idle period.
❑ Network issues
    ❑ Check for network timeouts (network protocol analyzer).
    ❑ Reduce components under test to isolate the problem component.

High CPU Utilization

❑ High user CPU (application server)
    ❑ Application needs tuning.
        ❑ Look at `String` processing, other Java best practices.
        ❑ Profile application, and reduce path length.
    ❑ Look at response time.
        ❑ Check for low response time. Perhaps high CPU is OK, and higher client loads still meet response time objectives.

❑ High system CPU (application server)
  ❑ If HTTP server is co-resident, reduce HTTP listeners or off-load HTTP server.
  ❑ Stop other processes on application server.
❑ High wait CPU (application server or database)
  ❑ Check for excessive logging.
  ❑ Check for sufficient disk space.
  ❑ For databases, consider adding platters to reduce contention.

Uneven Cluster Loading

❑ Network issues
  ❑ Check network hardware.
  ❑ Check firewall configuration.
❑ Routing issues
  ❑ Check IP affinity routing.

Summary Test Results Graph

Use the graph in Figure D.1 to plot the final client ramp-up results from your tests. On the x-axis, plot the concurrent user load. Start with a small number of users and increase the user load from left to right. On the y-axis, plot the throughput, typically in requests per second or pages per second, depending on your preference. The throughput graph should increase as concurrent users increase until the system reaches its throughput plateau. If you ran with an extremely high client load, the graph may also show a "buckle zone" for throughput.

On the alternate y-axis, graph the response time. This graph should also increase as client load increases. Once the system reaches its throughput plateau, expect the response time graph to increase linearly. See Chapter 1 for details on the expected relationships between user load, throughput, and response time.

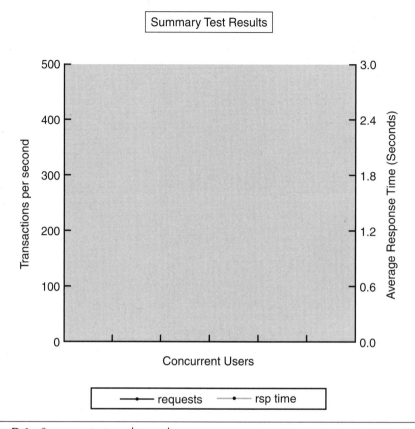

Figure D.1 Summary test results graph

BIBLIOGRAPHY

Alur, Deepak; Crupi, John; and Malks, Dan. *Core J2EE Patterns.* Upper Saddle River, NJ: Prentice Hall, 2001.

Asboeck, Stephan. *Load Testing for eConfidence.* Lexington, MA: Segue Software, Inc., October 2000.

Bulka, Dov. *Java Performance and Scalability.* Vol. 1. *Server-Side Programming Techniques.* Reading MA: Addison-Wesley, 2000.

Brown, Kyle; Craig, Dr. Gary; Hesler, Greg; Niswonger, Jaime; Pitt, David; and Stinehour, Russell. *Enterprise Java Programming with IBM WebSphere.* Reading MA: Addison-Wesley, 2001.

Cuomo, Gennaro. "A Methodology for Production Performance Tuning." IBM WebSphere Standard/Advanced White Paper, March 2000. IBM Corporation, March 2000.

Daconta, M.; Monk, E.; Keller, J.; and Bohnenberger, K. *Java Pitfalls: Time-Saving Solutions and Workarounds to Improve Programs.* New York: John Wiley & Sons, 2000.

Fowler, Martin. *Refactoring: Improving the Design of Existing Code.* Reading MA: Addison-Wesley, 2000.

Gamma, Helm, and Johnson, Vlissides. *Design Patterns: Elements of Reusable Object-Oriented Software.* Reading MA: Addison-Wesley, 1995.

Gunther, Harvey W. "Application Server Development Best Practices for Performance and Scalability, Version 1.1.0." IBM Corporation, September 7, 2000.

————. "Web Services Best Practices for Performance and Scalability, Version 1.0.0." IBM internal report, September 24, 2001.

Heiman, Richard V. "The Distributed Automated Software Quality Tools Market Forecast and analysis, 2001–2005." IDC Bulletin 25176–July 2001. <http://www-heva.mercuryinteractive.com/company/pr/idcreport/25176.htm>, December 27, 2001

Hunter, Jason, and Crawford, William. *Java Servlet Programming*. 2nd ed. Sebastopol CA: O'Reilly and Associates, 1998.

Killelea, Patrick. *Web Performance Tuning*. Sebastopol, CA: O'Reilly and Associates, 1998.

Reenskaug, Trygve. "ModelViewController." In *Portland Pattern Repository*. Retrieved February 28, 2002 from <http://c2.com/cgi/wiki?ModelViewController>.

Ueno, Ken, *et al*. *WebSphere V3 Performance Tuning Guide*. IBM Corporation International Technical Support Organization, March 2000, SG24-5657-00.

INDEX

Note: Italicized page locators refer to figures/tables.

More books from Addison-Wesley

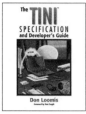

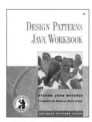

http://www.awprofessional.com

♦ Addison-Wesley

informIT

YOUR GUIDE TO IT REFERENCE

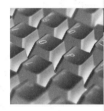

Articles

Keep your edge with thousands of free articles, in-depth features, interviews, and IT reference recommendations – all written by experts you know and trust.

Online Books

Answers in an instant from **InformIT Online Book's** 600+ fully searchable on line books. For a limited time, you can get your first 14 days **free**.

Catalog

Review online sample chapters, author biographies and customer rankings and choose exactly the right book from a selection of over 5,000 titles.